HEMCHAND GOSSAI is Associate Professor of Religion at Muhlenberg College. He is the author of *Power and Marginality in the Abraham Narrative* and *Justice, Righteousness and the Social Critique of the Eighth Century Prophets.*

NATHANIEL SAMUEL MURRELL is Assistant Professor of Philosophy and Religion at the University of North Carolina, Wilmington. He is also the co-editor of the award-winning *Chanting Down Babylon.*

Religion, Culture, and Tradition in the Caribbean

Religion, Culture, and Tradition in the Caribbean

Edited by
Hemchand Gossai
and Nathaniel Samuel Murrell

St. Martin's Press
New York

Library of Congress Cataloging-in-Publishing Data
Religion, culture, and tradition in the Caribbean / edited by Hemchand Gossai
    and Nathaniel Samuel Murrell.
        p.   cm.
    Includes bibliographical references and index.
    ISBN 0-312-23242-X
    1. Bible—Caribbean Area—History—Congresses.   2. Religion and culture—
Caribbean Area—Congresses.   3. Caribbean Area—Religion—Congresses.   I.
Gossai, Hemchand, 1954-   II. Murrell, Nathaniel Samuel.

BS447.5.C27 R45   2000
220'.09729—dc21

                                                                00–023368

Design by Letra Libre, Inc.

First edition: September, 2000
10 9 8 7 6 5 4 3 2 1

Contents

PART III

PLAYING WITH TEXT IN THE CARIBBEAN CONTEXT:
RASTAFARI, HERMENEUTICS, AND THE POLITICS OF LIBERATION

Acknowledgments

The editors wish to thank all of the contributors for making this fine anthology possible; we are specially grateful to contributor Leslie James for providing the cover photo on the book's jacket. We owe special gratitude to the Bob Marley estate, Rykomusic Inc, Fifty-Six Hope Road Music Ltd./Odnil Music Ltd./ Blue Mountain Music Ltd. for giving us permission to cite the lyrics of several reggae songs. Without the kind courtesy of William David Spencer, Clinton Chisholm, French journalist Helene Lee, and the Jamaican Archives in Spanish Town, Jamaica, it would have been impossible to publish the important chapter on the *Holy Piby*. We are indebted to our students who assisted us in editing the manuscript. For this, a special thank you is in order to Hilary Snow and Becky Heine of the University of North Carolina at Wilmington for making the first scoring of the index. We are much obliged to the copyeditor for St. Martin's Press, Brooke Goode, for doing a superb job helping us maintain consistency in the chapters written by different authors with diverse writing styles. Special commendation to Donna Cherry and Michael Flamini for their technical support and patience with us in this process.

Permissions

Introduction 🪶

Only in the 1940s and 1950s did scholars begin exploring seriously the cultural, racial, and religious traditions of the Caribbean area as an important field of study. But already much evidence of these traditions exists in the works of U.S. scholars such as Melville J. Herskovits, George Eaton Simpson, William R. Bascomb, and Leonard E. Barrett as well as several Caribbean scholars—Dale Bisnauth, Roger Bastide, and Idris Hamid to name a few. These initial explorations have yielded significant new insights into Caribbean religious thought. In the last few decades, religionists, sociologists, anthropologists, and historians have produced a number of touchstone books (as well as dissertations and a library of essays) on Voodoo, Santeria, Orisha, Shango, Yoruba, Rastafari, Islam, Hinduism, Christianity, and other Caribbean faiths. When Orbis Press published the book *Decolonizing Theology: A Caribbean Perspective,* a new day dawned for theological students with Caribbean roots. Many received and embraced these new ideas and saw a new way of entering the cultural and theological discourse—the possibility of decolonizing and ultimately contextualizing theology in the Caribbean. The book was therefore a precursor to many monographs, essays, and dissertations that raised questions about the nature, possibility, and content of a Caribbean theology—this in a region historically shaped by Eurocentric theology. Black theology to the north beckoned, while liberation theology flanked the shores of the Caribbean Sea.

For the most part, the study of the Bible prior to the last 30 years has focused largely on historical issues, and has been pursued by Western scholars. The importance of such work is unquestionable. But among the many hermeneutical schools, womanist and feminist voices have emerged in the last 30 years to give new and significant directions in the study of the Bible. Yet even here and now, scholars from the Caribbean are conspicuously underrepresented in the area of biblical scholarship. Comprised of voices shaped by Dutch, English, French, and Spanish, the very fabric of the Caribbean, in all of its textured existence, is complex. Rather than overlooking the possibilities that such complexity brings, one must begin the process of exploring new hermeneutical connections.

More recently, biblical scholarship has begun focusing attention on the Caribbean and the rich traditions for which it is now known. In 1994, the study of the Bible in the Caribbean saw new directions when *The Society of Biblical Literature (SBL)* authorized a three-year consultation on Caribbean culture and traditions as a formal and structured way to engage issues related to biblical materials within this neglected region. As is so often the case when one embarks on something new, the issue of where to begin is critical. It is not for the want of material or the lack of scholars and thinkers—there were already scholars blazing the trail in this field—but rather questions of methodology: the matter of organization, the question of scope, and the issue of substance. By having the consultation, we have been able to bring to the forefront and to the attention of the SBL and the American Academy of Religion (AAR) the importance of this region and the wealth of its historical traditions. In a region characterized by colonialism and now functioning in a post-colonial environment, with Christians, Hindus, Muslims, Rastafarians, etc., the possibilities and all their complexities for academic study are endless. As the consultation extended invitations for papers both within and outside of the Caribbean, we discovered immediately a great excitement at the prospect of what were genuinely new directions in biblical studies and the study of religions. Scholars from the Caribbean, Britain, and the United States explored a number of contemporary cultural, religious, and theological issues of great importance to Caribbean people and the field of Caribbean studies.

From the initial responses and throughout the consultation, we received a wide-ranging series of papers covering the fields of religious studies, theology, Bible, politics, history, and culture. The consultation was hailed as "an intriguing experiment in biblical research" and "a great success in the study of Caribbean culture and traditions" (participants' response). As a result, several publishers and colleagues who attended the consultation or supported our efforts encouraged us to make the proceedings available to a wider reading audience. The executive editor of St. Martin's Press, for example, expressed interest in this project on our first meeting and has stuck with us to make this publication a reality. As a positive and tangible result of the four-year consultation the book is a "first experiment" in Caribbean studies conducted under the auspices of the *Society of Biblical Literature,* and is in this regard a pathfinder.

More precisely, *Religion, Culture, and Tradition in the Caribbean* is a collection of readings on the dynamic interplay between scripture, politics, cultures, and traditions of Caribbean peoples as they have journeyed through their colonial and post-colonial experiences and come to terms with their own sense of identity and reality. Although these readings were first delivered to trained audiences at the academy, in this volume the material is directed to both scholars and the general reader who is interested in Caribbean current affairs, Caribbean history, politics, culture, theology, and scripture. The book does not replace other works in the study of Caribbean religions and culture but provides, in one volume, a valuable tool for studying those cultures and traditions as they relate to biblical materials. Since the chapters in this anthology have not appeared elsewhere, they offer new insights into the study of the Bible in the Caribbean.

The positioning of the chapters in this book reveals the tripartite nature of the anthology's content. In Part I, entitled *Whose Text Is It Anyway? Colonialism, Christianity, and History as Religious Contexts and Texts,* there are four chapters. At the beginning of this volume, Nathaniel Samuel Murrell aptly provides an extensive and insightful overview in the piece "Dangerous Memories, Underdevelopment, and the Bible in Colonial Caribbean Experience," which investigates the role that the Bible has played and continues to play in the colonization, enslavement, and underdevelopment of Caribbean peoples from the days of Christopher Columbus to modern times. Murrell advocates the need to read the Bible as texts for social change based on four models now operating in the Caribbean. From her extensive field research and many visits to Salvador Bahia, Brazil, Janet DeCosmo brings to us a carefully documented chapter, "Reggae and Rastafari in Salvador, Bahia: The Caribbean Connection in Brazil," in which she outlines interviews and insights elicited from Brazilian Rastafarians and their sympathizers. The importance of this piece is due in large part to the firsthand experience of DeCosmo in meeting the many individuals and sorting through the many nuances of their involvement in these religious and cultural traditions. Gerald Boodoo's chapter brings together two seemingly irreconcilable groups taking joint ownership of the Divina Pastora celebration in Trinidad. Boodoo, writing from a Trinidadian perspective in "The Faith of the People: The Divina Pastora Devotions of Trinidad," clearly illustrates the manner in which Roman Catholics and Hindus in that context engage in a practice that brings meaning to both groups and that is unique to this island community. In the final chapter of Part I, Miguel De La Torre in "Cubans in Babylon: Exodus and Exile" invites readers to see the various groups of Cubans who have come to the United States since the ascension to power of the Castro government as a new version of the Babylonian exile. De La Torre's work demonstrates the complexities in the reality of being a Cuban-American and underlines the similarities and differences among Cuban-Americans and the manner in which their experiences parallel that of the ancient Israelites in the Babylonian exile. De La Torre, in a provocative literary style, expresses critical ideas related to his people's experiences that only a Cuban-American can verbalize without being labeled politically incorrect and racially biased.

Part II of this volume, entitled *Discourse on Scripture, Culture, and Political Interaction,* contains five chapters covering a wide range of topics.

Horace Russell, in his article "Understandings and Interpretations of Scriptures in Eighteenth- and Nineteenth-Century Jamaica: The Baptists as Case Study," explores the missionary endeavors of Knibb and Liele and the manner in which they gave shape to the understanding and interpretations of the Scripture in Jamaica. John Holder's chapter, "Is This the Word of the Lord? In Search of Biblical Theology and Hermeneutics, the Eastern Caribbean," suggests that the story of Christianity in the Caribbean is inextricably linked to biblical interpretation. Holder seeks to trace the journey of this biblical interpretation by pointing to the many social elements that have led to this direction. Continuing under the umbrella of this second theme, Leslie James, in his chapter "Text and the Rhetoric of Change: Bible and Decolonization in Post–World War II Caribbean Political Discourse," explores the manner in which post–World War II colonialism was not only dismantled in the Caribbean, but how in the process Caribbean politicians began the arduous journey of giving shape to a new Caribbean identity steeped, in large part, in the biblical tradition. James argues that in using the Bible in public political discourse, several Caribbean politicians defined their political vision and contributed to the complex use of the Bible in the region. Hemchand Gossai's chapter, "Recasting Identity in Ruth and Hindu Indo-Guyanese Women," underlines the expansive nature of religious traditions in the Caribbean and highlights an often neglected strand of the Caribbean fabric. Using a typological approach and case study, the author draws parallels between central themes of "woman's identity" in the Hebrew novella *Ruth,* and Hindu Indo-Guyanese women. In a chapter on popular reggae culture entitled "Identity and Subversion in Babylon: Strategies for Resisting the System in the Music of Bob Marley and the Wailers," Richard Middleton creatively explores the *imago Dei* of Genesis 1 and the music of Bob Marley. Middleton brings together two seemingly unconnectable worlds. Placing the Hebrew epic within its ancient Near Eastern context and its composition in the era of the Babylonian exile, the author invites the audience to see Marley's music as reflecting the subversive nature of the creation story.

Part III of this volume, entitled *Playing with Text in the Caribbean Context: Rastafari, Hermeneutics, and the Politics of Liberation,* contains four chapters. Noel Leo Erskine, in his piece "Biblical Hermeneutics in Modern Caribbean Experience, Paradigms, and Prospects," reflects on his personal experience as one whose vocation was determined within the context of the church. Erskine's anecdotal introduction puts one on notice that his reflections on this subject are not distance learning or analysis, but are in some ways even hagiographic. Like other contributors to the volume, the personal experiences that Erskine shares so candidly shows one doing theology from the inside out, rather than a disinterested researcher from the outside. Erskine seeks a hermeneutic that will not simply maintain the status quo but take seriously the existential reality of the people in their environmental context.

Loretta Collins's "Daughters of Jah: The Impact of Rastafarian Womanhood in the Caribbean, the United States, Britain, and Canada" fills a significant void in Rastafari studies. From her many travels and extensive research on a Fulbright fellowship to Jamaica, Collins provides a very rich overview of the literature on Rastafari womanhood and the various perspectives developed. She underlines the complexity of the role of women in the practice of Rastafari, and posits important distinctions between the role of women in the Rastafarian movement and other well-established feminist movements. Collins's work is especially valued for bringing to public view the positive roles women play as "agency" in Rastafari, and the many community and international projects in which the "sistren" are involved. The chapter by Darren Middleton, "Riddim Wise and Scripture Smart: Interview and Interpretation with Ras Benjamin Zephaniah," provides readers with a very helpful glimpse into the life of the memorable Benjamin Zephaniah. In addition to citing some of Zephaniah's poetry, the author provides the text from an interview with him, allowing the poetry and the interview to serve as an important brief introduction to the man's thoughts. The final article in this volume, "Holy Piby: Blackman's Bible and Garveyite Ethiopianist Epic with Commentary," is an extensive introduction and commentary on the Holy Piby, an important Afrocentric Caribbean-American text, which has been used by scholars and Rastafarians alike, but principally through secondary sources. By making the text of this ephemera available for public reading in a sea of commentary and careful study, Murrell provides an important contribution to the field of religious studies on the Caribbean.

In general, the contributors to this volume genuinely seek to become actively immersed in the Caribbean, the theological project, or the way we read and play with biblical texts in the region. There is a call for hermeneutics to act not as a weapon against the oppressed, the marginalized, and disfranchised, but as a corrective to an aspect of the colonial missionary tradition that saves people's souls but leaves them enslaved, hungry, unclothed, and landless. The corrective is intended to liberate and empower the economically and politically oppressed peoples of the region, while at the same time sensitizing them to issues of their marginalization of "the other" and the misuse of power for personal and clannish purposes.

Part I

Whose Text Is It Anyway?

Colonialism, Christianity, and History as Religious Contexts and Texts

Chapter 1

Dangerous Memories, Underdevelopment, and the Bible in Colonial Caribbean Experience

Nathaniel Samuel Murrell

Thanks to the more than 500 years influence of Christianity, the Bible has been the mother of all books in the Caribbean and has had a most profound impact on the formation of the historical experience of the ethnically diverse peoples of the region. In many ways, the Bible has defined and continues to define the nature and quality of Caribbean people's existence, shaped their cultural traditions and ethnic compositions, influenced and redefined their morality and sense of community, and even informed their social and political ideologies. Since Columbus stumbled accidentally on the Caribs, Arawaks, Tainos, and other "Amerindians" in 1492, the Bible and *corpus christianum* have worked hand in hand to name and claim the islands and their peoples. St. Bartholomew, San Salvador, Santo Domingo, La Trinidad (the holy trinity), Saint Lucia, Saint Vincent, and Saint Eustatius are all Christian names, some of which are Bible-based. Biblical names of parishes and towns dot the map of the entire Caribbean archipelago of British-, French-, Spanish-, and Dutch-speaking island states and countries. For example, the names of 10 of the 12 parishes in the 166-square-mile island-state of Barbados came directly from the Bible: St. Andrew, St. James, St. John, St. Joseph, St. Peter, St. Paul, St. Philip, St. Mark, St. Thomas, and Christ Church—names as old as the British presence on the island.

The Bible is the most commonly read book in the Caribbean; it is in churches, in school prayers and "morning devotions," in hotels, and in motels. The Bible is everywhere. Caribbean peoples swear in court by the Bible "to tell the truth and nothing but the truth so help me God!" They make their sacred marriage vows on the Bible, and by the Bible decide individual, communal, and national morality. In Caribbean folklore and cultural myths, the Bible is divine and mysterious; it is a book to revere and obey, and a book to dread. Reading a verse from its sacred pages every morning brings one good luck, whether selling in the market in Kingston, Jamaica, or seeking a job in Georgetown, Guyana. So influential is the Bible in Caribbean culture that Jamaican sociologist of religion Ennis Edmonds said: "In the first half of the twentieth century, an education to which Afro-Jamaicans had access tended to come via the church. As a corollary, the education was rooted in the Bible, so much so that the only book with which the masses of Jamaicans were acquainted was the Bible. This resulted in a kind of 'biblicism' in which the Bible became the source of authority in all discussions and disputations."[1] So the Bible does not only provide a basis for religious faith and practice, it is also an essential part of public education and political discourse; students study the Bible in high school for their General Certificate of Education (the equivalence of the SAT) to qualify for university, and politicians use the Bible in political rhetoric to communicate with the masses. No separation exists between church and state in the region where the Bible is the mother of all books, and no other book holds the distinction of having such a mythic character and powerful grip on people in the place that Christopher Columbus named "West Indies."

Dangerous Historical Memories

The historical role that the Bible and Christianity played in the Caribbean experience was not just happenstance; it was planned as an essential part of the European expansionist program to make the Amerindians and their lands an extension of Western Europe. Pope Alexander VI (Roderigo Bogia) as Vicar of Christ and head of the *republica christiana* in Europe not only blessed Columbus's mission to the "Indies," but he commissioned the Genovese explorer to go and discover and claim lands, gold, and precious stones for the crown, spread the gospel, and convert the heathens to Christ and to the Christian Church. According to the Guyanese scholar of religious studies, Dale Bisnauth: "As explorers, discoverers, *conquistadores* and traders sought to open up the region for economic exploitation, missionaries and priests sought to introduce what they considered to be the blessings of European civilization to the indigenous peoples and to incorporate them into the fold of Catholicism—the religion of the *republica christiana*."[2] Later, a series of five Papal Bulls gave half of the world to Spanish sovereigns and authorized the veritable Christianization and civilization of the so-called heathens of the Americas.[3]

Using concepts of Christian evangelism and apologetics (spreading and defending the faith), Columbus named and claimed the peoples of the Caribbean for Queen Isabella and King Ferdinand of Spain and carried out the direct wishes of the pontiff, Roderigo Borgia. To the Spanish monarchs and the pontiff, Columbus had pledged himself an ambassador of Christianity and a defender of the faith against idolatry and heresies in Christendom. In one of his logs Columbus wrote: "Your Highnesses decided to send me, Christopher Columbus, to see these parts of India and the princes and peoples of those lands and consider the best means for their conversion. For by neglect of the Popes to send instructors, many nations had fallen to idolatry and adopted doctrines of perdition, and your Highnesses as Catholic princes and devoted propagators of the holy Christian faith have always been enemies of the sect of Mahomet and of all idolatries and heresies."[4] Columbus also promised to give a percentage of all his booty—gold, silver, precious stones—to the Church "for the recapture of Jerusalem from the Saracens . . . it had been his plan to pay for 100,000 infantry and 10,000 cavalry for the re-conquest of Jerusalem."[5] The eminent Caribbean historian and prime minister of Trinidad and Tobago, Eric Williams, says:

> Standing on the very threshold of the modern age of commerce and imperialism, Columbus' vision was focused on the past. He was the last of the medieval crusaders. The chief significance of the New World, in his eyes, was the opportunity it afforded of bringing multitudes into the Catholic faith. On his return from his first voyage, he ended his narrative of his exploits to the Sovereigns with the assurance that "God had reserved for the Spanish monarchs, not only all the treasures of the New World, but a still greater treasure of inestimable value, in the infinite number of souls destined to be brought over into the bosom of the Christian Church."[6]

Through biblical concepts and European expansionist mercantile and colonial principles, the Church blessed a program that set in motion a series of events, mechanisms, and activities that created a commercial legacy that left a history of dangerous memories for the unfortunate native peoples, Africans, and their descendants trapped in the European-Caribbean colonial enterprise. The colonials owned, controlled, exploited, enslaved, and oppressed the original peoples of the Americas, especially in the islands. Such a fate would also befall the Africans who joined them through sheer force of European firepower and African-European greed and inhumanity to fellow humans. With the Bible in one hand and the sword in the other, Columbus and those who succeeded him sought to convert the native peoples to Christianity by coercion while exploiting their human resources. In 1513 Martin Fernandez de Enciso advanced the theory that God gave the Indies to Spain to be Christianized as he had given the Jews the Promised Land to tell the world of his goodness. "The task of conquering the Indies was accompanied by that of Christianizing and civilizing them"[7]—a euphemism for enslavement, domination, and exploitation. The civilization-Christianization program functioned as a pretext for possession, oppression, and destruction. The natives, especially on the islands, who could not understand or accept the foreign religion and its foreign god, were either enslaved or destroyed. Those who escaped the edge of the sword and bayonet perished from European disease, airborne as well as sexually transmitted, died of grief or starvation, or committed suicide.[8]

In his *A Very Brief Account of the Destruction of the Indies* (1552), Bartolome de Las Casas, the first Catholic clergy ordained in the Americas (1507), gave a most horrifying account of the Spanish cruelty to the natives through the sword and in the *repartimento/encomiendas* system, essentially the earliest form of individual land and slave ownership designed by Columbus and endorsed by the Spanish government. In 1514 Las Casas, moved by his conscience, gave up his *encomiendas* in Santo Domingo and sold his "Indian" slaves. He "surprised his parishioners by preaching a Pentecost Sunday sermon severely condemning Spanish treatment of the native people,"[9] and later devoted his life to defending the defenseless Amerindians against Spanish brutality, enslavement, and destruction. Las Casas, who "refused to sacrifice the welfare of the Indians to the greed of the Spaniards," encountered decades of opposition and hostility from the clergy and the *encomienderos;* but he consented "to sacrifice the well-being of the Negroes to the preservation of the Indians. What he gave to humanity with one hand, he took away with the other."[10] When he finally succeeded in getting the king of Spain to support his efforts to save the natives, Las Casas's work was too little too late; the native populations in the island of Hispaniola had dissipated so rapidly that the aborigines were already reduced to a handful. But the dice were cast and the fate of the Africans—whose numbers had already increased substantially by 1528 when "Emperor Charles V granted to two German merchants the monopoly of supplying African slaves to the Spanish colonies"[11]—was now determined by the death of the Amerindians. To save a few natives, Las Casas, unintentionally perhaps, signed the death warrant of tens of millions of Africans by accepting "the solution proposed by the Dominican monks . . . to the King in 1511 to bring to Hispaniola many Negro slaves from Guinea."[12]

Because the evangelistic vision of Christendom that fueled the missionary enterprise was at the heart of the European expansionist explorations to the West, from the very beginning a Eurocentric theology was concocted from biblical materials to defend and support Europeans' interests and domination at Africans' expense. This theology was pressed into service to support the Christian culture that nurtured the oppressive institution of slavery in the Caribbean for over 375 years. European Christians found in the Bible's Great Commission the inspiration for conquering the foreign lands and their peoples (Matt. 28:18–20). A Catholic divine de Enciso argued with arrogance and impunity: "The King of Spain might very justly send men to require those idolatrous Indians to hand over their land to him for it was given him by the Pope. If the Indians would not do this, he might justly wage war against them, kill them and enslave those captured in war, precisely as Joshua treated the inhabitants of the land of Canaan."[13] Pauline and Petrine theology supplied the justification for enslaving the native American and African peoples (Eph. 6:5–9; Phil. 2:5–8; Col. 3:22–25; 1 Peter 2:5–25; and Philem.); and the Christians found in the Scriptures support for the culture and class structure that the colonial slave-based economy and society produced (Rom. 13:1–10; 1 Cor. 7:20).

During slavery in the English-speaking Caribbean, slaves were instructed and required to obey their masters as evidence of their obedience to Christ and a sign of their worthiness of baptism and communion, even when they were scarcely converted to Christianity. Preachers insisted, on the basis of their colonial reading of the Bible, that slaves must obey their masters and servants must be submissive to their lords. Disobedience and resistance were viewed as anti-Christ and anti-Christian and warranted severe punishments in the slave society even for simple infractions. The writings of the Baptist missionary to Jamaica and church planter, George Liele, show that in the 1790s even the Baptists, who would later defend the cause of the slaves, held their enslaved members to strict discipline and obedience to slave masters. To regulate member-slaves' behavior and alloy the fears of the plantocracy and the state about so-called "suspicious" church activities, Liele and his elders drew up a Twenty-one Articles document in 1795 in which they made it clear that no slave was permitted to take membership in the Church unless their master could first vouchsafe their good behavior (Article XV). Article XVII uses several biblical passages from Peter, Paul, and Luke to authorize capital punishment (usually severe flogging) of Christian slaves/servants whose only crime was disobeying their masters: "If a slave or servant misbehaves to the owners they are to be dealt with according to the Word of God . . . [they] shall be beaten with many stripes."[14]

Notwithstanding the declared religious and theological mission to convert enslaved Africans to Christianity and to teach them the Christian faith, on most large plantations the well-being of the slaves mattered only insofar as they were chattels, beasts of burden, and the chief economic means of production of goods and services for European consumption. As Eric Williams so ably argued, slavery was driven by economics first and foremost; religion was a mere tool of production and "racism was the consequence of slavery."[15]

On the plantation, Christianity and the Bible functioned as means of production, control, and domination. Some missionaries who owned slaves compromised the truth of the gospel in their Sunday sermons and homilies. Even the missionaries who did not own Africans as slaves were often used as tools of production and control; they were enjoined by their mission agency not to preach against slavery. Planters often supplemented the inadequate wages of the local parish minister and required him to teach the slaves obedience and subservience to their masters. In cases where the number of ministers was inadequate to cover Methodist circuits, lay preachers—some of them slave masters themselves—conducted Bible study and preached, the content of which was predictable.

Generally, on the question of slavery, many church officials interpreted the Bible as a servant not of Christ but of the purveyors of mammon. Such interpretation held the Scripture captive to European hegemony, economically and politically, so that the Bible was unable to liberate the oppressed African masses. The religion, designed to alleviate pain and suffering in human society from its beginning, became an integral part of the Caribbean problem. Essentially, colonial missionary Christianity attempted to save people's souls for heaven with the Bible but, with the same Bible, condemned their bodies to hell, dehumanized, brutalized, and robbed of their dignity. Under the hermeneutics of colonial power and political dominance, God was often viewed through European eyes, and the correct interpretation of the Bible was distanced from Caribbean people's life situation. In the intimate clergy/planter alliance, maintaining good relations and finding favor with peers were reckoned to be of greater importance than securing liberation for the captives, recovering sight for the blind, and healing for the brokenhearted, which the Christian gospel propounds (Luke 4:18). In 1827 the leading Episcopalian bishop in the southeastern Caribbean charged an official gathering of young clergy and newly confirmed members to be loyal subjects of the king, obedient servants to their masters, and content with slavery and the state of poverty (if necessary), knowing that their reward is in heaven.[16]

Since enforcing slave-protection laws in the Caribbean was difficult, for all practical purposes the slaves had little recourse to abuses and injustice apart from attempts at various methods of resistance and revolt. With few notable exceptions, primarily among the British anti-slavery abolitionist crusaders and the Baptists in Jamaica, the hermeneutics applied to Bible reading in this colonial context was tailored to facilitate the means of production, undergird *corpus christianum,* support the class structure, maintain the status quo, and keep slavery and colonialism in business. Missionaries regarded as their main calling the conversion and Christianizing of the slaves, though some worked for the amelioration of master/slave relationships. Very few missionaries joined the abolitionist movement since they were enjoined by their home office to be silent on the question of slavery.[17] Robert Stewart says, "the Moravians worked consistently under planter patronage and were allied with particular estates in the southwest region of the island" of Jamaica.[18] Methodists were enjoined to "refrain from meddling in secular disputes," for showing "circumspect behavior toward slave masters and civil authorities would gain the required toleration for missionaries to pursue their work." Stewart adds, "Methodist missionaries were directed to conform even to the prejudices of the whites."[19] The Methodists, like the Anglicans, Presbyterians, Catholics, and Moravians, had upheld a policy of "total silence on the civil wrongs of the Slave, lest injudicious language should interfere with the great and all-important objects which the Missionary has in view."[20] Up to the eve of emancipation, this official policy of silencing preachers on the abolition issue was still very effective.

During apprenticeship and the post-emancipation periods in the English-speaking Caribbean, 1834–38, no substantive change was evident in the European concept of Christian faith in mainline churches in the Caribbean. But this was not the case among the courageous and vocal British Baptist missionaries in Jamaica, whom the home office (mission agency) categorized as "nonconformists rebels."[21] Upon his arrival in Jamaica in 1825, Baptist missionary William Knibb expressed deep empathy towards "the poor, oppressed, benighted, and despised sons of Africa [who] form a pleasing contrast to the debauched white population."[22] Knibb, James Mursell Phillippo, Richard Merrick, and like-minded Baptists, who did not operate with a rigid separation of church and state ideology, sought to bring the kingdom of God to the whole African person to "show the poor people that [they] loved their bodies as well as their souls."[23] These missionaries fought for emancipation and, as Stewart notes, in the 1830s promoted the social and political welfare of Blacks in contrast and in opposition to the oppressive planterclass. Baptists were convinced that the Bible and the ordained ministry do not relieve the Christian's civic duty and involvement in social and domestic affairs of the state and its people.

But other church constituencies throughout the Caribbean supported the doctrine of laissez-faire, either occupying neutral ground or supporting the planterclass and colonial policies. The economic and political interest and ideology of class and colonialism that controlled biblical interpretation contributed to the lingering legacy of underdevelopment and impoverishment of Caribbean peoples into the post-colonial era. First under the mercantile system and then under colonialism, all goods were to be shipped in the colonial vessels, processed from raw materials in the "mother country" or "metropole," supported by colonial financial institutions (e.g., Lloyds Bank of England and Barclays Bank), and the manufactured goods had to be repurchased by the colonists; thus deriving huge profits for the metropole at the colonies' expense.[24] Little or no resources were invested in governmental infrastructure, or in providing adequate jobs for creole Caribbean peoples or the poor masses. In short, underdevelopment resulted from the fact that Europeans took as much as they could get out of the Caribbean and returned as little as possible.

This underdevelopment was marked by the exploitation of Caribbean human resources and land through a slave-based sugar monoculture, which netted substantial profits for absentee landlords and European commercial institutions; but it led to massive soil exhaustion, depletion in natural resources, and excessive population displacement, which are at the heart of modern Caribbean poverty, poor health, and malnutrition. Even in the post-emancipation period, Europeans brought large numbers of voluntary Africans, Chinese, Indians, and other races into Caribbean colonies and thus created growing populations on islands that, especially today, do not have the land space, technology, and food supply to sustain such massive demographic shifts. Emancipation thus laid the foundation for a large creole society subsisting on limited commercial capital and, especially in Jamaica, a very large peasantry to be exploited in a low-wage and underemployment economy.

Fighting Colonial Legacy of Underdevelopment

Africans enslaved in the Caribbean fought slavery and demonstrated resistance to the institution and its colonial Christian theology from the beginning of the sixteenth century. Slaves faked sickness and used go-slow tactics at the height of the sugarcane-cutting season. Some house slaves poisoned their slave masters, and female slaves aborted babies rather than bring them into a life of slavery.[25] Slaves planned revolts in British, Spanish, French, and Dutch colonies. Some slaves committed suicide and others ran away and formed the famous *cimarrones* or Maroon[26] community. "Formed around ever-increasing corps of runaway slaves—whose militancy, communal organization, and religious worldview were built on the basis of Akan cultural survivals—the Maroons battled the eastern and western mountain areas in the seventeenth and early eighteenth centuries until they were granted a somewhat circumscribed autonomy by the treaties of 1739."[27] In the late 1780s, the oppressed Black masses of Haiti rose up in protest against the French bourgeoisie and, with the help of Voodoo, destroyed the infamy of slavery and wrested their liberation from the jaws of French political power and the plantocracy in several episodes of a bloody revolution that ended in 1803. Although Voodoo had very little to do with the Bible, its battles with the Catholic Church in Haiti after 1804 went to new heights and inspired slaves elsewhere to challenge the institution and its colonial "Christian theology."

Paradoxically, out of the oppressive imperialist Christian culture arose a daring spirit of resistance and rebellion that challenged the very foundation of colonialism, slavery, and the underdevelopment of the Caribbean. Although Eric Williams's argument that the British government abolished slavery when it became unprofitable[28] is essentially sound, the anti-slavery religious and political agitation in Britain of Thomas Clarkson, William Wilberforce, Thomas Fowell Buxton, and others, on the basis of Christian principles, were also important factors in the abolition of slavery. In Jamaica the courageous and untiring efforts of British missionaries Knibb and M. Phillippo to obtain justice and improve the miserable lot of the poor black masses is unparalleled among missionary political activists in the Caribbean. Knibb's avant-garde (for his time) understanding of the Scriptures as demanding freedom and justice for all peoples, and particularly his agitation on behalf of the poor landless masses of Jamaica, was an inspiration to his parishioners, including Baptist lay preacher Sam Sharpe, the leader of the 1831 rebellion that hastened the abolition of slavery in British territories. Afro-Jamaicans staged an unprecedented national protest against oppression in the war of 1831, called the Baptist War. The protest was predicated on the reading and interpretation of biblical texts by lay preachers who understood the Gospel as demanding their liberation from slavery.

While Episcopalians, Methodists, Catholics, Lutherans, Presbyterians, and those of other faiths encouraged and supported the hermeneutics of oppression, the Baptist missionaries were viewed as "Negro lovers" who corrupted the minds of the slave with wrong ideas. The white Baptist British missionary William Knibb used Scripture to argue for better conditions and emancipation of slaves, as well as social justice in Jamaica in the post-emancipation era. In his Sunday homilies, Knibb supported the cause of the oppressed and the Baptist War, and he was severely persecuted for this stance. The enraged Jamaica's Committee on Assembly, meeting on January 28, 1832, charged Baptists with being the chief cause for producing evil, independent thinking in the minds of the slaves; and the court charged Knibb with being "a person of depraved, impious, and unquiet mind who, on December 4, incited the rebellion in the parish of St. James." The government and its white mob hunted down Knibb, his missionary friends, and their supporters with such savagery that the British government had to appoint a commission of inquiry into the brutal suppression of the pre-emancipation rebellion of 1831. According to Stewart, using "the electoral franchise to affect the legislature," and all available resources and avenues, Jamaican "Baptist[s] became a political force . . . in directing the ex-slave franchise toward the goal of shifting political power from the old plantocracy to the increasingly influential combination of colored lawyers, landowners, merchants, wealthy craftsmen, and Jewish entrepreneurs,"[29] in the decade following emancipation.

The "subversive" Christian idea of protest in the Caribbean was also actively behind the rebellions of 1865 and 1931 in Jamaica. The Morant Bay Rebellion of 1865 was a political action caused by the total absence of justice for Afro-Jamaicans, the landlessness of the poor masses who were willing to engage in agriculture, and embarrassingly poor minimum wages for workers in St. Thomas-in-the-East (the eastern parish of Jamaica). Baptist, Nativist Baptist, and other Afro-Jamaican religious leaders such as Paul Bogle and George William Gordon relied on the Bible to give leadership to prophetic political activities of the late 1800s.[30] In the 1880s and 1890s Alexander Bedward, dubbed strange and crazy for his apocalyptic theology, used the Scriptures to give a prophetic voice in defense of the oppressed Afro-Jamaicans.[31] In the nineteenth and early twentieth century, Edward Bleiden of St. Thomas, George Padmore of Trinidad and Tobago, Robert Love and Marcus Mosiah Garvey of Jamaica, and other Pan-Africanists (most of whom were Christians) led one of the longest protest movements that Christians of the diaspora have participated in, often motivated by a special understanding of the biblical text as a document of liberation, equality, justice, and the dignity of African peoples.

Caribbean people fought underdevelopment on other fronts. In the late colonial period, the church established elementary and high school education for some students, the fruits of which are seen in "the cream of the crop" of modern political, religious, and civic leadership. In the 1800s, Codrington College of the Church of England in Barbados began offering rather limited public education.[32] In the early 1900s, Spanish and French Catholic Creoles established a handful of primary and secondary schools in Trinidad, which were matched by two Anglican (Episcopalian) institutions on the island.[33] In Jamaica, Guyana, and the small islands the Church has an established record of cooperating with government to offer elementary public education to the masses and educating a small "talented tenth" of the population at secondary school and college levels. So clearly the Church performed a dual role in Caribbean historical experience: first as oppressor and later as advocate of public education and liberation. Of the Church's dual role in Jamaica, Noel Erskine says: "It was this very church that after slavery was abolished bought large plots of lands and subdivided them to the masses. The church built schools, hospitals, clinics, and water tanks for the masses of people in Jamaica."[34]

But unfortunately many of the activities of the Church were not widespread throughout the Caribbean, came too little too late, and proved inadequate to reverse the centuries of wrongs caused by Caribbean underdevelopment. A most troubling reality of underdevelopment is the fact that Caribbean youths have limited access to educational opportunities beyond high school. The three campuses of the University of the West Indies at Mona (Jamaica), St. Augustine (Trinidad), and Cave Hill (Barbados) could afford placements for only 3.1 percent of their high school graduates, and between .4 to .8 percent for graduates from the smaller English-speaking countries. Local private institutions and foreign universities educate another 1.1 percent of our students.[35] With more than 95 percent of our high school graduates terminating schooling without a college education, Caribbean people cannot compete in the world of science and technology, and continue to be dependent on foreign trade and commerce—a condition that make us slaves of consumerism. Technological advances that enhance the productivity and wealth of developed and developing countries have left the masses of Caribbean peoples stranded on the proverbial Jericho road, unable to access the superhighway of knowledge and information that could drastically change their situation and improve their quality of life. The efforts that Christianity made in addressing these problems reflect, at best, an appeasement for its double standard in the history of Caribbean morality and justice.

The double standard in the colonial theology of Christianity in the Caribbean legitimizes Karl Marx's classic criticism that "Religion is the sigh of the oppressed creature, the heart of the heartless world, as it is the spirit of spiritless conditions. It is the *opiate* of the people."[36] As Marx implies, the theological and moral passivity taught by colonial Christianity, which had little or no compassion for the wretched condition of the masses, drugged and doped the oppressed masses by numbing their senses so that they would not reflect on their miserable social condition. By so doing, the hegemonic powers attempted to stifle the spirit of resistance within the Church, the predisposition for revolt, and protest against the oppressive bourgeoisie who constitute and control the economic ways and means of production in society. Although for all practical purposes Marxism outlived its usefulness in the Caribbean and died an unexpected but necessary death in Grenada in 1983, perhaps Marx's criticism of the Christian religion is applicable to the region especially at the close of the twentieth century. In Marx's view, religion is intended to be a servant of the people and not their slave master. "Man makes religion, religion does not make man . . . Man is the world of men, the state [and] society. This state and this society produce religion, which is an inverted consciousness of the world because they are an inverted world."[37] The five-point summary of the classic Marxist criticism of Christianity might be worth hearing again by Caribbean persons who feel trapped in the colonial way of reading and playing with the biblical text:

One: "The social principles of Christianity justified the slavery of antiquity, glorified the serfdom of the Middle Ages and are capable . . . of defending the oppression of the proletariat, even if with somewhat doleful grimaces.

Two: "The social principles of Christianity preach the necessity of a ruling and an oppressed class, and for the latter all they have to offer is the pious wish that the former may be charitable" and obedient.

Three: "The social principles of Christianity place the Consistorial Counselor's compensation for all infamies in heaven, and thereby justify the condition of these infamies on earth."

Four: "The social principles of Christianity declare all the vile acts of the oppressors against the oppressed to be either a just punishment for original sin and other sins, or trials which the Lord, in his infinite wisdom, ordains for the redeemed."[38]

Marx concludes: "The social principles of Christianity preach cowardice, self-contempt, abasement, submissiveness and humbleness"; which the bourgeoisie do not preach to themselves. For these and other reasons, "The social principles of Christianity are sneaking and hypocritical"; but the proletariat must be revolutionary and courageous.[39] Few people in the modern Caribbean wave a Marxist flag today; and care should therefore be taken not to impose a foreign hermeneutics on Caribbean reading of biblical text. However, Christians who insist that the Church should not be involved in the political life of the people but should concentrate primarily on the mission of soul-saving and spiritual Christian responsibility[40] are proving the Marxist indictment correct. Jesus's parable of "The Good Samaritan" offers an apt paradigm with which to keep memory alive on both past and present aspects of the Caribbean religious experience. As the nameless man in Jesus's parable of "The Good Samaritan" was robbed and brutalized by thieves on the Jericho road (Luke 10:30–37), so too the modern Caribbean masses have been left to die on the treacherous roads of post-colonial underdevelopment, "polytricks" of our national leaders, natural disasters, lack of educational opportunities for the masses and, most recently, economic restructuring by the International Monetary Fund.

Reading Biblical Texts for Social Change

Throughout our four-year consultation on the historic role of the Bible in Caribbean culture and tradition for the Society of Biblical Literature (1994–97) we explored several ways in which the Church used the Bible to define and control Caribbean people's destiny and lives. We discovered that Christianity in the Caribbean fostered a paradoxical relationship to the society, one in which the Bible was used both to justify oppression and to challenge the very assumptions on which oppression and domination thrived. Because of this dual role that the church played in people's lives, Caribbean theology as a product of the Bible must be analyzed and understood as a social religious project that has definite political and economic implications. Any approach to reading the Bible in the Caribbean that wishes to be a viable and effective change agent must have as one of its objectives improving the quality of life of people in the society, especially for the oppressed, the marginalized, and the disenfranchised. Essentially, biblical interpretation must act as corrective surgery to the colonial theological legacy (or malady). The complex nature of that legacy and the multiple problems encountered in reading Biblical text in the region requires a hermeneutics that is itself diverse and many-legged. In recent decades several models have been proposed with regard to reading the Bible for positive change in the Caribbean. Because of their possibilities or potentials, I single out four of those models for special attention here: the Chaguaramas project; the Jesus model; land acquisition model; and Rastafari's messianic hope.

The Chaguaramas Project

One leg of the new approach to hermeneutics and theology recommended by modern Caribbean scholars is modeled after what I call the Chaguaramas project, a theological project and vision that was articulated at the Ecumenical Conference of the Caribbean Council of Churches (CCC) in Chaguaramas, Trinidad, West Indies, in 1971. This theological vision proffers a particular way of reading biblical texts intended to liberate and empower the economically and politically oppressed peoples of the region by analyzing a variety of experiences, situations, and realities vitally important to the quality of life of Caribbean peoples.[41] The first call in this project is for the Church to break with its colonial past of reading the Bible from the vantage point of the custodians of political and economic power and cultural dominance. The dominant political and cultural "narratives" that controlled and manipulated the play on biblical texts in the puzzling dance of Caribbean life, both in church and society, must be subject to the voices of the prophets who speak the word of the Lord in conversation with the people's own texts and contexts.

The new Caribbean hermeneutic that my colleagues and I proffer says that the moral and ethical responses of readers to the misuse of the Bible in the Caribbean Church should not discard the Bible with the Eurocentric "colonial bath water," as the Leninist Marxists of the now defunct People's Revolutionary Government of Grenada urged Grenadians to do in 1979, but rather should listen to the Bible with new ears. Theologians who have ears to hear, let them hear what the Spirit of prophecy (social, political, and religious criticism) says to the Churches of the Caribbean: put flesh and bones, arms and legs, hands and feet to the biblical texts when saying "Thus Saith the Lord" to the people. The Lord himself lives in the people's pantry in Grenada, drops in on their job interviews in Trinidad, sits at the bargaining table of labor union negotiations for just wages in Barbados, and hears their plea for better medical care and land ownership in Jamaica and Guyana. Like the mythic Santa Claus, the God of the Bible knows when our naughty and decrepit Caribbean politicians are stashing away millions of much needed, hard-earned taxpayers' dollars in their personal Swiss bank accounts while turning a deaf ear to the starving children and helpless people of our land.

This is precisely the point at which the perspectives of the hearers and the perspective of the text converge. Here the biblical text and its world interact with the text of the people's world. Here too the world of the experts, or biblical scholars interacts with the world of the "person in the street" without alienating the biblical text or the hearers and their contextual experience. This new approach to reading biblical texts does not make truth an abstraction far removed from people's kitchen, empty pantries, and bare wardrobes. As some of us in the academy have argued in different Caribbean publications, especially since the 1980s, both the reading and the hearing of the text must be done with a hermeneutic of suspicion and reflective criticism.[42] That is, we must be critical of the attempt to distance our reading and hearing of the biblical text from our own self-definition and identity as well as our social and political condition.

Biblical texts themselves are the real life stories, situations, and traditions of ordinary people whose struggles, aspirations, myths, and beliefs evolved over time in specific historical and social contexts. Therefore, the Caribbean Church must read and play with versions—and always sub-versions, never the original versions[43]—of those biblical texts in ways that address real life situations in our communities. But we must do so, critical of our own position of dominance in the modern Church since the Church has the reputation of functioning both as an oppressor and a defender of the oppressed in the Caribbean. Peoples in all walks of life in the Caribbean must be conscientized to the reality of their own propensity for the marginalizing of the other and their misuse of political power for personal aggrandizement. Since there is no notion of separation of Church and state in Caribbean life, the notion that the Church should not be involved in politics is foreign to the region. Elsewhere I have argued from the point of view of Romans 13:1–7 and Mark 12:7, that biblical materials encourage Christian involvement in the political process, as an advocacy for justice and peace, as a civic duty. Biblical materials do not prohibit a Christian functioning as a political leader, and it does seem quite in order for Christians to make direct input into the development of their nation. Paul contends that the principle of governing is established by God and its officials are God's servants to do good (Rom 13:4). So politics in and of itself is not evil, though it has a peculiarly violent character in a country like Jamaica.[44]

As David Jellyman and Noel Erskine of Jamaica noted recently, in Mark 10:35–37 Jesus rebukes the Sons of Zebedee—who asked him to allow them to sit one on his right and one on his left when he comes in his future glory—not for their wanting to get involved in politics but for their selfish attempt to wrest power for power's sake and use it for personal, clannish, and private purposes rather than in service to God and the people.[45] Such an approach to power that urges humility in political affairs is always timely in the modern Caribbean where political corruption is rampant and the possibility for the abuse of power is an ever-present danger. In this century the oppressive and decrepit administrations of the late Forbes Burnham of Guyana, Batista of Cuba, Eric Matthew Gairy of Grenada, Jean-Claude Duvalier (Papa Doc), his son Francois Duvalier (Baby Doc), and other dictators of Haiti, as well as those of the Dominican Republic have made this all too clear.[46] Caribbean people who read the biblical text from a Christian-specific point of view should attempt to model the life of Jesus of Nazareth.

Modeling Jesus

The politics of Jesus of Nazareth, when carefully understood, offers another paradigm in Caribbean hermeneutics and a marvelous model on which to construct a political theory for social change, one based on liberation, justice, and morality. At the very beginning of his ministry, Jesus declared his mission as one of service to humanity and obedience to the divine will. The same Jesus of Nazareth said: "The Spirit of the Lord God is upon me, because he has anointed me to bring good news to the poor. He has sent me to proclaim release to the captives and recovery of sight to the blind, to let the oppressed go free, to proclaim the year of the Lord's favor" (Luke 4:18, New Revised Standard Version [NRSV]). Throughout His three years of earthly ministry Jesus modeled the philosophy of servanthood as the path to true greatness and power. To read, hear, and play with the biblical text in the biography of Jesus is to see the shining example of a suffering servant in the face of Jesus of Nazareth. Instructive here is the memory of the paradoxical life lived by Jesus "who taught people to despise the best seats in the synagogues and the places of honor at feasts (Mark 12:39), who commanded [people] to love their enemies and to pray for their persecutors (Mark 5.44)."[47] To a young, politically ambitious would-be follower, Jesus said: "Foxes have holes, and birds of the air have nests; but the Son of Man has nowhere to lay his head" (Matt. 8:20, NRSV). Jesus taught the uncomfortable and humanly impractical doctrine of humility: that the way to save or gain one's life is to lose it, the way to true greatness is becoming like little children (Matt. 18:3), and the way to live in peace and community is not through self-defense and aggrandizement, but self-sacrifice. Luke records Jesus as saying: "If anyone strikes you on the cheek, offer the other also; and from anyone who takes away your coat, do not withhold even your shirt" (Luke 6:29, NRSV). Obviously, Jesus's use of the humility paradigm must not be read literally; Jesus is addressing people's attitude and their ability to be inconvenienced in some ways for the good of the community. Can that theology work in a Caribbean context where people have been humiliated and abused for hundreds of years? We will be damned if it does not!

In Pauline theology, Jesus shows the example of a servant leader par excellence when he decided to lay aside (divest) the glory and positions of power, equality, and authority that he had with his Father in heaven. He condescended to a lowly human state of a servant, obeyed God even to the extent of dying a cruel and shameful death on a Roman cross in order to serve the people of God. As a result of Christ's total obedience and humility, "God also highly exalted him and gave him the name that is above every name, so that at the name of Jesus every knee should bend, in heaven and on earth, and under the earth, and every tongue should confess that Jesus Christ is Lord, to the glory of God the Father" (Phil. 2:5–11, NRSV). This is a conception of love, servanthood, greatness, and glory on which the followers of Jesus are encouraged to set their gaze. They must have the mind of the servant, who did not attempt to grasp power for its own sake but gave of himself; who did not elevate himself above others but emptied himself of the desire to dominate and control others. If our Caribbean politicians could imitate even a modicum of that servant attitude of Jesus fewer leaders will be tempted to engage in political corruption and more of the people's tax dollars would be spent on developing community programs, economic projects, education, and government infrastructure than placed in personal accounts in foreign banks or squandered on party supporters in "Caribbean pork."

But paradoxically, the humble and obedient Jesus carried out a ministry of protest against false religion, injustice, and greed for political power and hegemony. According to Matthew 21:12–13, Jesus "entered the temple and drove out all who were selling and buying in the temple, and he overturned the tables of the money changers and the seats of those who sold doves." He did this not only because of the commercialization of the sacred place and its cultus but because of the exploitation of the poor worshipers. After this highly unpopular political action, Jesus, in the true spirit of the He-brew prophet (a social, political, and religious critic), said to the civil and religious leaders, "My house shall be called a house of prayer; but you are making it a den of robbers" (Matt. 21:13 NRSV). Another text says Jesus ran those who bought and sold out of the temple. Traumatized by this highly unusual political action of Jesus in the temple, and offended by his teaching against the establishment, "When he entered the temple, the chief priest and elders of the people came to him as he was teaching, and said, 'By what authority are you doing these things, and who gave you this au-thority'?" (Matt. 21:23 NRSV) Jesus was being very political and his as-sailants believed clearly that he needed authorization to do what he did. But actually, power and economic gains were as much their concern as political legitimacy.

Far from being a "little meek and mild" religious pacifist afraid to chal-lenge the root cause of human suffering under the guise of religious civility and obedience to civil authorities, the great paradoxical Jesus challenged the religious establishment of his day who separated the reading of the text of the Torah from the people and their own context. In a series of indictments (Matt. 23:3–36) the evangelist has the prophetic Jesus trumpeting more woes on the religious leaders than their ego and patience could bear; all be-cause of their laying heavy burdens on the weak and defenseless, gloating after places of honor and power, and being hypocrites whose actions locked people out of the kingdom of God. In that context Jesus outlined three sim-ple principles of true religion in this indictment: "Woe unto you Scribes and Pharisees, hypocrites! For you tithe mint, dill, and cumin, and have ne-glected the weightier matters of the law: justice and mercy, and faith. It is these you ought to have practiced without neglecting the others." (Matt. 23:23 NRSV). All of Judeo-Christian spirituality can be summed up in these three prophetic commands: Do justice! Love mercy! Walk humbly be-fore God and the world.

Caribbean people need to read and hear these texts in their own context so that they may exercise restraint in their use of positions of power and dominance while protesting against those who do not. Those who want to be the greatest among us must become the servant of all of our peoples, not just political favorites and party supporters. As the now popular saying goes, "power corrupts and absolute power corrupts absolutely." That the cultural, political, and economic ethos of the Caribbean require Christians to have "a sustained and vigorous protest against the love of prominence, prestige, and power which comes all too naturally to people,"[48] especially when it is mo-tivated by Machiavellian motives, is unquestionable. And what text has the better appeal to facilitate that ethos than the "Mother of all books" in the re-gion, the Bible?

Land Acquisition Solution Model

Another leg of the octopus called Caribbean biblical hermeneutics rests on the dire need for land acquisition for the people. As a solution to the colonial legacy of Caribbean impoverishment, underdevelopment, landlessness, identity crisis, and cultural negation, John Holder of Barbados will like to give Caribbean peoples a "Torah" in one hand—which keeps them theologically focused in the memory of their exodus experience of liberation from Egypt (slavery and colonialism)—and, in the other hand, a title deed to a piece of land or property from the other side of the Jordan (independent Caribbean countries), made possible by having a leader with the right ethic heading the government.[49] Holder's idea of responsibility, "hope, and memory," which ensure a people's right to land and property as an essential part of their social, economic, and spiritual redemption here on earth, is a helpful metaphor for playing with biblical texts in the Caribbean, as well as an ambitiously attractive proposal. In his interesting study on Deuteronomy 19, Holder argued that the Deuteronomist shows the engendering of hope in ancient Israel through their leader who reminds the people of an eternal bond between them, the land, and God.[50] They were to cherish and share the land and respect their neighbor's possession of it as a gift from Yahweh. The people must resist trading their gift of the land, their history, and their memory of God with those offered by other cultures. By so doing, not only will they preserve faith and memory in monotheistic Yahwism, but they will not be landless. If their king or political leader does not accrue to himself excessive political power, excessive wealth, an excessive harem, and upholds and respects the Torah, the blessings of Yahweh will attend the nation, and people will never be in want or distress.

In the Caribbean context where the upholders of what the Rastafarians call the "Babylon shitstem" have their peculiar hermeneutics and colonial approach to reading and playing with the same text to maintain their hegemony, the idea of memory and hope can be powerful tools in the fight against landlessness and political abuse. The problem is how to make Holder's dream a reality. Giving the people a Torah in one hand is easy; Caribbean peoples already have their "mother of all Torahs," the Bible. But the people must first have land before they can be grateful to Yahweh for it and use it to engender hope and memory of the goodness of God. However, moving the peoples from landlessness to land ownership is a very daunting task. The land must come from somewhere; and there are no free "crown lands" in Caribbean; Yahweh no longer owns the land as Holder implies. But even if God owned the land, how do we go about putting a title deed for a piece of real estate in the home of every Caribbean family?

The ancient Israelites "hijacked" the land by slaughtering and driving out earlier inhabitants of the land under the guise that Yahweh commanded them to conduct a form of "God-blessed invasion," a *jihad* of sorts. This holy war motif (driving out the heathens) pervades and drives much of the Deuteronomistic[51] presentation of the settlement of the wandering Israelite refugees from Egypt via the Wilderness and into the "promised land." One must pause to ask: Did Yahweh really give Israel the land or did they take it in his name? Has God really done all the evil things to the people and their lands that the biblical writers ascribe to God? Getting the people land by taking it from someone else in the name of God creates the kind of travesty of justice and barbarism the world has witnessed in the last few decades on the West Bank of Gaza with the resettlement of landless Jews on "Palestinian lands." In solving Caribbean economic problems, should we rob Peter to pay Paul? Holder's self-critical play with biblical texts would itself discourage a reading of Deuteronomy that encourages that sort of uprooting of families and destruction of communities in the name of religion and land settlement.

At the same time, Caribbean peoples have different approaches to the acquisition of real estate and "the good life." Peoples from foreign countries migrated to the Caribbean many generations ago and worked hard "pulling themselves up by their bootstraps," often doing the most menial of jobs and, after many years of sweat and toil, left the fruits of their labor to their offspring. Between 1848 and 1917, for example, the British, Chinese, and especially Indian immigration programs have brought about half a million East Indians and Chinese into Guyana, Trinidad, Jamaica, Grenada, and elsewhere in the Caribbean. These people worked on the plantations and at jobs that Afro-Caribbean people did not want. They were thrifty, enterprising, and operated cooperatives that allowed them to raise money to purchase large plots of land. Today, Indian descendants are the largest landholding ethnic group in Trinidad and Guyana. They are a great incentive to the cooperative effort to land ownership or economic enterprise, and an inspiration to those who are landless to work hard, be thrifty, and live in hope and memory of where Yahweh took them from and can take them to.

Holder's reading of Deuteronomy as a model for addressing the problem of landlessness in the Caribbean also advocates that the landholders should be local people and the king, or prime minister, must come from among them. This is a political necessity in the region because of our history and, especially in overcrowded Barbados, to prevent foreigners from owning too large a share of a Caribbean country's resources and to direct its foreign and domestic policies. The important question is how do we make Holder's "memory and hope" a dream come true for Caribbean people rather than a nightmare? Some scholars have suggested that we go outside of the church and look to the Messianic Hope of Rastafari for a workable answer. Three questions are pertinent to the Rasta messianic hope: How do Rastas read the biblical text? What is the Rasta messianic hope? And how would the messianic hope help the Caribbean church read biblical texts in the people's context?

The Rasta Messianic Hope and the Bible

I have attended Rasta open house and Nyabinghi celebrations in Jamaica and Barbados and on every occasion I was struck by the free, informal, and unorthodox way in which the Brethren "cited-up," quoted scripture to support their reasonings and Itations, a sort of testimony of one's belief in Haile Selassie and the movement coated with biblical citations and social and political commentary. The Bible of course, especially the KJV, is at the heart of the Rastafarian *axi mundi* (their cosmology), as an authoritative document of faith, and occupies a place of prominence and authority in the movement unrivaled by any other book. Rastas "cite-up the book" (quote the Bible) with almost religious devotion—in their "reasoning sessions, "jollification" (celebration), casual conversations, critical commentaries on government and West Indian society, oral discourse, and Rasta literary works. At a temple of the Youth Black Faith of the Nyabinghi Order in St. John, Barbados, where some of my students from the University of North Carolina and I attended a celebration in July 1998, the scriptures flowed from the lips of the Brethren as freely as their puffs of smoke filled the tent. Almost every political statement, every word of greeting, every social and cultural criticism of the "Babylon system" echoed in that peaceful and friendly gathering was punctuated with the exclamation of adoration and identity, "Haile I! Selassie I! Jah Rastafari!" and a range of scripture verses especially from the Psalms and the Hebrew prophets; psalms of adoration, imprecations and lamentations quoted from the KJV. So the Rasta ideology is Bible-based.

Because of the non-homogenous nature of the Rastafari phenomenon, Rastas have neither a unified nor a declared hermeneutic by which they all read and play with the biblical texts. They essentially "hijack" the Christian Bible by "citing-up" the text, using the "word-sounds" and language of the text to support their views on a subject with little regard for context and meaning of the text itself. In Rasta reasonings, a distinction is not always made between the literal and the figurative in the reading of biblical materials, between the original addressees and the contemporary Rasta reader, or between the writer *then* and the reader *now*. Every citation from the Bible is for "I-an-I" in the present; and, strange as it may be, the word-sounds is one of their greatest attractions. With this unique way of reading the Bible, Rastas bring specially creative "reasonings" to bear upon their playing with the text from their peculiar context of disfranchisement, "downpression" in Babylon (oppression in Jamaica and the West), and understanding of themselves as people of African descent. Rastas claim that the biblical personalities were all Black and the writers were all Black people before white folks corrupted the texts of the Bible. With this Black consciousness, Rastas identify themselves and their suffering in Babylon with the "Black" biblical characters, stories, and experiences. In this context, word-sounds, phrases, and ideas of the text are made to speak to specifically Black or Rastafarian historical, political, and economic situations.

As we have argued elsewhere, the Rastafarian biblical hermeneutics is informed by a strong sense of history, which places emphasis on people as "the subject of their own story," in this case Rastas who are conscious of their own historical experiences reflect on them in their reading of the Bible. They do this in association with the social, political, and cultural realities of their everyday lives.[52] Rastafarians neither claim to be unbiased in their approach to reading the biblical text nor do they believe it could be read as an apolitical document. They read the text with a hermeneutic of suspicion and Blackness and an "I-an-I" principle that shifts the center of attraction away from the text to the interpreter, from the text as object of inquiry to reader as the interrogator of the text. This is done in a "freestyle," unconventional "citing-up" of the Bible that allows Rastas to deconstruct the Eurocentric biblical interpretation that ignores the plight of the poor. Because many Rastas believe that Europeans corrupted the Bible, they also do not trust biblical commentaries (especially those published in Europe and America), exegetical studies, and tools used for biblical interpretation in the academy. Questions of grammar or syntax, original audience, and the context of the author are not matters of concern to Rastas as they move freely throughout the Bible citing-up text at will and reading them in such a way that word-sounds and texts speak to the conditions and needs of Rastafari. This is true of Rastas' reasonings on biblical warrant for marijuana as "the green herb" (e.g., Ps. 104:14, Gen. 1:29–30, Deut. 32:2),[53] in texts that speak positively about green herb (grass). It is also true of Rastas' discourse on Selassie as the Lion of the Tribe of Judah, king of kings and lord of lords, and his role in the collapse of Babylon spoken of in the book of Revelation.[54] And it is certainly true of Rastas' reasonings on Selassie as fulfilling the messianic hope.

Rastas "interpretive messianic approach to scripture is meant to confront what they perceive as the ideological captivity of the Bible and its interpreters and to liberate a message from the text that is relevant to them and their own situation. The appropriation of the Biblical message on this basis is in itself a liberating exercise."[55] The messianic hope of Rastafari is thus a three-legged animal: One leg is placed on the Garvey-inspired repatriation mission to Ethiopia, *Qua Africa,* as a means of escape from the Babylon "shitstem"; another leg is placed on biblical traditions from which messianic texts are hijacked and read for self-definition, identification, and liberation; and the third leg is grounded in Afro-Caribbean realities and traditions. These traditions are exalted above Eurocentric Babylon culture from which emerges the Rastas ethos—an ethos that is characterized by a mission to chant down Babylon through cultural dissonance, Nyabinghi and celebration, ritualization of ganja, reggae rhythms, and "ital living."

The messianic concept "gives Rastafari its distinct character in relation to similar movements that are usually characterized as millenarian religious sects. The concept of Messiah is thoroughly biblically based; it is influenced directly by the movement's own interpretation of selected biblical material that deals with messianic promise and hope."[56] In the Babylon imagery in the Bible,[57] especially in the Book of Revelation, Rastas find an interpretive context for their belief in the messianic hope designed to liberate Black people from their Babylonian captivity and oppression in Jamaica and the West. Babylon the Great Harlot, which Rastas interpret as the West, the Catholic Church, and the Jamaican establishment, will come crashing down on itself when Jah reigns judgment in punishment upon it for its iniquity and sins against oppressed peoples, especially people of African descent. When that happens, there will be a time of reversal of roles and positions; the powerful will be abased and the lowly and poor defenseless will be exalted. Rastafari is chosen to "Prepare the way of the Lord [Jah], make his path straight." For "Every valley shall be filled and every mountain and hill shall be brought low; and the crooked shall be made straight, and the rough ways shall be made smooth; and all flesh shall see the salvation of God" (Luke 3:5–6, KJV). The messianic hope inspires hope in the tomorrow for the poor and "downpressed" of Jamaica.

Here one finds that in spite of the death (Rastas say disappearance) of their deity Haile Selassie and recent events in Ethiopia, some Rastas are still convinced that they will experience full and final liberation through their repatriation to Ethiopia, qua Africa, and social and economic salvation here on earth. When Jah brings down the powerful Babylon shitstem, and reigns in the kingdom of God in which Rastas will feature prominently, their inheritance will be real economic "upliftment" and political power. But rather than sit and wait for this reversal to come as a "pie in the sky" in the "good bye and bye," as Marx says is expected in Christianity, Rastas proactively attempt to usher in the kingdom of Jah here and now through love "sounds," peaceful chants, and the reggae "rhythms." Rastas believe that the expected liberation could come in the here and now if everyone joins them in restructuring the political system and adopting the Rastafari social, economic, and political agenda spelt out in *The Rastafari Manifesto.*[58]

Notwithstanding their limited and questionable apocalypticism, an issue that one therefore finds most appealing in the Rastafarian messianic ideology is its attempt to contextualize theology within the Caribbean community. Rastas interpret the Bible in the social and political context of the Caribbean to make Scripture speak to social and economic issues of paramount importance to people of the African diaspora, and Jamaica in particular. At the 1971 ecumenical symposium on development held in Chaguaramas, Trinidad, discussed above, the Rastafarian representative outlined the social and political platform for Rastafarian action in the Caribbean: "The Rasta does not play a part in keeping up Babylon politics but would take part in the development of a just and true politics (a way of running the country), along that of the Holy Bible and any other equal and just way that would benefit the people of the Caribbean, Africa and the world."[59] *The Rastafarian Manifesto (EATUP)* has spelt out these principles clearly in its ambitious social, political, and economic agenda for solving economic problems in Jamaica. As Murrell and Taylor noted: "The messianic ideology of Rastafari conveys the distinct impression that the liberation . . . and hope is essentially a historical project. The expected liberation of the oppressed people held in captivity in Babylon is a reality in history. . . . Of course, the messianic vision that Rastafari espouses looks for the experience of full and final liberation beyond its immediate context of the captivity and oppression characterized as Babylon."[60]

Because of the peculiar nature of the reading of biblical text in Rastafari, the Church should not engage in an uncritical borrowing of the Rastafari hermeneutic or messianic hope in a manner that causes it to put new wine into old wine vats, or take a new piece of fabric (Rastafarian messianic hope) to patch an old garment (traditional Christian theology). In response to John's disciples' question as to why the disciples of Christ do not fast as the Pharisees do, Christ made it abundantly clear that new wine should be stored in new wineskins (bottles) or else the bottles will break and the wine will be destroyed. Christ used this metaphor to refer specifically to the uniqueness of the message of the kingdom of God in His preaching in contrast to elements in ancient Jewish religion. But the figure of speech is quite an appropriate message for us to hear in our changing Caribbean contexts. The Church needs new wine bottles (approaches to deal with contemporary Caribbean problems) but it must inquire into the nature of the "wineskin" and how well it will contain and preserve the wine, in this case the part of Rasta biblical hermeneutics and messianic hope that can be used to solve the social and economic problems of the region and what part should be discarded.

This partially answers Erskine's question, "What would it mean for the mainline Church to learn from the Rasta, and begin Bible study with a reading of the sociological text?"[61] The answer is: be creative like the Rastas in reading biblical text and interpret the Bible in the people's context with full knowledge of the dangerous memories of oppression, exploitation, landlessness, underemployment, underdevelopment, and other effects of colonialism. Knowledge of the critical times in which they live keeps the Church in tune with the people's needs and causes Christians to escape Marx's critique and Christ's indictment of the Pharisees and hypocrites who neglected the most important "matters of the law: Justice, mercy, and faith" which Jesus says the Church ought to do (Matt. 23:23). Like Rastas, we must read with the Bible in one hand and the newspaper in the other, to understand and respond to the times in which we live.

Notes

1. Ennis Edmonds, "Rastafarian Hermeneutics and the Politics of Liberation," a paper read at the Annual Meeting of the Society of Biblical Literature (hereafter AAR/SBL) (San Francisco: 1997), 4.

2. Dale Bisnauth, *A History of Religions in the Caribbean* (Jamaica: Kingston Publishers, 1989), 12.

3. Ibid., 11. See also Cinny Poppen, "Invasion," in *Dangerous Memories Since 1492* (Chicago: The Chicago Religion Task Force on Central America, 1991), 48.

4 Bartholome de Las Casas, "Digest of Columbus's Log-Book on His First Voyage," in *The Four Voyages of Christopher Columbus,* ed. and trans J. M. Cohen (New York: Penguin Books, 1969), 37.

5. Eric Williams, *From Columbus to Castro: The History of the Caribbean* (New York: Vintage Books/ Random House, 1970), 20.

6. Ibid.

7. Ibid., 13.

8. As late as the early 1700s, the last Carib resistance to French invasion and slaughter in Grenada terminated at Leapers Hill *(Le Morne Des Sauteurs)* in the parish of St. Mark with several hundred defiant Caribs jumping headlong to their death over a precipice of over 400 feet deep rather than surrender to the French (Williams, *From Columbus to Castro,* 95). See also Poppen, "Invasion," 50–53.

9. Bill M. Donovan, "Introduction" in *Bartolome de Las Casas, The Devastation of the Indies: A Brief Account,* trans. Herman Briffault (Baltimore: Johns Hopkins University Press, 1992), 4.

10. Williams, *From Columbus to Castro,* 37.

11. Patrick C. Hamilton, *The Struggles of the Caribbean People* (1492–1984) (Washington D.C.: Billpops Publications, 1984), 7.

12. Williams, *From Columbus to Castro,* 37. See also Poppen, "Invasion," 58–63.

13. Bisnauth, 13.

14. *The Covenant of the Anabaptist Church Begun in America 1777 and in Jamaica December 1783,* in *General Baptist Repository,* vol. 1, supplement (1802); also

Baptist Quarterly vol. 7 (1806), 20–26. Cited in Horace Russell, "Some Baptist Understandings and Interpretations of Scripture in Eighteenth- and Nineteenth-Century Jamaica: A Look at George Liele and William Knibb," paper read at the AAR/SBL in Philadelphia, 1995, 3.

15. Eric Williams, *Capitalism and Slavery,* 9th ed. (London: Andre Deutsch, 1944), 7; *From Columbus to Castro,* 280–90.

16. Bishop William Heart Coleridge, *Charges Delivered to the Clergy of the Diocese of Barbados and the Leeward Island* (London: J. G. & F. Rivington, 1835), 263–4. Cited in John Holder, "Is This the Word of the Lord? Caribbean Theology and Hermeneutics," paper read at the AAR/ SBL Bible in Caribbean Culture and Tradition Consultation (Philadelphia, 1995), 3.

17. Robert J. Stewart, *Religion and Society in Post-Emancipation Jamaica* (Knoxville: University of Tennessee, 1992), 13.

18. Ibid., 10.

19. Stewart, 14. See David Brian Davis, *The Problem of Slavery in Western Culture* (Ithaca, NY: Cornell University Press, 1966), 388.

20. *Missionary Registrar* (August 1832), 328. Cited in Stewart, *Religion and Society,* 14. Cf. Methodist Missionary Society instructions for missionaries, 1834, Article 5, cited in Dorothy Ann Royall, "The Organization of the missionary societies, the recruitment of the missionaries in Britain and the role of the missionaries in the diffusion of British Culture in Jamaica during the period 1834–1865," Ph.D. diss., University of London, 1959.

21. Horace O. Russell, "The Church in the Past—A Study on Jamaican Baptists in the 18th and 19th Centuries," *Jamaican Historical Society Bulletin* 8 (1993): 204–71.

22. John Clarke, *Memorials of the Baptist Missionaries in Jamaica* (London: Baptist Missionary Society, 1869), 156. Cited in Stewart, 12.

23. Richard Merrick in *Baptist Herald* 1 (March 1843): 25; Stewart, 17.

24. Williams, *Capitalism and Slavery,* 98–107; *Columbus to Castro,* 156–71.

25. See Barbara Bush, *Slave Women in Caribbean Society 1650–1838* (Bloomington: Indiana University Press, 1990), 51–81.

26. Williams, *From Columbus to Castro,* 66–7.

27. Stewart, 50.

28. Williams, *From Columbus to Castro,* 280–92.

29. Stewart, 18–19.

30. Gad Heuman, "A Tale of Two Jamaican Rebellions," *The Jamaica Historical Review,* vol. XIX (1996): 1–6; Don Robotham, "'The Notorious Riot,' The Socio-Economic and Political Bases of Paul Bogle's Revolt," working paper no. 28 (University of the West Indies, Jamaica: Institute of Social and Economic Research, 1981): 17–24.

31. Nathaniel Samuel Murrell and Erica Campbell, "Should Christians Be Involved in Jamaican Politics?" *Caribbean Journal of Evangelical Theology,* vol. 2 (1998): 47.

32. Sehon S. Goodridge, *Facing the Challenge of Emancipation: A Study of the Ministry of William Hart Coleridge First Bishop of Barbados,* 1824–1842 (Bridgetown: Cedar Press, 1981), 31–67.

33. See Bridget Brereton, *A History of Modern Trinidad* 1783–1962 (London: Spottiswoode Ballantyne, 1981), 122–7.

34. Noel Erskine, "The Bible as Source and Resource," paper delivered at the Annual Meeting of the American Academy of Religion and the Society of Biblical Literature, Chicago, 1996): 1

35. "Editorial," Barbados Advocate (February 1998).

36. Karl Marx, "Toward the Critique of Hegel's Philosophy of Law: Introduction," in *Writings of the Young Marx on Philosophy and Society,* trans. and ed. Lloyd D. Easton and Kurt H. Guddat (New York: Doubleday Anchor, 1967). "Religion is the Opium of the People," in John Lyden, *Enduring Issues in Religion* (San Diego, CA: Greenhaven Press, 1995), 27.

37. "Religion Is the Opium of the People," 27.

38. Ibid., 30–2. It is interesting to note here that the Rastafarians debunk the notion of original sin since they believe original sin, if it does exists at all, is sin committed against black people.

39. Ibid., 31.

40. L. H. Fletcher, "The SDA Facing the Challenges of the 80's," sermon published in *The Caribbean Pulpit,* ed. C. H. J. Gayle and William W. Watty (San Fernando, Trinidad: 1986).

41. In the last three decades, many Caribbean theologians have underscored the need for this project and have attempted to articulate it as a vision: the late Idris Hamid, William Watty, and Bishop Abdullah of Trinidad; Burchell Taylor, Lewin Williams, and David Jellyman of Jamaica; Roy Neehall and Dale Bisnauth of Guyana; John Holder and Robert Cuthbert of Barbados, and a cadre of others including this author from Grenada.

42. Nathaniel Samuel Murrell, "Wrestling with the Bible in the Caribbean Basin: A Case Study on Grenada in Light of Romans 13:1–7," *Caribbean Journal of Religious Studies* vol. 8, no. 1 (April 1987): 12–23.

43. As Walter Brueggemann noted, interpretation (and preaching) involves giving "an alternative version of reality." It is a sub-version because we never have the original version; and what we offer sub-verts the dominant version of the cultural narrative of the society (Walter Brueggemann, "Preaching as Sub-version," *Theology Today* vol. 55, no. 2 (July 1998): 199–200.

44. Murrell and Campbell, 45–63.

45. Erskine, 6. David Jellyman, "Protest, Pattern and Power," *Caribbean Journal of Religious Studies* vol. 1, no. 2 (July 1976): 2–29.

46. These political leaders fleeced our people of hard-earned money in taxes in order to stash away millions of dollars in their personal foreign bank accounts.

47. Erskine, 6–7.

48. Ibid., 7.

49. John Holder, "Some Deuteronomic Themes in a Caribbean Context," *Caribbean Journal of Religious Studies* vol. 14, no. 2 (September 1993): 12–16.

50 Ibid.

51 Someone was responsible for piecing the large chunks of materials together in the Torah and "The Former Prophets," whom scholars call the Deuteronomist. According to the so-called Deuteronomist, the people who moved into the land of Canaan after their wilderness wandering drove out the original inhabitants and slaughtered others in order to take possession of the land through bloody battles in the name of Yahweh.

52. Nathaniel Samuel Murrell and Burchell Taylor, "The Messianic Hope of Rastafari," *Chanting Down Babylon, The Rastafari Reader* (Philadelphia: Temple University Press, 1998), 391–2.

53. Issembly of Elders of Jahrastafari, *The Ethiopian-African Theocracy Union Policy: EATUP* (Kingston: Jahrastafari Royal Ethiopian Judah-Coptic Church, n.d. ca. 1989), 12, 25.

54. John Moodie, *Hath the Lion Prevailed?* (Boynton Beach, FL: Future Printing and Publishing, 1992).

55. Murrell and Taylor, 396.

56. Ibid., 391.

57. As other contributors noted above, Babylon is symbolic of a complex of oppressive forces represented by slavery, colonialism, imperialism, and the structures, systems, and ideologies that enforce and sustain their interests.

58. EATUP, 18–24.

59. Haile Mikael Yenge Flagot Kezehemohonenow, "The Role of Rastafarians in the Caribbean," unpublished paper delivered at the Caribbean Symposium, Chaguaramas, Trinidad (November 1971), 3.

60. Murrell and Taylor, 398.

61. Erskine, 20.

Chapter 2 🎋

Reggae and Rastafari in Salvador, Bahia

The Caribbean Connection in Brazil

Janet L. DeCosmo

As is the case in other parts of the world, Rastafari[1] made its way to Bahia by way of Jamaican reggae music, in particular, the music of Bob Marley and the Wailers. As elsewhere, Rastafari in Bahia may be described as a continuum of beliefs, ranging from the orthodox on one end to free-wheeling individualists on the other. In its orthodox version, Rastafari stands opposed to indigenous forms of Bahian religion and culture, such as *Candomblé*[2] and Carnival. Yet other Rastafari in Bahia happily participate in both. This chapter begins with a description of the social, cultural, political, and religious background from which Rastafari emerged in Bahia. Then, selective quotations from Bahian Rastafari are used to illustrate similarities and differences between an "ideal type" of Jamaican Rastafari and those forms found in Salvador. Suggestions for the direction of future research, as well as tentative conclusions, will follow.

Salvador, Bahia

Tragically, Brazil is distinguished by having the largest gap between rich and poor of any nation on the planet.[3] There is high inflation, a huge foreign debt, millions of abandoned children, and rapid urbanization, which has led to the formation of slums *(favelas)* and urban blight. It is the largest Black country outside of the African continent, with only Nigeria having a population larger than that of the more than 70 million African descendants who reside in Brazil. In general usage, the term "Bahia" (a region in northeast Brazil) refers to "Salvador," the third largest city in the country. São Paolo, the largest, is the third largest city in the world, behind Mexico City and Tokyo. The 1991 Brazilian census (which offers "colors" as racial categories) reported that of Salvador's population of 2,075,273 inhabitants, 14.5 percent were black, 64.2 percent were brown, 20.4 percent were white, .1 percent were yellow, and .2 percent were red (indigenous).[4]

The urban barrio in Salvador in which this study was carried out, Pelourinho, is rich with historical significance. It is where African slaves were first whipped and beaten in public; in fact, the word "Pelourinho" means "whipping post" in Portuguese. The average monthly income in the area, where approximately 75 percent of the population is illiterate, is about $120.[5] Unemployment is high, and there are a number of impoverished street kids in evidence. Over and over again, I was told about problems with alcohol, prostitution, and crack, and about how Rastafari (and practitioners of *Candomblé* before that) have been discriminated against and brutalized by the police, especially during the period of military dictatorship. The difference between the tourist areas in Pelourinho—including bars, hotels, and restaurants reminiscent of the French Quarter in New Orleans—and the black ghettos, which are only blocks away but hidden behind the façades of colonial structures, is shocking. Tourists in Pelourinho feel secure due to the presence of armed guards stationed on most corners; they never see these "invisible" ghettos unless they make a determined effort to do so. About 80 percent of the population of Salvador lives in poverty, and there is no government welfare or "safety net" for the poor. On several occasions I observed many persons sleeping in doorways alongside main urban thoroughfares around Pelourinho. Vehicles carrying Church members often appear in these areas at certain prescribed hours handing out food. While talking to a Rastafari friend one evening, he suddenly rushed off, returning in a few minutes with a paper cup full of corn chowder, which a local Church group was distributing to hungry street people.

A second Rastafari informant provided me with the following description of the ghetto in which he and many others like him lived: "The situation in Salvador, it's very poor. . . . People are hurting here. The activists, the militants, are . . . repressed by the police. Movements dedicated to revitalization are being put down very strongly. . . . A majority of us don't have jobs, and we don't have a chance and opportunity. . . . We survive by miracles. We evoke the all-powerful God and we use the positive, supernatural powers. Like people were fed for 40 years in the desert, like our patriarch Moses, the leader of our people invoked the all-powerful God and the all-powerful God sent food to us. We don't have basic help of any kind. . . . We are thrown and confined to the concentration camps that in Brazil they call *favelas*. . . . Here is hell."

Despite its poverty, Salvador is a legendary city, "a land of the imagination produced by generations of novelists, songwriters, poets, ethnographers, historians, artists, musicians," as one scholar put it. The bay in Salvador is known as *"Bahia de todos os santos"* (Bay of All Saints). Guides throughout the city are fond of repeating the often-heard claim that Salvador contains as many churches as days of the year. Although this is an exaggeration, I was able to photograph a dozen Catholic churches in a 45-minute period on foot one day. As anthropologist Jim Wafer describes it, Bahia is indeed a magical place.[6] As is typical of many parts of the Caribbean, Bahia is culturally rich while materially poor. Yet because Afro-Bahians have refused to give up their heritage, cultural and religious pluralism have managed to prevail over acculturation to European norms.

Bahia, like most of Brazil, has a long history of racial discrimination and political repression. The institution of slavery was particularly brutal in Brazil due to the fact that the largest numbers of Africans were imported into Brazil. Because of a surplus of cheap labor power, it was economically more efficient for sugar plantation owners to work slaves to death and purchase replacements, rather than keep them alive for as long as possible.

After emancipation in 1888, Afro-Brazilians began the long, laborious task of making a place for themselves in society. A significant and public part of this quest involved participation in the Catholic pre-Lenten festival, *Carnaval* (Carnival). African Carnival groups *(blocos)* joyfully celebrated their newfound freedom along the public thoroughfares in the weeks before Ash Wednesday. As was the case in many parts of the Caribbean, conservative Catholic authorities soon became appalled at what they considered to be the "excesses" of Carnival, and in 1905 the African groups were expelled. They were not to reappear again until the emergence of the Sons of Gandhi *(Filhos de Gandhy),* formed by black and mulatto dockworkers in 1949.[7] The group thrived until the advent of the military regime in 1964 when it went into hiding, to reemerge with the beginning of political liberalization in 1974. At this point, Carnival groups of all sorts came to the forefront as the bearers of a new Black consciousness. With the established channels of power cut off from them (electoral politics and bureaucratic structures), Afro-Bahians produced cultural organizations that were later to give them political leverage. As historian Kim Butler put it, "Afro-Bahians have created one of the most vital alternative communities in the Afro-Atlantic world, with institutions such as *Candomblé* through which people of African descent maintain a distinct value system and worldview. Through these institutions, Afro-Brazilians find the personal dignity, self-worth, and social power that is so frequently denied them in the larger society."[8]

In Brazil generally, Black consciousness has been expressed in such nonpolitical forms as religious brotherhoods, samba schools, Carnival *blocos,*

African religious organizations, mutual aid societies, and recreational clubs, all of which kept a low profile during the military dictatorship when laws such as the National Security Law banned all speech on the subject of race relations. These groups maintained their own spaces, seeking recognition and legitimacy from alternative power bases. The Carnival groups emerging from the *Candomblé* houses serve as an example. *Ilê Aiyê* (founded in 1974) led to efforts to educate the marginalized, and thus transform them, through work in building self-esteem, educating Afro-Bahians about their ancestral legacies, and providing counterhegemonic analyses of daily life. Participation by dark-skinned (black and brown) Afro-Brazilians was strongly encouraged. The ultimate goal of *Ilê Aiyê*, as described in one of their educational booklets, is to use culture to create citizens who can exercise political power.[9] Their slogans include words such as "maturity," "dignity," "integrity," "Black consciousness," "resistance," and "power." Similar groups, dozens of which emerged from the *Candomblé* houses throughout the 70s and 80s, used Carnival lyrics, hairstyles, and costume to teach the African heritage.

Serving as meeting spots for activists, *Candomblé* thus helped lead the way out of the repression of the nineteenth and early twentieth centuries to become an important focal point for Afro-Brazilian cultural politics. As Butler put it: "Poor and elderly black women who, in mainstream society, could not dream of entering the highest spheres of power because of their color, sex, age, and poverty, could become mighty leaders in the world of *Candomblé*. *Candomblé* valued the wisdom of age, the ancestral links to Africa, and the power of women."[10] In addition, institutions were created that provided a link between cultural groups and the government. In most of the 22 states of Brazil today, there are active "federations," or umbrella organizations, which mediate between individual religious centers and the wider Brazilian society, in particular governmental institutions. For example, there is a national umbrella organization for Afro-Brazilian religions known as CONTOC: "Conference of the Tradition and Culture of the *Orixás*," which provides representatives to the International Congress of *Orixá* Tradition and Culture.[11] The Unified Black Movement (*Movimento Negro Unificado*, or MNU), formed in 1978 for the purpose of political activism, also uses cultural institutions to generate political awareness. Butler stated that "by the mid-1980s, a sizable activist core working through such outlets as Afro-Bahian newspapers, *blocos afros*, reggae radio programs, and reggae bars had positioned itself to make an impact on the electoral politics of the newly restored democracy."[12] As center-left coalitions came to power in Salvador, socialist and communist parties actively began to recruit Afro-Brazilian militants and express openness to issues of race. In this regard, I was told by a Rastafari informant that a socialist politician had sponsored his Carnival *bloco, Amantes do Reggae* (Lovers of Reggae), in 1998. A document approved by participants in the First National Encounter of the Abolition of Slavery Centennial, held in Bahia in 1987, stated that Afro-Bahians would continue the struggle to gain space in the formal political arena without disregarding the racial question, and to strengthen ties with other social movements, "especially those which represent living forces in Brazilian society." They would also struggle to "reverse domination by the elites."[13]

Another example of the complex dialectic of social transformation in Bahia is the story of the internationally known percussion group, *Olodum,* founded in 1979. Before the run-down barrio of Pelourinho became a tourist mecca, *Olodum* held its practices in its center. Highly visible as well as audible, the practices soon became a meeting place for the Afro-Bahian community, many of whom were dreadlocked. Its leaders were activists, using music to promote awareness of history and social issues. Their logo was the peace sign and their colors were the Rastafari colors: red, green, and yellow. Soon foreigners, as well as formerly hesitant middle-class Bahians, ventured into the area. When the new form of music invented by *Olodum*—samba-reggae—was featured on Paul Simon's 1990 album, *Rhythm of the Saints,* the government finally caught onto the economic and commercial potential of the area, promising to renovate the crumbling but magnificent historic colonial architecture. Between 1991–93, many buildings were restored in Pelourinho, but hundreds of longtime residents were paid only $400-$800 for the apartments they were forced out of.[14] Police were then stationed in the area to keep "undesirables" from bothering people, and "marginals" were continually harassed and arrested, to keep them away from tourists.

As a result of their newfound success, *Olodum* opened a new headquarters in a restored townhouse and began to stage concerts for tourists, with paid admission and strict security. The group continued to serve as a source of local employment and cultural programming. By 1992, a school, a boutique, a theatre group, a touring professional band, a youth percussion group comprised of over 300 children, and a Carnival *bloco* were all under *Olodum*'s umbrella. One of their founders, Joao Jorge Rodrigues, was named head of the *Fundacao Gregorio de Mattos,* a state cultural agency that provided resources for Afro-Bahian organizations. The icing on the cake was to come when Spike Lee directed a video for Michael Jackson in Pelourinho featuring *Olodum,* with Jackson wearing one of their T-shirts.[15]

Not surprisingly, as these groups opened up new spaces, the elite began to use them for their own ends. Black culture has been commodified and is now for sale in the tourist markets of Bahia. Many vendors seek commercial gain through the use of popular reggae and Rastafari imagery. One finds tams with long dreadlocks for sale in Pelourinho; caps with Baiana hair[16] in blond, brown, and black (some available with *Olodum*'s logo on the front); pencils with Rasta heads at the ends; T-shirts with Carnival groups' logos on the front, etc. Bob Marley T-shirts, posters, flags, and calendars abound. In fact, the Caribbean influence in Pelourinho is so strong that one of my informants called it "the second Jamaica." Another told me, "you can see Jamaica in the streets." Recently, a very exclusive Jamaican *"Bar, Hotel, Restaurante e Bou-tique do Reggae," Suite Quilombo do Pelô*, was opened in Pelourinho by a Ja-maican and his Bahian wife. While most of the other stores in the area offer Brazilian-made versions, the posters and T-shirts of Marley in this boutique are imported directly from the Marley Museum in Kingston. Although it serves meat, the restaurant's menu stated that it also serves "Ital" food, but "Ital" was spelled "I*n*tal." The owner's wife had not been aware of the mistake until my Rastafari friend and I told her about it. Although this supposedly "authentic" Jamaican place had been created with scant ties to, or knowledge of Rastafari culture, its advertisement in the *Folha do Reggae* claimed that it was the "most exotic **RAS**taurante in Pelourinho."[17]

Another example of the cooptation and commodification of culture has occurred with *capoeira,* a crucial marker of Afro-Bahian identity, which has helped provide psychological and spiritual support and employment to many people in the area. In the 1980s, *capoeiristas* sought to raise cultural awareness by holding public festivals. Adapted from an Angolan dance/the-atre/martial art form, *capoeira angola* is to be distinguished from *capoeira re-gional,* a form purged of African elements and thoroughly bureaucratized. The latter form was taught to the Bahian police during the military regime to defend Brazilian society from supposed "internal enemies."[18] In their will-ingness to perform for profit, instructors of *capoeira regional* have not only taught policemen the skill but have sold shows to local hotels and restau-rants, drawing tourists away from the traditional *capoeira angola* academies, causing some of them to go bankrupt.[19]

Given the context in which it is found in Pelourinho, it is now clear why one of my informants, an orthodox Rastafari and *capoeira angola* instructor, refuses to take any money from his students despite intense pressure to do so. After staging a special *capoeira angola* practice with his students (which included both boys and girls) so that I could videotape it, I was able to see his school's uniforms. They consisted of loose-fitting green pants with an elastic waist and a white T-shirt designed by the instructor. On the front of the T-shirt was a rainbow of red, yellow, and green with a Star of David un-derneath it. At the top were the words, "Jah Rastafari I Selassie I." In the red part of the rainbow was written *"Academia De Estudos Da,"* in the yellow part, *"Capoeira Angola,"* and in the green was written the name of the infor-mant's instructor, "Joao Pequeno." Under the rainbow, "Jesus Christ Is Our Teacher" was written in Portuguese, and in very small print, the location and date of the academy's founding were noted. The *berimbaus* that he made,[20] one of which he gave me, were also inscribed with the words important to his faith. A large Star of David with a fish in the middle of it was burnished into the gourd. Along its rim were three smaller stars and the words "Jah Rastafari Selassie I." At the top of the bow were the date of the instrument's making and an address in Pelourinho. In the middle, the words "Jah Rastafari Selassie I Amen" were inscribed. Toward the bottom were the words *"capoeira angola"* and his own name as instructor. Although he was happy to give me the *berimbau,* he told me that he could not give me one of the academy's T-shirts—they were for members only.

Reggae

Reggae, and with it, Rastafari, seems to have been introduced into Bahia in the 1970s by Gilberto Gil and Caetano Veloso.[21] While Brazil festered under a military dictatorship, the two men were exiled in London (Gil had actually been jailed for a time) just when Bob Marley and the Wailers' *Catch a Fire* was becoming an international success. When they returned to Salvador, the new "heartbeat" rhythms of Marley, Jacob Miller, and Jimmy Cliff came with them. One of my informants explained his attraction to reggae upon first hearing it:

> I, like thousands and thousands of young men in Brazil, grew up listening to Black music, American Black music. It comes without saying that I didn't know a word in English. When I heard reggae the first time I discovered it was the beat of my heart. Something happened to me. I felt like light. And it was not important what the words were saying because I was made conscious to my spirit; it made me feel good to my soul, to my being. I was very interested to know what the people were singing in the reggae music. In truth what they said had a lot of things to do with me. And it was my own history that was being translated in the words of the songs and from then on, [listening to] reggae was like to eat and drink well every day.

The first reggae composition to be recorded in Portuguese was Gil's rendition of Marley's "No Woman No Cry," which however did not remain loyal to the English lyrics. Then in 1980 (or 1981)[22] Gil arranged the first reggae concert in Bahia, featuring Jimmy Cliff. Since then, many other reggae performers, including leading exponents of Rastafari such as dub poet Mutabaruka, have appeared there. FM radio stations regularly offer special reggae shows with their own regular time slots, and as many as 15 or 20 reggae bands currently exist in Bahia, although only a few are comprised of "orthodox" Rastafari.

William David Spencer noted that most of the dreadlocked musicians in Brazil were not Rastafari, and quoted musician and composer Caetano Veloso on the subject: "Some people in Brazil . . . behave in a Rastafarian way. I mean, they look like Rastafarians and they kind of dance like Rastafarians. But I don't know if there are real Rastafarians in Brazil. I mean, with all the religious implications and all of the fantasies that belong to that belief."[23] This remark is very similar to that of a dreadlocked sculptor/composer informant who distinguished between a "Rasta" and a "Rastafari." He considered himself to be the former because of his active participation in *Candomblé*. He related the following:

> Rastafari is something very spiritual. I dreamed three times about my hair being curled [locksed] before I curled it [grew it out]. I went a little deeper into Rastafari and tried to understand what Rastafari is. I do not consider myself Rastafari, but I consider myself Rasta because of the dreads. Rastafari I see as a religion, as a spiritual following; it has a deep connotation that I really don't know if in Brazil people follow. Being a religion I do not consider myself a practitioner of this religion. I practice *Candomblé*. But I believe Rastafari is a religion and the beliefs of Rastafari have their own processes. The Rastafari do not eat meat, or red meat. They have spiritual practices, they use kaya, or marijuana, but in a very intelligent way inside the ritual. . . . I eat meat. That's why I do not consider myself Rastafari. I have a lot of friends that are Rastas; however, they are not Rastafaris.

Spencer maintained that popular music is more likely to promote Afro-Brazilian faiths, and stated that reggae was not "pure" there since it was usually blended with other Brazilian rhythms. This is indeed the case with the samba-reggae associated with *Olodum*, which sounds more like samba than reggae. But the majority of reggae bands who identify themselves as such sound very similar to Jamaican reggae bands. It is certainly the case that not all dreadlocked musicians who sing reggae are Rastafari. For example, there is a dreadlocked singer in Bahia named Sine Calmon, whose song "Nyambing [*sic*] Blues" was the reggae hit of the 1998 Carnival. Calmon, a beardless ganja-smoker, claimed that Rastafari is idolatry. While the lyrics to this song contain phrases such as "fire in Babylon" *(fogo na Babylonia),* Calmon's religious references are to light and love, and God and Jesus—never Jah, Rastafari, or Haile Selassie. His songs might therefore be considered a form of Christian reggae. My orthodox Rastafari informants, who remain on friendly terms with Calmon, told me that he had a severe drug problem. The Rastafari reggae bands during Carnival all did covers of the hit song. When I asked them why they would play a song whose composer they disapproved of, one of their wives somewhat irritatedly exclaimed, "Because it's a good song!" And indeed it is.

For reggae band members in Bahia who are Rastafari, reggae is most definitely a form of social protest and a tool of consciousness-raising, liberation, and evangelism. In addition, many of the *"blocos Afros"* of Carnival have incorporated the icons and colors of Rastafari or are comprised of dreadlocked musicians (some of whom identify themselves as Rastafari), such as *Olodum, Muzenza, Ska Reggae, Amantes do Reggae, Aspiral do Reggae* (Breath of Reggae), *Filhos de Jah* (Sons of Jah), and *Unidade Real* (Real Unity). Individuals joining the smaller reggae *blocos* to dance down the street do not necessarily have to purchase the costume if they can't afford it (T-shirts, or T-shirts and shorts, are generally $40 or less) and are not kept away from the bands by a circle of rope handlers. The more popular groups insist on costumes and employ rope handlers to keep non-members out. Class stratifications are thus highly visible during Carnival.

The Informants and
Why They Identify as Rastafari

The fieldwork for this study was carried out in Pelourinho during the Carnivals of February 1997 and 1998, and during the summer of 1997. Of eight male informants ranging in age from 32 to 50, one was formally interviewed three times, three were interviewed twice, and four were interviewed once. Many were interviewed informally a number of times. They include an artist; a craftsman/reggae musician; a *capoeira angola* instructor and reggae singer/composer; a musician/instrument-maker; a reggae musician and self-described "psychotherapist, sociologist, and theocratic"; and three artist/musicians. All wear dreadlocks and identify as Rastafari in some form or fashion. As Butler reminded us, "[a]lthough it might be tempting to think of all Afro-Bahians as a single 'community' linked by their African heritage, it must be remembered that there is no monolithic Afro-Bahian culture, identity, political ideology, or ethos."[24] The same holds true for Rastafari. The informants make a basic distinction between two ends of a continuum, separating themselves into "cultural/political" Rastafari and "religious" Rastafari (also called "orthodox" or "Protestant" Rastafari). Members of the former group wear dreadlocks and consider Rastafari to be a way of life involving cultural resistance against a system that oppresses them ("Babylon"). Those who define Rastafari as a religion that requires vegetarianism, like the artist/composer described earlier, do not align themselves with the orthodox Rastafari but do consider themselves to be Rastafari in some sense.

Members of the orthodox group maintain that Rastafari is primarily spiritual, smoke ganja in informal reasoning sessions, and usually wear beards and dreadlocks. (While most of the Rastafari interviewed in the latter group have descended from African slaves and identify with the Black underclass, some of them are very light-skinned and have hair that, although long and very curly, is not worn in dreads because, one presumes, they don't care to devote the extra time and attention it would take to artificially "locks up.") Among this group's friends was a straight-haired blond woman from Germany with dreads. Both cultural Rastafari as well as religious Rastafari distinguish themselves from mere "dreadlocks." As one informant put it, "a lot of people use Rastafarianism as a style. They use dreads, the style of Rastafari, but they don't really know Rastafarianism. Because it's very beautiful, everybody wants to know. But [it's used] more as a style." Although ganja-smoking seems to have been in existence in Bahia for quite some time before, the wearing of dreadlocks, reggae bands, and Rastafari all came to Bahia as a direct result of exposure to Jamaican reggae. As Carole Yawney and John Homiak have noted, Rastafari may be the only religion that has spread globally through popular culture.[25]

Although one informant said he had been Rastafari since birth (and later did not catch himself when he mentioned a time "before" he was Rastafari) and another said he had been Rastafari since the age of ten when he got involved with *capoeira angola,* most of the informants said that reggae music was what introduced them to the ideology. Five of the eight informants are members of reggae bands. When asked when they "sighted" or became Rastafari, depending on their ages, my informants gave dates ranging from the late 70s to the late 80s. While all the informants stressed the supreme life-changing importance of Bob Marley and reggae music and were either indifferent to, or actively defended, the use of ganja, their notions about Ethiopian emperor Haile Selassie, meat-eating, and repatriation are quite different from those in Jamaica. This points out the problematic nature of defining a global Rastafari.

Informant #1 is a well-known outgoing 42-year-old artist from the island of Itaparica just off the coast of Salvador. He is separated from his wife but supports three children in school. He grew up within *Candomblé,* and describes himself as "40 percent Rastafari." He wears 12-year-old, narrow dreadlocks, smokes cigarettes and cigars, doesn't smoke ganja, eats meat, and drinks alcohol. Besides colorful market scenes and the streets and people of Pelourinho, he paints the *orixás* of *Candomblé* and portraits of Amazonian Indians. One of his self-portraits contains the words "Rastafari" and "500 Years." He also serves as an official but informal guide in the Pelourinho area. Although he said he was not too familiar with the Bible, he has some knowledge of Haile Selassie's claim of descent from Solomon and Sheba, and mentioned the importance of Marcus Garvey within Rastafari, as well as the symbolic importance of the ring given to Bob Marley by Selassie's family. He dances in Carnival with the *bloco Afro, Ska Reggae.* When I observed him in

February dancing behind the trio, he did a perfect imitation of Marley's eclectic jumping around, with arms waving and locks flying as his head shook violently from side to side in time to the music.

This informant identified with Rastafari, he said, "because I believe in human rights. The first position of Rastafarianism is human rights—to put all of us equal to each other. We are all brothers and sisters. When the human being thinks of another being as a brother, you don't need anything else because there's no individualism. There's a strong identification of Rastafarianism against oppression, against discrimination. This is the life philosophy that says that 'the color of a man's skin should have no more significance than the color of his eyes.'"[26] He stated that "Rastafarianism is not really a religion. It's a philosophy of life—open, free, and democratic. It's a very strong democracy. Rastafari is a very strong resistance, a very active resistance . . ."

Informant #2 is an itinerant 32-year-old instrument-maker and musician of "all types of music," *capoeira angola* in particular. He is single, wears dreadlocks, eats meat, and most likely smokes ganja and drinks alcohol. On my third visit to Salvador, I was told he had moved to São Paolo. He stated: "I identify as a Rastafari in my way of life. It's a transformation that happened inside myself. I started with this story when I was 10 years old. It's going to be 22 years now that I've worked with this. The first thing that made me look inside myself was *capoeira* and I began to build instruments like the *berimbau*." He makes a distinction between "the Rastafaris" and "the dreadlocks," adding that "really, in Bahia there are few Rastafarians. There are a lot of curly-hairs but few Rastafaris because Rastafaris, for sure, dwell in the religion, in the Rastafari religion. And they feed themselves with natural things. In Bahia there are few Rastafari who feed themselves with natural products, who only dwell in the religion itself."

Informant #3, age 32, is a friend of Informant #2 and a T-shirt designer/painter and part-time reggae musician with a local band, *Aspiral do Reggae* (Breath of Reggae). He identified with Rastafari, he said, "because of the lifestyle that I have. I started letting my hair grow about ten years ago. I define Rastafari as a way of living. Rastafari means the belief not to eat meat, not to cut your hair. Rarely do I eat meat, almost never, even when I was a young man. Through the rhythm, through the music . . . I identify myself [as Rastafari] because of this."

Informant #4 is a friend of Informant #1. He is a 43-year-old sculptor and composer who lives with his older sister, his nephew, a dog, and a cat in Paumiudo, the poorest Black ghetto in Bahia. His long dreadlocks, which he began to grow in 1982, fall almost to his waist. He eats meat, drinks beer, and may or may not smoke ganja. He is an active participant in *Candomblé* and has taken several years to sculpt an amazing wooden image of the *orixá*,

Ogun, which takes up almost the entire space in a small studio near his house. He gave me a leaf sacred to Ogun while I was there. This is the informant, described earlier, who makes a distinction between "Rastafari" and "Rasta," describing himself as the latter.

Informant #5 was brought to me by Informant #1, and is a philosophical 50-year-old artist and musician with long dreadlocks. His acquaintances refer to him as "the philosopher." He is an active member of the Carnival *bloco, Filhos de Gandhy,* which he said represents *Candomblé* in Carnival: "We only refer to peace, the slogan is peace. Mahatma Gandhi was the divine inspiration for freedom, he supported all of the people and like Jesus Christ was betrayed by his followers, a Sikh killed Gandhi." This informant eats meat and smokes ganja. He mentioned having a son, but apparently he travels constantly and does not appear to be attached to a family. During my last visit he was with a female friend from Argentina. During the initial interview this informant expressed his objection to the phraseology of one of my questions, which asked why he identified with Rastafari. He answered, "I do not *identify* myself with Rastafari. I *am* a Rastafari. Since I was born I started with this." Concerning dreadlocks, he explained: "There are two choices: to have long hair; and not to have long hair. I'm a Rastafari and I chose to have long hair. A lot of people say that to be a Rastafari you don't have to have dreadlocks. In my conception you have to have dreadlocks. It's a way to say no to the system." Concerning vegetarianism, he maintained that a Rastafari "can eat anything that he wants; he's a Rastafari because he uses the dreads, as we say here. My family does not accept Rastafari. They don't tell me anything, but they think I'm a Rastafari to smoke marijuana. Long ago before I became Rasta, in the 70s, I was a teenager back then and it didn't cause me any damage. But today I'm very politically conscious about my position, my thoughts, and my way of being. I would like to assume the political side of Rasta."

This informant went on to define Rastafari as the "perfect anarchism." He explained: "The biggest tendency on this planet is anarchism. Rastafari tends toward anarchism, not to put things down, but the nature of the thing is to fight for freedom. Christ fought for his freedom, Gandhi fought, Buddha fought for his own integrity, Hare Krishna and many others that we know of . . ." He vehemently objected to defining Rastafari as a religion. "Rastafari is a philosophy, yes it is. Religion, never. I particularly do not believe in religion. I believe more in the football fan club than religion . . ." "The philosopher" also believes that Rastafari's concern for nature will help the world's ecology. He said: "You can see the forests dying, and the oceans are dirty, and our cause is to give more love to people. There would be less killing on the planet. Here is still a paradise, even though Adam and Eve were expelled from the paradise. I want to take advantage of the paradise. If we have to construct this world again, Rastafari will build this world, because we are from Ethiopia, we are from Africa. And then? Respect for Rastafari, respect for Rastafari, respect for Rastafari."

Informant #6, age 37, the self-styled "psychotherapist, sociologist, and theocratic," lives in a communal ghetto haphazardly built of wooden shacks constructed inside the facade and three walls of a roofless, historic building (which, he told me, the inhabitants owned). There is one small standpipe providing running water on the ground level. This informant's back and upper arms are covered with tattoos of Bob Marley and other images, about which he said: "These tattoos are a letter, the name of this letter is 'words of wisdom.' With this letter what happens? People will not relate to me by the color of my skin; they deal with me because of intelligence, because of love. I am respected not by how I look outside but the kindness, justice, and truth of Jah inside of me. I'm a mural because on my body I go back to the roots of the African people, of the less fortunate poor ones. But even the very small can give a rich spiritual presence." The informant's dreadlocks are wide and matted. He told me that Rastafari men look like Jesus, and that a lot of people don't accept that: "Some people ask me, 'Your hair is so soft, why do you leave it in such misery?'"

This informant explained how he sighted Rastafari: "I identify myself as Rastafari because I transformed through Jah and the Holy Ghost the segments of Babylon that were inside of me. I started when I was 18 years old, when I went into the army. I found some brothers who liked Bob Marley and who identified themselves with me because I had already heard Marley, and I had heard reggae music. And because of my own lifestyle and my environment I was touched by the Holy Ghost. Jah transformed my life, and I became his disciple, his lamb." Describing himself as a man with mystical powers, he added, "The people who hurt me are afraid of me because [they think] I am a demon. They don't understand the knowledge that is in me. They don't understand that Rastafari is the spirit of light, that I'm in the light of God. They do not understand what's written in the word in the name of the master Jesus Christ. I could drink anything that could kill me, and it wouldn't kill me. I could touch the snakes that spoke in tongues, I could put my hands on the hearts of people and cure them. Me, in Brazil, I live from miracles."

This informant vigorously condemned the capitalist system: "I do not believe in capitalism. Capitalism was taken away from my life. To maintain this hair, I cannot invest in the system. Not a cent. I live from the powers, like Daniel, like Joshua. I live like Jesus Christ. I live spirit because I am spirit. If I live in spirit, I have to walk in spirit. People do not understand why I do not need money to live. I do not need the form of government. I live theocracy." For him, the way to fight Babylon is through the music. He said:

Jesus Christ has given me the consciousness that I'm a living fire, a living stone foundation, a tool to annihilate the system of lies. I want freedom, fraternity, sharing. No guns, atomic weapons (disarmament), heavy machinery. We have the music to fight this system of lies. In a simple clear way, money brings confusion. We can't prostitute the music. We have to be our own producers. All of you who have a boom box, a bass, a drum, a guitar, let's get together and do a project the same way Jesus did through Marley. We can do the same. If you don't want reggae, the beats of the heart, tell the truth with any kind of music—salsa, merengue, waltz, bolero, any music—but say the truth.

About political power, he said: "When we get the chance to get in the government, in power, we're going to start a new program, planting and sharing and dividing. We are all partners on the land. Why didn't we have participation in Brazilian oil and gold? We are a people of the planet. Why aren't the universal riches of the world invested in us? We have to do that. When we ascend we have to give people what they deserve: dignity. What I understand by dignity is that man is an instrument for love, to love. Love your neighbor like you love yourself. Let's start this feeling, this mental posture, fraternity, to see in each human being a brother. Fraternity. To give up, extinguish, and banish away capitalism from the earth. No money. Culture of Jah, yes. Amen."

Informant #7 is a friend of Informant #6 and *capoeirista* and reggae vocalist/composer for *Amantes do Reggae*. In his mid-to-late 30s, he is light-skinned and has short, fine, thick dreadlocks. He has a small tattoo of a *berimbau* on his upper arm, eats meat, and smokes ganja. He lives with his Argentinean wife and two small sons in an apartment that they own in a building inhabited by other reggae artists and friends, which has a communal yard behind it for washing, for growing herbs, and for reasonings. He works about 90 hours a week taking care of his fruits and vegetables on a small plot of land (a *terreno*) that he owns in a distant barrio and teaching *capoeira* gratis to children and adults at four different locations in Salvador. His wife is paid for teaching Portuguese to families working at the Argentinean Embassy.

On my first visit to Bahia, after telling me that he was going to answer my questionnaire in a "very philosophical" manner, he proceeded to answer as if he were Jah. He volunteered no personal information about himself, which the questionnaire was designed to elicit:

WHAT IS MY NAME? His name is Jesus Christ, Jah Rastafari.

MY AGE IS? He is the Creator, and nobody created him. He is the power not created by anyone, who created all the power, all the energy.

WHERE DO I LIVE? Jah lives in the heavens of heavens. He lives with Jesus Christ and with the Holy Ghost and has his archangels and cherubims, 24 old men that are in the front of his throne and four animals that are around his seat singing a song that we're going to listen to now. Praised is Jah, the all-powerful God, the one that was, is, and will be all the power. Amen.

WHAT IS MY PROFESSION? Jah is Rastafari. His is the profession of love. He supports himself through his own spirit, through his creation.

WHY AM I RASTAFARI? Because Jah Rastafari is the recognized Holy Ghost and he convinced us that that is the truth.

WHEN DID I START WITH THIS? Jah started this a long time ago, before the foundation of this planet, when Jesus Christ was already here to recover the humans from this earth. Jah is all over. He's the head, we are the members of this large body. Jah is in all of us; he never leaves us. Amen.

ARE MY FAMILY MEMBERS RASTAFARI? Those who do not abandon father, mother, son, daughter for Jah Rastafari is not dignified to be with Jah.

Informant #8 is a 40-year-old man who is a close friend of Informants #6 and #7. He is a reggae musician in a group called *Unidade Real* (Real Unity). He said that his songs were inspired by the Bible. Presently having no visible means of support, until his tools were stolen he was a craftsman, making jewelry out of coconut shell. He is separated from his wife and daughter. His wife is Rastafari but works full time in order to live in a comfortable environment—he told me that often women have no use for unemployed men. He said that he has a house where assorted people stay for various lengths of time, but I did not visit it. Like Informant #7, he said he never refuses people in need and some people have stayed at his house for as long as a year before leaving. He often sleeps and showers at Informant #7's apartment in Pelourinho or in the *terreno*. He wears somewhat matted, thick dreadlocks, smokes ganja, eats meat, and drinks beer. He is eager to collect and read everything in print on Rastafari, defining himself as Rastafari "because the person of Jesus Christ in accordance with the New Testament turned me into a son of God." He explained: "I, like any other being under the sun, was dead, and the spirit of Jah through Jesus Christ took the sins away from me and revived my spirit. I in Rastafari and Rastafari in I."

This informant stated that his group's reggae is "orthodox": "We play reggae because we believe reggae is the Song of the Psalms, the song of the kings, right? We play reggae, nyabinghi, to say good things to the Creator of everything. We sing songs to everyone." He said that there were many dreadlocks in Bahia, but few Rastafaris: "Some of them call themselves Rastas but when you see the practice you know they're not Rastas." He explained why the Bible is so important to him and his friends: "The little information that comes to us from the rest of the continent, the rest of the world, sometimes it is changed and altered. That's why the Bible is our faith book, our ruling book in practice. Everything that's not in accordance with the teachings of the Creator, of Jah, it's not literally worth our respect." The informant maintained that Rastafari was both a way of life and a religion. It is a religion, he said, "because the literal meaning of religion is to keep yourself from the corruption of the world. . . . Rastafari is the correct way of life. It's love. Love is the accomplishment of the law. Christ said, I'm the way, the truth and the life. Allelu-jah. Rastafari. Amen."

On Bob Marley

Bob Marley's influence on the Rastafari of Salvador cannot be overemphasized. As one informant put it, "life will not be the same after listening to his music." Often familiarly referring to him as "Bobbie," informants consider him a brother and a prophet equal in status to Marcus Garvey. He is often compared to Jesus and is claimed to have shown people what freedom truly is. One informant stated that his music "is like an open book of the Rastafari character." Even though they do not always understand the English lyrics, they sing along any time a Marley tune is being played. His image is pervasive and his music is to be heard all over the streets of Pelourinho—in restaurants, bars, stores, and ghettos. One of the informants involved with *Candomblé* said that the influence of Marley had "everything" to do with who he is and that Marley was a "cosmic influence." An orthodox informant said that Marley's influence on him was "very deep—everything that I am, I say thank you to Jesus Christ through Bob Marley. For us in Bahia, he is our older brother. We started becoming closer to the music of Jesus Christ through Marley . . . We live in Salvador, Bahia, in Jamaica." But a close friend of the previous informant answered the question of Marley's importance to him in the following way: "His importance to me? It's none. The importance of Jah is total, Rastafari. Bob Marley, our brother in Christ Jesus, is an instrument of Jah Rastafari. His reggae music is an instrument of Jah."

On Haile Selassie

In contrast to the three orthodox Rastafari, the five cultural/political informants stated that Haile Selassie (or Ras Tafari) is not God. I saw only one image of Haile Selassie in Pelourinho, a poster in the *Suite Quilombo do Pelo,* the Jamaican shop where products from the Marley Museum in Kingston are sold. Apparently, the orthodox Rastafari place no great emphasis on the image of the emperor. It appears that the latter believe he was/is God in the same way that they themselves are God, with the difference between themselves and the emperor lying in the degree of inspiration by, or indwelling of, the Holy Spirit. They said that, like Marcus Garvey or Bob Marley, the Ethiopian emperor was a prophet filled by the Holy Spirit of God, which the title "Haile Selassie" (might of the trinity) indicates. It appears that those who use the term "Jah Rastafari" are not referring to the emperor (the man himself), but to the Holy Spirit within the man. "Jah Rastafari" seems to be used synonymously with "God," "Lord," and "Jesus," all of which contain the Holy Spirit, which can enter into various individuals.

Informant #6 explained his view of Haile Selassie this way: "I consider Tafari Makonen to be a guide, salt, and light to the world. I'm also salt, I'm also light, like Jah lives in me and lived in him [Makonen] because Jah is alive. According to the words of Jah, according to his ethical principles and social principles, he is God like we are God. The messenger Jesus Christ told us that we were God because we're manipulated by God the father." And according to Informant #7: "Haile Selassie is God, and the emperor of Ethiopia is God in the person of Ras Makonen. God took Ras Makonen to the glory and his resting for the resurrection of the dead in the day the Imperial Majesty will come and embrace to his kingdom, to the right words, the lambs. How do I understand Rastafari? Rastafari is the King of Kings, the Seer of Seers, the Conquering Lion of the Tribe of Judah, the Majesty. He's everything in all. Amen."

On my third visit to Salvador, I asked Informants #7 and #8 to clarify their views about Haile Selassie. I told Informant #7 that many images of the emperor can be seen in Jamaica and that some claim that one *must* believe that Haile Selassie is Jah in order to be considered a true Rastafari. He replied that Tafari Makonen was a prophet, not God, and to say that he is God is idolatry. He said that Jesus was/is the only Son of God. Haile Selassie, he said, is the light of the trinity, the Holy Spirit of Jah Rastafari that is in all of us. Jah is in us, in nature, in everything, he said. By contrast, Tafari Makonen was "a man, even a dictator." Bob Marley, Marcus Garvey, and Tafari Makonen were all prophets. And although the emperor's words might be right and just, this informant said that Jah's words were to be found elsewhere: in the Bible. He therefore didn't seem particularly interested in reading the emperor's speeches, although he knew that the words to Marley's "War" came from one of them. Unlike Informant #8, who wants to read everything in print about Rastafari (even if it's in English, which he can barely understand), the second informant seems only to want to (or have time to) read the Bible. The primary medium for communicating his beliefs to others is the Bible and reggae, the music of Jah.

When I asked Informant #8 to clarify and explain his views about Haile Selassie, I drew a diagram. I wrote "God" at the top of a piece of paper, put "Jesus" underneath to the left, and "Holy Spirit" underneath to the right. I then asked him to tell me where Haile Selassie fit in. He drew a circle around the three words and then drew two arrows: one to the right of the circle with the words "1 *pessoa so*" (one person only) written under it, and another arrow under the circle with "Haile Selassie I" written under it. When I indicated my lack of comprehension, he shrugged and said that I should "put on God's glasses and think like God thinks" so I could "understand these spiritual matters." Thus, either the informants declared outright that Haile Selassie is/was not Jah or the Messiah, or they answered affirmatively that Haile Selassie had been especially imbued with the Holy Spirit. In either case, the emphasis one finds in Jamaica on the emperor—especially his image—is not present in Bahia.

On *Candomblé*

Those informants who were raised within *Candomblé* do not condemn it. Rather, in the case of Informant #1, it inspires his art. Informant #2, who also grew up in the tradition, made a distinction between what he called "tourist" *Candomblé* and authentic *Candomblé*. He advised me to try to experience the latter, because "the tourist is too commercial." Although no ceremonies were underway at the time, on my first visit to Bahia I had been able to visit a well-known *casa de Candomblé* on the outskirts of Salvador and make photographs of the building and surrounding gardens. Some of the orthodox Rastafari have participated in the rituals of *Candomblé*, including Informant #7, but now soundly reject it as a "low form of spirituality" leading to violence, drug-taking, prostitution, uninhibited sexuality, self-mutilation, and other forms of "satanizing."[27] Yet they appear to understand the aesthetic attraction of the *orixás* and drums to visitors and artists. Informant #7, for example, showed me the invitation to an opening of an exhibition by an Argentinean painter friend of his who had attempted to capture the energy and beauty of *Candomblé* on canvas. He wasn't particularly happy about the subject matter, but he didn't condemn her outright for her choice either. It is likely that most of the orthodox Rastafari were brought up in the Protestant tradition, like Informant #7, who did tell me that he had been brought up in the Baptist Church. He said that he and his two sisters played music in the church when they were children, and that his father played bolero music.

When asked if he participated in ceremonies in honor of the *orixás*, Informant #4 replied: "Of course, of course. My everyday *orixá* is Ogun. I'm the son of Ogun. I practice Ogun every day. Tuesday I eat white meat. Friday I eat white meat. I'm incorporated. Ogun, Exu, all of them. Radically, in the root, with BIG letters." He vigorously defended *Candomblé*, calling it "the religion of religions." He said that the Catholic Church learned a lot from *Candomblé*, because it had been around for 5,000 years before Christ. "Forgive me," he said, "[but] all the other religions are followers." He defined *Candomblé* in the following way and was very irritated about its detractors: "*Candomblé* transforms what exists. It's a transformation. I say that because each people has its own spiritual religion. Why does the Black people's religion have to be understood as diabolical and persecuted? *Candomblé* is the religion of religions. I don't want to talk any more about that. Finished."

However, this informant was not finished. He continued: "My people are not educated. But *Candomblé* has everything, from levitation . . . It's one of the oldest things on the planet. If the music's Black, if our people are Black, we are always going to be learning new experiences through the search, through the practices. I'm open to everybody else, to everyone, and to other cultures. And I do not discriminate against anything. But I do not accept that people can step on me. . . . I myself, I did not come from slaves. My ancestors are kings and queens."

When I asked him about his participation in *Candomblé,* Informant #5 (who is a member of the *Candomblé*-inspired group, *Filhos de Gandhy*) suggested that there was still some danger associated with belonging to an Afro-Bahian religious group. He would not answer the question, replying: "When you ask me, do you participate in events in honor of the *orixás?* This question is too complex. It wouldn't be too good to answer that question. What kind of event? Where? It's very dangerous to answer that, OK?"

Informants #6, #7, and #8 all condemned *Candomblé.* Informant #6 stated:

> *Candomblé* is anti-culture. *Candomblé* in Bahia, like any part of the world, is used to retain us, to hold us back in our evolution. . . . I hate *Candomblé* because I was part of the lower spiritism. I tried to find myself. I was involved with the prince of darkness, with this low culture. *Candomblé* is missing culture. It's a corruption. . . . When I lived for *Candomblé* I mutilated myself. I cut my own body, and I fed violence. *Candomblé* is the opium of the world. . . . It destroys. I participate in several cultural events but not to the *orixás,* no. I'm the *orixá.* Jah made me an *orixá.* I'm holy. I'm the guide. I and I. The *orixá* of *orixás,* Jesus. The guide of the guides, Jesus Emanuel. The *caboclo*[28] *of the caboclos,* Emanuel. And we are *orixás.* Jah made us holy.

Informant #7 defined *Candomblé* as "a popular movement of spiritual African gods." He continued: "In Bahia this name is bad news because *Candomblé*—the celebration party of the African cults—it's the rhythm of the drum. In Bahia it's very corrupt. It's very misused. It's a cult to other gods, gods that have no real power. It's a fantasy. . . . It's not from the Bible. According to the Bible, sacrifice of animals and adoration of other gods do not go with the thinking of he who knows the true God and the only living God." Informant #8 regards *Candomblé* as "the low spiritism." He said: "*Candomblé* doesn't have any relation to the people of God, neither with the sons of God. *Candomblé* is idolatry. *Candomblé* divinizes strange gods, praises strange gods. And Jah, the true God of eternal life, the creator of heaven and earth, abominates idolatry. Rastafari, or the Son of God, does not bend his knee to idols. Rastafari is only afraid of the name of Jesus, in the person of Jah, Rastafari, Selassie I the First."

In sum, those informants who were brought up within *Candomblé* consider it to be their religion, yet at the same time identify with Rastafari ideology. This was the case with Informants #1, #2, #4, and #5. The orthodox Rastafari (Informants #6, #7, and #8) who have come from the Protestant tradition (although they may have experimented with *Candomblé*), tend to define Rastafari more narrowly, as a religion. They condemn *Candomblé* and insist on the necessity of reading the Bible, often using biblical phraseology or scripture to explain and justify their beliefs.

On Carnival

Hundreds of thousands of people, from as far as Holland, Japan, and Australia, come to Bahia every year to attend Carnival. Thousands from Rio de Janeiro consider Bahia's Carnival to be superior to their own and make the trip every year. Because these tourists bring millions of dollars into the city, authorities have made sure to provide for them in various ways. They provide security,[29] place mobile health units in strategic locations (indicated in the Carnival program) to provide free health care to all but locals, hand out free condoms,[30] and employ people to help clean up after each day of Carnival. Hotels, restaurants, stores, T-shirt and trinket vendors, photographers and videographers, and food vendors (including many "baianas" on street corners selling their Yoruba dishes made of cornmeal, shrimp, palm oil, and okra) enjoy a brisk business during Carnival. Young boys walk about all day giving away "free" colorful ribbon bracelets with the names of the *orixás* on them; however, they do not leave tourists alone until they have given them a "donation" for these good luck charms.

It is during Carnival that *Candomblé* becomes highly visible—the Carnival groups inspired by it are categorized in the program as *Afoxé (Filhos do Congo; Olorum Baba Mi; Arca de Zambi; Alaxé Oyá; Filhos de Gandhy; Ilê Aiyê; Filhas D'Oxum; Ilê Oyá)*. Group members sometimes number in the thousands, with those in different sections of the *blocos* wearing identically colored clothing and head-wraps inspired by Africa or the *orixás*. Their dance movements are slow and deliberate. Songs are sung in the Yoruba language. Exposed flesh is not to be seen. The trucks upon which they perform are small.

Another type of Carnival music is termed *axé* music. It is the popular music of the Bahian youth, and is a form of dance music with little or no socially or politically relevant content. The more popular and well-funded of these groups perform on the tops of the large 16-wheelers known as "*trios electricos.*" Band members and dancers often dress very skimpily or wear very tight clothing. Many of the female performers whose natural hair color is black, dye it blond. The reggae groups and some of the larger percussion groups (such as *Ilê Aiyê* and *Olodum*) are categorized as *Afro,* while smaller percussion groups are considered to be *percussao.* Some groups, inspired by Amerindians, are termed *Indios (Apaxes do Tororo, Comanches do Pelô).* There are groups categorized as *travestidos* and *alternativos* as well. Unlike Carnival in Rio, nudity is rare, although I videotaped a "fantasia" (a contest among cross-dressers and transsexuals for Carnival "Queen") in which most of the contestants wore little or no clothing.

Hundreds of groups perform during Carnival, so many that one person cannot possibly see them all. The 1998 celebration, which lasted from February 18–24, took place simultaneously in Pelourinho and along three main parade routes *(Circuito Centro Histórico, Circuito Dodô,* and *Circuito Osmar),* as well as in an additional seven barrios. Usually beginning around noon, Carnival groups continue to parade until dawn. Those with wealthy sponsors perform during the peak hours of Carnival; those without sponsors often perform at 3:00 or 4:00 A.M., thus reducing their exposure. A sign of the success of Informant #7's group, *Amantes do Reggae,* is that they were seen at the beginning at one of the Carnival routes during peak time this year, contrasted to last year's entry in the early morning hours.

Bahians have a saying that Carnival is "the festival of the devil blessed by God."[31] While most of my informants take part in Carnival, the three who are orthodox Rastafari would agree with the first part of the saying but not the last part. They take part in what they consider to be a Babylonian festival encouraging the weakness of the flesh only to proselytize through reggae music. Informant #4, who has composed music for *Ilê Aiyê,* stated: "Today I don't participate as much because I do not see much in Carnival . . . But the Carnival is a popular celebration, the biggest celebration of the world. It's a paradox, because one of the richest countries of the world [culturally] is one of the poorest. They use the people. If the people don't participate . . . they use people and reproach them. I don't understand these impositions."

Informants #6, #7, and #8 had the most to say about Carnival. When Informant #6 was asked if he participated in Carnival, he answered: "Inside the Carnival I try to fight this structure. We talk about the Carnival as alienation, it's the money of people, it's the prosperity of people badly distributed as an instrument of demonization, as massification. It's why people die in darkness, why people live in poverty. And people are alienated from this fake celebration, this Babylonian celebration. They fool everybody else with this festivity that's pervasive with promiscuity. Carnival is sick. It's propagation of sexual diseases. Carnival, it's rotten." Said Informant #7, "We come into Carnival because Jah determined this. Inside the Carnival we praise the word of Jah so that people wake up to reggae music, but we don't play Carnival music. Neither are we a part of the celebrations of Carnival. We give the message of Jah to the people during Carnival because Jah determined that we come to the Carnival to give the message of Jah. Today it's possible to do that in Bahia through reggae music. Amen." And Informant #8 stated:

> Carnival is Babylon. The meaning of Carnival literally is "party of the meat, of the flesh." Jah tells us to walk not according to the flesh but according to the spirit. And Carnival here in Salvador is a popular celebration where people liberate themselves, liberate all the fruits of the flesh. But we are not flesh. We are the spirit made alive by the Holy Ghost of God and the works of Jah are all manifested. . . . In truth we play reggae in Carnival to deal with the matters of Jah, to notify the population of the extreme necessity to discover the knowledge of God. And through the real spirit, the truth of the spirit, they free themselves from the works of the flesh. In Carnival all kinds of transgressions, physical and also moral and cultural, happen. Carnival, in truth, is an authentic cultural genocide.

On Repatriation

When asked about going back to Africa (there is no Portuguese word that is a direct translation for "repatriation"), most of the informants said they would love to have the opportunity to visit Africa so that they could discover their history, their roots, and their African heritage. Some said that if Jah sent them there, they would go. Although all of the informants would identify themselves as "Afro-Bahians" and consider their heritage to be African, none of them spoke of moving to Africa permanently. None expressed belief in a massive exodus brought about either by divine or human agency. Informant #7 expressed the view that they were already there in spirit. He said: "If Jesus leads me to go to Jamaica, yes. To want and to do something comes from Jah. If it is his desire I will come to all these places. But we know that spiritually we are in all these places."

Informant #8's answer to the question of whether or not he wanted to go to Africa contained a reference to a spiritual unification at some future time or place (perhaps the apocalypse) when Jah would bring everyone together again:

> I have a lot of interest in going to Ethiopia. . . . Yes, I'd like to know my brothers and sisters who live in Jamaica, who live in Grenada, who are in Martinique, who are in Surinam, who are spread all over the entire planet.

However, one day all of us will be together. We are going to be meeting there where there's no tears and crying, because the light of the celestial father, Jah, Haile Selassie the First and the Only, . . . is going to shine every place and our tears and differences here in Babylon will be extinguished from our minds and from our hearts.

In the history of Bahia there have been many repatriates, beginning in the nineteenth century soon after emancipation. Mostly these trips were made for the purpose of gaining the necessary information and skills to return to Bahia to found houses of *Candomblé*. For example, geographer Robert A. Voeks tells us that after emancipation in 1888, "a black woman born in Cachoeira, Bahia, named Isadora Maria Hamus, moved to Lagos, spent eight years learning Yoruba and English, and returned to Bahia to become a leader of a house of *Candomblé*."[32] As Voeks puts it, for Afro-Bahians "Africa is no vague mythical land. . . . It is a living reality, whence many of the objects they use in their rituals are imported, where people they know have visited and . . . where their fathers or grandfathers came from."[33] In the post-abolition era, *Candomblé* houses were conceptualized as "recreated African homeland[s] in microcosm."[34]

It is impossible *not* to think of Africa while one is in Bahia, especially in Pelourinho. There are African museums, exhibits, restaurants, fabric stores, *baianas* selling African food on the street corners, and images of *orixás* everywhere in the public spaces of the historic district. As far as they are concerned, the Rastafari of Pelourinho already live in the midst of Africa and Jamaica. Thus, the goal is not to abandon where they live, but to transform its Babylonian elements.

Conclusion

One reason for the similarities between Rastafari in Jamaica and Bahia may be attributed to their having shared a common colonial and neocolonial history. Like most former colonies that relied on labor power from the African continent, the same problematic issues of miseducation, and of race, class, and gender exist in Bahia as they do elsewhere in the diaspora. As in Jamaica, it is obvious from Bahian informants' responses that an identification with (or as) Rastafari helps them to locate themselves within an oppressive and racist society. Wearing their hair in dreadlocks (and, for two of the informants, wearing tattoos) are signs of their opposition to the system. As in Jamaica, pronouncing words differently from the norm,[35] using a specialized vocabulary, writing graffiti in public places, using the colors of Rastafari, and inscribing Rastafari phrases and symbols on their arts and crafts accomplishes the goal of establishing themselves as separate and apart from Babylon.

While reggae music in Bahia presents some degree of resistance against the system, it does not necessarily represent the views of the orthodox Rastafari. There is a clear distinction made between those reggae musicians who are Rastafari and those who are not. Although one informant used the word, "nyabinghi" and is familiar with Ras Michael's music, I do not believe that Jamaican-style nyabinghi chants are practiced in Bahia. As in Jamaica, all the informants see self-expression through art, poetry, and music as having the power to liberate. And, as in Jamaica, some Rastafari in Bahia express a desire to be more politically active, while others refuse to participate in politics but will use the system when it benefits their cause. Since all but one of the informants eat meat (and he, too, eats it occasionally), an "ital" diet is not followed. Some Rastafari in Bahia use ganja and some do not; for those who do, the experience is a way to discover divine truth within themselves.

Although I have not yet had the opportunity to interview Rastafari women, Bahian men appear to share the same patriarchal view of the role of women found in Jamaica. The orthodox Rastafari are more conservative on this issue than are the cultural/political Rastafari. When asked why there appeared to be so few Rastafari women in the area, all of the informants responded that women were not up to the pressures and hardships of struggle, or were needed to support the "real" warriors (the men) or raise children at home. Yet, at the same time, I observed Informant #7 quite cheerfully and willingly take on such domestic and childcare duties as washing dishes, sweeping, washing and hanging out clothes (by hand), and washing off the soiled bottom of his baby boy. Although I noticed that this informant's wife usually wore long skirts (or pants) and tied her long, straight hair back, other female friends of the family who came to visit or who lived in the same building wore short skirts, shorts, and tank tops. The idea that women should dress modestly, however, was expressed by many of the orthodox Rastafari, who took a dim view of what many of the female singers wore (or failed to wear) when they performed in public during Carnival. As Maureen Warner-Lewis pointed out, elements in a belief system like Rastafari can be profoundly traditional and conservative at the same time that other elements of their vision are "radical, even revolutionary."[36] Further research needs to be carried out regarding gender issues among the Rastafari of Bahia.

Yawney suggested that the factors that influence the various shapes Rastafari takes outside the Caribbean include "pressures such as racism, criminalization, and commodification."[37] I would suggest that the religion and culture of the colonizers, as well as the cultural and religious upbringing of those who identify themselves as Rastafari, are also essential elements. Another explanation for the differences between the "ideal type" of Rastafari in Jamaica and that in Bahia has to do with the way in which Rastafari was introduced in Brazil, and that is through popular culture. Unlike in Jamaica where Rastafari organically emerged from the Garvey movement and developed through reasoning sessions with elders, in Bahia Rastafari beliefs emerged directly from reggae music, largely that of Bob Marley. To my knowledge, Rastafari elders have not visited Bahia.

None of my informants, except Informant #8, possesses much written literature by or about Rastafari abroad, and unfortunately I was not able to see his collection. He and his friends are eager to receive all the books, articles, and videos that I could send him. Many Bahian Rastafari also cannot understand English, and some cannot read Portuguese well either. Thus, their understanding of reggae lyrics coming from abroad has often been limited. Written Portuguese translations do not seem to abound in Salvador. I found translations of popular Marley songs in the *Folha do Reggae,* but their accuracy leaves much to be desired.

In her 1994 book, *Arise Ye Mighty People!,* Terisa Turner has crafted an inclusive definition of Rastafari. She described what she calls "New Rastafari" as "one of many expressions of indigenous people fighting for their rights. It unites first nations peoples with those of the African diaspora, including exiles, migrants, refugees and their children. For instance some of the aboriginal peoples of New Zealand are identifying themselves as Rastafari and are pursuing land claims. New Rastafari is a global cultural practice, an expression in particular of black people and especially of black women, but one which is also inclusive of revolutionary white women and men."[38] According to Turner, what unites these groups is their passionate demand for social justice and a fair distribution of power. Belief in the divinity of Haile Selassie, wearing dreadlocks, smoking ganja, being vegetarian, and being black are not necessarily essential to New Rastafari.

In Bahia I observed quite a few Europeans who had forced their straight hair into dreadlocks and who dressed in the manner of "hippies" but I was not able to interview them about their beliefs. Informant #7's band contained at least two members who are light-skinned and whose hair is long and curly, but not dreadlocked. Although I did not get an opportunity to interview these two, while they were around the informant they participated in reasonings and smoked ganja, thus appearing to be a part of the orthodox Rastafari community. In addition, it appears that other light-skinned Bahians who do not necessarily "look" like Rastafari or wear dreadlocks may, in fact, identify themselves as such. Some may be Rastafari "sympathizers" or "apologists," sharing the vision and engaging in the struggle to end Babylon's domination. As Yawney suggested about those who are not Black but are nevertheless attracted to the movement, "We need to determine precisely what are the specific aspects of Rastafari that form the basis of its resonance where it has gained a footing beyond the black community."[39]

In Kingston at a Rastafari rally to legalize marijuana in March 1996, I heard a brother by the name of Ras DaSilva express the idea that Rastafari was "the new shining light" when he said that what they hoped to do was "Rasterize the world." All of my informants in Bahia, too, base their hope for the future on the efforts of the Black underclass. Regardless of how they define Rastafari, they all have a mission: they all feel the heavy burden and responsibility of educating and proselytizing, through whatever medium of self-expression is available to them, the hope and potential of Rastafari. As Informant #5 (the philosopher) puts it: "My profession is [fostering] hope." In Bahia, the Rastafari hope is alive and well, although the forms of its cultural expressions are conditioned by the Brazilian cultural context, historical circumstances, and *Candomblé*.

Notes

1. Since the terms "Rastafarianism" and "Rastafarians" have been rejected by its adherents, the term "Rastafari" is used herein to refer to the ideology/religion/way of life itself, as well an individual or a group of proponents.

2. *Candomblé* is one of several Afro-Brazilian religions found in Bahia. Characterized by members who are possessed by (or go into trance with) African deities known as *orixás,* the most well-known group within *Candomblé* uses Yoruba dress, rituals, and language.

3. Approximately 10 percent of the people of Brazil own 54 percent of the wealth; 80 percent of the land is owned by 5 percent of the people, and 32 million Brazilians own nothing.

4. Hendrik Kraay, "Introduction," in *Afro-Brazilian Culture and Politics: Bahia, 1790s to 1990s,* ed. Hendrik Kraay (Armonk, NY: M. E. Sharpe, 1998), 9.

5. In regard to illiteracy, I observed a sign-maker having to recarve a beautiful, hand-painted wooden sign for a bar because he had misspelled "Pelourinho" by leaving out the "u."

6. Jim Wafer, *The Taste of Blood: Spirit Possession in Brazilian Candomblé* (Philadelphia: University of Pennsylvania Press, 1991), 8.

7. This group contains thousands of men, perhaps as many as 8,000–10,000. They wear white and blue beads in honor of the *orixá,* Oxalá, wear white turbans made of towels around their heads, and carry small containers of a green liquid (that may be aftershave), which they squirt on onlookers for good luck. They move to the rhythms of *Candomblé.*

8. Kim D. Butler, "Afterward: *Ginga Baiana*—The Politics of Race, Class, Culture, and Power in Salvador, Bahia," in Kraay, 159.

9. *Caderno de Educaçao do Ilê Aiyê,* vol. I, *Organizacoes de Resistencia Negra* (Salvador, Bahia: Projeto de Extensao Pedagogica, 1995), 5.

10. Butler, in Kraay, 163.

11. Wafer, 4.

12. Butler, in Kraay, 168.

13. Abdias do Nascimento, *Brazil: Mixture or Massacre? Essays in the Genocide of a Black People* (Dover, MA: Majority Press, 1989), xv.

14. The forcible removal of tenants and owners is still taking place in Pelourinho. I read a sign during a protest at the end of the 1998 Carnival that read, "I want to live where I was born."

15. I heard some grumbling on the street about *Olodum* when I was in Pelourinho during the 1998 Carnival, suggesting they were a "sell-out" and even racist. During one local street parade/protest occurring after the Carnival, cardboard signs painted by local artists were carried that listed the faults of various local hotel owners, bar owners, politicians, and others. One sign claimed that *Olodum* didn't value their black members "100%" and another claimed that *Olodum* didn't pay its rope-handlers. Two large banners were also carried by the group of protesters: one that read in English, "S.O.S. Children of the Historic Center—Let Us Live" and the other, in Portuguese, that quoted the U.N. Declaration of Human Rights' statement that each human being has a right to live.

16. Baiana hair—a result of miscegenation—is long, brown or black, curly hair, which forms itself into narrow spirals or tendrils. It is seen by many to be the ideal hair, or "good" hair, to use African-American parlance.

17. *Folha do Reggae*, Salvador, Bahia, *Janeiro de 1997, ano 1-no. 2*, 3.

18. Jocelio Teles dos Santos, "A Mixed-Race Nation: Afro-Brazilians and Cultural Policy in Bahia, 1970–1990," in Kraay, 128.

19. Ibid., 129.

20. A *berimbau* is an instrument used in *capoeira* that is made from a bent piece of wood that forms a bow, held taut by wire. Attached to it is a dried gourd half of which is pressed against the abdomen while the wire is hit with a stick held by the right hand, which also holds a small shaker basket at the same time. The sound this instrument makes is a unique one, and it appears to be a difficult instrument to learn. Other instruments used in *capoeira angola* include an instrument similar to the tambourine, and a conga drum.

21. A reggae newspaper in Salvador printed a three-part article last year explaining the history of the recent presence of reggae in Bahia. *("Reggae in Bahia: Historia de Uma Presenca Recente," Folha do Reggae, Janeiro de 1997, nos. l, 2, and 3.)*

22. *Folha do Reggae*, no. 1, gives both dates.

23. William David Spencer, "Chanting Change around the World through Rasta Ridim and Art," in *Chanting Down Babylon: The Rastafari Reader*, ed. Nathaniel S. Murrell, William D. Spencer, and Adrian A. McFarlane (Kingston: Ian Randle, 1998), 271.

24. Butler, in Kraay, 173.

25. Carole Yawney and John Homiak, "Yard Roots to International Branches: Popular Culture and the Globalization of Rastafari," abstract for American Academy of Religion paper, Orlando, Florida, November 1998.

26. The informant was quoting the words to Marley's "War" based on a speech by Haile Selassie.

27. Although rituals that involve animal sacrifice and small cuts or incisions made during initiation are described, academic researchers do not condemn *Candomblé* in the manner of these informants. For example, geographer Robert A. Voeks, who investigated the pharmacopoeia of *Candomblé* in Bahia, wrote that at first he was attracted to its "exotic nature." Then "as *Candomblé* appeared less and less arcane and mysterious, I developed a healthy respect for many of its leaders. These are men and women of considerable intelligence and charisma, people limited in their upward social mobility only by their race and class." Robert A. Voeks, *Sacred Leaves of Candomblé: African Magic, Medicine, and Religion in Brazil* (Austin: University of Texas Press, 1997), xvi.

28. A *caboclo* is an Indian spirit in *Candomblé*, as distinct from the *orixás* of African origin.

29. Often, long lines of police or some sort of militarily outfitted authority, would march single-file right through Carnival dancers. They looked harmless to me, but were a threat to my informants. When military personnel suddenly appeared in the crowd, although my inclination was not to rush to "jump aside" to let them pass, my friends insisted that I do so, going so far as to push me away from them when I did not respond fast enough.

30. There is a Carnival band called *Bloco da Saudade,* comprised of older adults who, as they dance down the streets, hand out condoms on rope necklaces to the crowds.

31. Wafer, 10.

32. Voeks, 154.

33. Ibid., 153.

34. Kim D. Butler, *Freedoms Won: Afro-Brazilians in Post-Abolition São Paulo and Salvador* (New Brunswick: Rutgers University Press, 1998), 192.

35. Just as in Jamaica some Rastafari pronounce "Jesus" as "Jes' Us" rather than "Jeez-us," I was told by my translator that the orthodox Rastafari in Bahia do not use the normal pronunciation either. When they speak the word, it sounds like "Je-soo-iss." It may be part of the regional dialectic of the area, or a distinctive Rastafari pronunciation.

36. Maureen Warner-Lewis, "African Continuities in the Rastafari Belief System," *Caribbean Quarterly* vol. 39, nos. 3, 4: 122.

37. Carole D. Yawney, "Tell Out King Rasta Doctrine around the Whole World: Rastafari in Global Perspective," in *Latin America, the Caribbean and Canada in the Hood: The Reordering of Culture,* ed. Alvina Ruprecht, (Ottowa: Carleton University Press, 1995), 57.

38. Terisa E. Turner and Bryan J. Ferguson, eds., *Arise Ye Mighty People! Gender, Class and Race in Popular Struggles* (Trenton, NJ: Africa World Press, 1994), 15.

39. Yawney, 59.

Chapter 3

The Faith of the People

The Divina Pastora Devotions of Trinidad

Gerald Boodoo

The island of Trinidad is situated just above ten degrees latitude in the Caribbean Sea. It is the southernmost island in the Caribbean, under 5,000 square kilometers in area and only about 10 to 15 kilometers from Venezuela. According to the 1994 annual statistical digest of Trinidad and Tobago, the population is just about 1.1 million persons with a denominational breakdown as follows: 29.3 percent Roman Catholic, 23.6 percent Hindu, 10.9 percent Anglican, 7.4 percent Pentecostal, 6.8 percent Muslim, 3.7 percent Seventh Day Adventist, and 3.4 percent Presbyterian/Congregational. The remaining 14.9 percent consists of Baptists (2.9 percent), Jehovah Witnesses (1.3 percent), Methodists (1.2 percent), with 9.5 percent having none or no stated religion. Though this breakdown shows that the island is predominantly Christian there is still a large (30.4 percent) Hindu and Muslim community that is accounted for by the history of colonization and the policies of post-colonialism in the island. This will also explain the wide ethnic cross section found even within the Roman Catholic Church.

The inclusion of Trinidad into the Spanish Empire began with Columbus's arrival in 1498. This set the tone for the Roman Catholic dimension to the island whose denominational hold was threatened by the surrender of the island to the British in the late nineteenth century. It was at this time that Anglicanism was introduced into Trinidad along with Protestantism in general. Though Anglicanism was given the status of the official religion of the island for a few decades in the mid-nineteenth century, it neither diminished the continued influence of the Roman Catholic Church in the island nor brought about a serious religious shift from the Roman Catholic to the Anglican Church. Within this diverse religious environment were of course the Africans, who constituted the bulk of the population and who thus unofficially made up the vast majority of Christians in Trinidad. Of more interest to us here, though, is the arrival of about 144,000 East Indian indentured laborers in Trinidad from 1845 to 1917. It was especially during those years that the island received the influx of French planters from the rest of the West Indies, especially Saint Domingue now Haiti, Grenada, Guadeloupe, and Martinique. The Chinese and Syrian merchants and shop owners that joined the established Christian churches of the island also arrived during those 72 years. As a result of this mix of ethnic and religious traditions, Trinidad became a very cosmopolitan country with a diverse religious heritage.

Obviously, with the established Churches upholding and furthering in general the aims and policies of the ruling colonizing powers,[1] the popular religious expressions of the former slaves and indentured workers and their descendants were always suppressed and looked upon with disdain as of a "lower" religious form. But with the island claiming independence from the British Empire in 1962, there came a rise in indigenous leadership at both secular and religious levels. The popular religious expressions of the people gained greater ascendancy and asserted their right for "respectable" inclusion in the cultural diversity of the country. It is in this scenario that the dreaded Obeah, as the dark side of influencing spirits, and Shango/Orisha, the syncretic merging of traditional African Yoruba religion and Christianity, especially with regard to the ancestral spirits, the saints and the Virgin Mary, are to be understood as gaining importance. However, there is one popular religious festival that is unique to the Trinidad situation and shows how the religious impulse of a people cannot be stifled, and that is the Divina Pastora/Suparee Ke Mai feast. This feast is celebrated mainly by Roman Catholics and Hindus, but also to an extent by other Christians as well as Muslims and persons of other faiths. This is not to say that Roman Catholics and Hindus are in agreement with regard to this feast, but over the years a hesitant respect has grown with regard to the feast being a shared rite and not solely the province of the Roman Catholics. Before getting into a presentation of the feast, let me give a brief socioeconomic picture of the island, especially with regard to religion and to some extent class, since they are fairly intertwined in Trinidad.

Under colonial rule the island was chiefly a sugar economy that was average in terms of its financial worth. In that system, Christians were the administrators, landowners, merchants, professionals, civil servants, and anyone of "worth" in the island. Hindus, Muslims, and others performed the menial tasks of the island, especially in terms of field work. To belong to the Christian Church was thus a measure of class and, to the Roman Catholic Church, a sign that one had "reached." This explains the mostly East Indian population of the Presbyterian Church in Trinidad, since it was the only Christian Church that accepted Hindu and Muslim converts as part of its missionary thrust. The induction of well-to-do East Indian families into the Roman Catholic church came later. With the oil boom of the 1970s, the island achieved a measure of wealth that served to bolster the courage of those who were traditionally looked upon as belonging to "lesser" Churches. Coupled with the Black Power movement of the early 1970s, financial security translated into the desire and need to give more vent to local expressions, religious and otherwise. This gave impetus not only to the Christian Churches but also to the East Indian and other communities to be more confident of their own localized and indigenous religious expressions, and moreover to present these fearlessly and with some pride. Unfortunately, this optimism and the financial security that bolstered it has gone, and now in the 1990s it seems that the Churches and the island have not risen to and implemented the religious and social visions of the 1970s.[2] It is in this light that popular religiosity in Trinidad and indeed in the Caribbean is being seen anew as the locus that requires explicit attention and involvement insofar as it is the expression of the vital and gut-level concerns of people in the region. In this context let me now turn to the festival of La Divina Pastora/Suparee Ke Mai.

The feast of La Divina Pastora (the Holy Shepherdess) and Suparee Ke Mai (Mother Kali) are the Christian and Hindu aspects of a celebration that is rooted in the cultural and religious values of the people of Trinidad. Over a period of 100 years it has attracted Hindus, Muslims, as well as non-Catholic Christian groups to a shrine in Siparia (a village in the southeast-central part of the island) dedicated to La Divina Pastora. The Roman Catholic feast is itself celebrated on the second Sunday after Easter, but Hindu and Muslim devotees especially go on pilgrimage there on Holy Thursday and Good Friday.

The Catholic origin of the feast[3] hails back to Andalusia in southern Spain in the early eighteenth century where it is held that Mary, the mother of Jesus, appeared to a monk, Isidore of Seville, in the guise of an Andalusian shepherdess and made known to him that her role is to bring people into the sheepfold of her divine son. Isidore was a Capuchin monk and this order brought the Holy Shepherdess devotion with them as early as 1715 in their mission to the South American mainland, especially to what is now known as Venezuela. In 1759 they formed a mission in Siparia in Trinidad, apparently fleeing persecution by the Amerindians from the South American mainland, which had begun from as early as 1730. With them, apparently, came the statue, which is held in reverence in the shrine. The statue itself makes for an interesting comparative study with other statues of Mary. It is short, possesses long, black hair, copper-colored skin, small cheeks, kindly eyes, and a tiny nose. It is this statue that is carried in solemn procession through the streets of Siparia, during which the rosary is recited and Marian hymns sung. Of course the popularity of the devotion is also due to the many miracles said to have taken place and innumerable favors granted. Siparia itself, at the time of the arrival of the Capuchins, was a center for the Guaranon Indians, known as the "Warwarrhoons," who carried out a lively trade in Trinidad in the nineteenth and early twentieth centuries. This popular devotion found easy identification with them especially with its feasting, litany praying, procession with a statue, and favor-seeking—all similar elements of the Amerindian religious way of life.

The Roman Catholic Church has traditionally interpreted the feast as an opportunity to shepherd all into the fold of Jesus Christ, an opportunity for evangelization that has caused many a parish priest to attempt to convert, with insignificant success, non-Catholic devotees of La Divina Pastora to Roman Catholicism. Further to this, Roman Catholics also think of the feast as really "their feast," which has been, and is being, distorted by other Christian denominations. However, along with all other devotees, Roman Catholics also understand the Holy Shepherdess as an aid in time of need and one who grants favors and ensures proper guidance and protection. As we will see, this is no different from either the Hindu, Muslim, or other religious devotees' understanding of the Mother of Siparia.

The East Indian dimension to the feast grew out of events that occurred during their period of indentureship. Originally, East Indians came to Trinidad (from 1845) on a labor contract, first for three, then for five years. This was extended to ten years with a guaranteed free return passage to India. So for the first 20 years or so the East Indian immigrant had no intention of settling down in Trinidad. The chief aim was to finish one's contract in the sugarcane fields, save as much money as possible and then return to India. Trinidad was an alien land to the East Indians, and their encounter with the Africans and the Christian religions was a strange and bewildering one. However, two events occurred in Trinidad that had consequences for the feast of La Divina Pastora with respect to the East Indians.

In 1870 Governor Gordon decided to give a block of crown lands to the East Indians who were desirous of making their home in Trinidad in return for their free passage to India. The response was so good that other East Indians began to apply for lands and as a result East Indian villages began to spring up mainly in the north-central, central, and south-central parts of the island. The next event was the opening up of the interior of Trinidad with the coming of the railway in the 1870s and its extension in the 1880s. This allowed easy access to the south of the island and Siparia then became accessible to East Indians using the railway. It is not known exactly when they began to identify La Divina Pastora with Suparee Ke Mai, which really is an acknowledgement of Mother Kali, one of the more popular goddesses of the Hindu belief system. By 1890 however, the statue of La Divina Pastora was already attracting a large number of East Indians, especially Hindus, but also Muslims.

It is easy to understand the East Indian attraction to La Divina Pastora. Goddess Kali is the Goddess of famine, destruction, plagues, epidemics, illnesses, and other forms of disaster. Indentureship in Trinidad was a grueling time for the East Indians in that they encountered here not only a hostile environment but also had to endure harsh sugar plantation life, which was a new form of slavery. Their living conditions were subhuman, they contracted all kinds of illnesses, consumed large quantities of alcohol, smoked ganja, and were subject to a fair amount of murders as a result of marital infidelity. When it was brought to their attention that favors were granted through the intercession of Mary as represented by the statue, they readily came to her and saw her as Mother Kali. To her they poured out their woes, sorrows, and distress. Barren wives would ask for children, young children would have their first long locks cut off as a sign of dedication and offering. The sick would ask for healing, young girls for proper husbands, and beggars for the alleviation of distress. As the East Indians were under the planters' control, the public holiday of Good Friday was their chosen day to do homage to the Goddess Kali, when they would travel by train singing Hindu devotional hymns. Important for these devotees was the offering of jewelry, gold and silver bracelets, chains and rings, candles, oil and money, either in supplication or in thanksgiving. Usually for thanksgiving, Indian dances would be performed by colorfully clad dancers, and help would be given to beggars and less fortunate members of society as acts of piety.

The East Indian attachment to the feast, though not having an "evangelizing" component to it, is not dissimilar to the Christian understanding of the same, in that both understandings circulate around the intercessory, restorative, placating, and generative powers of La Divina Pastora/Suparee Ke Mai. And it is to be noted that the method of devotion to La Divina Pastora/Suparee Ke Mai has not changed significantly since the nineteenth century. Devotees still bring offerings to her and young children still have their first haircut in her presence. Indeed, over the years the real problem with La Divina Pastora/Suparee Ke Mai has not been with regard to its efficacy but with regard to "whose feast" is it really? In that regard the Roman Catholic Church has always laid claim to it. In the 1920s the Roman Catholic Church made attempts to prevent East Indians from coming to the shrine, and a notice to that effect was made public in five languages. The police were even called in to implement the decree, but the attempt proved a failure.

Over the years, some parish priests have attempted various strategies such as moving the statue out of the shrine, but the resultant upheaval (among Catholics themselves who want the statue in the shrine) has always seen the statue and the locus of devotion returned to the shrine. In more recent years the feasting aspect of the festival has gained prominence so that the days in and around the feast are now known as Siparia Fete. In 1993 the community of Siparia argued with the parish priest over his decision to bring the feast forward by one week. They argued that "Siparia owns La Divina and La Divina owns Siparia,"[4] in other words the feast really is a "community thing," where the community could derive some commercial profit, and not only a "church thing." It would seem that all expressions of popular religion eventually have to deal with this commercial aspect to them, but let us now attempt some clarification of the issues offered to us by the feast of La Divina Pastora/Suparee Ke Mai in Trinidad.

Clearly, the feast has correlatives in many other parts of the world in that the worship of a Black Virgin is not uncommon to this part of the world (Our Lady of Guadalupe for instance) nor does the popular devotion to Mary lack enthusiasm the world over. As a matter of fact, there was a time when such enthusiasm was discouraged in Roman Catholicism because it seemed to supersede the "official" liturgical expressions. So another popular religious festival to Mary is of itself interesting but hardly new. What, however, is unique in the Trinidad experience is the use of the feast, and of the statue, by Hindus regarding it as a representation of Kali. More than this, that this sort of devotion should survive the attempts to stamp out such "superstition," and also resist conversion, is a striking and instructive event in the religious life of a people. It hints at a reality that we must take into account if we are to appreciate seriously and respectfully popular religiosity and if we are to understand the possibilities (if at all) of multifaith dialogue in such contexts.

First, it seems that popular religious expressions arise out of the perceived hopes and desires of persons. This is why they persist and this accounts for their enduring character. More than this, it also accounts for why popular religious expressions will always find an avenue of expression, in that they survive as forms of resistance more than as formal structures with clarified metalanguages (theologies). Indeed, it is as such that La Divina Pastora/Suparee Ke Mai continues to thrive, despite the attempts by the Roman Catholic Church, in the persons of the various parish priests of Siparia, to regulate and formalize the proceedings.

There is a lesson to be learnt here. As much as we would like to harness the vibrant and compelling impulse found in the Siparia devotions and in all popular religiosity, it would seem that one has to be careful to allow the expression under study to remain what it is, not what we would like it to be.

Clearly, we have to be careful that we do not go along with popular religiosity because it suits our purpose in terms of imposing our own understanding of reality and events on others. The significant aspect about popular religiosity, however, is that it resists such an incorporation reflexively. Parish records in Siparia clearly show that converts are not had simply because diverse peoples share a common physical and geographical referent and thereby seemingly have "common" ground. On the contrary, the Hindus in the main have remained staunchly Hindu, and other Christians and religious devotees have also maintained the structures of belief they came with in their devotional practices to La Divina Pastora/Suparee Ke Mai.

While in Guyana on an interfaith conference in early April of 1993, a member of the Winty religion—a "popular religion" in Suriname similar to the Shango/Orisha in Trinidad, Pocomania in Jamaica, and Voodoo in Haiti—told me that he gets angry when so-called "established" religions want to understand Winty so that they can incorporate or translate some of their elements in order to attract Winty followers. He was angry at the arrogance and lack of respect shown to Winty followers and also at the branding of the religion as "popular," meaning that it is not really a cohesive unit with a solid core of basic beliefs and understandings. I think we must take this critique seriously and question the whole raison d'être for our wanting to understand popular religiosity. Is it so that we can exploit that which seems to work well for others in order to use its devices to our own ends?

Second, what is liberating about the La Divina Pastora/Suparee Ke Mai feast is not so much the symbolism involved, but the opportunity to invoke and restore such symbolism in the lives of a people. It is in the midst of the hardship of indentureship that the East Indian in search of a "home" finds that home not only in a physical sense but in the religious sense that covers his/her range of expression. In effect, Suparee Ke Mai allows the worship of the Goddess Kali just as the Caroni River takes the place of the river Ganges for the local Hindu. So that once there is that space, either created or already established (as in this case) to allow for the adequate expression of the hopes and pains of a people, there we will find the vibrancy that supports and carries popular religiosity. This is something that the "established" churches need to consider. Where is the "space" for the average believer and worshipper to adequately express their hopes and pains?

Third, the creation of this space of confrontation (in resistance and survival) is only an initial step for the believer. As important as the issue of survival is for the popular religious believer, is not salvation more important? We rightly acknowledge the importance of the themes of resistance and survival in popular religiosity, but isn't salvation the goal for the genuine religious believer? And sometimes as a denial of survival? I think at this point we could begin some critique of popular religiosity instead of uncritically proclaiming its "goodness." Remember that the contemporary problem in Trinidad for the Divina Pastora celebrations is no longer about its religious significance but its economic and social impact. Its survival in terms of its growing success has strangely enough diminished its salvific qualities. Is this the route of popular religiosity, or of any "successful" religion? Are the goals of resistance and survival in today's religious expressions sacrificing the salvific content of religion for the sake of survival geared towards success by all means possible? If there is evidence to claim that this is happening in a significant manner then we are dealing merely with ideological substitution, the replication of systems of domination dressed in more localized garb. The use of popular religiosity then becomes the latest fad in the marketplace that allows access to a greater piece of the pie. Nothing more and nothing less. For the faith of the people, and for any religion, to retain its salvific qualities there must be some sustained reflexive and reflective drive towards salvation, which builds upon, and is not replaced by, its survival strategies. Thus far, popular religion does not seem able to carry that weight. Whether it can is another issue.

Endnotes

1. See Idris Hamid, ed., *Out of the Depths* (San Fernando, Trinidad, St. Andrews Theological College), for a collection of papers that echo this theme.
2. This is one of the more important points brought out in a consultation on theological education within the Caribbean held in Jamaica from January 23–29, 1993. See Howard Gregory, ed., *Caribbean Theology: Preparing for the Challenges Ahead* (Jamaica: Canoe Press UWI, 1995).
3. Taken from an introduction to Novena Prayers written by Thomas Harricharan O.S.B.
4. "Holy War Brews in Siparia," *Sunday Express,* May 9, 1993, 2.

Chapter 4

Cubans In Babylon

Exodus And Exile

Miguel A. De La Torre

There are two Cubas. On the island are the revolutionaries, crusading to construct a Cuba that combats any attempt to subjugate her spirit to U.S. hegemony. On the U.S. (main)land are the modernists who look to the United States as guide and hope for revitalizing a post-Castro Cuba. Due to these fundamental political and cultural differences, the Cuban community is a people divided against itself. We look beyond each other for our mentors because we do not know how to look at ourselves. The individual who chooses to address our two groups from any perspective other than the official one would be suspected of secretly abetting the opposing camp and might succeed only in uniting both groups to condemn her or his initiative.

The purpose of this chapter is to look within our own Cuban cultural legacy to construct an *ajiaco* Christianity. *Ajiaco* is a renewable Cuban stew consisting of different indigenous roots. A native dish, it symbolizes who we are as a people, and how our diverse ethnic backgrounds came to be formed. *Ajiaco* Christianity allows us to read the Biblical text with Cuban eyes. We read the text hoping to explore avenues that might lead to peace and solidarity among Cubans by debunking the Exilic Cuban ethnic identity, constructed to mask and normalize the position of power occupied by the Exilic Cuban elite. *Ajiaco* Christianity rejects the Anglicization of our culture by constructing an ethics of reconciliation that seriously considers the reality of our diverse backgrounds within the context of the intra-Cuban struggle for legitimate self-rule based on self-identity and self-determination. Founded on the sociohistorical reality of Exilic Cubans, *ajiaco* Christianity equates salvation with reconciliation (both with the deity and each other). Hence, the post-Castro libertarian society created for implementation by the Exilic Cuban elite is immoral for it expands the social structures of race, class, and gender oppression existing from Miami to the Cuban island.

Ajiaco Christianity

The Amerindians gave us the *maíz, papa, malanga, boniato, yuca,* and *ají.* The Spaniards added *calabaza* and *nabo,* while the Chinese added oriental spices. Africans, contributing *ñame* and, with their culinary foretaste, urged a meaning from this froth beyond the necessity of clever cooking. We are "a *mestizaje* of kitchens, a *mestizaje* of races, a *mestizaje* of cultures, a dense broth of civilization that bubbles on the stove of the Caribbean."[1] In effect, we eat and are nourished by the combination of all of our diverse roots. *Ajiaco* symbolizes our *cubanidad*'s attempt to find harmony within our diverse roots, aspiring to create Jose Martí's idealized state of a secularized vision of Christian love that is antiimperialistic, antimilitant, antiracist, moral, and radical.[2] Unlike the North American melting pot paradigm, maintaining that all immigrants who arrive on these shores are somehow placed into a pot where they "melt down" into a new culture that nevertheless remains Eurocentric in nature, an *ajiaco* retains the unique flavors of its diverse roots while enriching the other elements. For this reason, our *ajiaco* is and should be unapologetically our own authentic reality, our *locus theologicus* (theological milieu), from where we Cubans approach the wider world.

Why an *Ajiaco* Christianity? Most Exilic Cuban theologians have dealt with the Exilic Cuban experience from an overall Hispanic context. Absent from the discourse is the application of a hermeneutic of suspicion of ourselves as Exilic Cubans. While it is important to position the Exilic Cuban within the larger Latina/o community, misunderstanding occurs when we fail to realize the radically different social space occupied by Exilic Cubans, specifically those who reside in Miami. By lumping Exilic Cubans with Mexicans, Puerto Ricans, and other Latin Americans under the term Hispanic and/or Latina/o, our power and privilege that comes with our racial composition and upper- and middle-class status, are masked. Also, absent from such a discourse is the Exilic Cuban attempt to identify themselves from within the white, Anglo-dominant culture, and thus against other Hispanic groups. The desire of Latino/a theologians to evoke a pan-Hispanic unity diminishes the reality of how racism, classism, and sexism are alive and well within the Exilic Cuban's constructed social space. Casting ourselves solely as victims obscures the dubious role we also play as victimizers. In respect to a theology of liberation we are simultaneously both the oppressed

and the oppressors, a fact that is inconvenient and therefore sometimes ignored by those who would lump us all together as the Hispanic Other to
U.S. hegemony.

Exilic Cubans' mean family income of $39,600 is closer to the United
States population's mean of $44,500 than any other Hispanic group. Con-
trast this to Mexicans at $29,300 or Puerto Ricans at $26,600. About 63
percent of Exilic Cubans own businesses (the highest rate among Latin
Americans) contrasted to 19 percent of Mexicans, or 11 percent of Puerto
Ricans. Unemployment rates of 4 percent for Cubans are lower then the national average, while Mexicans are at 11 percent and Puerto Ricans are at 8
percent.[3] Only 14 percent of Exilic Cubans find themselves below the
poverty line, as opposed to 25 percent of Mexicans and 37 percent of Puerto
Ricans. Finally, 22 percent of Exilic Cubans hold managerial or professional
employment, much higher than the 9 percent of Mexicans or 12 percent of
Puerto Ricans.[4]

These figures illustrate the difficulty for Exilic Cubans to find a space
within an overall Hispanic theology that attempts to construct a perspective
from a position of marginality, poverty, *mestizaje,* solidarity, and exile. While
discrimination against Exilic Cubans is a reality and is reflected in the distribution of income, they still earn higher average incomes and more frequently occupy professional-level jobs than any other Hispanic group.[5] The
ascension of Exilic Cubans to positions of power is a relatively new phenomenon. In the early 1980s, anti-Cuban referendums in the form of an-
tibilingual ordinances were passed overwhelmingly in Miami. An attempt to
solidify the political hold of the Anglo-elite was in full swing. The endeavor
to disenfranchise Exilic Cubans created a backlash leading toward a concerted effort to wrest control from the old guard. By the 1990s, the majority of city commissioners were Exilic Cubans, as was the mayor. Also, the
presidents of a number of banks (about 20), Florida International University, Dade County AFL-CIO, Miami Chamber of Commerce, and the
Greater Miami Board of Realtors were Exilic Cubans. We became an integral part of Miami's political, economic, and social power structure, using
our position of power to marginalize our others.

While Exilic Cuban theologians construct a supposedly seemless
Latina/o perspective, that effort is not beyond criticism. Few of us address
the Exilic Cuban theological location from within our context of power in
the Miami community. When the Exilic Cuban perspective is discussed, it
is usually done within the pre-1980s rubric of being an alien. To contribute
to the overall Hispanic liberationist discourse, we have tended to speak either within a pan-Hispanic space (which in fact does not exist), or within
some other Latino/a tradition. Within the Mexican and/or Puerto Rican
communities are Mexican and Puerto Rican theologians who construct

their theology exclusively from their own social location in order to enrich the overall dialogue. My suggestion is that we Exilic Cubans do the same.

Why are so few Exilic Cuban theologians willing to speak from our own constructed space in Miami? We generally ignore this space because of the obvious difficulty of "doing theology as an oppressed people," when in fact the overall Exilic Cuban community is economically well-established, has a most effective U.S. lobbying group (Cuban-American National Foundation, CANF), and is the center of the political, economic, and social power in Dade County, Florida. It is difficult to cry "oppression" once middle-class status is achieved. This chapter does not attempt to create a new body of theological tenets under the rubric *ajiaco* Christianity nor does it reflect any specific religious movement in Miami. In the tradition of the Hebrew prophet Amos, *ajiaco* Christianity is a Biblical ethical response from out of our multicultural roots, within an exilic location that occupies a space of power and privilege. As such, *ajiaco* Christianity is more a prophetic call *to* liberate than a cry for liberation.

> *Beside the Miami River we sat and wept at the memory of La Habana leaving our conga drums by the palm trees.*

In *la sagüesera* (southwest Miami), on *Calle Ocho* (Eighth Street), is a restaurant called Versailles, dubbed *El palacio de los Espejos* (the mirrored palace). Like other popular restaurants in Miami, Versailles attempts to copy the exclusive night spots of La Habana. What makes this particular restaurant unique are the mirrored walls. Sitting at the table in the crowded salon, one constantly sees oneself reflected on one of many heavily-gilded mirrors. As we look in the mirrors surrounding us, we are in fact searching for our ontological origin: not so much what we are, but what we see ourselves as being. Versailles serves as a vivid illustration of Jacques Lacan's theory of the Mirror Stage. While I look at myself, I assume that what I see is a reflection of a self, a secondary reflection, faithful (more or less) to the likeness of an existing original self. Lacan would propose the opposite, that the image in the mirror is what constructs the self. My encounter with the mirror literally reverses the direction, and serves the function of forming my "I." Lacan's theory describes the fact that the delusive reflection of the Cuban in the mirror constructs an Exilic Cuban "self" captivated by the belief in the projected "imaginary," where both future and past are grounded within an illusion. In short, the ideal formed in the mirror situates the agency of the "ego" in fiction, while projecting the formation of the "self" into history.[6]

My Cuban eyes see in the mirror the anticipated maturation of the power I desire to possess and read into my history, the illusion of a "golden Exile." This is why it is so important to go well-dressed and wearing all my jewelry, not so much to be seen by others but so that I can see. Our striving for power creates a history where we tell ourselves that before we Cubans came to this place, "*Miami era un campo con luces* (Miami was a village with fancy lights)." We who possess the power to transform a tourist town into the epicenter of U.S. trade with Latin America, see within ourselves a superior distinction when compared to other ethnic groups who have not transcended the barrio or ghetto. But as Lucan would ask, which is the illusion, the self or the reflection? To see myself as an Exilic Cuban through the mirror's "imaginary" places the subject "I" in a privileged space of observation, while imposing an oppressive gaze upon other Cubans who do not look like me, such as those who came through Mariel in 1980, or those who stayed on the island. They become my Other (as well as Mexicans and Puerto Ricans), categorized by their class and skin pigmentation.

How I see my Other defines my existential self. To "see" implies a position of authority, a privileged point of view. "Seeing" is not a mere innocent metaphysical phenomenon concerning the transmittance of light waves. It encompasses a mode of thought that radically transforms the Other into an object for possession. My subjective "I" exists when I tell the "I" who I am not. The subject "I" is defined by contrasting it with the seen objects *"Marielito"* or "Resident Cuban." In socially constructing "I" out of the differences with the "them," there exist established power relations that give meaning to those differences. Specifically, when I look in the mirror I do not see a *"Marielito"* or "Resident Cuban." By projecting my "I" into *Marielitos* and Resident Cubans, I am able to define myself as a white *macho* who is civilized and successful. As long as I continue to reconstruct myself in the mirror, any type of reconciliation between the two Cubas is futile. Our task is to learn how to see authentically by debunking the image in the mirror.

Seeing our "self" in the mirror is internalized, naturalized, and legitimized in order to mask our position of power as we shape Miami's political and economic structures along the tenets of our false religion. We initiate an active self-formation complete with a long and complicated genealogy, so that we can blame our Other for their deserved constructed space. The ethnicity we construct attempts to imitate the dominant culture, the same culture whose neocolonial ventures on our island caused us to be refugees now. Emasculated by the United States' neoimperialism, we look toward our oppressor to define our manhood. Paulo Freire's "submerged consciousness" helps explain why the first two waves of Exilic Cubans desired at all cost to resemble their oppressor, yearning for equality with the "eminent" men of the United States.[7] Hence, we construct a genealogy that proves we are a white people coming from a white nation, fleeing tyranny with only the clothes on our backs and leaving behind *la Cuba de ayer* (the Cuba of yesterday), which encompassed a seemingly idyllic way of life. Remembering *la*

Cuba de ayer becomes a strategy against oblivion, a tactic by which we can survive as a people.

Looking in the mirror, I reread my history as that of one who escaped. Batista's departure from Cuba on New Year's Eve, 1959, triggered panic as party-goers rushed to their houses to collect their sleeping children, moneys, and anything of value. Those who were able to leave arrived in this country still in their tuxedos and dress uniforms, in formal gowns and high heels. These first refugees arrived with "class," not so much in the elegance of their attire, but in their high economic social stratum. Unlike other contemporary examples of refugees, both the Babylonian-bound Jews and the United States-bound Cubans belonged to the privileged upper social class. The Biblical account tells us that Nebuchadnezzar carried off *"all* Jerusalem into exile [emphasis added]." "All" is defined as the officers, the mighty men of valor, craftsmen, and the blacksmiths. Those left behind were the "poorest of the land" (2 Kings 24:14).

These Exilic Cubans, like their Jewish counterparts, were not necessarily numerous. Yet they represented the top echelons of their country's governmental and business community, facilitating our reestablishment in a foreign land, while creating a "brain drain" that literally emptied the resident community of trained personnel, indispensable for the socioeconomic development of the country. Undoubtedly, the mass exodus of Cubans from the island created regrettable consequences for both communities. The surreal scene at the Miami airport, of well-dressed refugees, was caused by the same forces that brought about the Babylonian exile. In both cases, the hegemonic Northern power was responsible for the circumstances that lead to refugee status. Cuba's political system (especially the Batista regime) was designed to protect the commercial interests and assets of the United States.[8] As vassals, both Cuba and Judah were desirable prizes: Judah as a buffer zone between the powers of the North and South, and Cuba as a key to the entire hemisphere. While Judah's exile was triggered by the physical invasion of Babylon, Cuba's revolution was a reaction to the hegemony of the United States.

The economic restructuring of Cuba by the United States created presocialized refugees. An influential elite that formed a linkage with upperclass groups in the United States and Latin America was created to protect United States interests. Clearly, these refugees represented the political, economic, and social structures of the neocolonial United States' Republic of Cuba. As a means of protecting themselves economically against Cuba's political instability, they hoarded their capital and educated their children in the United States. Most of the elite managed to transfer their assets out of Cuba prior to Castro's victory while others held the bulk of their investments abroad.[9] Protected capital eased the transition to Exilic existence.

This first wave (1959–62) brought to these shores 215,000 refugees who could be considered "political exiles." Demographically, these new Cuban refugees were quite homogeneous. The vast majority composed an elite of former notables who were mostly white (94 percent), middle aged (about 38 years old), educated (about 14 years of schooling), urban (principally La Habana), and literate in English.[10] Unity existed in their bitterness at lost status and their commitment to overthrow Castro in order to regain their assets. Not wanting to minimize the trauma and hardship of being a refugee, those of us who settled in Miami had an advantage denied other immigrating groups of entering a social environment made familiar through years of prior travel and business dealings. South Florida, especially for the *habanero/as,* was seen as a pleasant vacation hub from which to await Castro's immediate downfall. The second wave (1962–73) brought 414,000 refugees who were predominately white, educated, middle class, and willing to work below minimum wages. While in Cuba, they mostly represented those who directly relied on economic links with the United States. On average, they were semiskilled working-class who capitalized on the emerging economic enclave being established by the first wave Cubans. Our hatred toward communism facilitated our usefulness as a Cold War propaganda tool for the dominant culture in the United States. A "golden exile" was constructed to contrast with Castro's Cuba. The United States allowed virtually any Cuban arriving legally or illegally to stay, and assumed a great deal of the financial responsibility to help "those escaping the horrors of communism, yearning to breathe the airs of freedom."[11]

"Sing," they said, "some mambo." How can we sing our rumba in a pagan land? Mi Habana, if I forget you, may my right hand wither.

Every Exilic Cuban has heard Celia Cruz sing the popular tearjerker *"Cuando salí de Cuba* (When I left Cuba)." No other song better summarizes the pain of our existential location. "Never can I die, my heart is not *here.* Over *there* it is waiting for me, it is waiting for me to return *there.* When I left Cuba, I left my life, I left my love. When I left Cuba, I left my heart buried." This popular Cuban ballad, written by a Chilean and sung as a hymn of the faith, illustrates the denial of accepting the reality of being, living, and most likely dying on foreign soil. Both Exilic Jews and Cubans were forced to deal with this incomprehensible pain. Ancient Judaism was constructed in Babylon through the pain of questioning the sovereignty of a God who would tear God's people from their homes and plant them in an alien land. Likewise, we Exilic Cubans subconsciously reconstructed ourselves in Lacan's mirror. We internalize and naturalize our image in the mirror so that we can begin to shape outside structures, always masking our drive toward mastering them. This reconstruction took the form of *la Cuba de ayer* (the Cuba of yesterday).

La Cuba de ayer on United States soil created a landless Cuban territory with its distinct cultural milieu and idiosyncrasies, which served to protect us from the pain of the initial economic and psychological difficulties caused by our uprooting. Cuba became more than just the old country, it was the mythological world of our origins. Cuba is an ethereal place where every conceivable item *es mejor* (is better): from the food, to the skies, to pests. Everything *aquí* (here) when contrasted with *allá* (there) is found lacking. Unlike the stereotypes of other immigrant groups, who left painful memories of the old country behind, joyfully anticipating what they perceived was a new country where "the streets were paved with gold," Cubans did not want to come to what we perceived to be an inferior culture. Like the Babylon Jews, we rejoice every time someone says, "Let us go to our house" (Ps. 122). Remembering *la Cuba de ayer,* we forget the reality of yesterday and exaggerate the atrocities of today. In our attempt to avoid our pain, we construct a mythical Cuba where every *guajiro/a* (country bumpkin) had class and wealth, where no racism existed, and where Eden was preserved until the serpent (Fidel) beguiled Eve (the weakest elements of society: Blacks, the poor, etc.) and brought an end to paradise.

Is it any wonder that when Exilic Cubans read Psalm 137 we are stirred to the core of our souls? We fully comprehend the tragic pain of sitting by the rivers of an alien land unable to sing to a God the Psalter secretly holds responsible. Landlessness, which comes with the 90-mile crossing of the Straits of Florida, radically disenfranchises us. The hope of returning to one's land becomes a foundational building block for the construction of our Exilic Cuban ethnicity, yet with the passing of each year, the cemeteries of Miami hold evermore headstones engraved with Cuban surnames. Rather than proclaiming, "next year in Jerusalem," we tell each other, "this year Castro will fall," as though this one person is the only thing that prevents us from "going home." In reality, the hope of returning home has been replaced with a private desire to adapt and capitalize on our presence in this country.

Jeremiah writes a letter to the Exilic Jews to forget about their hope for a speedy return. He tells them (29:5–9): "to build houses, live, plant gardens and eat their fruits; . . . [they are to] seek the peace of the city [to which exiled] . . . and pray to Yahweh for its peace, for in its peace there will be for you peace." Like the Jews, Exilic Cubans are forced to relinquish the old world and deal with the realities of the new space they occupy. Our adherence to Jeremiah's dictates was facilitated through our former contacts with elites in other Latin American countries, the possession of the necessary language skills and cultural links to deal with these contacts, and our connections with U.S. corporations developed when we were their representatives back in the homeland.

These advantages created a space that allowed us to bring new businesses to Miami and gain positions of power within the banking industry. We established "character loans" as a way of providing entrepreneurs the seed money required to start up businesses. This action helps create an ethnic enclave.[12] Labor was easily obtained from both family members and other more recent refugees. With time, Exilic Cubans with business acumen acquired in La Habana filled an economic space in Miami by offering U.S. products to Latin America. Even though Exilic Cubans constitute 4.8 percent of the Latino/a population in the United States, a third of all the large Hispanic corporations are based in Miami.

The Central Intelligence Agency also contributed to the influx of capital helping establish the Exilic Cuban economic enclave. According to reports published by the United States Senate Select Committee to Study Government Operations with Respect to Intelligence Operations in the mid 1970s, Zenith Technological Services, known by code name JM/WAVE, served as a front operation on the campus of the University of Miami. By 1962, JM/WAVE was the largest CIA installation in the world outside of Langley. Funds to carry out CIA missions contributed to the operation of more than 54 front businesses, including an "air force" known as Southern Air Transport and a navy disguised as merchant vessels.[13] The proactive presence of the CIA provided Exilic Cubans with employment opportunities in numerous service industries including boat shops, gun shops, travel agencies, and real estate agencies.

The creation of an economic ethnic enclave eventually led to replacing the old Anglo political elite with rising Exilic Cuban entrepreneurs. Like the Exilic Jews, Cubans suffered no unusual physical hardship. On the contrary, life in exile opened up opportunities that never existed in the homeland. Similar to the Babylonian Jews, Cubans entered trade and grew rich, with some like Nehemiah ascending the political structures to hold power over those who did not go into exile. The United States became the space where Exilic Cubans placed their hope. As Jerusalem was falling, however, Jeremiah bought a plot of land (32:9–11). His message juxtaposes God's judgment with deliverance. The true hope for Jerusalem did not lie in Babylon, rather it was rooted in the homeland. Similarly, Exilic Cubans see their exilic experience as positive due to their individual economic advancements. While we look toward the United States to define the future of Cuba, we also look toward Cuba to define our present reality in this country. The historical activity of remembering *la Cuba de ayer* protects us from the apocalyptic danger of having our history come to an end. The greatest danger of landlessness is the ushering in of the end of history for a people. Separated from our land, *la Cuba de ayer* protects us from extermination, and creates the hope of one day returning to the "promised land."

Self-deception and denial are manifested in the construction of our ethnic identity. Identity as an Exilic Cuban is a social construction created from the pain of living in *el exilio*.[14] A foundational tenet of this construction claims we are victims who "fled" tyranny. In the 1960s, the United States lost Cuba to the communists (assuming Cuba had belonged to the United States and thus could be lost), and was defeated at *Playa Girón*. These were major setbacks in the ideological struggle against the Soviet Union. But the image of Cubans getting off rafts and kissing U.S. soil provided powerful propaganda showing the superiority and desirability of capitalism over communism. "Fleeing communism" also afforded Cubans benefits that simply did not exist for other immigrating groups, specifically $2 billion in resettlement aid and immediate resident status. It hid the fact that later refugees were not so much fleeing tyranny, but were seeking economic prosperity. They closely resembled "classical immigrants" who were "pulled" by the glittering allure of economic opportunities found in the United States, as opposed to being "pushed" by the Castro regime.[15] The economic "pull" to the United States complicates the reductionist explanation that the sole reason for Cuban immigration is political. It ignores the natural flow of people from underdeveloped to developed countries, a trend that has existed in Cuba since Cortés left for the greater riches of Mexico. While the overall rubric for an individual to leave a country may be expressed as a dissatisfaction with the current situation, it is impossible to discern any clear dividing lines between political, economic, or psychological reasons.

The 1980 Mariel exodus best illustrates this point. As the 1970s came to a close, the Cuban economy experienced a sharp decline of commodity prices, rising interest rates, rapid increase in costs of industrial goods, and a budget deficit that reached $785 million by 1982. The situation was exacerbated by natural disasters, crop diseases, and machinery breakdowns that reduced the industrial output. These conditions worsened Cuba's economic situation as the country reduced spending in the dominant social economy in the late 1970s by eliminating previously gratuitous services as bus fares, utilities, and infant day care.[16] In spite of the vehement denunciations of the Castro regime by United States-bound Mariel refugees, it appears that their immigration was more a result of being "pulled," like Haitians, due to economic difficulties in the homeland. Unlike Haitians, the Mariel wave was not "as black" and benefited from the then emerging political and economic clout of the established Exilic Cuban community.[17]

The construction of our ethnicity remembers Cuba as a white nation. This remembrance is rooted in the fact that 99 percent of Exilic Cubans prior to 1980 were white. Cuban census information has always been manipulated prior to and after Castro's revolution to insure the reputation of a predominance of Whites even when the black population throughout the century has ranged from 50 to 80 percent. The construction of Cuba as a white nation was challenged by the 1980 Mariel boatlift. Unlike the elite first wave, or the middle-class second wave, these Cubans best resembled the population's masses. Forty percent of these refugees were biracial. An immediate distancing between the established Exilic Cuban community and these new arrivals began due to racism and classism. They came to be known as *Marielitos,* in an effort to differentiate this group of Cubans from all previous Exilic Cubans. *Marielitos* occupied their own constructed space, defined by both Exilic and Resident Cubans as "criminals, homosexuals, and scum."

The negative images of *Marielitos* surfaced in the midst of the established community (both Anglo and Cuban) through the reporting done by the *Miami Herald.* While it is true that more than one-fifth of all *Marielitos* had prison records, the vast majority of these incarcerations were as political prisoners or traders in the underground market. Less than 2 percent were hardcore, recidivist criminals, and only a few thousand suffered from mental illness.[18]

Marielitos' darker skin provided a scapegoat for the Exilic Cuban's flawed character. They were seen by the established white Exilic community as a threat to their social construction of "model immigrants." According to a 1982 poll conducted by the Roper Organization about attitudes of the U.S. public toward U.S. ethnic groups, only 9 percent felt Cubans have been good for the country, while 59 percent saw Cubans as making the country worse. The remaining 32 percent had mixed feelings or did not know. The transition from "model citizen" to the least favored ethnic group in the nation caused the established community to blame the new arrivals from Mariel. Not surprisingly, three years after arriving, 26 percent of polled Mariel refugees believed they were discriminated against by Anglos, while 75 percent believed they were discriminated against by the more established Exilic Cubans.[19] *Marielitos* quickly became our Other.

Ironically, part of the white Cuba construction is the assertion that Cuba was free of racism. While discrimination may have existed in some sectors, it was presented as never as bad as in the United States. Love and respect supposedly existed between the races in Cuba. As expected, this view is mostly held by those Exilic Cubans who are white. The economic and political structures of *la Cuba de ayer* and the Miami of today are designed so Cuban Whites with privilege can foster an ideology that justifies and maintains white rule over black nonexistence. Paradoxically, those of us who constructed ourselves as white, are only white in Miami. Once we leave Miami, we are seen by the dominant U.S. culture as non-white, non-center.

Finally, our constructed ethnicity stresses being model citizens who embraced the North American work ethic. During the early 1960s, the U.S. media broadcasted numerous stories of penniless Cubans rising from adversity to success. These stories stereotyped us as "the Cuban success story." The rags-to-riches discourse benefited both the United States and the Exilic Cuban community. The Cuban success story was created when the civil rights movement was beginning to be established in Miami. While the city's black community began to organize and make demands for justice, Cubans began to arrive. This created a diversion for the white establishment, who could then ignore and avoid dealing with the issues the black community raised. The Miami power structure was able to point to the Cubans and in effect urge the black community to stop complaining and look at the "amazing Cubans" who came with only the clothes on their back, not speaking the language. They have pulled themselves up from their humble beginnings.

On a local level, it was important for Exilic Cubans to succeed to serve as a counterpoint for the black community. On a national level, the success of Exilic Cubans served as a viable alternative to communism by perpetuating the myth that *any*body can make it in this country. For the Exilic Cubans, it facilitated their ability to replace the Miami Anglo establishment. The inclusion of the "rags to riches" discourse in our identity construction serves as a form of resistance to the Anglo-dominant culture. It was necessary for Exilic Cubans to master the structures of oppression, not only to get the attention of the dominant culture, but to replace it. The public narrative of "those amazing Cubans" allowed the Exilic Cubans to move from refugees to model immigrants, and now to Miami's ruling elite. Croucher shows how the social and political construction of the Exilic Cuban success story created a public narrative that reflected and reinforced the changing character of power and politics by forging the success story "truth" and linking it to power.[20]

> *Yahweh, remember what the communist did—a blessing on him who takes and dashes their babies against the rock!*

The psalmist prayed for the enemy's babies to be dashed against the rocks. Mimicking the psalmists, the Exilic Cuban U.S. Congressman Diaz-Balat (ironically a nephew of Castro) called for a post-Castro Cuba to launch a campaign of retribution against anyone who participated in "collaborationism with tyranny." Ten years in prison will not be enough for those who are guilty. The congressman even called for the abduction of foreign investors presently doing business with Cuba, and to have them brought to the island to be punished.[21]

Hatred is not limited to one side of the Florida Straits. While the Exilic community calls you "a Castro agent" for suggesting any deviation from the tenets of *la lucha,* the Resident community calls you a *gusano* (worm) for leaving the island in the first place. Each Cuba sees itself in the mirror as the true remnant. Resident Cubans see themselves as the true Cubans just as King Zedekiah's nobles who remained in Judah saw themselves as true Jews (2 Kings 25:7–30). Similarly, Exilic Cubans see themselves in their mirror as God's "good basket of figs" as opposed to the "bad basket of figs" with which Jeremiah (24) represents King Zedekiah and all those who remain behind. Resident Cubans are seen as pseudo-Cubans in need of being educated in the ways of capitalism and democracy. *La lucha* is reduced to a struggle to promote new oppressors.

Before we Exiles attempt paternalistically to educate Resident Cubans, we of *el exilio* must first recover from our amnesia. Jeremiah strives to overcome the Babylonian Jews' attempt to displace blame. He explains that their condemnation is due to "no one doing justice." Our own sins, and the sins of those to whom we have become vassals, are the causes of our exile. Our reconstruction of *la Cuba de ayer* ignores the reality that La Habana was an exotic space constructed by the United States where the repressed libidinous appetites of the Anglos could be satisfied. The commercialization of vice afforded North Americans the opportunity to experience life outside of their accustomed moral space. La Habana of 1958 was a U.S. brothel with Mafia-controlled casinos, holding the infamous distinction of being the sex and abortion capital of the Western hemisphere. As a playground for North Americans, Cuba developed an unequal distribution of wealth and violated basic human rights. Jeremiah's condemnation of King Jehoiakim also applies to Cuba's elite who profited from this arrangement. They built their house through the oppression of people (Jer. 22:13–17). No communal covenant based on justice and compassion existed between the elite and the masses. By continuing to scapegoat the communist, we deflect attention from our own responsibility. Castro is not the one responsible for our landlessness. The Cuban elite who profited from the United States' neocolonial venture is responsible. Today, many of those responsible are today's Exilic Cuban elite.

Maintaining *la Cuba de ayer* insures the condemnation of our perceived enemies today, while it mythically creates the Cuba of tomorrow, a post-Castro Cuba based on horizontal oppression, where Resident Cubans will be subjected to Exilic Cubans. The overwhelming support of the embargo by Exilic Cubans denies Resident Cubans basic medical supplies and causes death among the sick, the elderly, and infants. From a sanitizing distance, we are dashing the "enemy's" babies against rocks when we deny insulin to those born diabetic. Most Exilic Cubans have no desire to move physically to Cuba. Any type of physical return would mean a tremendous economic sacrifice. Like the Exilic Jews, we have become well-to-do, taking away motivation for any possible rush back to the homeland.[22] The hardships required in nation building do not outweigh the luxuries of living in Miami. While a willingness to financially support the venture may exist (Ezra 1:4,6), polls suggest that few are willing to participate.

While our two Cubas struggle with each other, the United States is positioning itself to reimpose its hegemony. In the same way that the Persian court created a post-exilic Jewish community to secure its national interests, the United States has promised to "rebuild" Cuba, ensuring that any post-Castro government sacrifices its sovereignty.[23] Such a future would create a hierarchical community dominated by those dedicated to the economic concerns of U.S. business people.

CANF, operating as the ultraright government in exile, was established to reinstate U.S. hegemony. The creation of CANF transformed the United States' foreign policy on Cuba into a domestic interest group issue. Elgarresta, working for Richard Allen who was then national security adviser to President Ronald Reagan, created the Exilic Cuban political action committee to funnel monies to U.S. candidates, thus affecting mainstream politics. CANF was started in 1981 when Allen took personal charge in handpicking the 50 white Exilic Cuban business*men*, who paid $10,000 each to purchase a seat on the board of directors. CANF wrote a constitution for a post-Castro Cuba complete with legal codes and a sector-by-sector economic analysis. In the early 1990s, CANF created the Blue Ribbon Commission for the Economic Reconstruction of Cuba.[24] The commission envisions a libertarian Cuba where all of the nation's infrastructures would be run and operated by the private sector. Upon Castro's downfall, CANF plans to send to the island "a ship of hope," full of investors, stockbrokers, and bankers.[25] Obviously, impoverished Resident Cubans lack the necessary capital to refurbish and head power plants, airports, railroads, or utility companies. This task will fall into the hands of foreign corporations.

By August 1990, the University of Miami's Research Institute for Cuban Studies began to collect data to produce a *Registry of Expropriated Properties in Cuba.* The purpose of these land registers is to compensate previous Exilic owners for the loss of their property and assets. CANF prefers commercial properties be auctioned off to the highest bidder rather than go to the pre-Castro owners, giving a clear advantage to those who can outbid the previous owners. Even if Exilic Cubans were to take advantage of the Helms-Burton Act, allowing those who lost properties during the Castro regime to sue corporations presently benefiting by their use, they must wait two years after all U.S. corporate claims are made. Proposed horizontal oppression amongst Cubans is thus masked by patriotism (patriotism at a profit). The question not asked is, What will happen to those presently occupying these properties?

From the periphery of the Jewish Exilic community's epicenter of power, a prophet arose who became a subversive yet redemptive voice. While we do not know his name, his work is found in the later chapters of Isaiah. Appealing to the community's old memories, he plots a new trajectory to discern reality, a reality that conflicts with the self-deception of the exiles. Second, Isaiah's vision is inclusive (49:6; 56:1–8; 66:18–21), calling the Exilic community to become "a light to the nations, that [God's] salvation [reconciliation] may reach to the end of the earth." The focus is on a God who acts on the side of the afflicted. Such a God opposes the partisan politics rampant in the post-Exilic Jewish community. Rejecting this prophetic voice, Exilic Cubans are aggressively taking the opposite role, that of the Zadokite priestly party.[26] The inclusiveness of Second Isaiah's community is met with accusations of being "communist dupes or agents." Biblical scholar Paul Hanson points out that the Zadokite: (1) moved away from Second Isaiah's (60:21; 61:6) egalitarian call for a nation of priests by firmly holding power in their own hands; (2) replaced Isaiah's (56:3–7) mission to the nations with a pragmatic and parochial strategy of domestic consolidation; and (3) confused the sovereignty of God with that of the Persian emperor, even to the point of proclaiming that God elected a pagan, Cyrus, to be His messiah.[27] Thus the Zadokite hierarchy struggled against those who embraced Second Isaiah's egalitarian vision. The failure to pursue Isaiah's vision can be traced to the Persian Court's self-serving support of the Zadokites. The construction of a post-Exilic Judah was possible because it contributed to Persia's international goal of creating a buffer between them and their enemies, the Egyptians. As such, Judah's existence depended on Persia's good will (Ezra 7:11–18). The nation was rebuilt at the price of being a vassal (583 to 332 B.C.E.) to its more powerful northern neighbor. The parallels to modern Cuba are striking.

Ezra (7:25–26), with legal and financial support from Persia, was sent to create this buffer zone where the inhabitants would strictly obey the "laws of your God *and the law of the [Persian] king* [italics added]." Absent was any negotiation for land. Instead, land was controlled by the returning Jews. Like Ezra's approach, Exilic Cubans are preparing to demand that Resident Cubans "put away their foreign wives." Some of those "wives," however, may be worth keeping (such as high literacy rates, a 100 percent social security system, a high doctor per patient ratio, a low infant mortality rate, and a long life expectancy). Ignoring Second Isaiah's egalitarian call, the post-Exilic community soon found itself weakened by internal economic abuses. Exilic Jews benefited from the economic misfortunes of the Resident Jews, while concealing their profiteering in piety (Isa. 58:1–12; 59:1–8). The Resident poor found themselves enslaved as they lost their lands to the returning Exiles (Neh. 5:1–5) and were cheated from wages by returning Jews who set up new businesses (Mal. 3:5). The book of Ruth, written during this period, becomes an alternative voice to the imposition of the Zadokite power structure (priestly clan) among the Jewish priestly elite and captures the spirit of Second Isaiah. Here, God uses a "foreign wife," a Moabite, similar to the ones put away by Ezra, to represent society's most vulnerable members. Ruth is saved by the egalitarian laws that the exilic leaders aborted.

This Biblical paradigm of domination will repeat itself. The planned post-Castro community will lead to the subjugation of Resident Cubans by Exilic Cubans, who in turn will be subjugated to the U.S. hegemony. The options available to Exilic Cubans are similar to those faced by the Babylonian Exilic Jews. We can follow the example of Ezra, forcing Resident Cubans to "put away their foreign wives," establishing a vassal political system that enriches the Exilic community elite to the determent of the Resident community. Or, we can follow Second Isaiah's egalitarian vision, which attempts to construct a reconciled and just community. As long as Exilic Cubans maintain our mirror-like construction of ethnic identity, along with participating in the false religion of *la lucha,* and as long as Exilic Cubans theologians define our theological location in terms of some general Hispanic perspective "from the margins," reconciliation between the two Cubas remains impossible. On the contrary, the *Ajiaco* Christianity I propose here constructs our identity based on our sociohistorical reality, unmasking the power and privilege held by Exilic Cubans and debunking our ethnic construction, which prevents dialogue between us and our Other. A liberationist approach to theology liberates the oppressed as well as the oppressors. As present oppressors in Miami, and as future oppressors in a post-Castro Cuba, Exilic Cubans are in need of an *Ajiaco* Christianity of liberation and reconciliation.

Notes

1. Fernando Ortiz, *Los factores humanos de la cubanidad* (La Habana: Revista Bimestre Cubana, XLV, 1940), 165–9. Fernando Ortiz was the first to use *ajiaco* as a metaphor for the Cuban experience. He used this term within the context of a Cuba that was a country of immigrants who, unlike the United States, reached the island on the way to someplace else. Rather than accenting the immigrants, I used this term to refer to the distinctive nexus of our people's roots, specifically our Amerindian, African, Spanish, Asian, and Anglo roots.

2. José Martí (1853–95), Cuban journalist, revolutionary philosopher, and patriot is credited with organizing the physical invasion of Cuba to bring about her independence from Spain. A prolific writer (whose *Obras Completa* consists of 73 volumes) and precursor of *modernismo,* Martí is regarded as the father of Cuba by both Resident and Exilic Cubans. He was killed a month (May 19, 1895) after landing in Cuba during a skirmish with Spanish troops at Dos Ríos. His death made him a martyred symbol of Cuban liberation.

On the eve of his death, he wrote on a notepad, "Cuba must be free from Spain and from the United States."

3. Frank L. Schick and Renee Schick, eds., *Statistical Handbook on United States Hispanics* (Phoenix: Opyx Press, 1991), 176.
4. Marlita A. Reddy, ed., *Statistical Records of Hispanic Americans* (Detroit: Gale Research, 1995), 223, 510, 589, 653, 762, 868–9.
5. Schick and Schick, 186–7.
6. Jacques Lacan, *Écrits* (Paris: Seuit, 1966), 94–5.
7. Paulo Freire, *Pedagogy of the Oppressed,* trans. Myra Bergman Ramos (New York: Continuum, 1994), 44–5.
8. Hugh Thomas, *Cuba: The Pursuit of Freedom* (New York: Harper & Row, 1971), 971. Batista's utility to the United States was best expressed by William Wieland, Cuban desk officer at the State Department, who said, "I know Batista is considered by many as a son of a bitch . . . but American interests come first . . . at least he is *our* son of a bitch, he is not playing ball with the Communists. . . ."
9. Marifeli Pérez-Stable and Miren Uriarte, "Cubans and the Changing Economy of Miami," in *Latinos in a Changing U.S. Economy: Comparative Perspectives on Growing Inequality,* ed. Rebecca Morales and Frank Bonilla (Newbury Park, CA: Sage Publications, 1993), 135.
10. Richard R. Fagan, Richard A. Brody, and Thomas J. O'Leary, *Cubans in Exile: Disaffection and the Revolution* (Stanford, CA: Stanford University Press, 1968), 19–28.
11. Silvia Pedraza-Bailey, "Cuba's Exile: Portrait of a Refugee Migration," *International Migration Review* 19 (1985): 4–34. For the first time in U.S. history, this country became an asylum for a large group of refugees by assuming the financial burden of resettling them. Total aid of approximately $2 billion was disbursed through the Cuban Refugee Program. Over a 12-year period, aid consisted of direct cash assistance, guaranteed health care, food subsidies, retraining and retooling programs, college loans, English-language instruction and financial assistance for establishing small businesses. Even though most assistance was contingent on resettlement to another part of the United States, Miami's economic base was greatly impacted, triggering the transformation of South Florida.
12. Alejandro Portes and Alex Stepick, *City on the Edge: The Transformation of Miami* (Berkeley: University of California Press, 1993), 132–5. The flight of capital from Latin America to the economic and political security of the United States provided an economic space for Exilic Cubans to manage said funds leading to the creation and growth of banks. Once secured in banking positions they provided "character loans" to their compatriots to encourage business. It mattered little if the borrower had no standing within Anglo banks, little collateral, or spoke no English. Loans (usually from $10,000 to $35,000) were provided, based on the reputation of the borrower in Cuba. This policy was discontinued in 1973 because the new refugees, who were not from the more elite first wave, were unknown to the lenders. This practice contributed to the development of an economic enclave.

13. Joan Didion, *Miami* (New York: Simon and Schuster, 1987), 88–91.

14. *El exilio* is a term mainly used by Exilic Cubans to name our collective identity. The term connotes the involuntary nature of displacement and constructs us as sojourners in a foreign land. *El exilio* is an in-between place, a place to wait and hope for a return to our homeland. It is more then geographic separation, it encompasses dis-connection, dis-placement, dis-embodiment. *El exilio* is existence in a reality apart from what one loves. *Exilio* exists for the Exilic Cubans who were forced to wave goodbye to their homeland and loved ones, as well for the Resident Cubans who watched us leave. In Miami, longing for Cuba or the "rhetoric of return" becomes the unifying substance of our existential being, yet this hope is being replaced with a stronger desire to adapt and capitalize on our presence in this country. Taking our cue from Martí, *el exilio* becomes a sacred space making morality synonymous with nationality. Living in exile is a sacrifice constituting a civic duty representing a grander moral basis.

15. N.V. Amaro and A. Portes, "Una sociologia del exilio: Situación de los grupos cubanos en los Estados Únidos," *Aportes* no. 23 (1972): 10–14.

16. Franklin W. Knight, *The Caribbean: The Genesis of a Fragmented Nationalism,* 2nd ed. (New York: Oxford University Press, 1990), 254.

17. In spite of the extreme repression in Haiti, Haitian refugees were categorized as fleeing the island due to economic difficulties, while Exilic Cubans fled for political reasons. The latter gained entrance into the United States while the former were repatriated.

18. Mark F. Peterson, "The Flotilla Entrants: Social Psychological Perspectives on Their Employment," *Cuban Studies/Estudios Cubanos* 12 (July 1982): 81–6.

19. Alejandro Portes and Juan M. Clark, "Mariel Refugees: Six Years Later," *Migration World* 15 (Fall 1987): 14–18.

20. Sheila L. Croucher, *Imagining Miami: Ethnic Politics in a Postmodern World* (Charlottesville: University Press of Virginia, 1997), 102–108.

21. Patrick J. Kigar, *Squeeze Play: The United States, Cuba, and the Helms-Burton Act* (Washington, D.C.: Center for Public Integrity, 1996), 57.

22. John Bright, *A History of Israel,* 3rd ed. (Philadelphia: Westminster Press, 1959), 362–3. Bright documents the success of the Exilic Jews by pointing out that their names frequently appear in business documents from Nippus (437 and afterwards). Also, he quotes Josephus (Ant. XI, 1, 3) as stating, "they were not willing to leave their possessions," to be their excuse for not returning to Jerusalem.

23. A 24-page report titled *Support for a Democratic Transition in Cuba,* submitted to the U.S. Congress on January 28, 1997 by President Clinton, outlines the administration's intention of providing $4 to $8 billion to establish an approved governmental and political system. The conditions for replacing the ongoing 35+ year trade embargo with this assistance package includes the departure of the Castro brothers ("horizontally or vertically" as per Senator Helms), the release of all political prisoners, the dismantling of the in-

terior ministry, and the holding of a U.S.-style public election. The report also calls for a possible renegotiation of the soon-to-be expired lease of Guantanamo Bay, where a United States military presence still exists.

24. Patrick J. Kigar, 31–2. Members of the Blue Ribbon Commission for the Economic Reconstruction of Cuba include Republican presidential candidate Malcolm Forbes Jr., former U.N. Ambassador Jeane Kirkpatrick, U.S. senators Bob Graham and Connie Mack, economist Arthur Laffer (whose "Laffer Curve" served as the foundation of Reaganomics), Hyatt Hotels Corp. CEO Jay Pritzker, and a special appearance by Ronald Reagan.

25. Peter Slevin, "60 Minutes Examines Mas Canosa," *Miami Herald,* October 19, 1992, A-10.

26. The Zadokite priesthood was responsible for the reforms made during the reign of King Josiah in 622 B.C.E. They held exclusive responsibility for the temple cult, facilitating their leadership status within the Exilic Jewish community. Their leadership expanded to civic matters with the mysterious disappearance of the Davidic prince, Zerubbabel. Just as CANF holds official sponsorship by the U.S. government and has set out to create plans for the "restoration" of Cuba, the Zadokite were also officially sponsored by the Persian court and given the task of restoring Judah as vassal to Persia.

27 Paul D. Hanson, *The People Called: The Growth of Community in the Bible* (San Francisco: Harper & Row, 1986), 255.

Part II

Discourse on Scripture, Culture, and Political Interaction

Chapter 5 🖼

Understandings and Interpretations of Scripture in Eighteenth- and Nineteenth-Century Jamaica

The Baptists as Case Study

Horace O. Russell

Within the context of the role of the Bible in Caribbean culture and tradition, this chapter examines two important case studies of Christian interpretation of the Bible in Jamaica in the 1700s and 1800s. This evaluation, the Baptists' understandings and interpretations of Scripture in eighteenth and nineteenth century Jamaica, begins in Bristol, England, and Savannah, Georgia, two places from which the early Baptist missionaries to Jamaica came. In particular, George Liele and William Knibb, on whom this chapter focuses, derived their earliest understandings of the faith within the context of the Evangelical Movement in America and England respectively.

George Liele

George Liele (1750–1828?) was the son of two Virginian slaves, and in the course of time came under the ministry of Rev. Matthew Moore, pastor of the Bulkhead Creek Baptist Church.[1] He was licensed to preach and pursued an itinerant ministry, which was to influence David George, who established Baptist work in Sierra Leone, and Andrew Bryan, the pioneer of the National Baptist Convention of the United States, while he himself went on to establish Baptist witness in the Caribbean island of Jamaica. Liele was certainly in contact with Daniel Marshall (1706–84) and Shubal Stearns (1706–71), who were of the itinerant tradition and laid emphasis upon personal experience of regeneration and separation from the world. The preaching was emotional, but as with the Separate Baptist tradition it tended to be concerned with every aspect of life. There is little doubt that Liele was influenced by this tradition, which had been successful in attracting the poor and illiterate. Michael Sobel has observed that "Baptists in the South, both because of the social strata of their members and their world view, rapidly gained a reputation as dangerous and contemptible. Many were widely considered law breakers and a 'menace to society.' Their belief in regeneration after baptism was regarded as a license to break the law without fear of damnation." A contemporary charged that with this view of baptism "you take off all religious restraints from men of abandoned principles, who having once dipped in your happy waters are let loose to commit upon us murders and every species of injury, when they can do it secretly so as to avoid temporal punishment. The Baptist laymen of this period were the poor and the disinherited and for the first time their Christian churches uniformly included many blacks."[2]

The background of George Liele, therefore, was the Great Awakening, or Evangelical Movement, as it came into Georgia with a strong antislavery, antiestablishment but nevertheless a "fundamentalist" Biblical message. The antinomianism quoted by Sobel was not common but was symptomatic of that bent toward freedom and liberty in the gospel so characteristic of the New Lights. Among the features of Church life were, apart from Baptism, the Lord's Supper and Foot Washing. An importance was attached to weddings and funerals, and several of the songs reflected these concerns. Singing was important and, among the Separatists, the folk tradition of song began to claim pride of place. This can be understood since these events were a part of the First Awakening with its rich tradition, not only of song but of Psalmody and hymnody.

George Liele's approach to the Bible had much in common with the history of Baptist belief and practice. William Brackney of Mac Master University and a prolific writer on Baptist matters, has observed that "to say Baptists 'believe in the Bible' is to identify a basic emphasis that the Bible is the sole authority of determining matters related to the Christian faith. All doctrines and practices, individual and corporate, are to be tested in the light of the Scriptures, particularly the New Testament because it is 'an absolute and perfect rule of direction for all persons, all times to be observed.'"[3] For early Baptists, interpretations and understandings of the Bible were linked closely to the idea of Covenant, and by the time Baptist witness had come to the Americas in the seventeenth century this appears to have been a standard feature. This was because, by that time, Covenant had become a recognized pattern of the Church organization of the Puritan Commonwealth and was incorporated with the coming of the Awakening. Thus, the Covenanting community became the expression of a regenerate membership in which the covenanting behavior was the mark of the people's discipleship. It was within this covenant community, and for it, that Scripture was interpreted.

George Liele arrived in Jamaica in September 1783 and established a Baptist work in Kingston. In the next decade, the work had become so significant that the established Anglican Church, which was then being influenced by the High Church movement in Britain, began to take significant notice of it. The Baptist Church was, of course, a dissenter Church and was seen as a part of the wider Evangelical Movement that came out of Britain. The Evangelical Movement, in contrast with the High Church, was antislavery, appealed to the poor, had an emotional appeal, and used folk imagery and song. Nevertheless, unlike its counterpart in the United States, it was still wedded to the *Book of Common Prayer* and the traditional liturgy of the Anglican Church.

The Baptists, therefore, aroused suspicion within the Jamaican slave society because it had roots in the Evangelical Movement and it was alien to the Jamaican colonial society. Partly to allay this fear, Liele published, on Christmas Day, 1795, a document signed by all the elders of the Church called *The Covenant of the Anabaptist Church Begun in America, December 1777 and in Jamaica December 1783.*[4] This covenant, outlined in several articles, gives us an insight into early Baptist interpretations and understandings of Scripture. There are 21 Articles in all, covering the Lord's Supper, Foot Washing, the admission of young children, praying for and anointing the sick, laboring with one another, the appointing of judges and the prohibition against going to courts presided over by "the unjust" and not "the saints." Further prohibitions were against swearing, sexual irregularities, and the shedding of blood, which meant not to take any life. It is important to comment, in some detail, on some of these articles because they illuminate current understandings of Scripture and suggest how the early Baptists used Scripture.

Liele begins Article I with a statement that, "We are of the Anabaptist Persuasion because we believe it *agreeable to the Scriptures,*" and he quotes Matt. 3:1–3 and 2 Cor. 6:14–18 in support of his position. While the Matthew reference appears clear, the Corinthian passage seems polemical because it attempts to set Baptists apart from everybody else. Verse 14 speaks of "unbelievers" and of "not having fellowship with the unrighteous." One may ask, within such a divided society based on theological principles, who are the unrighteous and the unbelievers? Was this a way of speaking in code about the membership of the Established Church? Liele does not say.

Article II outlines the ways in which the Church conducts itself. Its public worship involves singing psalms, hymns, and spiritual songs, and preaching. This is supported by an appeal to Mark 16:2–6; and Col. 3:16. Both proof texts are complementary, but it is possible that the Markan passage was a strong appeal to establish Sunday, the first day of the week and resurrection day, as the legal day of worship and rest. This Article was in conflict with the prevailing practice of using Sunday as a market day for slaves. Article III speaks of Baptism in a river or at a place with much water. Here the Covenant contains more proof texts than in most other articles. Liele quoted Matt. 3:13–17, Mark 16:15,16, and Matt. 28:19, and invited the Baptist membership to participate in what he called an Ordinance. After all, this is understandable—Liele is a Baptist minister.

Article XV reads, "We permit no slaves to join the church without first having a few lines from their owners of their good [behaviour]." This is followed by Bible references (proof texts) from 1 Pet. 2:13–16 and 1 Thess. 3:13, which speak about the reverence to be given to kings, rulers, and potentates. The use of these texts raises the question as to whether, in this Covenant, Scripture was being used as a device to regulate the behavior of the congregation so that there would be less tension between the slave and the Plantocracy and the State. Liele's background as an employee of the Governor, and as a slave holder himself, appear to give credence to this view.

Article XVII, "If a slave or servant misbehaves to the owners they are to be dealt with according to the Word of God" (1 Tim. 1:6; Eph. 6:5; 1 Pet. 2:18–21; Titus 2:9–11) certainly underlines obedience to the slave master. Article XVIII has as its proof text Luke 12:47, which reads, "And that servant which knew his Lord's will and prepared not himself, neither did according to his will, shall be beaten with many stripes" and appears to be even more explicit than Article XVII. There seems little doubt that this Covenant and its proof texts may be read as providing underlying support to, and for, the slave society. But there are other regulations and texts within it that imply otherwise.

Article XX, after dealing with transgressions and heresy, says, "They shall have no right or claim whatever to be interred into the burying ground during the time they are put out should they depart this life . . ." (2 John 1:9,10; Gal. 6:1,2; Luke 17:3,4). These proof texts address forgiveness and reconciliation but they were also a warning or sanction against slave disunity, since the belief existed that only a Christian burial would allow the spirit to return to Africa. Common among enslaved Africans was the belief that when they died their spirits would return to Africa as a free agent. Thus, to inform on another had the consequence of eternal ancestral separation. Coultart, a British Baptist missionary, complained that he could not get the truth because no slave could be induced to inform on the other. So this article served a double purpose—of declaring forgiveness, but also punishing disunity.

Article VIII, which speaks of laboring together according to the Word of God, is a strange one. The proof text, Matt. 18:15–18, refers to the "binding and loosing" as well as the plea for agreement in prayer. This suggests that the Covenant had a broader meaning that set it not only within the general witness of the Church, but within the particular context of the slave society. Two things can be stated for certain about the George Liele Covenant. First, each Article concludes with the phrase "according to the Word of God" or "agreeable to the Word of God," after which follows the "proof text." Here one sees clearly the Baptist Tradition of submitting all Church teachings to the Scriptural test but it is Scripture within a context, the context of life. The second observation derives from the first and shows that no aspect of life is excluded from the Scriptural test. So, for instance, as is common to the Arminian tradition—the precursor to Anabaptists and Baptist—Article XIV forbids the wearing of costly raiment, as such is superfluity (1 Pet. 3:3,4).[5]

Among the early converts to the Baptist persuasion in Jamaica was Moses Baker, an immigrant like Liele, a lapsed Episcopalian from New York who, with his wife Susannah, settled in Liguinea, on the edges of the city of Kingston. A look at the narrative of his conversion throws further light on the ways in which Baptists used and understood the Bible. John Ryland reports in the *Evangelical Magazine of 1804,* that Baker wrote:

> One day as Mrs. Baker and myself and child were sitting at the door for breakfast, this old man (Cupid Wilkin) came and stood at the door. We sat down carelessly without giving thanks to God for what we were about to receive; which the old man perceiving he turned round to another and said, Whence have these people come I could wish to learn if they know that God made them? I overheard him speaking thus and instantly got up and spoke to him in the following manner: "Old man, can you read?" "No," he replied, "but I know that both of you can." "As you cannot read how dare you thus reprimand me?" The old man immediately humbled himself and said, "Master, if you will not be angry I will tell you where to search Scriptures and you will find there that you are not only to thank God, but to return love, prayer and Thanksgiving for what you are going to receive in the name of Jesus Christ."[6]

In his confession, Baker reported that during his absences to do business in the city, Cupid Wilkin asked Mrs. Baker to read the Scriptures to him and, in discussion with her, Cupid discovered that Moses, her husband, was prone to drink. Cupid then told her that if Moses read the Scriptures and got religion, the first thing to go would be the drink. The narrative continues, "On my return Mrs. Baker was continually importuning me to incline me to religion. . . . A few nights after, my mind was impressed with the thought that I would go and hear whether these people could pray or speak any sense at all. Accordingly, I got up one night and heard them singing and praising God. I drew near and found them in a small hut on their knees in prayer. I immediately approached the man who was praying and fell on my knees also with an intention of hearing his prayer. I heard that he asked for so many things agreeable to the Scriptures, as astonished me and made me almost believe that he had more knowledge than myself."[7] This narrative of Baker is reminiscent of slave narratives that relate their conversion to the Scriptures because of the recognition of their own situation in Scripture. This bears a close resemblance to the experience of Liele himself who reported that Matthew Moore, his pastor, "omitted no opportunity of instructing them in the truths of Christianity and, in the intervals of labor, employed himself in reading the Scriptures and in singing Psalms with them."[8]

Baker also appended to his narrative a Covenant that resembles the Liele Covenant, but without "proof texts" and with significant differences in some articles. Baker's covenant has no provisions for the admission of young children (Liele VI). This is probably due to theological differences between the two on the subject of Baptism in the early years. Liele was known to have close links with Stephen Cooke, a prominent Methodist layman who had introduced him to the British Baptists.[9] It is further known that one of Liele's leaders, Nicholas Sweigle, had asked Thomas Coke to take over the Baptist Church in Jamaica, which Coke refused to do because of theological differences.[10] The absence of Article VI suggests that perhaps Liele and Baker might have differed on this matter. Another possibility exists, that the property on which Baker worked was owned by a Quaker. Quakers did not stress either baptism or the Lord's Supper, and the Covenant reflected this. Absent also from the Baker Covenant was the clause prohibiting slaves to join the Church without a "few lines" from the master (Liele XV). This was probably due to differences in circumstances. Baker did not operate as an independent witness but rather as a chaplain to the plantations on which he lived.

Rippon throws further light on the eighteenth and nineteenth century Baptist use and understanding of Scripture. *The Register,* which he published, was a compendium of correspondence between Great Britain, the United States, and the Caribbean, and contains letters that give insight into this question. Nicholas Sweigle, referred to earlier, punctuates his letters with Scriptural references. In one letter, he writes of being called "from the state of darkness to the marvelous light of the gospel" and continues, "We were living in slavery to sin and Satan and the Lord both redeemed our souls to a state of happiness to praise his glorious and ever blessed name." Sweigle also writes of a "pocket companion," which Rippon describes as a collection of scriptures directed toward Church members. This collection used as a catechism was given free of charge to the slaves, whether literate or not. If they could not read they were expected, as was the case of Cupid Wilkin, to ask someone to read it for them. This had the advantage of allowing the slave owner to be appraised of what was being taught, and also served as an evangelistic and social device.[11]

In his correspondence with Rippon, Liele also gave an account of his conversion. Of the event he observes, "the more I heard and read, the more I saw that I was condemned as a sinner before God; till at length I was brought to perceive that my life hung by a slender thread and if it was the will of God to cut me off at that time I was sure I should be found in hell, as sure as God was in heaven. I saw my condemnation in my own heart and I found no way in which I could escape the damnation of hell only through the merits of my dying Lord and [Saviour] Jesus Christ, which caused me to make intercession with Christ for the salvation of my poor immortal soul." He goes on to say that he confessed Jesus Christ as Lord and Master and asked what work he should do for the church. He continues, "I agree to election, redemption, the Fall of Adam, regeneration, and perseverance knowing the promise is to all who endure in grace, faith and good works to the end, shall be saved."[12] In 1792, Liele writes again to Rippon telling him that he has sent a copy of the Covenant, which he describes as:

> a collection of some of the principal texts of Scripture which we observe both in America and this country [Jamaica] for the direction of our practice. It is read once per month here on sacrament meetings that our members may examine if they live according to those laws which they professed, covenanted and agreed to; by this means our Church is kept in Scriptural subjection. As I observed in my last letter, the [chieftest] part of our society are poor illiterate slaves, some living on sugar estates, some on mountains, pens and other settlements that have no learning, no not to know so much as a letter in the book; but the reading of this covenant, once a month when all are met together from different parts of the island keeps them in mind of the commandments of God. And by showing the same to the gentlemen of the legislature, the justice, the magistrates, when I applied for a sanction it gave them general satisfaction; and whenever a Negro servant is to be admitted, their owners after perusal of it are better satisfied.[13]

Scripture, then, is understood not only as the word of God but also as a manual for living, providing for social as well as personal identity.

The Covenant functioned not only as a document for the instruction of the membership but was also an apologia (a defense) for the very existence of the Church in its national setting; and perhaps this explains the juxtaposition of texts that clearly speak favorably of the master-slave relationship while, at the same time, address the way in which the master should treat the slaves. Liele, like Sweigle, refers to "the Ethiopian Baptists of Jamaica" when he requests the prayers of the British church.[14] This identification with Ethiopia was at first thought to be used by people of African descent only, as their own Christian identity. However, it was a common designation at that time for all persons of African descent, certainly in parts of the United States. Abraham Marshall, a leading figure in the Baptist Convention of Georgia, in recommending members of the Savannah Church writes, "This is to certify that upon examination into the experience and character of a number of Ethiopians . . . it appears that God has brought them out of darkness into the light of the Gospel." In another correspondence with Rippon, Marshall said the "Ethiopian Church of Jesus Christ at Savanna, have called their beloved brother Andrew to the work of the ministry."[15]

Mention must be made of the place of singing as an integral part of the understanding and interpretation of Scripture because singing was of great importance among the early Baptists. There is some evidence that the hymns used by Liele and Baker came from the popular edition of "Watts and Rippon."[16] These hymns were largely a paraphrase of the Scriptures and helped to reinforce the biblical message. Incidentally, it was the same hymn book William Knibb used in Bristol, England; so hymnody forms an important link between the early foundations laid by the Baptists of America and the subsequent development of the Jamaican witness by the British.

William Knibb

William Knibb (1803–45) was the fifth child of Thomas and Mary Knibb of Kettering, England, and grew up under the preaching of Dr. John Ryland in Bristol. John Ryland (1753 –1825) and John Rippon (1751–1836) were foundation members of the British Baptist Missionary Society in 1792, with its tendencies to Particularism or a strict Calvinist interpretation of Scripture.[17] Ryland was president of the Bristol Baptist College and pastor of the Broadmead Church. He was one of the persons who had responded to Jonathan Edwards with favor, which, as they put it, led them to a strong sense of God's purpose and a disciplined study of the Scriptures. Under his ministry, the Bristol Education Society, under whose auspices the College came, responded to the appeals of the newly formed Missionary Society by sending suitable candidates to help William Carey in India. Knibb was an active member of the Broadmead Church, engaged in its outreach ministry and, although not a student at the College, was sent out to Jamaica after some training at the Borough Road School in London—which specialized in the Lancastrian method of teaching—to take his brother's place as a teacher in Kingston. The Lancastrian method used the senior pupils to teach the younger ones and so maximized personnel. This allowed the school to develop in senior students, very early, spiritual leadership and personal responsibilities, badly needed in a repressive slave society. It also meant that it allowed for the "free" interpretation of Scripture.

Knibb arrived in Jamaica in 1825 and took charge of the mission school at East Queen Street in Kingston but soon found himself preaching at the naval base in Port Royal and in a mountain village, Mount Charles. Unschooled as he was in academic theology, he fell back upon the simple evangelical training he had received. He was a prolific letter writer, and we are fortunate that his biographer, John Hinton, the Baptist minister in Oxford and a member of the Baptist Missionary Society, kept many of his letters and quoted them verbatim in his work. Writing to a friend about a baptismal service, Knibb quotes the hymn, "Jesus and shall it ever be, a mortal man ashamed of thee" and goes on to report that he baptized in the name of the adorable Trinity. Despite his lack of formal theological education, Knibb showed an understanding of Christian doctrine that was balanced. If he tended in any direction it was toward the Particularism (Calvinism) espoused by his pastor, John Ryland, who was strangely committed to the salvation of all. William, writing to his brother Thomas from Bristol, quoted loosely from Luke 15:10: "there is joy in the presence of God over one poor Negro that truly returns to God through the death of his son."[18] William appears to have embraced the same theology.

Knibb's letters were full of scriptural allusions and quotations used in the same way that Liele had used his "proof texts" as a part of his argument. In a letter to his mother, Knibb writes, "Here is a ray of light among the dark gloom. This cheers the heart of your son which would otherwise sink. To proclaim liberty to the captive and the opening of the prisons to them that are bound, is a delightful employment and here would I dwell that I may be thus employed"[19] (Isa. 61:1, 2; Luke 4:18,19). This feature of incorporating the Scriptures into everyday usage was not uncommon among the preachers of the day since their frame of reference was the Bible. Thus Knibb's letters were full of these scriptural references and allusions and there was a certain feature that bound them together. While his quotations were from both Testaments, most references reflect a social and political consciousness. Writing to his sister Mary in 1825, he tells her that his sermon text was, "This day is salvation come to this house," and goes on to say he longed for the slaves' salvation.[20] Similarly, when an altercation developed with the clerk of the peace in Port Royal over whether he had the legal authority to preach or not, he preached from the text, "Be not deceived, God is not mocked."[21]

This pattern of social and political comment can also be seen in the Spa Fields speech of 1833 in which Knibb used the exilic Psalms as a background for his attack on the system of slavery. He said, "But I need not say that all is lost that our harps are hung upon the willows and that the voice of praise is no more heard in the streets. A combined Satanic effort has been made to root out all religion; the sanctuaries of God have been broken with axes and hammers and the infuriated yelt; Rase it, rase it even to the foundations there of"[22] (Ps. 137:2,7 and 66:8). However, Knibb's understanding and interpretation of the Scriptures did not always coincide with that of the official stance of the Baptist Missionary Society. John Dyer, who was at that time the secretary to the Society, reissued instructions to the missionaries when the situation in Jamaica became unsettled on the eve of emancipation. The instructions said: "The Gospel of Christ you well know so far from producing and countenancing a spirit of rebellion or insubordination has a directly opposite tendency. Most of the servants addressed by the apostle Paul in his epistles were slaves and he exhorts them to be obedient to their own masters in singleness of heart fearing God; and this not only to be good and gentle but also to the forward"[23] (Eph. 6:5; Col. 3:22). Knibb did not absolutely concur with this. When this passage was quoted to him by an ordained clergyman of the Church of Scotland as a rebuttal in a debate on the abolition of slavery, Knibb asked, "Why did not the reverend gentleman continue reading a little longer? If he had done this, he would have found it written, 'Masters give unto your servants that which is just and equal knowing also that you have a Master in heaven"[24] (Col. 4:1).

The importance of the use of Scripture in the abolition debate was not lost either on the British government or, as we shall see later, on the slaves themselves. In the evidence before the House of Lords after the 1831 Christmas uprising in Montego Bay, which implicated the Baptists, Knibb was asked if he found it difficult to separate the spiritual concerns of the black population from their temporal situation. Knibb replied that it was difficult but every good man would do it. When asked specifically about "freedom," Knibb answered with the policy sent down by Dyer, that there is a separation between the freedom of the spirit and the freedom of the body. But in reply to another question, Knibb said he preached the whole counsel of God. When asked if that meant he could preach the Christian doctrines and not speak of freedom, Knibb replied, "No."[25] The evidence before the House of Lords is interesting because it shows that Knibb was not a systematic theologian. He had a bias toward the emancipation of the slaves and the elimination of slavery which he worked out in stages using scriptural categories. His hermeneutic was contextual. With the coming of freedom, for instance, he chose on that occasion to preach from Neh. 12:42–43, which speaks of "the singers and the sacrifices of joy with celebrations given by the women and children" when the city wall was dedicated. Knibb was not singular in his bias in the way he used Scripture, as was made abundantly clear when August 1, 1833, was set as the day for the abolition of slavery. On that day the Baptists without exception interpreted the day as the Day of Jubilee

(Lev. 25) while slavery continued to be compared with the plagues of Egypt (Exod. chapters 7–12).[26]

The abolition of slavery in 1833 meant that although children would no longer be slaves, adults were not completely free. Knibb and his colleagues in Jamaica and Britain addressed the situation and described it as "half-freedom" but, at the same time, as "being associated with the extension of the Messiah's reign."[27] By 1834 freedom was beginning to take on new meanings for Knibb, his colleagues, and the freed slaves. From the correspondence available, it appears that there was a search for a more positive understanding of liberty. What did the "extension of the Messiah's reign" imply? Knibb suggested that "it demanded that there should be a sharing of the gospel with Africa."[28] It also meant that the freed slave should receive what he termed "equitable and fair wages." In response to a suggestion that the value of the services of an apprentice ought to be regulated by the market and that it should be no more than one shilling, Knibb, in a sermon, replied that he desired "to see every vestige of slavery completely rooted out. You must work for money. You must pay money to your employers for all you receive at their hands. A fair scale of wages must be established and you must be entirely independent . . . to be free, you must be independent. Receive money for your work; come to market with money, purchase from whom you please and be accountable to no one but that Being above who I trust will watch over and protect you."[29] The sermon goes on to say that with fair wages the freed slave would be able to secure education for the children, put by something for sickness and old age, contribute to the support of the church, and relieve the distressed in society.

When charged that his approach to these questions was political, Knibb replied that to sympathize with the oppressed, whether black or white, was not a political matter. "I pledge myself by all that is solemn and sacred never to rest satisfied until I see my black brethren in the enjoyment of the same civil and religious liberties which I myself enjoy, and see them take a proper stand in society as men."[30] While Knibb does not apply Scripture to the working of the labor market by this stance, he was clearly aware of its consequences and sought ways to address its worse effects. It was this that lay behind the creation of the Free Villages. The Free Villages were designed to create a free landowning peasantry. Knibb, together with others, had been influenced by the ideas of Joseph Sturge (1783–1859), a Quaker from Birmingham who had been significantly involved in the liberation movements among the Russian serfs. The need to create a new society based on the peasant did not originate with Knibb, but he together with James Phillippo, another Baptist missionary, adapted it to the Jamaican situation as the best model to secure the personal liberty that he believed the Christian faith demanded. He says as much in a letter to Sturge in September of

1839. He writes, "It may be that a few less pounds of sugar are made (and who can expect a free man to work as incessantly as a poor slave was obliged) but what matters this? It is but small dust in the balance. We have the germ of a noble free peasantry and I assure you that to assist them in the attainment of their civil and religious liberties is to me a source of pleasure only surpassed by the proclaiming of that mercy by which they are freed forever"[31] (Isa. 40 and 61).

The holistic approach to religion and life that had marked Knibb's work up to this point had not been significantly challenged by the island leadership led by the governor who, understanding the mood in Britain, knew that the days of slavery were numbered. However, when Knibb began to relate his understanding of Scripture to the buying of land and subdividing it so that each family would have a vote, then the governor came out in opposition. Sir Charles Metcalfe (1785–1846), had arrived in 1839 at a time when the High Church Party had gained some ascendancy in the Church in England, and the Tories were being resurrected in Parliament. Pusey had been known to have dismissed the compensation to the slaveowners as a waste of money on an "idea." And the Oxford hierarchy and historians were hostile to antislavery interests, which the Baptists epitomized. So, when later that year the governor, who was related to one of the professor of history at Oxford, singled out the Baptists for criticism, in response Knibb and his associates retorted: "Are Protestant dissenters to be frightened by the bugbear of political expediency? Do you call yourselves the followers of Luther and of those who in Smithfield, ascended in their fiery chariots to heaven?"[32]

Two other consequences derived from the understandings of freedom in Baptist circles in the 1830s. The first had to do with education. Knibb himself put great store on education and when he first arrived in Kingston had devoted himself to it. With the coming of freedom, the Baptists maintained that a greater effort was needed because, as an editorial in the *Baptist Magazine* suggested, "the [coloured] population was to be instructed."[33] In February of 1837 the Baptist missionaries in Jamaica, under the chairmanship of a senior missionary, Joshua Tinson, with Knibb as secretary, drafted a letter to the Society of Friends in England asking for help to sustain a Baptist Education Society, which had just been formed to respond to the demands of freedom. Integral to general public education was moral education. At the Bethephil School in St. James it was reported that apart from reading, spelling, writing, arithmetic, English grammar, and Jamaican geography, "their Scripture knowledge was highly satisfactory."[34]

The second consequence was a literal interpretation of Psalm 68:31, "Ethiopia shall stretch forth her hand." George Liele, Moses Baker, and Nicholas Sweigle had quoted this verse extensively as a way of describing themselves, but Knibb used it as the proof text for a missionary mandate and an African mission. It is not quite clear when the idea of an African mission came to Knibb. Of course, the importance of Africa had begun to make itself felt in Europe and America ever since the slave trade, but now the emphasis was different. A strong body of opinion had developed in Church circles that if Africa was to be evangelized no one is better suited to do it than Africans themselves. This thesis had already gained considerable acceptance with the Buxton group in anti-slavery circles in England and, through him, with the Church of England. As far as Jamaican Baptists were concerned, perhaps Knibb's sermon at Eagle Street in 1839 gives a clue to their general thought. His text was Psalm 68:31, and in the sermon he argued that because God was the moral governor of the universe, everything that occurred had a purpose, even the institution of slavery. Developing this text, he observed that "it will be our [endeavor] this evening in taking farewell of you to direct you to some of the results which we firmly believe will be brought about in connection with that Emancipation Act that has lately stamped glory on our land and happiness on the sons and daughters of Africa."[35]

Slavery had posed difficult questions for many Christians and now that it had been abolished answers were sought from the scriptures. In this sermon Knibb used the text to link the evangelization of Africa with the "providential design" theory of slavery. This link between the Emancipation Act and a mission to Africa led to the interpretation that the Act was an answer to "direct prophecy," but that in order for prophecy to be fulfilled in its entirety education was necessary. For Knibb and his fellow missionaries slavery had already been identified with Egyptian bondage, so that emancipation could only be the Exodus, and the abuse of slaves who had confessed Christ, "the marks of the Lord Jesus," reflecting a Pauline phrase. "The marks of the Lord Jesus" appears to reflect the Anabaptist emphasis on the necessity of suffering as a refining process and became an important feature in the postemancipation hermeneutic of Knibb. He often observed that the freed slaves had been in "the school of adversity" but that theirs was "the last moan of the captive." Toward the end of the Eagle Street sermon, the Isaiah 61:1–3 passage quoted by Jesus (Luke 4:18,19) occurs, and Knibb declares that if Africans preach the gospel in Africa "there shall come a voice from the Isles of the West speaking better things than the blood of Abel—there come those who proclaim liberty to the captive and the opening of the prison door to them that are bound—if there are found there those who shall tell of Him, who though he was rich yet for Africa's sake became poor, that they through his poverty may become rich; then shall we say indeed, Africa is compensated for all the wrongs that have been heaped so unjustly upon her."[36]

In his later years, Knibb became more literalistic especially when he contemplated an African mission, perhaps fearing that "his" freed peoples may not measure up to the expectations of the Missionary Society. In a report to the Society, he observed that "the Christian Church will have to learn a new lesson; she will have to find out what men who can speak of Jesus will do for the enterprise. We want cultivated men to carry some departments, I know; but there are men who simply feel the love of Christ in their hearts and they can talk of that love to others. I, if I be lifted up will draw all men to me. I am more than ever convinced that the simple exhibition of the cross of Christ is the great means of the renovation of the world."[37] The social and ethical implications of the Scriptures as it now related to peasant life, as Knibb saw it, was now also more evident. Perhaps it was because in some Christian circles moral rectitude was viewed as ultimate proof of evangelization and not a "ritualistic" approach to the faith. So in writing to the Churches of Falmouth, Waldensia, and Wilberforce, he asked them to "live near to God in your cottages. Live as Christian husbands and wives ought to live. Train your children for heaven. Hail sinners to the cross . . . As God has blessed you with freedom, let the world which is looking upon you see that you are desirous of improving the blessing, then will you be instruments in extending the mercies you enjoy to thousands of your fellow men who are still deprived of the liberty they ought to possess. Be it your aim to glorify God in your bodies and in your spirits which are his."[38]

On his final visit to England, Knibb encountered severe criticisms of his missionary methods. The controversy between the Baptists, the Congregationalists, and the Presbyterians is adequately covered in several places. Knibb saw the attacks as attacks upon the "freedom" he had given his life to obtain and also as an affront to the voluntary principle so dear to Baptists at that time. At a meeting in Norwich he met the criticism head on and observed that if the Christian allowed the charge of "politics" to hinder action nothing would be done. He declared:

> I am one of those individuals who believe it is my duty and by every means in my power to protect the injured man, let him be found wherever he may or whatever the circumstances in which he is placed. That fact is this, that politics have entwined themselves around our dearest rights. We cannot touch anything that is human, we cannot redress any wrong, we cannot sustain anything that is right if we are to be terrified by this bugbear which men of the world have set up. . . . Providence has caused us to pass, to denounce wrong as wrong—to denounce sin as sin—to denounce unrighteousness as unrighteousness whether it be clothed in linen or covered with [mitre], or whether it be found in the law books of our country; but in all our opposition we want it to be understood that we use no weapons but those of calm reason and deliberate thought . . . We wish not to obtain alteration by physical force; we wish only to establish in all omnipotence the eternal principles of justice assured that they will do their work.[39]

Knibb was not unmindful that behind this criticism were economic and political interpretations of freedom and a struggle within the Church of England. Referring to certain High Church criticisms he declared, "Our missionaries, not only in the East but in the West, are now denounced by these striplings from Oxford and Cambridge as men who ought not to touch the sacred ark of God. Tracts are sent among our [labourers] headed thus—'The sin of attending dissenting places of worship.' They have placed their little basin where the cross of Christ should stand, they have placed the sacrament of the Lord's Supper where the atonement should shine forth in all its power." And in a subsequent section he observed that while this is not a condemnation of all Episcopalians he did feel hurt that after years of toil for freedom some "striplings who were not even born or were playing marbles in Oxford and Cambridge" should set themselves up as the established religion but did not wish to pay for it. So he bluntly put it, "I am for free trade not only in sugar but in religion too."[40] For Knibb, the Scriptures were plain for all to interpret in freedom and with liberty. Nevertheless freedom and liberty had certain ethical, social, and political consequences.

Phillippo and Slave Narratives

Not many documents exist that reflect the interpretations by Jamaican slaves themselves. Slave narratives exist but were reported for specific reasons and the few slaves' narratives that exist are included in the writings of missionaries and annual reports and are used for propaganda purposes. Phillippo in his *Jamaica, Its Past and Present State,* published in 1843, narrates a few anecdotes that throw some light on the interpretations and understandings of Scripture by some slaves at this time. Phillippo describes a slave in a church meeting responding to questions about his testimony, a common feature in Baptist churches before baptism. The questions ranged from matters of conversion to the doctrine of the Trinity and, in some of the responses, the words "God's holy word says" or "the good book says," occur, suggesting the candidate needed some acquaintance with the Scriptures and its orthodox interpretation. In other cases, conversion was linked to inner knowledge probing acquaintances with Quaker tendency. In a discussion reported by Phillippo between a soldier and a slave, the soldier asked whether the slave was converted. The slave replied that he was "convinced" before he was converted.[41] But it is in the slaves' prayers that the depth of Scriptural usage and understanding is reflected. In a Kingston church a slave was heard to pray, "O do [dou] root [dem] out same as Massa Jesus did cast out the [debils] out of [de] man wandering [mong de tombs' an] may we sit down like him at de feet of Jesus clothed and in we right mind," or "come [dis] night, hungry and thirsting, to eat de bread of life, an bring me empty pitcher, like de woman of Samaria."[42]

"The History and Proceedings of Salters Hill Church," already referred to, contains the testimonies of former slaves as well. While the main preoccupation of the speeches appear to have been the defense of freedom, they also reflect free slaves' understandings of Scripture in that part of the island. Knibb, perhaps, influenced the way the slaves addressed the need to work for a full wage and not to be asked to pay oppressive rents. In his remarks, Robert Scott, a slave, suggested that one reason for the opposition of the Planters was "they knew that our ministers bring us knowledge and that knowledge makes us free."[43] This emphasis on the "rational" (knowledge) is of great significance because one of the arguments for the continuance of slavery was the irrationality of the Africans and their inability to grasp the truth. Scott places the ability "to know" in the acceptance of the gospel, and there seems little doubt that this is the same understanding he refers to when he alludes to John 8:32, "Ye shall know the truth and the truth shall make you free." Speaking in the Bethephil church at about the same time, Stephen James maintained: "They were not to listen to any other calls but those of the Bible alone. They must hold fast the instructions of the Bible, till God took their immortal souls."[44] William Russell, in his testimony, linked religion, education, and freedom together and argued that religion must be open. The gospel command was to "Go into all the world and preach my gospel to every creature" and, to do this, God gave the Bible, the ministers, and the schools. He maintains that this world was not just Jamaica but includes Africa and America, which were not free. He went on, "Oh my friends, think of Africa—pray for Africa, never rest satisfied until the gospel finds its way to Africa."[45]

Of course, some reports were as supportive of the missionary hermeneutic as they were a necessary part of missionary propaganda. In order to have a more accurate assessment of those activities, it is important to look at what the opponents of the Baptists had to say. The most comprehensive anti-Baptist account is a document drawn up by the Congregationalists and the Presbyterians called the "Remonstrance or Exposition" and circulated widely in Britain in the 1840s. It goes without saying that it did much to undermine Baptist confidence in themselves and their reputation. The basic criticism was that the Baptist methods of Church discipline were un-Scriptural. Baptists had prided themselves that the Bible was the foundation of all they did, and that their preaching and teaching derived from it. Barrett and his associates suggested that the Leader system, by which the Church was divided into class groups—a system taken over from the Moravians and the Methodists, was unscriptural. Barrett says it "ought to be sufficient objection that no pattern of it can be found in the sacred Scriptures. But not only so there is no principle in the New Testament applicable to the ruling of churches and to the extending of Christianity with which it agrees."[46]

Barrett goes on to describe how a candidate for Church membership is received. First the candidate kneels or prostrates himself or herself on the ground after which there is a prayer, and the candidate is raised up with the words, "in the presence of the Father, and of the Son and of the Holy Ghost." Then the candidate becomes available for instruction and subsequently, after examination, baptism. While Barrett does not think the system is essentially bad, he objects to the quality of candidate selected for Leadership, especially in light of the changed national mood in Jamaica. He is also critical of the "tickets" that were given to candidates with texts on them. These tickets were renewed quarterly, and since many members took the opportunity to pay their dues at that time, there grew up an unfortunate association between the money and Church membership. Tickets were called "water tickets" because they were given out at the time of baptism.

Barrett warms to the subject by reporting the testimony of Thomas Burke, a former slave, about William Hall, a Leader. Hall is reported to have told the candidate, "If we no baptize in the river, we full up with sin. When we baptize we see our pardon."[47] Thomas Burke, who had left the Baptist Church to become a Congregationalist, went on to say that he had thought, from Hall's teaching, that John the Baptist was God. He reported that every Friday was a fast, and that the fast was broken in the evening by drinking from white cups only. Burke continued to report that at that time he had two wives and did not know that that was forbidden.[48] Little doubt exists that there were differing interpretations by European missionaries and freed slaves of what baptism meant. This is understandable in view of the denominations involved. Among the slaves, Myal beliefs (African ancestral practices) were never far from the surface, and many often were compatible with Scripture. For instance, Myal accepted dreams as a medium of divine communication and this coincided with the stories of the Old Testament. Similarly, the emphasis on divine healing and the expulsion of evil spirits was consistent with New Testament teaching. So, for the Africans, accommodation was easy, and Barrett and Vine were right in their observation that this presented problems of syncretism. They had brought to the situation a different hermeneutic.

Knibb did not seem as troubled about the suggestion of syncretism as he was about another matter. He saw the remonstrance as the emergence of old imperial assumptions that peoples of African descent, or as Knibb called them, "his poor Negroes," could not look after their own affairs. Knibb had built upon the Liele legacies and had fashioned an idealistic picture of a new society somewhat akin to the noble savage of romantic literature: a Christian peasant drawn from the pages of Scripture, the redeemed person. This had been derived from a naive literalistic interpretation of Scripture. The symbols of the Old Testament had been used liberally to symbolize the plight of the enslaved. Bible phrases such as bondage of Egypt, Babylonian captivity, the rivers of Babylon, triumphant notes of Jubilee, deliverance from bondage, Covenant, and Truth had all been pressed into service.[49] Other symbols like Zion and Jubilee found their support not only in the Bible itself but were reinforced by the memorizing and use of Rippon's Psalter. The frequent pointing to Isaiah 61, as well as its use by Jesus in Luke 4, helped to sacralize the concept of liberty. Moreover, the belief that freedom was integrally linked to the land as "promise" was clearly an Old Testament idea and was related to the Free Villages created to develop in Jamaica a Christian peasant class with economic and political rights.[50] All this was at stake as Knibb and his contemporaries saw it and not so much the "purity" of the gospel or the Church. The remonstrance–exposition undermined, as the Baptists saw it, the social implications of the Scriptures as they had interpreted them. Freedom was threatened. While this may have been true, it was also a clash of hermeneutical approaches and differing understandings of Scripture.

Conclusion

The lasting legacy of Liele, Baker, and Knibb and their contemporaries has been the bequeathing to succeeding generations in Jamaica of the use of the Scripture to create new social and political models. That there were other influences, for example economic ones as Eric Williams[51] has demonstrated, cannot be denied. Yet even here, as in the humanitarian movement and ideology, the socio-political models appear to have been taken from Biblical categories. In fact, the King James Version of the Bible gave the design for the new society. The Bible and its social and personal categories were used by Jamaican Baptist political activists Paul Bogle and William Gordon, not discussed in this chapter, to define the society that was beginning to emerge in their day and led to the peasant uprising of 1865. In more recent times, despite the Bible controversies and a multiplicity of versions that have had some effect upon Church leadership, the rank and file membership— through the Street Preachers of the 1890s, Bedwardism[52] at the turn of the century, and Garveyism[53] in the 1920s—appear to have kept this older Biblical legacy alive. Today there are changes on the horizon, the social and political models operative from the 1930s through the 1960s were not based primarily on the Biblical models.[54] Nevertheless, the old ideas of the peasant society—although almost totally submerged in the new urban interrelationship for which as yet not many Biblical models have been developed—still persist. They are present not so much in ecclesiastical organizations, except among the Rastafarians, but in the music of the Reggae artists and the artistry of the Dub poets.[55] These symbols still hold the same power and freshness although they no longer come from the pulpit but from the stage.

Notes

1. Grant Gordon, *From Slavery to Freedom: The Life of David George—Pioneer Black Baptist Minister* (Hansport: Lancelot Press, 1992), 23–4; also Clement Gayle, *George Liele Pioneer Missionary to Jamaica* (Kingston: Baptist Press, 1983).

2. Mechal Sobel, *Trabelin' On: The Slave Journey to an Afro-Baptist Faith* (Princeton: Princeton University Press, 1979/88), 85, 99–108. Sobel's discussion on the sources of the Baptist Faith at the end of the eighteenth century in the southern United States is very informative.

3. William Brackney, *The Baptist* (Westport: Praeger, 1994), 24 (includes also John Smyth). See also pp. 44–50, for a discussion on the relationship between Bible and Covenant.

4. *General Baptist Repository,* vol. 1, supplement (1802). A similar Covenant is reproduced in *Baptist Quarterly,* vol. 7 (1934–35): 20–6, with an explanatory article by Ernest Payne. Compare this with comments by Mechal Sobel, 139–80.

5. Arminianism assumed great importance at this time. Both Rippon and Ryland were writing incessantly about it because of their pro-Calvinist outlook. Arminianism emphasized faith and experience, and this contrasted with Calvinism; both of these have had important implications for the missionary movement and the evangelical experience.

6. *Evangelical Magazine* (1804), 366. This magazine was published by a group of ministers belonging to several denominations in England, Scotland, and Holland. Its proceeds went to the Widows Fund of Gospel ministers.

7. Ibid., 367.

8. *General Baptist Repository,* vol. I supplemental (1802): 229–31.

9. John Rippon, "The Baptist," *Annual Register,* vol. 1 (London: 1790–93): 338–9.

10. Thomas Coke, *History of the West Indies, Containing the Natural, Civil and Ecclesiastical History of Each Island:* With an Account of the Missions Instituted in these Islands, from the Commencement of their Circulation but more especially of the missions which have been Established in that Archipelago by the society . . . in Connection with the Rev. John Mesley, 3 vols., vol. 1 (Liverpool, 1808); vols. 2 and 3 (London: 1810, 1811): 410 ff.

11. Nicholas Sweigle, Annual Register, vol. 1 (1790–93): 542, vol. 3 (1790: 212–4, vol. 4 (1790–93): 973–5 and 1144–6.

12. *Annual Register,* vol. 1 (1790): 336. See also Letter from Liele d/d 1791.

13. Ibid., 343–4.

14. Ibid., 542; dated January 1793.

15. Ibid., 340–1; also letter dated January 19/20, 1788. Abraham Marshall was from Kioke and had participated in the ordination of Andrew Bryan 1782. The Georgia Association (1784) ratified the ordination to everyone's surprise. See James Simms, *The First Coloured Baptist Church in North America Constituted at Savannah, Georgia, Jan. 20 AD 1788* (New York: Negro Universities Press, 1969), 20,24,26.

16. According to *History and Proceedings of the Church at Salter's Hill* (London: Watts and Rippon nd.), James Coultart in a letter to John Saffrey included reports that Mrs. Baker made children say grace before meals. They were also required to repeat by heart Watts's hymns and parts of the Old and New Testaments. In another report, this time from Annatto Bay, the pastor reported that several persons could read passages from the Bible and commit them to memory (Isaac Watts, "Second Catechism and Divine Songs," *Baptist Magazine,* vol. v 3 (1841): 130–1.

17. Norman Moon, *Education for Ministry—Bristol Baptist College, 1679–1979* (Bristol: Bristol Baptist College, 1979), 18–21.

18. John Hinton, *Memoir of William Knibb* (London: Houlston and Stansman, 1849), 20.

19. Ibid., 49.

20. Ibid., 66.

21. Ibid., 92.

22. Ibid., 143. In this excerpt there is a conflation of texts drawn from the suffering of the people either during the time of the Exile or at other times when there was oppression. Psalm 137 is still popular in the Caribbean as an expression of Hope for deliverance, e.g., the Bob Marley and Bonni Em 1975 reggae hit, "By the Rivers of Babylon."

23. Ibid., 50–1.

24. Ibid., 170–1.

25. Ibid., 177–8. The full text is to be found in parliamentary papers of the time.

26. Ibid., 273. The Day of Jubilee (Leviticus 25).

27. Ibid., 276. In letters to his friend Dr. James Hoby, Knibb complains of the unjust nature of apprenticeship.

28. Ibid., 280.

29. Ibid., 288–9.

30. Ibid.

31. Ibid., 315; also letter dated September 14, 1834.

32. Ibid., 354: a speech in Exeter Hall in 1840 in reply to Governor Metcalfe's accusations.

33. See "Religious Intelligence Comments," *Baptist Magazine,* vol. xxix (1837): 546.

34. Report of the Jamaica Education Society, (1838), 36. Appended to the Annual Report of the Baptist Missionary Society (BMS) entitled "Freedom in Jamaica on the First of August 1838," published in London, November, 1838. Beginning in 1838 there was an annual report of the Jamaica Educa-

tion Society (JES), which is devoted to the education work of Baptists. The JES annual report was appended to the general report.

35. William Knibb's sermon at Eagle Street Baptist Church, London, "The Spiritual Prospects of Africa" (Regents' Park College Library), 3.

36. Ibid. Here Knibb is referring to the compensation given by the British government of £20 million pounds and comparing it with the treasures of the Gospel.

37. Hinton, 363.

38. Ibid., 382–3. Knibb wrote another letter to the churches reminding them of their spiritual responsibilities. He writes, "Watch over the purity of the church . . . Yearn over the young. Pray for the lambs in Christ's flock . . . Visit the sick. O prepare, prepare for heaven" (p. 386).

39. Ibid., 484.

40. Ibid., 494–500. The final speech touched upon these issues: freedom, voluntaryism, the African mission, and the disestablishment of the Anglican church. For a full discussion of voluntaryism and its inclusivity, see William Brackney, *Voluntaryism—The Dynamic Free Church Principle* (Hayward Lectures, Acadia Divinity College, 1990).

41. Hinton, 318–320.

42. Ibid., 342–3. For a similar story of literal interpretation, see 366–7; a slave cares for the person who sold him into slavery (Rom. 12:20,21, "if thine enemy hunger," etc.).

43. *History and Proceeding of the Church,* 38–9.

44. Ibid., 54–5.

45. Ibid., 60–1.

46. *Baptist Mission in Jamaica: An Exposition of the System Pursued by the Baptist Missionaries in Jamaica by Missionaries and Cathecists of the London Missionary Society in That Island* (London, 1842), 7–8. Note that the Presbyterians added an appendix of support although the original research was not their own.

47. Ibid., 15.

48. Ibid.

49. Barry Higman's work on the significance of the *First of August* establishes without doubt that the day assumed a permanent social significance related to Exodus 12:14, "This day shall be to you a memorial." See Barry Higman, "The First of August: Jamaica 1838–1972," unpublished paper, postgraduate seminar, University of the West Indies, 1973.

50. Horace Russell, "The Emergence of the Christian Black: The Making of a Stereotype," *Jamaica Journal* vol. vvi, no. 1 (1983).

51. Eric Williams, *Capitalism and Slavery* (London: Andre Deulsch, 1944). This thesis modified the humanitarian thesis of Matheison and Coupland. Williams argues that economics played as large a part as religion in the abolition of slavery.

52. Bedwardism was a revivalist movement that created quite an up-stir in Kingston. See: Patrick Bryan, *The Jamaica People 1880–1902* (London:

Macmillan, n.d.), 38–45; *Race, Class and Social Control* (University of Warwick: Warwick University Caribbean Studies, 1991).

53. Marcus Garvey did not begin a religious movement, but one developed. For further reading, see Rupert Lewis, *Marcus Garvey: Anti-colonial Champion* (Africa World Press, 1988), and *Marcus Garvey and the Vision of Africa,* ed. John Henrik Clarke (New York: Vintage Books, 1974).

54. Michael Manley: *The Search of New Solutions* (Maple House, 1976); for another perspective, Rex Nettleford, *Mirror, Mirror* (Collins-Sangster), 1970.

55. See: Yoshiko Nagashima, *Rastafarian Music in Contemporary Jamaica: A Study of Socio-Religious Music of the Rastafarian Movement in Jamaica* (Institute for Study of Languages and Culture of Asia and Africa), 137–58.

Appendix

Baker's Covenant

We are of the Baptist persuasion because we believe it agreeable to the Scripture (Same as Liele's).

We hold to the keeping of the Lord's Day throughout the year in a place appointed for public worship in singing psalms, hymns and spiritual songs and preaching the gospel of Jesus Christ (Same as Liele's).

We hold to be baptized in a river or a place where there is much water in the name of the Father, Son and Holy Spirit and receiving the Lord's Supper in obedience to his command (Liele's III and IV).

We also hold with washing one another's feet, praying over the sick and anointing them with oil in the name of the Lord Jesus (Liele's V and VII).

We hold to appoint judges and such other officers among us to settle any matters according to the word of God (Liele's IX).

We held not to the shedding of blood and think ourselves forbidden to go to law one with another before the unjust but to settle any matters before the saints (Liele's X and XI).

We are forbidden to swear at all; and account ourselves bound not to eat blood for it is the life of a creature (Liele's XII and XIV).

We abstain from things strangled and from meat offered to idols (Liele's XIII).

We are bound to submit ourselves to every ordinance of man for the Lord's sake, whether to the king as supreme or unto governors as unto them that are sent by him, for the punishment of evil doers and for the praise of them that do evil.

To avoid fornication, we permit none to keep each other, except they be married according to the word of God (Liele's XVI).

If a slave or servant misbehave to their owners they are to be dealt with according to the word of God (Liele's XVIII).

If anyone of this religion should transgress and walk disorderly and not according to the command we have received in the covenant of our Lord, he will be censured according to the word of God (Liele's XVIII).

If a brother or a sister should transgress any of the articles written in this covenant so as to become a swearer, fornicator, an adulterer, a covetous person, an idolater, a railer, a drunkard, an extortioner or should commit an abominable sin; and doth not give satisfaction to the church according to the word of God, we hold that such a one should be put away from among us, as we must not keep company, nor eat with excluded persons (Liele's XIX).

We hold to all other commandments, articles, covenants and ordinances recorded in the Holy Scriptures as are set forth by our Lord and Master Jesus Christ and his Apostles and to live to them as nigh as we possibly can, agreeably to the word of God (Liele's XXI).

"If ye abide in me, and my words abide in you, herein is my Father glorified, that ye bear much fruit so shall ye be my disciples." This is his commandment, "That ye love one another as I loved you." "Greater love hath no man than this, that a man lay down his life for his friend." "Ye are my friends, if ye do whatsoever I command you." [*Evangelical Magazine,* September 1803].

Chapter 6

Is This the Word of the Lord?

In Search of Biblical Theology and Hermeneutics, the Eastern Caribbean

John Holder

The story of Christianity in the Caribbean and in more recent times the story of Rastafari is the story of the interpretation of the Bible in a manner that allowed it to speak to the conditions within which it was being interpreted. This chapter traces the story of this interpretation by drawing attention to the many social elements that conditioned each interpretive exercise. I hope to demonstrate that in the Caribbean biblical theology and hermeneutics have been and still are conditioned by many factors, not the least of which is the desire to keep God aboard the religious activity whatever may be the social conditions. As I will show, this is especially the case in what I call the high point of Caribbean biblical theology and hermeneutics, the 1970s.

In November 1971 an exciting event swept through the Caribbean on the wave of the spirit of independence and marked a first for the established Churches in the region; the first large-scale ecumenical gathering in the region took place at a consultation on development. Delegates representing 25 Christian denominations, other religious traditions, 16 nations and territories met from November 15–21 at Chaguaramas, Trinidad. During the conference the best theological minds of the Caribbean wrestled with the shaping of a Caribbean theology and searched for new paths in biblical theology and hermeneutics. They were guided by the basic principle that new social and religious order must, in a radical way, speak directly to the experiences of the Caribbean masses.

The gathering in Trinidad, entitled "The Caribbean Ecumenical Consultation for Development,"[1] was a watershed for an emerging Caribbean theology that explored new and exciting ways of understanding and interpreting the biblical traditions. It was in many ways a "Call to be,"[2] and a challenge to move out of the old inherited biblical theology (with its rather docile way of interpreting the Bible) to search for new ways of understanding and interpreting the Bible within the Caribbean. The Bible was seen as crucial in efforts to create new theological perspectives that would address Caribbean issues and concerns, the basis upon which a new Caribbean theology could be built. The Bible became a mandate for change, the legitimizing agent of the call for radical changes in all areas of Caribbean life. The keynote speaker at the Chaguaramas meeting, Roy Neehall, found support for these radical changes in the Christian Gospel when he said: "The Gospel projects the total liberation of man and society, condemning the forces that oppress and projecting a new society based on justice and solidarity. For this end God is seen to be at work among [men], incorporating the acts of human liberation with the larger context of the salvation of the world, offering the kingdom of God upon earth as the consummation of the human struggle for freedom from internal and external forms of oppression."[3] Here is an interpretation of the Gospel tradition that places it on the side of liberation and development and, consequently, against all persons, institutions, and social structures that impede liberation and development. At work here is an understanding and interpretation of the biblical traditions that allows the message of specific sections of the Bible to speak to concrete experiences of Caribbean peoples. These experiences for Neehall were of the type that cried out for liberation and spoke directly to the most pressing need in the Caribbean: "From the Exodus, through the Exile, incarnation, resurrection, and future hope, the [centre] of God's activity is the liberation of men from within their historical situation."[4] Neehall, like many others at that November gathering in Trinidad, represented a new breed of Caribbean theologians who were prepared to reject most, if not all, of the inherited European understandings and interpretations of the biblical traditions.

Pre-1970 Biblical Interpretation

The new interpretations of the Bible that emerged in the Caribbean in the 1970s must be understood against a background of three centuries of biblical hermeneutics that hardly ruffled the status quo of Caribbean society. For more than 300 years, this status quo consisted of socioeconomic conditions that militated against the uplifting of the majority of Caribbean peoples,[5] as they attempted to relate traditional interpretations of the biblical tradition to their experiences that seem to be far removed from what the good, loving God of the Bible would demand. An acute tension existed between traditional biblical theology and hermeneutics, and the experiences of the majority of Caribbean people. While there were attempts from very early in Caribbean history to engage in the type of biblical theological reflection that spoke directly to the experiences of Caribbean peoples, the official theological tradition was little more than an attempt to legitimize the position of the ruling dominant group and justify the status, or lack of it, of the underclass.

In early Caribbean society, where sharp divides of class structure existed, biblical theology was invariably skewed to support the privileged position of the dominant group and to justify the position of the underclass. This use of biblical traditions is ably demonstrated by a sermon preached in 1827 by the Anglican/Episcopal bishop of Barbados, William Hart Coleridge, after a confirmation. In an admonition to the newly confirmed, he urged them to:

> Consider well through life the relation which you bear to your fellow creatures, whether as rulers or subjects, masters or servants, parents or children, married or single, young or old, rich or poor, bond or free. In all things and in every station, strive to approve yourselves the chosen of God . . . being diligent as rulers, loyal as subjects; just and equal as masters, obedient as servants; as parents kind, as children dutiful, faithful in marriage . . . liberal in wealth, contented in poverty, if bond, with good will doing service, if free, not using your liberty as a cloak of maliciousness, but as servants of the Lord.6

Coleridge's sermon, preached some seven years before the emancipation of slaves in the British West Indies,7 was clearly a call to maintain things the way they were in Barbadian society. The bishop drew heavily on the Bible as he marshaled Eph. 5:15–33; 1 Pet. 2:11–25; 3:1, 13; Titus 2:1–15; 3:1, 2; Rom. 12:6–21, and 13:1–7 in support of his admonition to slaves and servants, or some other group, for example women, to be obedient and submissive. Here are a few examples:

> Eph. 5:22:Wives, be subject to your husbands . . . (cf. 1 Pet. 3:1)
>   1 Pet. 2:18:Servants, be submissive to your masters with all respect, not only to the kind and gentle, but also to the overbearing.
>   Titus 2:9,10:Bid slaves be submissive to their masters and to give satisfaction in every respect; they are not to be refractory, nor to pilfer, but to show entire and true fidelity, so that in everything they may adorn the doctrine of God our Savior.
>   Titus 3:1,2:Remind them to be submissive to rulers and authorities, to be obedient, to be ready for any honest work, to speak evil of no one, to avoid quarreling, to be gentle, and to show perfect courtesy to all men.

> Rom. 13:1: Let every person be subjected to the governing authorities. There is no authority except from God, and those that exist have been instituted by God. Therefore, he who resists the authorities resists what God has appointed, and those who resist will incur judgement.[8]

Through the selection of these texts, the Bible became a ready and useful ally in support of a system whose very existence depended upon the submissive nature of the underclass, especially the slave population. No other use of the Bible could be of greater importance to the planters of Barbados. They found a ready ally in Coleridge and his interpretation of the Bible.

The use and interpretation of the Bible reflected in Coleridge's sermon was undergirded by a number of assumptions. The first was the hermeneutical one that the Bible can speak to any human condition and is an authoritative guide in all human relations. There can hardly be any arguments against this assumption and the attending exegetical process of developing an interpretation of the biblical texts that allows them to speak to contemporary conditions. But when all this was conditioned by the second assumption that the text was interpreted to support an oppressive social and economic system rather than to challenge for change, then clearly the hermeneutical exercise was reduced to an effort to legitimize the colonial status quo. As Coleridge's sermon shows, the Bible in that slave society is not interpreted in a manner that would provide a biblical basis for protest against slavery.

Another important assumption that conditioned the understanding of the hermeneutical task in that era is that Caribbean slave society worked toward the civilization of the enslaved, that is, the Africans. Slavery under European dominance was understood to be far better than freedom back home in Africa. Biblical theology, and theology in general, were shaped to support this conviction. This view finds expression in the words of the Protestant Church leader, Count von Zinzendorf, who sent missionaries to Jamaica and elsewhere in the Caribbean a century before the time of Coleridge. He told the slaves in St. Thomas in 1739: "God punished the first Negroes by making them slaves, and your conversion will make you free, not from the control of your masters, but simply from your wicked habits and thoughts, and all that makes you dissatisfied with your lot.[9]

Behind these sentiments is the notion that the European is superior to all other races, a conviction that wreaked havoc on attempts to develop a biblical theology that questioned and challenged social structures, especially those of the slave society. The conviction was fairly widespread across the Caribbean Protestant spectrum and was reflected also among Roman Catholics. A Jesuit priest, Father Ignatius Scoles, who worked in Guyana (then British Guiana) in the latter half of the nineteenth century, held this opinion of people who were not Europeans: "It can hardly be fair to take poor Blacks and expect from them all firmness of character which Europeans like to boast of. They must rather be compared to over-grown children, ready to do what they are told, and often not doing it, often going astray and often returning . . ."[10] Views of Blacks, the Bible, and theological positions such as these, were employed by the dominant Christian groups within the Caribbean during slavery and for many decades to follow. Such views were enchained by race, class, and power relations in the region. From positions cemented by privilege of race, class, and power, those entrusted with the proclamation of the word of God engaged in a form of hermeneutical exercise that was sure to enhance their positions or, at least, not to challenge them.

The biblical theology and hermeneutics that were shaped during slavery, and functioned to legitimize European dominance and the subjugation of Africans, persisted in the post-slavery colonial Caribbean. The Eurocentric hermeneutics of colonialism was formulated in the era of conquest, consolidated in the era of slavery, and remained very much intact until the postcolonial era. The Eurocentric interpretation of the Bible was challenged in Jamaica mainly by the slaves themselves, especially in the Baptist tradition. Once the colonial theology was introduced to the slave population in the Caribbean,[11] the slaves found in the same Bible that was interpreted to justify their enslavement a message that justified resistance to and rebellion against slavery. Among these slaves was Sam Sharpe, who led the famous Sam Sharpe Rebellion in Jamaica in December 1831.[12] Mary Reckford and Philip Sherlock attested to the influence of the Bible on Sharpe in his attempts to secure the freedom of the slaves in Jamaica. According to Reckford: "Sam Sharpe, a domestic slave who worked in Montego Bay . . . was a member of the Baptist Church there. Sharpe was literate, intelligent and ambitious, and, like many of his kind, he found an outlet and a stimulant for his ambition in a mission church. . . . From his own reading of the Bible he became convinced that slaves were entitled to freedom."[13] Philip Sherlock tells us: "Daddy Sharpe and his leaders, by nature brave and gentle, were no visionaries, though like other 'spirit Baptists' they read divine meanings into their dreams. They had no grand messianic message, only the message of the Bible, that freedom was their right and that all men were equal in the sight of God the Father."[14] The understanding of the Bible and its interpretation by Sharpe reflected the basic hermeneutical assumptions identified earlier in the message of Bishop Coleridge of Barbados: The message of the Bible can and must speak to the contemporary and the concrete experiences of those being addressed. Unlike Coleridge, however, Sharpe found in the Bible not the justification and the legitimization of the status quo, that is slavery, but a rejection of it.

The 1971 Watershed in Caribbean Theology

When the group of Christians from across the Caribbean met at Chaguaramas from November 15–21, 1971, they were ensuing the great expectations and excitement of the early days of the post-colonial era. The use of the Bible as the basis for the call for liberation and development within the Caribbean contained choes of slaves who used the Bible as the basis of their protest against slavery[15]—a protest that had become one against colonialism and soon turned into a protest against the consequences and effects of colonialism. The Bible became for Caribbean theologians the best of allies against colonialism and all its debilitating effects. It was also for many an essential tool for carving out a Caribbean theology and a Caribbean identity, which were seen as essential if the post-colonial Caribbean was to move forward. In their use of the Bible, Caribbean theologians opted for those biblical motifs and personalities that could at one and the same time be a rejection of colonialism and a guide beyond the post-colonial era.

The most popular biblical motifs were those that are found in the Exodus tradition. One of the most vocal and articulate of Caribbean theologians in the post-colonial era, Idris Hamid, found in the Exodus tradition an understanding of God that, according to him, was hardly, if ever, used in the slave or colonial eras. The God of the Exodus, Hamid points out, is a God who, when bargaining failed, "walked off the bargaining table and set his people free."[16] Hamid saw his task as engaging in the type of Biblical theology and hermeneutics that would release the God of the Exodus who was hidden from the eyes of the Caribbean people.[17] The Exodus tradition not only provided the important theme of liberation but also the truth for Caribbean theologians of the 1970s that "liberation is salvation." This understanding and integration of the Exodus tradition is clearly reflected in William Watty's commentary on a verse from the story of the event at the sea. Exodus 15:21, which says "Sing to Yahweh for he has triumphed mightily," leads Watty to conclude that "the God whom Israel accepted as Sovereign, and whose rule they acknowledged over their lives in the relationship of covenant, was the God who had liberated them from the power of Egypt."[18] In essence, the Exodus tradition proclaims liberation that is salvation.

Attention is given also to the figure and role of Moses, who became a model of persons in the Exodus tradition infused with God's liberating zeal. In his paper delivered at a conference on theological reflection held in Trinidad on May 29–30, 1973, the (then) Anglican Bishop of Trinidad and Tobago, Clive Abdullah, found in the role of Moses a powerful message that spoke directly to the conditions of the Caribbean at that time. As he puts it: "Certainly the milieu of the Caribbean forces us to identify with the word of the Lord spoken by his prophet Moses some twelve centuries before

Christ. That word was: Let my people go." Abdullah claims that "for us he (Moses) is particularly relevant since he encompassed all the factors that still persist in the Third World today."[19] In the approach to biblical texts of Hamid, Watty, and Abdullah, we see an attempt to use a biblical tradition and character interpreted to speak directly to Caribbean conditions and experiences. Here, biblical hermeneutics were employed to support what is identified as being essential for the well-being of modern Caribbean society. If in the eras of slavery and colonialism what was thought to be "best" for Caribbean society was ensuring that the status quo is maintained, in the 1970s the "best" was nothing short of a total transformation of the social order. The theologians felt that to this radical transformation, the Exodus tradition with its special role of Moses spoke with profound insight.

Out of this interpretation of the Exodus tradition emerged an understanding of God that was projected as being peculiarly relevant to the Caribbean condition. So the God of the Exodus, the God of Israel, "was a God who was on the side of the weak and oppressed and against the power and dominance and privileges which oppressed and dehumanized men."[20] This understanding of God, drawn from the Exodus tradition, was regarded as antithetical to the dominant European idea of God's relationship with humans in the slave and colonial eras. Clearly, these contrasting interpretations of biblical traditions point to two diametrically opposed understandings of God. Idris Hamid captured this sharp divide when he said: "The God of traditional Caribbean Christianity has not been presented as a God who is identified with the live issues of Caribbean man. He is seldom presented as a God who breaks the yoke of the oppressed, who smashes the bars asunder and sets prisoners free. The God of the Exodus . . . is not the God whom we know by and large."[21] Therefore, the God of liberating power proclaimed by Caribbean theologians in the 1970s was, in contrast, proclaimed as the God of the Exodus and the God of Moses.

Robert Cuthbert, another Caribbean theologian of that era, pushed the Watty-Hamid-Abdullah hermeneutics of liberation and salvation to the boundaries of development in a climate of gross underdevelopment. Cuthbert looked beyond mere liberation to the creation of conditions that would be the very opposite of those that then existed under the constraints of the legacy of colonialism. Using the Bible as a base upon which to construct his theological perspectives, he argued that development is liberation, and cited as support for this conviction Luke 4:18; 1:51–53; Isa. 65:20–22; Amos 8:4–6; and Mic. 4:3–4. These passages contained what was for him the ideals of development, which he spelt out this way:

Imagine a world without blindness, without prisons, without malnutrition and infant morality. Imagine a world without tenant farmers and slave labor.

Imagine with Amos a world without commercial exploitation (Amos 8:4–6). Imagine with Micah a world where "nation shall not lift up a sword against nation . . . but they shall sit every man under his fig tree, and none shall make them afraid" (Mic. 4:3–4).[22]

Like fellow Caribbean theologians who used the liberation theme and the character of Moses from the Exodus tradition to address the need for freedom from colonial legacy, Cuthbert uses the biblical prophetic tradition to describe the conditions that should ensue after liberation has been experienced. The glorious expectations of Isa. 65:20–22 were seen as grounded in Caribbean reality and, like Mic. 4:3–4, were articulated in terms of: liberation from "hunger which saps the energies God gave us to use; liberation from the tragedies of infant morality and of violent conflict; liberation from man's exploitation of his fellow man. Liberation, in short, from all those things that 'dehumanize' people by limiting needlessly the development of their God-given potential."[23] The Bible thus becomes the basis for an understanding of development that will be nothing short of a total transformation of Caribbean society. A rejection of an *other worldly* interpretation of the biblical tradition was obvious in biblical theology and hermeneutics of Caribbean theologians in the 1970s. For them, there is no spiritualizing away of issues, but the Bible is brought to bear on the harsh realities of Caribbean experience in order to provide the guidelines for the development of a process to tackle these experiences. Between the liberation and the state of development, quite a few things had to be done. An effort and a great one was needed if the Caribbean was to reach the goal of development. Cuthbert saw in the work of the prophets what was demanded in the Caribbean. Like the figure Moses, the prophets provide the model of the type of work that was necessary to lead the Caribbean from liberation to development.[24] The Bible once more provided the character that was deemed to be necessary to push the Caribbean forward.

Cuthbert found in the "speaking forth" ministry of the prophets an element that was essential to the process of moving toward development in the Caribbean. He declared:

> We address the prophetic word not only to secular groups and institutions in the area, but also the institutionalized Church. Christians did just that in the days of slavery when some church members were slaves others were slave-owners. We are doing it today with our insistence that—without denying our debt to foreign missionaries—the time has come for church leaders in the Caribbean to be drawn from the Caribbean church.[25]

Here the prophetic word speaks directly to what for Cuthbert is one of the most pressing issues that had to be addressed as the Caribbean moved toward development. The weight of the prophets is placed on the side of the call for the indigenization of the Church in the Caribbean. The hermeneutical assumption behind this use of the prophetic tradition is that as the prophets spoke directly to the issues of their day, so they could be interpreted to speak directly to the issues of the Caribbean in the 1970s. The Old Testament prophets could, therefore, become for the Caribbean Church models of rejection and resistance, of radical transformation and change. All these were seen as being absolutely necessary if the Caribbean was to halt on its present path to the path of development. This shift would only come about, however, if the Church in the Caribbean, under the influence of the prophets, subscribed to "Prophetic radicalism." This was the opinion of Patrick Gomes, a lecturer in rural sociology at the University of the West Indies, who says, "To subscribe to prophetic radicalism is to invite the current institutions to undertake a liberating transformation."[26] The prophets become a source of radicalism that, if embraced, leads to liberation and transformation.

Although the Old Testament was very popular among Caribbean theologians in the 1970s, it was not used to the exclusion of the New Testament. The powerful message of liberation that was found in the Old Testament was also discovered in the New Testament text, which was interpreted as speaking to the issues of life and, consequently, the pressing issues of Caribbean life. One is struck by Bill Watty's interpretation of Mark 10:29–31, an interpretation that drew in some of the relevant issues of the Caribbean in the 1970s. On this text, William Watty comments:

> Jesus calls men away from houses, lands, etc; but that assumes that they have houses, land, etc., which they can give up; and it is because they can find more houses, land, etc., in the present life. Land-distribution and land-use are crucial for the Caribbean peoples' understanding of their history as Salvation-history and their future as a Divine calling into covenant.[27]

This Markan passage is rescued from any *other-worldly* interpretation and made to speak to what was yet another pressing Caribbean issue of the 1970s, land distribution. Jesus was placed firmly on the side of all those persons in the Caribbean who were demanding a better and fairer distribution of the land resources of the region.

The attempts to place Jesus firmly within the Caribbean, in order to listen to his message addressing Caribbean issues, was made nearly four decades before the efforts of Watty and others of the 1970s. Another son of the Caribbean, the revered Trinidadian trade unionist Uriah Buzz Butler, who was also a local preacher, made a gallant effort to interpret the word and message of Jesus in a manner that directly addressed what for him was the most pressing issue of his day, the welfare of workers, especially those of the lower classes. Like Watty, Butler found in the message of Jesus a basis from which he could launch his call for the improvement of the life of the working class. At the launching of his political party in 1936, Butler invited the "dispossessed to rally around the banner of Jesus to attack the bastions of the blue-eyed devils."[28] He saw Jesus at work in "a new political organization known as the British Empire Workers and Citizens Home Rule Party of Trinidad where he took evidence of the suffering of his people."[29] The significance of Butler's understanding and interpretation of Jesus is its discovery of an "underground" understanding of Jesus that was radically different from the official understanding of the churches, and existed from very early in Caribbean society.[30]

It was the "underground" understanding of Jesus that broke free in Caribbean theology, and was proclaimed as the understanding of Jesus that was necessary for the Caribbean of the day since it spoke directly to Caribbean issues. The task of the Caribbean biblical theology was therefore an urgent one, of providing for the region an understanding of Jesus that would address Caribbean issues. This task involved revamping the inherited Eurocentric Jesus, brought to the Caribbean with the European settlers and honored by the traditional Churches during the past centuries. This was the view of another Caribbean theologian, Clifford Payne, who, in an article published in 1977, addressed the issues from a position that was all too familiar to the Black theologians of North America of that era: the position of color.[31] One of the several features of a Caribbean Christ identified by Payne is one that becomes progressively Black.[32] The Caribbean theologians of the 1970s projected Jesus as one whose mission and ministry were to liberate the downtrodden and lead them into new and exciting experiences of God's salvation. He was presented as the model of the type of radical transformation that was needed in the Caribbean.[33] It was this mission, clearly spelt out in the Gospel tradition, that should be embraced by all Christians. In keeping with the model left for us by Jesus, those who become a part of this mission must work to bring about a "socio-political restructuring of relationships among the people of God," according to Harold Sitahal.[34] The Jesus of the New Testament provided the message that pointed along a path that many theologians of the 1970s believed was the way that the Caribbean should go.

Perhaps no other decade of Caribbean history has witnessed as intense a wrestling with the understanding and interpretation of the Bible as the 1970s; many theologians felt that the time had come to carve out a new understanding and interpretation of the Bible that differed radically from the inherited ones. It was only by so doing that the Caribbean Church would become a catalyst for the type of transformation and development needed in the region. As Idris Hamid insisted, the "God of the plantation" had to be replaced with the "God of the Exodus."[35] The religious fervor of the 1970s, which gripped the Caribbean Church and its theologians and set in motion new trends in Biblical theology, also had its effect upon both religious and nonreligious groups. It was reflected in the teachings of "indigenous sectarian groups."[36] As Hamid points out, in the traditional Churches there was "the conspicuous absence of the Exodus event as a meaningful symbol" and "it was left to a few, and more so to the indigenous sectarian groups like the Rastafarians in Jamaica, to lay hold upon the event which so closely paralleled their condition and aspiration."[37]

Even before the Caribbean theologians of the 1970s interpreted the Bible in ways that called for liberation from a colonial past and development into a brighter and better future, the Rastafarians were interpreting the Scriptures in ways that spoke of the liberation of Jamaicans' "Babylon,"[38] that is, from what they perceived to be an oppressive Jamaican society and world. Other contributors to this volume and the recently published *Chanting Down Babylon: The Rastafari Reader* by Temple University Press (1998) have done the most extensive studies of Rastafarian hermeneutics, which need not be repeated here. Important to note is the fact that for Rastafarians, the Bible became a ready ally in the movement's attack on established society, especially European society. The image of the Old Testament Babylon, an image of oppression and conquest, captured for the Rastafarians all the ills of Western society. So in yet another case, Biblical theology and hermeneutics are being conditioned by what is perceived to be the most important issue of those involved in the process. For the Rastafarians, it was liberation from "Babylon" and the preservation of African Caribbean identity and pride; they use certain biblical texts to support the priority of cultural identity and liberation.[39]

Interpretation and Challenges of the 1980s and 1990s

If the desire to break out of a colonial past and create a Caribbean understanding of God was the most dynamic force shaping biblical theology and hermeneutics in the 1970s, in the decade of the 1980s the need to relate God to the crisis experiences of the Caribbean was the driving force. The crisis was multidimensional and resulted from: the erosion of the colonial support system as the Caribbean plunged headlong into independence, self-reliance, and self-determination; the exporting of capital to foreign banks, and the withdrawal of foreign investments in places like Jamaica and Trinidad; the restructuring policies of the International Monetary Fund; and natural disaster. In an address to a consultation in Guyana in November 1984, sponsored by the Caribbean Conference of Churches (CCC), the CCC general secretary, the Rev. Alan Kirton, painted this picture of the region: "The Caribbean prophet sees a region that is becoming increasingly a waste land devastated by disaster, both natural and man-made, parched by drought, inundated by flood, ravaged by hurricanes, stifled by pollution and stripped by erosion."[40] If nature was this devastating, the man-made disasters were probably worse, at least in the view of Kirton. The Caribbean prophet sees people polarized by participation in a political process that has created a veritable jungle in which only the most brutish can survive; with economies shattered, not only as a result of global economic and monetary policies, but also due to irresponsible mismanagement and ineptitude of local leadership. Thus, the poor become desperate and those who have no helper turn to chemical dependency and to arms as possible solutions. So in the Caribbean we are faced with declining morals, low morale, despair, and cynicism.[41]

Biblical theology and hermeneutics had to relate to the crisis of the decade, by the middle of which the tone of Caribbean theology had changed. That bubbling enthusiasm that characterized the theological enterprise of the 1970s had subsided; by this time, scholars realized that it was no longer a simple case of using the Bible to support the exorcising of the past and the creation of a glorious future. Caribbean peoples now controlled their own present and their future, and their experience in the present had to be addressed. This was a present that had not lived up to all the great social and theological expectations of the 1970s. This condition of despair demanded a different use of the biblical tradition, a use that favored certain themes over others. For Kirton, the biblical theme demanded in the context of despair was the theme of hope held out by the prophet Jeremiah whose purchase of a piece of land contains a powerful message that proclaims hope. Kirton's interpretation of the story in Jeremiah 33, and his application of this interpretation to the Caribbean makes very interesting reading:

> Where are the places and what are the ways in which we buy our piece of land? And, particularly, how are we as Christian people and churches in our time being called upon, ourselves, to make a purchase. I believe that there is a challenge . . . to the Christian community in general and to individual Christians in particular, to buy our piece of land, to make an investment in hope, to be part of programs for the reconstruction of our communities and our societies [emphasis added].[42]

Were we still in the 1970s, one could expect an interpretation of Jeremiah 33 to lead to such discussions as the centrality of land ownership by Caribbean people for genuine Caribbean development to take place, and so the need for the redistribution of land. Now in the 1980s hope, which is still hope to change and reconstruct Caribbean societies, lacks, however, the socioeconomic and political cutting edge that characterized Caribbean theology of the 1970s.

Other Caribbean theologians engaged in a form of biblical interpretation that attempted to address the pessimistic reality of the decade of the 1980s while holding up a torch of hope. At the CCC consultation in Guyana, William Watty did an important study of 2 Kings 18:17–37, entitled "Big Brother and Weaker States."[43] In his interpretation of this passage, Watty, like Hezekiah and Israel in 2 Kings 18, contends that the Caribbean lives in the shadow of a "Big Brother." Israel, in the days of Hezekiah, lived in the shadow of Egypt as the Caribbean lives in the shadow of the United States. The words of the Rabshakeh in 2 Kings 18:21 becomes for Watty very instructive for the people of the Caribbean:

> The backup of Egypt seemed to be his (Hezekiah's) policy of resistance to Assyria. Isaiah had warned him repeatedly about this in as much the same way as the Rabshakeh now taunts him: Don't look to Egypt. Forget Egypt. Egypt is unreliable. Egypt will leave you in the lurch. In superpower politics there are no Big Brothers . . . Caribbean people would do well to heed this admonition. . . . [44]

Watty's interpretation spoke directly to the conditions that obtained in the Caribbean in 1984. The Grenada Marxist experiment with its heavy dependence upon its communist ally Cuba had self-destructed and was finally wiped away by superpower United States.[45] Grenada had paid the price of believing there were big brothers in superpower politics. Whatever lessons it learned from the Kennedy missile crisis, the Soviets kept its forces at home while the United States "cleaned up" her backyard.

The point that Watty makes is not that there was not a more salutary side to "Big Brother." The Rabshakeh tried to give salutary promises to the very ones whose liberty he was taking away. Watty finds parallel with the Caribbean-U.S. relationship: "Promises! Promises! The sound of coins jingling in the pocket, the vision of supermarket shelves well stocked again, the anticipation of 'happy days are here again.' Everyone will sit under his own vine and under his own fig-tree and drink water out of his own cistern (2 Kings 18: 31)."[46] The issue is firmly grounded in the Caribbean reality: "The doors of opportunity are open wide. Visas are to be had for the asking, Green Cards galore!"[47] Rabshakeh's words, loosely paraphrased, resounding the realities of the Caribbean-U.S. relations: "I will bring you back to my own land of plenty, where streets are paved with gold and where the sky is the limit in the shining city on the hill."[48] What is evident in Watty's interpretation of 2 Kings 18 is an attempt to fit, what to many was an insurmountable problem of U.S. hegemony, into the Caribbean belief that Caribbean peoples were still God's people, and that God was still at work in the Caribbean. That God seemed far removed from the experience of

Caribbean peoples in the middle of the decade of the 1980s, even as he seemed far removed from Hezekiah and his people in 2 Kings 18, was for Watty an indication of his freedom. The God of liberation, judgment, and development of the 1970s, a God so well-presented in the Exodus tradition, in the Old Testament prophets, and in the life and ministry of Jesus, seemed far away. The experience of the 1980s dictated that another understanding of God had to be worked out. Once more the biblical tradition provided building blocks for the construction of this understanding.

It was an understanding that affirmed God's presence in the face of numerous contradictions that beset Caribbean society. The Bible was no longer interpreted to provide the impetus to remove the contradictions but, instead, it was interpreted to help Caribbean peoples to identify, understand, and live with the contradictions. In response to one of these contradictions, the U.S. invasion of Grenada, theologians placed peace on the Caribbean theological agenda with some urgency. Leslie Lett, one of the pioneers in the development of a theology of peace for the Caribbean, declared: "Peace must be seen as an urgent historical necessity. For the Churches this means that peace theology must begin with an analysis of the contemporary situation. Theology must have two points of reference: the Scripture and an analysis of specific social situations and our actual involvement in these situations."[49] Lett identified the "forces against peace" as weak economies, multinationals, the possibility of foreign intervention, violations of human rights, "constitutions of entrenchment," etc.[50] The Christian is called to struggle and work against all of these. The Bible provides the ammunition for the struggle and the strength for the work: "Any search for peace must reckon with the Kingdom of God as fundamentally a social movement, and only secondarily a message of salvation to individuals. The new [Man] in Christ (who is our peace, Eph. 2:14f) is a social reality. Man made in the image of God is a community of persons."[51]

The thematic shift from the dominant themes of the 1970s to those of peace did not result, at least for Lett, in a dramatic theological and hermeneutical shift. The Bible was still made to address the Caribbean condition. In contradistinction to the wave of fundamentalist brands of Christianity that were invading the Caribbean from North America, and were proclaiming a theology that interpreted the Kingdom of God as a place we will go after death,[52] Lett insists that experiences of the Kingdom are to be had here and now. The Kingdom is about social transformation here and now. The work for peace and the work for the Kingdom were, therefore, synonymous. This work also involved for Luis Riviera working for justice as well. As he pointed out, "peace and justice are two indissolubly linked concepts."[53] Riviera found support for this link between justice and peace in such texts as Isaiah 11:1–10; 65:17–25; 2:4; Psalm 72, and James 2:5.[54]

Both Old Testament and New Testament, he argues, come from an op- pressed people, and hence the dominant themes of freedom, justice, and peace.

As peace became the companion of justice, so it became the champion of human rights. Here once more, the Bible is interpreted to support a popu- lar concern. Peace only comes about when all the many conditions that vi- olate human rights are removed. So the "true nature of peace," Knolly Clarke says, is summed up in Isaiah 9. The one who oppressed and exploited the people of Yahweh, that is, the one who violated their human rights, is defeated as part of the process that ushers in conditions of peace.[55] Conflict was related to peace with the assistance of the Bible as was militarization and sectarianism. Cecil Prescod's use of the Bible to treat peace and conflict re- flects what became the standard hermeneutical approach for most Caribbean theologians, the legitimizing of social analysis by innovative in- terpretation of the Bible.[56]

In Ashley Smith's exposition of the peace-conflict tension, the Bible once more was drawn into the discussion and became a supportive base for the analysis of the problem of militarization. According to Smith, "In whatever language or mood a biblical/theological analysis of the phenomenon of global militarization is attempted . . . the basis of any such analysis is to be found es- pecially in the Books of Genesis and Exodus, the Prophets and Paul's exposi- tion on human nature and of sin, its implications and its consequences for the individual sinner and for the rest of the human family."[57] In many ways this can be interpreted as an attempt to cut the giant down to size, to the size of the dwarf, using the Bible as the tool in the exercise. The giant and the dwarf are subjected to the same limitation, sin; a limitation that the military giant does not accept. Smith gives us the reason why. It has to do with the power that derives from the military-industrial complex. The Bible helps us to understand all this: "The Military-Industrial complex . . . represents the very essence of human prideful attempt at the abolition of the God of the Bible and the idolatrous replacement of him. It is undoubtedly a reenactment of the drama of the tower of Babel."[58] As was the case in the 1970s, God, as he is understood in the biblical tradition, especially in the Old Testament, is presented as standing on the other side of human power, alongside the pow- erless. In the face of the overwhelming might of the military-industrial com- plex of the 1980s (the manifestation of "hubris"), Smith affirms "God's power over both created order and demonic forces. . . ."[59] This is the power that is proclaimed in the traditions of the Hebrew prophets, in the story of the Ex- odus, and in the account about the limitations of the power Nebuchadnez- zar. So, for Smith, hope lives in spite of the presence of the "demonic expression of 'hubris.'" For, with an understanding of history based on con- victions about God's sovereign power and lordship and unconditional love for that which God has created, the faithful remnant presses on, not with optimism as do the devotees of the deities of the military-industrial complex of East and West, but with hope based on faith in Him whose covenant with his people is everlasting.[60]

Biblical theology and hermeneutics in the Caribbean of the 1980s were like torches trying to point a way through a maze of contradictions: some homegrown, some imported, some exported and imposed, which bedeviled the Caribbean. Even if these theological reflections lacked in some ways the sharp, incisive thrust of the 1970s, they still released from the Bible a voice that spoke directly to the Caribbean experience. This is the voice that is needed in the Caribbean of the millennium. Any exercises in biblical theology and hermeneutics should be exercises that, like those of the decades of the 1970s and 1980s, allow the Bible to speak to the realities of the Caribbean experience. In the 1990s, the era of one superpower who still possesses all the characteristics of Watty's "Big Brother,"[61] and whose religious-cultural shadow threatens to block out the theological sun in the Caribbean, the need exists for a concerted theological effort to retain the theological identity of the Caribbean. The invasion by U.S. Pentecostals, ultraright radio stations, and preachers threatens to undermine the "this-worldly" approach to biblical theology and hermeneutics carved out in the 1970s and reshaped in the 1980s. The fundamentalist simplistic interpretation of the Bible that hardly addresses the Caribbean experience does not allow the Bible to speak to the experience of Caribbean peoples in a "humanistic" way. It comes in an attractive package and pretends to provide all the answers to life's many complex problems and contradictions, while the biblical hermeneutics of the 1970s model points the way that one should go in search for answers and social transformation.[62]

There is a strong feeling that Caribbean biblical theology and hermeneutics in the decade of the 1990s have been hijacked by the religious right of the United States and are being used to ensure the U.S. cultural/religious, if not political, hegemony in the Caribbean. A mechanism employed in the process is to avoid the biblical/theological approach that addresses communal concerns and to use approaches that address personal/individual salvation. Howard Gregory, in reflecting on the development of Caribbean theology, notes how sharp the contrast between the communal and the individual approaches is. He argues that a "major point of criticism of western theology is located in its emphasis on individual salvation. Such a perception of the faith is seen to be distorted, divisive, and destructive of Christian community. In rejecting the emphasis on individualism, a corresponding emphasis in Caribbean theology on community and social transformation emerged. It is through an affirmation of community that loyalty to the biblical tradition is seen to reside."[63]

In spite of the theological-hermeneutical approach that stresses individual salvation, the efforts to preserve the legacy of the 1970s and 1980s, and allow the Bible to speak to the pressing issues of the Caribbean, are undaunted. *The Caribbean Journal of Religious Studies (CJRS)*, now subtitled *A Forum for Discussion of Religious and Pastoral Issues Affecting the Life of Caribbean Peoples,* represents a concerted effort to preserve this legacy, as seen in two articles published in the 1993 editions. In a study of Exodus 1 and 2, Joseph Nichols attempts to relate three themes to the experiences of Caribbean peoples. He posits some contradictions in the Exodus passage that reflect some of the contradictions that Caribbean peoples are called to face. Pharaoh's concern about the loyalty of the Hebrews should he be attacked by an enemy is juxtaposed with his refusal to allow them to leave. Nicholas comments: "The fact that the argument comes in this obviously confusing way is probably testimony to the difficulty that one can face when the whole story cannot be told."[64] The story has another side that is not being revealed by Pharaoh, so confusion sets in. Nicholas likens it to high-level diplomacy[65] where there is more to the story than is told. He finds some parallels in the attitudes toward Caribbean emigrants in some metropolitan countries. He said, "Maybe it should not surprise us that much that even though we hear of problems with Caribbean emigrants, there is no anxiety to repatriate. In fact, despite the occasional complaints, there are still official provisions for our people to migrate to those same parts."[66]

The Bible thus becomes, through Nicholas's hermeneutical approach, a means to help Caribbean peoples face the several contradictions that are characteristic of their paradoxical relationship with the metropolitan United States. The first two chapters of the book of Exodus can help Caribbean peoples understand these contradictions, which include acceptance-rejection attitudes toward Caribbean peoples, but also the willingness of many of those persons, especially professionals, to accept employment in the United States that is normally regarded as below their profession.[67] Just as the Hebrews contribute to the wealth of Egypt while consolidating wealth among themselves and improving the welfare of their group, so Caribbean emigrants provide a service in the larger countries, but are aware of the benefits this service can provide for themselves and their children. As Nicholas puts it: "Providing service [has] other benefits in terms of the opportunities provided, exposure received and experiences acquired. All these may then become important elements in the building of a new life for the Caribbean person or for the whole family."[68]

Nicholas is in the hermeneutical path pioneered by Hamid, Watty, and others in the 1970s, and sustained by other Caribbean theologians in the 1980s. It is a path that takes seriously the experiences of Caribbean peoples and attempts to relate these experiences to the theological insights of the biblical tradition. So the pivotal role of women in Exodus 1 and 2 does not escape Nicholas. It is the type of role Caribbean women, especially those of the working class, have played very well in the past, and continue to play well in the present.[69] In an article entitled "Some Deuteronomic Themes in a Caribbean context" in the same volume of *CJRS,* I attempted to relate some important themes in Deuteronomy to the experiences of Caribbean peoples. The hermeneutical assumptions behind this exercise were the same as those behind the work of the Caribbean theologians of the 1970s and 1980s; the Bible as the word of the Lord can speak to and illuminate the experiences of Caribbean peoples. Using the theme, "Land, Identity, and Leadership," I attempted to relate these Deuteronomic themes to the Caribbean experiences. The *nahalah* challenge of Deuteronomy proclaims a right to land ownership. When applied to the Caribbean experience, it leads to the realization that "land ownership is still outside of the grasp of many Caribbean people, given the ownership patterns that have developed over the years. The *nahalah* challenge of Deuteronomy is one that demands a response from the governments of the region. Theirs is the power to ensure that the people of the region are able to experience, as Deuteronomy would demand, their *berakah* through their relationship with their *nahalah.*"[70]

One of the persistent problems facing the peoples of the Caribbean is that of identity. Built on the cultural foundation of Europe, and in more recent times swamped by the culture of North America, especially that of the United States, the identity of Caribbean peoples seems never to have had the space to grow and firmly establish itself. Clive Thomas once wrote: "The penetration of North American ideology, particularly through the electronic media, press, and school system, . . . is taking the lead in the region's cultural development . . . and taking the lead in the region's economic development."[71] This condition led me to Deuteronomy, a book strong on identity, to find some theological insights about identity that can address the Caribbean condition. The people to whom this book is addressed are a people whose identity is under threat from cultural penetration.[72] Deuteronomy responds to this crisis by taking the community back into its past. This reminds us that, "We can only cope with where we are, if we fully understand and appreciate from whence we came."[73] The book, therefore, provides for Caribbean peoples some theological and pedagogical insights that can help them make creative use of their past as the building blocks for creating a unique Caribbean identity. This carries a "stern warning about the destruction of identity, and the consequential creation of facelessness, a condition that inevitably leads to annihilation."[74] The "omnipresence" of CNN and the satellite dish, McDonald's and Kentucky Fried Chicken, the "invasion" by hundreds of thousands of tourists—who, of course, the Caribbean economy needs for survival—make Deuteronomy's concern about identity one that speaks directly to the Caribbean experience.

The discussion of the theme of "Leadership" in Deuteronomy and especially the six stipulations of the "Law of the King" (Deut. 17:15–18)[75] offers an understanding of leadership that can speak directly to the Caribbean. The stipulation that the king should be a national points to the need for continuity. Should the king be a nonnational, he would be lacking, Deuteronomy assumes the sense of history and continuity. These are never to be sacrificed. The implications of this for the Caribbean, as I understand them, is that "the national leader and party must preserve the memory, that is, they must not try to negate and destroy the past all for the sake of immediate political advantage."[76] In all of the other stipulations profound insights surface about leadership that are all relevant to leadership in the region. The stipulations demanding that the king should be versed in the way of the Torah is another of those insights. As I pointed out previously, "The insistence that the king must be subjected to the Torah is a reminder that leadership in all areas and at all levels need the assistance of rulers and conventions. These work to curb the glamour for power and prestige, gained at the expense of those being led."[77]

Out of this comes a very important point that speaks directly to the Caribbean experience: "The embracing of the Torah by the king may well rule out the type of leadership that has flourished in the Caribbean for several decades; this is the charismatic type of leadership. Not that this type of leadership has not served the Caribbean well. But it often can lead to . . . 'populism and personalism.'"[78] Influenced by the theologians of the 1970s and the 1980s, I was able to read Deuteronomy in a manner that could release its powerful message to address the experiences of the Caribbean peoples. This hermeneutical approach was, and indeed is, based on the conviction that the biblical tradition can come alive and speak to us in our own peculiar set of circumstances as Caribbean peoples.

Conclusion

As we enter the new century, the need to engage in the type of biblical theology and hermeneutics that will allow the Bible to address Caribbean issues is as pressing as it ever was. The "cultural magnet" of the north is as strong as ever. The question of the relevance of a Caribbean biblical theology and hermeneutics in a region where the pull and the power of the cultural magnet can proclaim both the irrelevance and the inferiority of things Caribbean cannot be ignored. The need exists for concerted effort and space to pursue the theological task in the Caribbean that *CJRS* is now facilitating. As we move into the twenty-first century, the following guidelines for interpreting the Bible in ways that allow it to speak to the experiences of Caribbean peoples can be instructive:

1. We must hold onto the conviction that the Bible can be interpreted to speak to the experiences of Caribbean peoples;
2. We must see our biblical theology and hermeneutics as being as valid as those of other peoples;
3. We will draw on the experiences, scholarship, and traditions of others, but we reserve the right to use them in ways that will sharpen the message of the Bible for us in the Caribbean;
4. We will not sacrifice the biblical communal interpretation of the Bible for an individual interpretation that can play down the need for communal responsibility and communal salvation;
5. We will engage in our theological exercise, convinced of the guidance of the Holy Spirit, who can lead us into the truth.

Only if we follow these guidelines and remain faithful to them will we be, at the same time, faithful to the great legacy left for us by the pioneers of Caribbean biblical theology. We will be able to understand the Bible in a way that would allow all our people to proclaim: This is indeed the word of the Lord.

Notes

1. Robert Cuthbert, ed., *Called to Be: Report on the Caribbean Ecumenical Consultation for Development* (Bridgetown: Caribbean Conference of Churches, 1972).
2. Ibid.
3. Ibid., 24.
4. Ibid.
5. On these conditions, cf. Kortright Davis, *Emancipation Still Comin! Explorations in Caribbean Emancipatory Theology* (New York: Orbis, 1990), 29ff.; Irene Hawkins, *The Changing Face of the Caribbean* (Bridgetown: Cedar Press, 1976).
6. William Coleridge, *Charges Delivered to the Clergy of the Diocese of Barbados and the Leeward Islands* (London: J. G. & F. Rivington, 1835), 263–4.
7. The emancipation of slaves in the British Empire took place in 1834.
8. Coleridge, 264.
9. William Watty, "De-Colonization of Theology," in *Troubling of the Waters,* ed. Idris Hamid (San Fernando, Trinidad: Rahman, 1973), 70.
10. Geoffrey Williams, "Classicism and the Caribbean Church," in *Out of the Depths,* ed. Idris Hamid (San Fernando, Trinidad: St. Andrew's Press, 1977), 57.

11. On the introduction of Christianity to the slaves in the Caribbean, cf. Isaac Dookhan, *A Pre-emancipation History of the Caribbean* (London: Collins, 1974), 124ff.

12. Cf. Jan Rogozinski, *A Brief History of the Caribbean: From Arawaks and Caribs to the Present* (New York: Lengrun, 1992), 152–73; Mary Reckford, "The Slave Rebellion of 1831," *Jamaica Journal* (June, 1969): 26–8.

13. Philip Sherlock, *Shout for Freedom: A Tribute to Sam Sharpe* (London: Macmillan, 1976), vii.

14. Sherlock, x.

15. Dale Bisnauth, *History of Religions in the Caribbean* (Jamaica: Kingston Publishers, 1989), 101ff.

16. Idris Hamid, ed., *In Search of New Perspectives* (Barbados: CADEC, 1971), 5.

17. Idris Hamid, "Theology and Caribbean development," in *With Eyes Wide Open* (Bridgetown: CADEC, 1973), 125.

18. Watty, "De-colonization of Theology," 71.

19. Clive Abdullah, "Any Word from the Lord?" in Hamid, ed., *Troubling of the Waters,* p. 15.

20. Watty, "De-colonization of Theology," 71.

21. Hamid, "Theology and Caribbean Development," 123.

22. Robert Cuthbert, "Development and the Caribbean Christian," in *With Eyes Wide Open,* 112.

23. Ibid.

24. Cuthbert, 117ff.

25. Ibid.

26. Patrick Gomez, "Religion and Social Change: Problems of Prophetic Radicalism and the Institutional Churches," in *Out of the Depths,* Hamid, ed., 158.

27. Watty, "De-Colonization of Theology," 76.

28. Harold Sitahal, "Rethinking Missions for the Caribbean," in *Out of the Depths,* Hamid, ed., 40.

29. Ibid.

30. Cf. Hamid, "Theology and Caribbean Development," 125.

31. On black theology of the era, cf. William James, *Is God a White Racist?* (New York: Anchor/Doubleday, 1973); Albert Cleage, *The Black Messiah* (Kansas City: Sheed and Ward, 1968); James Cone, *A Black Theology of Liberation* (New York: Lippincott, 1970); *Black Theology and Black Power* (New York: Seabury, 1969).

32. Clifford Payne, "What Will a Caribbean Christ Look Like," in *Out of the Depths,* Hamid, ed., 5ff.

33. Sitahal, 43ff.

34. Ibid., 44.

35. Hamid, "Theology and the Caribbean Development," 126.

36. Ibid., 125.

37. Ibid.

38. On the use of the term "Babylon" by Rastafarians, cf. Joseph Owens, *Dread: The Rastafarians of Jamaica* (London: Heinemann, 1976), 69ff.
39. Ibid., 39ff.
40. Alan Kirton, "There is a Balm in Gilead," in *Consultation for Ministry in a New Decade,* ed. Alan Kirton and William Watty (Barbados: CADEC, 1985), 5.
41. Ibid.
42. Ibid., 6.
43. William Watty, "Big Brother and Weaker States," *Consultation for Ministry in a New Decade,* 9–18.
44. Watty, "Big Brother," 15.
45. On the Grenada issue, cf. *Point Salines, for What Purpose,* ed. Leslie Lett (Barbados: CADEC, 1984); Hugh O'Shaughnessy, *Grenada: Revolution, Invasion and Aftermath* (Great Britain: Sphere Books, 1984); Fitzroy Ambursley and James Dunkerley, *Grenada: Whose Freedom?* (London: Latin America Bureau, 1984).
46. Watty, "Big Brother," 17.
47. Ibid.
48. Ibid.
49. Leslie Lett, "Working for Peace in the Caribbean," in *Peace: A Challenge to the Caribbean,* ed. Alan Kirton (Barbados: CADEC, 1982), 27.
50. Ibid.
51. Ibid.
52. On this theology, cf. Kortright Davis, *Emancipation Still Comin'* (Maryknoll, New York: Orbis Press, 1990), 78–9.
53. Luis Riviera, "Peace and Justice in the Bible," in *Peace: A Challenge to the Caribbean,* 21.
54. Ibid.
55. Knolly Clarke, "Meditations on Peace," in *Peace, Human Rights and Development* (Barbados: CADEC, 1982), 2.
56. Cecil Prescod, "Peace and Conflict: A Christian View," in *Peace, Human Rights and Development,* 7–12.
57. Ashley Smith, "Militarization: Whose Security? A Theological Reflection," in *Peace, Human Rights and Development,* 19.
58. Ibid.
59. Smith, 26.
60. Ibid.
61. Cf. Watty, "Big Brother."
62. Kortright Davis says this branch of Christianity "sometimes takes fundamentalism so seriously that it has slighted more urgent problems of Christian engagement in the social Emancipatory process" (29).
63. Howard Gregory, "En Route to a Pastoral Counseling Model for the Caribbean: A survey of the Methodology of Caribbean Theology," *Caribbean Journal of Religious Studies* vol. 11, no. 2 (1990): 5.

64. Joseph Nicholas, "Wealth, Women, and Wit in Exodus 1 and 2," *Caribbean Journal of Religious Studies* 14 (1993): 29.
65. Ibid.
66. Ibid.
67. Nicholas, 30.
68. Ibid.
69. Ibid., 39.
70. John Holder, "Some Deuteronomic Themes in a Caribbean Context," *Caribbean Journal of Religious Studies* 14 (1993): 8.
71. Clive Thomas, *The Poor and the Powerless* (New York: Monthly Review Press, 1984), 324.
72. Cf. E. W. Nicholson, *Deuteronomy and Tradition* (Oxford: Blackwell, 1967), 101.
73. Holder, 11.
74. Ibid., 13–4.
75. Ibid.: cf. Gerhard von Rad, *Old Testament Theology* vol. 1 (Edinburgh: Oliver & Boyd, 1962), 75.
76. Holder, 16.
77. Ibid., 22.
78. Ibid., 22–3.

Chapter 7 🔆

Text and the Rhetoric of Change

Bible and Decolonization in Post–World War II Caribbean Political Discourse

Leslie R. James

Introduction

"No one would deny," declared Orlando Patterson, "that today freedom stands unchallenged as the supreme value of the Western world."[1] To Patterson the rhetoric of freedom is pervasive in Western discourse: philosophers debate its nature and meaning endlessly; it is the catchword of politicians, the secular gospel of the economic "free enterprise" system, and the foundation of all Western cultural activities. It is also the central value of Christianity: being redeemed, being freed by, and in, Christ is the ultimate experience and goal of all Christians. Freedom is the one value that many people seem prepared to die for. During the Cold War, leaders of the West had even divided the world into two great camps, the free world and the unfree, and were prepared to risk a nuclear holocaust to defend the sacred ideal called freedom. Orlando Patterson's argument is that the vision of Israel that emerged from the bondage of Egypt makes the Exodus experience and the passion for freedom the core value in Israel and the biblical text and vision.

Patterson's comments on freedom's centrality in Western consciousness provide an appropriate framework with which to explore and define the functional/historical juxtaposition between the biblical text and Caribbean political rhetoric in the post–World War II imperial disengagement in Caribbean society. The Caribbean horizon was significantly shaped by a history of colonialism and the indigenous struggles to accommodate, or resist and transcend European and other hegemonies, as did the biblical horizons in the ancient Near East. Just as Israel's vision of freedom emerged from Egyptian bondage, so did the vision of Caribbean autonomy proceed from the quest to transcend New World slavery and colonialism. The biblical text, in other words, was shaped by a world that was similar to that of the Caribbean, one in which freedom was the underlying force driving history toward an emancipatory eschatology or end.[2] Indeed, a hermeneutic of freedom or emancipation is central to the biblical text, as is seen in the Exodus tradition and liberation from Babylonian captivity. This liberating hermeneutic gave the biblical text a vitality that is relevant to the evolution of Caribbean society and culture from slavery to freedom.[3]

The end of World War II marked the end of Western European domination of planet earth. From 1945 onward, Great Britain, in the light of changing fortunes, was intentional in dismantling her extensive empire, which included a significant part of the Caribbean.[4] The imperial custodians of the Caribbean were to facilitate the genesis of new nations emerging from the colonial womb. The imperial plan fought to integrate these fledgling colonies into a new multiracial commonwealth whose members shared a common maternal affection and respect for Britain and its values, including the Judeo-Christian religious ideal of freedom. Ironically, the colonial plan did not work out as expected. Instead, a generation of nationalist messianic Caribbean politicians emerged, determined to lead their people into a new dispensation of freedom and prosperity. Caribbean politicians who had a strong background in Christianity used biblical vocabulary in their attempt to communicate the path Caribbean people should take to make their independence a reality. The public use of the Bible in Caribbean political rhetoric became a noted feature in the rhetoric of decolonization, which defined the politicians' sense of the historical moment. This chapter illustrates this phenomenon, relative to decolonization, in reference to several contemporary Caribbean politicians: Michael Manley (Jamaica), Eric Williams (Trinidad and Tobago), Maurice Bishop (Grenada), and Jean-Bertrand Aristide (Haiti). My central assertion is that the Bible and Caribbean post–World War II political discourse can be interpreted from a rhetorical perspective. Caribbean politicians, through their use of the biblical text in their rhetoric of change in the post–World War II decolonization era, developed, in varying degrees, a unified view of history in which the sacred and the secular realms of human existence were integrated.

Text and Context: Garvey and Patterson

The post–World War II era witnessed the decline of European colonialism and the worldwide increase of proletarian consciousness. Decolonization entailed the exodus of Caribbean and other peoples from the aegis of colonialism to a new day of freedom and nationhood. The biblical text, with its images and visions of national messianism, became a powerful tool in the rhetoric of mobilizing the newly independent masses for freedom and the future of national construction. The post-colonial era posed significant challenges for Caribbean politicians, who were forced to define an alternative society in relationship to their local and metropolitan frames of reference. In the process, they established a fundamental convergence between biblical emancipatory historical consciousness and Caribbean emancipatory historical consciousness. In other words, their participation in the politics of "setting at liberty the oppressed" connected them with the spirit of freedom manifested in the biblical text but also at work in the world in terms of human and historical transformation. Inevitably, as Caribbean politicians promoted freedom in their own societies, like Jesus of Nazareth in his, they participated in a universal project of human liberation. The political figures treated in this study, despite their different approaches to merging biblical imagery with a rhetoric of decolonization, participated in the process of promoting global freedom.

Gordon K. Lewis argued that with independence the West Indian society faced, after the fifteenth-century Columbian discovery and nineteenth-century emancipation from slavery, its third seminal period.[5] The first period of colonialism, because of its heavy reliance on imported slave labor, left a legacy of excessive population increase in relation to the economic resources.[6] Post-emancipation, because of its use of indentured labor, left behind a legacy of low-wage economy, with living standards kept artificially low by the maintenance of a reservoir of unemployed and underemployed persons. Unlike emancipation, independence was merely a redefinition of the legal status of the society; it did not necessarily bring the anticipated social change in improving the lives of the masses and thus inherited the problems created by the slave and Creole societies. This is the context in which Caribbean politicians were challenged to remap their societies through the politics of transformation. The challenge was to recreate their peoples and Caribbean communities by giving the people back to themselves that they might become subjects of their own history. The result was the rise of a prophetic emancipatory rhetoric that expressed the people's commitment to widen the horizons of Caribbean freedom in the decolonization era. This rhetoric was often laced with biblical language and ideas, a language designed to persuade, impress, and move the will in order to direct human existence in fresh directions.

The biblical text and post–colonial Caribbean rhetoric have a similar emancipatory thrust; both envisage transformation when they question the present social structure. In the biblical world, as in the Caribbean situations, divorcing religion from politics or the sacred from the profane is very difficult. Biblical vocabulary is political or at least has profound political resonance. This resonance stems, in part, from the fact that, according to Orlando Patterson, the idea of freedom in its religious and secular expressions, is the core value of Western civilization. Caribbean history and experience, as a product of Western civilization, is a tragic manifestation of Western failure to be always true to its self-espoused ideal of freedom.[7] Furthermore, as Patterson argues, the idea of freedom in the West correlates with the struggle to transcend slavery.

Like biblical rhetoric—which in its major thrust is a rhetoric of change and liberty—Caribbean political rhetoric is a rhetoric of change. It is a subversive rhetoric, one that denounces the present social configuration and announces a new *(the novum)* or alternative social framework. It is an emancipatory rhetoric, which announces the deliverance of Caribbean people from the entrapments of history and causes a shift in the colonial paradigm. The late Prime Minister of Trinidad and Tobago, Eric Williams, announced an historical paradigm shift when he publicly declared in 1961 *"massa day done!"*[8] Williams's proclamation had equal rhetorical value to Luke's Jesus messianic proclamation of "good news to the poor," "release for prisoners," "recovery of sight to the blind," letting "the broken victims go free," announcing "the year of the Lord's favor" (Luke 4:16–30). Though distant in time, the "good news" of the two proclamations was the emancipation of the oppressed. Such rhetoric, whether Williams's or Jesus of Nazareth's, has the power to remap the social space of Israel, Trinidad and Tobago, the Caribbean, and the world. As Jesus was seen as a popular hero to many in the Palestine of his day under Roman colonialism, so was Eric Williams seen as the popular hero in the Trinidad and Tobago of his day under British colonialism. Jesus of Nazareth was Rabbi, and Eric Williams was "The Doc." As prophetic figures, they announced the renewal of their people's lives, the return of their freedom, and the restoration of their fortunes. Political activism against injustice was central to Jesus's and Williams's messages. As oracles, they proclaimed freedom for the oppressed, clothes for the naked, food for the hungry, education, health, housing, and opportunity for the nation. The message of Jesus and that of Williams are similar in their hermeneutic of national regeneration.

Discussion of the juxtaposition between the biblical text and the rhetoric of change leads to the consideration of both Scripture and Caribbean political rhetoric as "inspired" and spirit-led. The category of the spirit is not a difficult one for Caribbean peoples to understand. For them, the Bible is cast within the framework of the spirit, which makes "all things new" (Rev. 21: 1–5). John, the Seer of Patmos, sees the future filled with the promise of a transformation so complete that there will be a new heaven and a new earth. When John's vision is integrated into Caribbean history it becomes the vision of a new Caribbean.[9] The renewal process can only be possible within a framework of freedom. It follows that if Luke 16: 16, with its three periods in the history of salvation, is accepted as the hermeneutical center of the Luke-Acts collections, then history is characterized by the maximization of freedom. The author of Luke-Acts saw the Church in the center of the struggle for an emancipatory history. Western Christianity entered the Caribbean with Columbus's encounter with the New World in 1492. Consequently, the Bible, from the coming of Montesinos to Aristide, has played a critical role in the religious-political consciousness of the Caribbean. Radical contact with the prophetic emancipatory spirit of the Bible in Caribbean history has always been accompanied by the desire for change and justice in Caribbean society. It is an historical process in which the emancipating word or hermeneutic of Scripture becomes incarnate in Caribbean history. This is a process of historical reversal in which the Caribbean is placed at the center of its own history, a history that must begin with an indigenous "Exodus." In Lukan eschatological terms "the first becomes last and the last becomes first"[10] (Matt. 5: 3–10; Luke 6: 20–23).

Caribbean societies are deeply religious. In addition to Christianity, Hindu and Islamic traditions are potent forces in Trinidad and Tobago, and Guyana. Caribbean societies are also marked by a significant African diaspora population for whom African religious traditions persist.[11] In African religious traditions such as Shango, Voodoo, Santeria, Pocomania, and Jordanites, the spirit is a major reality and the religion is inseparable from the culture. Christian churches, synagogues, mosques, and temples house public schools, their leaders create political parties and elect and support political candidates, and bishops and Hindu pundits prophesy political doom or victory for the nation. It is even conceivable in the Caribbean world for a political figure to be considered a more authentic spokesperson of the spirit than a religious professional.

Caribbean people travel miles to listen to and spend long hours with their political leaders, something they will not do for their religious leaders, no matter how much they might be appreciated. This must be predicated on expectations or aspirations of the Caribbean populace, even as it did with those who went out to hear Jesus and the prophets before him. In ancient Israel, prophetic speech took place in the public, political arena. Later, in light of Israel's subsequent history, especially the Babylonian Exile, prophetic traditions were written down by disciples and scribes and later codified in canons to preserve national memory and a sense of historical consciousness. In the same way, the early Christians codified and preserved the prophetic utterances of Jesus for the preservation of the historical consciousness of the community of believers. Parallels can be drawn between Caribbean history and the biblical prophetic traditions.[12] The case of Marcus Garvey, the black Jamaican messianic figure, is instructive in terms of social vision and transformation under the aegis of British and other imperial hegemony. Any discussion of the juxtaposition of the biblical text and Caribbean political rhetoric in the post–World War II era cannot exclude Marcus Garvey, a major forerunner to post–World War II Caribbean politics.

Tony Martin argued that Garvey's political struggles in Jamaica were both a failure and a success as in the case of his North American activities.[13] Garvey failed insofar as he was thwarted in his bid to consolidate his party and move toward black majority rule, self-government, and West Indian federation. He also failed to realize his visionary black universal kingdom in Africa. However, he successfully demonstrated that political parties could work in Jamaica, and in the process indoctrinated and politicized the workers and peasants on a scale probably more massive than they had experienced before. The hundreds and thousands who followed Garvey and attended his meetings were well-represented among the rioters and strikers of the late 1930s. The leaders who emerged from these later struggles were more fortunate than Garvey; they built on foundations that he laid.[14] Alexander Bustamante and Norman Manley were able to reap the benefits of widespread challenges to British colonialism. Garvey, argued Martin, often cautioned his followers, at least publicly, to be "constitutional,"[15] but there is no telling what might have happened if he had been fortunate to walk into a ready-made situation of mass unrest, such as was the case in 1938. The post-Garvey upheaval was pan-Caribbean in nature and came at a time when British imperialism was about to be severely weakened as a result of World War II. Garvey could have used those events to his advantage. S. J. Garrick, a JLP (Jamaica Labor Party) organizer, was correct when he observed in 1941 that "if there wasn't a UNIA (United Negro Improvement Association) there could be no People's National Party or (PNP)."[16]

From 1935–45 there was an increase in the number of political parties throughout the Caribbean. These followed riots for higher wages and better living conditions in St. Kitts, St. Vincent, Trinidad, Barbados, Guyana, and Jamaica. Labor unions grew out of these troubles, and some of their leaders were able to transform the labor organizations they controlled into political parties. Such leaders included: Robert Bradshaw (St. Kitts), Vere Bird (Antigua), Grantley Adams (Barbados), Grenadian-born Uriah Buzz Butler (Trinidad and Tobago), Alexander Bustamante and Norman Manley (Jamaica). Proletarian consciousness, on the rise in the Caribbean from the 1930s, continued to rise in the post–World War II period and affected the process of decolonization as well as Caribbean biblical interpretation. On the rising tide of Caribbean popular expectation it was easy to see the God of Israel and Jesus Christ as the God of the oppressed. Garvey was not negligent in making a contribution in this regard. He cleared the way for many Caribbean politicians who followed him. As the Biblical idiom goes, he had "to decrease" so they "could increase" in strength and popularity.[17] Garvey certainly appreciated the relevance of the biblical text to its social world and the Caribbean; he brought the text into dialogue with the black diaspora experience.

Rastafari, which builds its ideology on aspects of Garveyism, uses an apocalyptic biblical subtext which, according to Theophus H. Smith, focuses on the biblical books of the Psalms, the Prophets, and Revelation.[18] The Babylonian Captivity or Exile is also eminent in Rastafarian religious thought.[19] Repatriation, an essential requirement for black redemption in Garvey's teaching, is dominant in Rastafarian ideology. Garvey made the concepts of exile, black redemption, restoration, and black Zionism central unifying themes in his Caribbean political religious vision. His successors built on the foundations he laid by extending his basic ideas to Caribbean people as a whole. Michael Manley, the late prime minister of Jamaica, sought to apply a unified view of history by juxtaposing the biblical text with the struggle for creating a just, participatory, and self-sustaining Jamaican society. In order to do so, Jamaican society had to be remapped; the country needed to experience the wind of change.

Text and the Politics of Change: Manley, Williams, and Scripture

The Spirit of change, an integral category of Michael Manley's political philosophy and rhetoric, is described and outlined in his work, *The Politics of Change*.[20] In the Old Testament, Joshua, the successor of Moses, led the children of Israel across the Jordan River into the Promised Land of Canaan. Manley, grandson of an English clergyman and scion of Norman Manley, veteran Jamaican politician, used the biblical figure of Joshua as his persona. Manley often assumed the persona of Joshua at public political rallies in ways that held his audience spellbound. He frequently used a rod, a symbol of the rod of Moses, to stir up his audience in the course of political oration, another display of the juxtaposition of biblical thought and Caribbean political rhetoric. The rod used by Manley on such occasions was given to his father by the Emperor Haile Selassie of Ethiopia. To the Rastafarians of Jamaica, Haile Selassie was a direct descendant of the Davidic-Solomonic dynasty and divine; Haile Selassie (Power or Might of the Trinity) was also King of Kings, Lord of Lords, Conquering Lion of the Tribe of Judah, Elect of God, Light of the Universe. As Emperor of Ethiopia, Haile Selassie was a symbol of that which the Western European nations were not able to defeat and colonize. He represented the ultimate reversal of Africa's colonization and thus the ultimate black liberator and messiah, anointed by the Lord to defeat Ethiopia's and Africa's enemies.

By extension, Manley's use of the rod given by Haile Selassie to his father recalled Yahweh giving Moses a rod as he is sent to Egypt to deliver the children of Israel from Egyptian slavery. Rastas believe this same rod was given to Joshua after he succeeded. Manley's use of the rod as part of his political rhetoric therefore cast him in a Mosaic and Joshua role. He was clearly drawing on the Exodus paradigm and relating it to his political discourse. Biblical imagery thus undergirded Michael Manley's political rhetoric. Such rhetoric, in deeply religious Jamaica, had tremendous efficacy in directing Jamaican historical and eschatological consciousness toward an emancipatory destiny. Indeed, the politics of change was liberating and emancipating as it generated a nonstatic, "unitive" understanding of faith. The subtitle for the treatise of his political philosophy is scriptural: *A Jamaican Testament*. For Manley, the politics of change was also a politics of promise. It was appropriate that he, Manley, be Joshua, invoking the powers of the rod of Moses. Would that Pharaoh would recognize the signs and miracles that Moses performed with his rod and let the children of Jamaica/Israel go. In biblical terms, Exodus implied the movement of Jamaican society from a so-called Egyptian slavery, or Babylonian captivity, into the Promised Land, led by Manley, as Moses and Joshua led the children of Israel out of Egypt into the Land of Promise. A new day had dawned in Jamaica's history.

According to Manley, in the early post-colonial phase of a developing country, only political movements devoted to the politics of change have relevance.[21] The politics of tinkering with the status quo, argued Manley, is inadequate to the Jamaican situation because an analysis of the legacies of colonialism suggests a degree of social debilitation and economic and social malformations so grave as to make that variant of politics irrelevant.[22] It was necessary to bring an end to the existing world. What then did Manley propose? His response was that "nothing less than transformation can provide answers to the dilemmas within which we are currently trapped."[23] The role that Manley perceived religion playing in terms of social transformation, particularly the Church in Jamaica, indicates the correlation between the biblical text and the politics of change in Manley's political rhetoric. By bringing biblical faith into radical dialectic discourse with Jamaica's post–World War II, Cold War-era problems, Manley was able to generate an understanding of Christian ideology as dynamic, socially and historically transforming. Biblical faith thus has potential or strategies for change. There

are foundations in Christian faith upon which to make a valid contribution
to social reconstruction.[24]

Knowledge of Jamaican society and religious history discloses the rhetorical strategies involved in Manley's discourse as he refers to Jamaica's religious
ethos and appeals to the Jamaican Baptist tradition. Among other things,
Manley, like Marcus Garvey before him, was actually reaching out to a significant religious-political constituency in Jamaica that had been traditionally disenfranchised but had struggled for effective integration and
participation in Jamaican society. In other words, Manley was invoking the
history that the Baptist tradition in particular had made in relating biblical
faith to social transformation in Jamaica. In reality, he was attempting to
promote his political agenda through recollection of the way in which several Jamaican national heroes, who were Baptist deacons, translated their
biblically based faith into historical transformation on behalf of oppressed,
marginalized, and landless Jamaicans. If the Church had played a part in ef-
fecting change in Jamaica in the past, it could do so in the present.

To Manley, the Church should "play a crucial role in the development of
a country like Jamaica."[25] Jamaicans are a church-going people, brought up
in a strong "God-fearing" tradition and deep instinctive respect for the
clergy. Traditionally, this respect has been limited to spiritual guidance, very
often to the exclusion of temporal concern on the part of the clergy. Nevertheless, some Christian denominations, notably the Baptist, have a strong
activist tradition. The Baptist Church, argued Manley, played a tremendous
part in the development of the early land settlement schemes that followed
the abolition of slavery and was constantly in the forefront in the battle for
land reform.[26] The Jamaican national hero, Sam Sharpe, a Baptist deacon,
paid the ultimate price with his life in this fight in the early 1830s, and Paul
Bogle, another Baptist deacon, was hanged for his leadership in the abortive
revolution of 1865; his cause was land reform. Jamaican national heroes, like
Sharpe, George William Gordon, and Bogle had a unified view of history in
which the sacred and secular realms of life were not separated. As national
heroes or messiahs they have been placed at the center of Jamaican history
because they create Jamaican history. Their biblical archetypes are Moses and
Jesus Christ; the former led the children of Israel from out of Egyptian slavery and the latter announced the arrival of Yahweh's regime in history and
the dawn of a new future of freedom for all people. Paul, the Apostle to the
Gentiles, consequently declared, "There is neither slave nor free, there is neither male nor female; for you are all one in Christ Jesus" (Gal. 3: 28).

Manley's observation, with respect to the demarcation in the spheres of
power between Church and State, that all Churches "have been firmly united
in the view that the State must never interfere with, or dictate to, the men of
God and have often proved willing to concede a reciprocal separation,"[27] sets

up a scenario for noting a paradigm shift in understanding the relationship
between faith and history in the post–World War II Caribbean. Since independence this tendency has been reversed substantially and now, in Jamaica
and throughout the Caribbean, a great new wave of concern has arisen
amongst the clergy that the Church should play an active part in the life of
the people in the various territories, particularly on behalf of those who suffer. Although there are still strong feelings about the need to keep the Church
out of party politics, a growing recognition exists, particularly among the
younger clergy, that Christian faith must be concerned with humankind's
condition on earth as an aspect of divine purpose including the metaphysical
questions of the afterlife.

Here, Manley, the Jamaican Joshua who carries Moses' rod, brings the
biblical context into dialectic tension with Jamaican and Caribbean realities
within his rhetorical framework. "Clearly," he argues, "increasing inspiration
is derived from the miracles of healing and the symbolism of the feeding of
the multitudes as examples of Christ's concern for the sufferers and the disinherited." Underlying Manley's thought is a unified view of history in
which the spiritual and the material, the sacred and the secular aspects of
human existence are not disjointed but integrated. In other words, following Christ, according to Manley, is a commission to making people truly
human. In a situation where there is the tendency of the politics of freedom
to create division, and in a country where the clergy is influential, where
every politician is to some extent compromised by party affiliation, the
clergy person is the one individual who transcends politics nationally and
within each community, she/he can teach the lesson of national unity and
cooperation. One can safely assume that the Church accepts racial equality
and justice as the social expressions of the fatherhood of God. Manley's
rhetoric unambiguously expresses his option for a unified view of history,
one that merges the biblical horizon with the decolonization process. He
said, "One must also assume that they accept Christ's ministry as embracing
temporal concern."[28]

Michael Manley's politics of change shows that it was influenced significantly by a type of biblical humanism modeled on the Judeo-Christian
Scriptures. He saw this humanism as originating from such notions as the
Fatherhood of God and the ministry of Jesus Christ. Manley's identification
with biblical figures/icons such as Moses, Joshua, and the Seer of Patmos,
who bade the faithful to "stand firm" in the face of overwhelming persecution by the empire, also is clear. Manley's dependence on biblical humanism
gave him an openness to the future and the capacity not to be overcome by
despair and disappointments when he encountered frustrations and political
change of fortunes. Manley struggled to bring biblical faith, with its notion
of social justice and equality or egalitarianism, into dialectic discourse with

the existential situation of Jamaica. Like the prophets and Jesus before him, he discovered that, as valid as his ideas were, transforming societies such as Jamaica is by no means easy. Whereas many poor blue-collar workers supported Manley, dealing with the traditional beneficiaries of the Jamaican status quo was a completely different matter. Manley, on the basis of a unified view of history, was implicitly attempting to secularize theology or incarnate the Judeo-Christian text as a praxis of social transformation in post–World War II Jamaica. He was to learn that people's political consciousness is not easily transformed, and that there is always great resistance to the secularization of the biblical text, especially on the part of those who stand to lose the most from the process. Jamaicans are not unique in this regard, although in Jamaica the process involved considerable conflict; it was marked by considerable violence and a national cry for peace. At the grassroots level in Jamaica, the argument was made that where there is no shedding of blood there is no atonement for sin. The process of including the marginalized in the rhetoric of change is traceable throughout the Caribbean in the post–World War II era. Although Trinidad and Tobago is a more pluralistic society than Jamaica, the process or the politics of inclusion was also manifested there in the period under discussion. Eric Williams of Trinidad and Tobago also used a unified view of history when he declared the eclipse of the master/slave era in Trinidad and Tobago, as I noted above.

Text, Rhetoric, and Caribbean Future: What Shall it Profit a Country?

Eric Williams, like Michael Manley, was committed to a politics of change in the post–World War II Caribbean. Trinidad and Tobago, like Jamaica, became independent in 1962 under the leadership of Eric Williams. Williams was very aware of the plural nature of Trinidadian society and the dominant American presence in the region. Independence therefore had to forge a national identity, "out of many one," (Trinidad Motto and Court of Arms) forged by the love of liberty. Nationalism warrants a unified view of history, a sense of national identity, and that a state be internally self-defining. William's rhetoric of decolonization was shaped by these factors. He forged his People's National Movement (PNM) from a coalition of Afro-Trinidadians, Christian, Hindu, and Muslim Indo-Trinidadians, and remnants of the Portuguese, French, and English groups.[29] The People's National Movement dominated Trinidadian politics from 1956 to 1987,[30] at a time when the Caribbean was perceived as the American Mediterranean.[31]

What were the prospects for the future of Caribbean nationalism and real independence in the face of American hegemony in the post–World War II era? The Caribbean states faced a dilemma like that of biblical Israel; can they establish independent and sovereign existence in a world dominated by superpowers? Israel's experience was shaped significantly by its constant struggle for self-determination in the face of Babylonian, Assyrian, Egyptian, Greek, and Roman domination. Biblical materials are filled with the hopes and fears of a small nation struggling to maintain its Exodus culture of freedom in the face of threats posed by surrounding superpowers. The prophetic vision of peace and social justice is conditioned by its experience of a fragmented nationalism. The historical-communal-eschatological vision, a unified view of history that marks the Judeo-Christian Scriptures, reflects Israel's desire for national integrity and health within the family of nations. This same desire is resonated in secular terms in Eric Williams's rhetoric.[32]

At the end of the 1960s, Williams raised the question of the future of the Caribbean. He summed up his discussion of the issue by portraying the contemporary Caribbean as an area characterized by instability; economic, psychological, cultural, in some cases political dependence; large-scale unemployment; economic uncertainty; unresolved racial tensions; potential religious conflicts; the restlessness of the youth; and an all-pervading fear of the United States. Within the framework of his description, Williams asked, "What, then, is the future of the Caribbean?"[33] In language recalling Israel's frustrated national experience, Williams argued that given its past history, the future of the Caribbean could only be meaningfully discussed in terms of the possibilities for the emergence of an identity for the region and its peoples. The whole history of the Caribbean so far can be viewed as a conspiracy to block the emergence of a Caribbean identity—in politics, in institutions, in economics, in culture, and in values. Viewed in historical perspective, the way forward for the peoples of the Caribbean must be one that would impel them to start making their own history, to be the subjects rather than the objects of history, to stop being the playthings of other people.[34]

Despite his realism, Williams, reading the *signs of the times*[35] in the Caribbean, was optimistic concerning the region's future. In its quest for identity and self-realization, the Caribbean in 1969 showed certain favorable conditions—young populations and the idealism of youth, relatively high rates of literacy and education, relatively high levels of per capita income, and a long history of contact with the Western world—a condition not of the entire Caribbean. Williams saw a new global consciousness or sense of community and humanity emerging. In his thought, the goal of history is an eschatological recovery of global community; a corollary of a unitive view of history. This, indeed, is intrinsic to the Pauline vision (Gal. 3:26–28). An historical interpretation of Gal. 3:26–28 from within the Caribbean context must take into consideration the struggle for integration of Caribbean society. It is a political process in which those who are marginalized in

Caribbean society are brought into the corporate and collective life of Caribbean community. This is the process in which those "beyond the boundary" are included as meaningful partners and players in Caribbean life.[36] In the final analysis, however, a radical dialogue between the biblical text and Caribbean decolonization rhetoric recommends that the new paradigm for Biblical studies and education be cross-cultural and international.

Economic and social transformation, and the achievement of a national identity are imperatives that confront contemporary Caribbean reality. However, for Williams, national identity cannot be sacrificed for anything else. The Puerto Rican path seems to Williams to have had certain economic gains as the cost of national identity and independence. Williams juxtaposed the Puerto Rican case with biblical idiom and the rhetoric of change when he asked: "What shall it profit a country if it gains the whole world and loses its own soul?"[37] (Matt. 16: 25–26; 4:1–11; Mark 1:12–13; Luke 4:1–13). The conclusion is Caribbean states must resist the temptation to sacrifice national identities for economic gains through uncritical allegiance to superpowers. Remembering the vulnerability of the small states and the fragmented nature of the Caribbean condition, Williams advocated the strategies of regional community, integration, harmonization, unity, and functional collaboration to empower the region to deal with extraregional threats to subvert its autonomy.[38] To this end, he shared the vision of Theophilus Albert Marryshow of Grenada, "the Father of West Indian Federation," whose work on behalf of Caribbean integration is well-known.

For Williams, Commonwealth Caribbean countries must become aware that the goals of greater economic independence and the development of a cultural identity will involve them in even closer ties with one another at economic and other levels. With a somewhat utopian idea, Williams envisioned a reign of peace in the Caribbean when true integration among all the units of the Caribbean and all the vestiges of political, economic, cultural, and psychological dependence, and racism were removed from the Caribbean; only then would the Caribbean take its true place in Latin America and the New World and put an end to the international wars and interregional squabbles that, from Columbus to Castro, have marked Caribbean history.

Marcus Garvey, Michael Manley, and Eric Williams were prophets of freedom in the Caribbean who struggled to incarnate liberation in the Caribbean and the world. They challenge one to read the Bible and the newspaper together. Their struggle for human rights in the Caribbean in the post–World War II era unified our biblical liberative hermeneutics, the politics of change, and the process of decolonization. The merger of biblical text and political rhetoric has created a sense of the underlying unity of history, solidarity, and integral liberation. Garvey, Manley, and Williams thus made significant contributions to a transforming biblical faith for post–World War II Caribbean people. The remaining sections of this chapter show how a younger generation of Caribbean politicians have continued in the footsteps trod by those "who have come up from the abyss of slavery"[39] and indenture to national leadership. I will show that whereas Maurice Bishop, as a change agent, did not fully or explicitly embrace a unified view of history, Jean-Bertrand Aristide (Haiti) is a classic example of one who did.

The Text in a Revolutionary Context: Gairy, Bishop, Aristide, and the Bible

The Grenada revolution (1979–83) occurred at the height of the Cold War. It coincided with the end of the Manley regime in Jamaica and the last days of Eric Williams at the political helm in Trinidad and Tobago. In many ways, the Grenada revolution was a configuration of the various aspects of the Caribbean struggle for emancipation and authenticity. It brought into sharp focus several concerns that the older Caribbean leadership had over the possibilities for regional autonomy. The rise and fall of the revolution therefore had a tremendous impact on the future of the regional integration movement. The revolution had brought an end to the dictatorial and abusive regime of Eric Gairy, a shepherd-King gone bad.[40] Gairy, himself a classic example of a Caribbean politician able to juxtapose biblical texts and religion with political rhetoric and showmanship, increased his domestic abuse as he increased his infamous reputation internationally. Gairy was a tragic figure in the sense that he corrupted and abused the political system in Grenada but was unable to exit the political scene in the rising tide of discontent and youthful restlessness that was sweeping the Caribbean and much of the world in the aftermath of the 1960s. In many ways, Gairyism facilitated the rise of the New Jewel Movement (NJM), led by Maurice Bishop, and the Grenada revolution. The Gairy regime had become dictatorial, and its human rights record a great embarrassment to Caribbean people. Due to Gairy's oppressive history, the Grenada revolution burst onto the historical stage with enormous popular support in the region. Several factors, within and without, contributed to the revolution's demise. Among these were the revolution's adoption of the Cuban model and close association with the Castro regime; these limited the extent and the way in which the revolution juxtaposed the biblical text with the their rhetoric of change. In biblical terms, frequently on the lips of the average Caribbean citizen, the revolution ignored the saying that humankind "shall not live by bread alone but by every word that proceeds out of the mouth of God" (Deut. 8:3; Matt. 4:4; Luke 4:4).

In the Judeo-Christian tradition the Bible was fundamentally seen as mediating life in all its dimensions. Life should by no means be reduced to specific theoretical reductionism. The Deuteronomic historian makes this point in his tradition (Deut. 8:3); the Evangelists Matthew and Luke deal with the issue in Jesus' temptation (Matt. 4:4; Luke 4:4); and John's Gospel also deals with the issue in its declaration that Christ's coming was to bring life in all its fullness (John 3:16). Dialectically, it is difficult to conceive of Caribbean people who, like their Hebrew counterparts, have had to rise from the crucible of slavery, thinking of life in reductionist terms. Just look at their annual Carnival celebrations! In other words, Bishop's regime, in its excessive reliance on the Cuban model, arrogantly breached a basic tenet of Caribbean folk wisdom by not adopting a unitive view of history. His vision for change sounded too secular in its orientation. One cannot afford to be naive here. The question is, what was the revolution's ideological position with respect to religion, the Church, and the clergy? What role did the revolution have for dialogue in the democratic process?

The Cuban model, despite the high admiration in which it is held throughout the Caribbean and Latin America but its limited success in surmounting pervasive Caribbean problems in the areas of public health, unemployment, illiteracy, and inequitable resource and wealth distribution, was not attractive to all Caribbean governments and people.[41] It is difficult to imagine the Anglophone Caribbean, with its Westminster parliamentary democratic culture, opting for a Cuban totalitarian model. On March 13, 1979, Bishop, in his first radio address to the people of Grenada, Carriacou, and Petit Martinique, declared that the revolution was for work, food, decent housing, and health services, and a bright future for "our children and grand-children."[42] Church-State relations must be considered one of the areas in which the Grenada revolution contributed to its own death. Most of the leadership of the people's revolutionary government, including Bishop, were sons and daughters of the Church. Bishop was a product of the Roman Catholic Church, the largest Christian denomination in Grenada. Other leaders of the revolution were Protestant lay preachers. Bishop ended his first address with the cry: "Long live the People of Grenada! Long live Freedom and Democracy! Let us Together Build A Just Grenada!"[43] The revolution helped to center Grenadians in their own history. The desire to create a just society, a cardinal biblical prophetic principle, is clearly stated in Bishop's call to Grenadians to create a new society (Mic. 6: 8). The difference lies in the fact that the commitment to build "a just Grenada" was not set within a religious but a secular framework. From the present historical vantage it seems that in the pursuit of freedom, the central Western value, religious and secular, good and evil coexist. Grenada, like the rest of the Caribbean, is deeply religious. God is invoked in both the national motto and anthem of Grenada, but the secular model of liberation had inherent problems.

In 1980, religious and secular freedom were already in conflict in revolutionary Grenada. In a national broadcast over Radio Free Grenada on February 15, 1980, Bishop gave "a permanent, standing commitment to freedom of worship and religion" under his regime. This commitment later underwent serious questioning especially when certain sections of the Grenadian Christian community were seen as counterrevolutionary, a perception that led to the relationship becoming antagonistic. The conflict stemmed from the regime's perception, allegedly derived from a letter someone wrote titled "Dear Jonathan," which intimated that the Church in Grenada was to be used as a base by members of the Dominican Order of the Roman Catholic Church to subvert the revolutionary process in Grenada. In responding to the claims of the mysterious letter, Bishop redefined the government's understanding of the role of the Church and the State in revolutionary Grenada. In his response Bishop juxtaposed the biblical text with his Marxist revolutionary rhetoric.

Bishop's position was that the Church and the State had two separate roles to perform.[44] According to Bishop "Grenadians look to their church for spiritual guidance and to their Government for political leadership."[45] The Bishop regime believed this separation of Church and State to be correct.[46] In a rather simplistic fashion, Bishop defined his government's position on Church-State relations by appropriating the biblical text "Render to Caesar the things which are Caesar's and to God the things which are of God's." (Matt. 22:15–22 KJV) The text, argued Bishop, represents a correct belief that the functions of the Church and of the State are and should be different.[47] Bishop's exegesis of Matt. 22:15–22 (cf. Rom. 13:1–7) ultimately proved fateful. In simple terms, the late prime minister's exegesis of Matt. 22:15–22 helped to strengthen the growing perception that the Bishop regime was godless. This definition of Church-State relations and perception of the Bishop regime alienated many religious Grenadians from a popular revolution with which they had previously identified. On the one hand, Bishop might have been reacting to pressures from certain Leninists in his administration who perhaps did not care to understand their own Grenadian culture deeply. On the other hand, their ideological absolutism or "Puritanism," which Bishop himself was apparently trying to modulate, in the end led to the destruction of the "new dawn of freedom" in Grenada. In the process, Bishop and a host of other Grenadians lost their lives in a tragic "holocaust" that reminds one of Good Friday.

Had Bishop adopted, or been able to adopt, an integral view of salvation, one that does not bifurcate spiritual and material existence, the Grenada revolution might have had a different end. The Bishop regime was very fearful of attempts to subvert the Grenada revolution. Such fears even led to the regime confiscating a shipment of Jerusalem Bibles. In the post-revolutionary era, the Bible has become a significant text for some of the former leaders of the revolution. Who is to say that some of the most creative biblical interpretations in the Caribbean might come from those who look at Scriptures from a post-revolutionary perspective? However one evaluates Maurice Bishop and the Grenada revolution, it must never be forgotten that Bishop's political career—the New Jewel Movement (NJM), which he led, and the Grenada revolution—were catapulted into existence as a result of gross human rights violation in Grenada which Bishop tried to heal. This is an appropriate point at which to turn to Jean-Bertrand Aristide and Haiti.

The Bible and Liberty for the Deprived

Jean-Bertrand Aristide emerged on the Haitian political scene with a rich post–World War II Caribbean political tradition to guide him; the political careers of all those discussed so far in this study, Bishop included, were available to him. Haiti's Aristide is comparable to Grenada's Bishop. Duvalier was to Haiti what Gairy was to Grenada. Aristide had to take Haiti beyond Duvalierism, as Bishop had to take Grenada beyond Gairyism. Aristide and Bishop rose to political prominence on the tide of mass proletarian support. However, whereas Aristide explicitly operated with a holistic view of history, Bishop did not. When one looks at post–World War II Caribbean politics in its entirety, it can be argued that Aristide's rhetoric offered a corrective supplement to Bishop's in terms of a holistic view of history, one in which the sacred and secular are not separate. This offers integral salvation in which the spiritual and material aspects of humankind are fulfilled. No post–World War II Caribbean politician so intentionally and explicitly brought the biblical text into dialogue with the contemporary struggle for freedom and social justice in the Caribbean as Jean-Bertrand Aristide. Aristide's training and ministry as a Salesian priest, and the deep religiosity of the Haitian peasantry, empowered him to integrate the biblical text in his political rhetoric.[48] Aristide made his biblical knowledge a practical force in transforming Haitian society.

In his *Aristide: An Autobiography,* Aristide states the central thesis that underlines his juxtaposition of the biblical text and political rhetoric in post–World War II Haiti and the Caribbean. According to Aristide, "The Bible, more than ever a message of liberation, proclaimed liberty for those who are deprived of it."[49] Aristide's liberationist biblical hermeneutic, the source of his "unitive" view of history, correlates with his praxis of Haitian liberation. Furthermore, his recognition that "the human being is, at one and the same time, unique and plural" permitted him to relate the Haitian struggle for democracy to the Caribbean community and the world. Aristide recognized that a "unitive" view of history carries with it the liberation of all humankind and the cosmos. Garvey, Manley, and Williams, like Saint Paul, recognized this truth (Rom. 8:22; Gal. 3:26–28). Aristide took his biblically based political rhetoric beyond Haiti to the Caribbean and world community. Haiti, the Caribbean, and the world had to note that "a prophet was in their midst" (2 Kings 5: 8; Luke 7:16–17; John 4: 44). The prophetic presence among the people served to mediate the mind of the Divine to the people. It was a force to direct the people toward the future; to transcend the limits of the present. What was significant about Aristide is that he grounded his politics in the religion and culture of Haiti. Two biblically derived images Aristide would have accepted for himself are those of priest-president and prophet-president.[50] "I am priest and president," he declared. "But I remain what I have always been . . . : I am a militant in the midst of a people who want to merge from the shadows."[51] In words that define his self-understanding, perhaps his understanding of Israel, Haiti, and the Caribbean, Aristide argued that "anyone who assumes his or her responsibilities, who is not afraid to say what he or she sees, can be regarded as a prophet, or, better, as the spokesperson of a prophetic community." As a priest, he understood himself as a bridge, leading his people from out of the past into the future. As spokesperson for a prophetic community, Aristide saw himself as the one to articulate the collective consciousness of the Haitian people; the consciousness of a new Haitian people. In keeping with his self-understanding, Aristide recovered and reinterpreted the Mosaic covenant for the Haiti of his day. Like Moses, Aristide enunciated "The Ten Commandments of Democracy in Haiti" to the United Nations General Assembly on September 25, 1991:

The first commandment: liberty or death.

The second commandment: democracy or death.

The third commandment: fidelity to human rights.

The fourth commandment: the right to eat and to work.

The fifth commandment: the right to demand what rightfully belongs to us.

The sixth commandment: legitimate defense of the diaspora, or tenth department.

The seventh commandment: no to violence, yes to *Lavalas*.

The eight commandment: fidelity to the human being, the highest form of wealth.

The ninth commandment: fidelity to our culture.

The tenth commandment: everyone around the same table.[52]

Aristide thus sought to retell the Haitian story through the recovery and application of a biblical praxis of liberation to the oppressed in Haitian society and the world. The tenth commandment of democracy, with its egalitarian, communal-historical-eschatological vision of "everyone around the same table," was a fusion of Christ's eucharistic table fellowship and a vision of the Haitian community.[53] Aristide's vision stemmed from the fact that he saw his political praxis as an extension of his prophetic ministry in faithful obedience to the will of God. In this respect, he is unique amongst the Caribbean politicians considered in this study.[54] He is the type of clergy person that Michael Manley saw emerging in the post–World War II Caribbean who incarnated a biblically based praxis of freedom leading to human transformation. He is also the type of "subversive" prophetic clergy the Grenada revolution feared. He might be the type of consummate revolutionary admired by the late C. L. R. James. Time will tell whether Aristide prefigured the future Caribbean politician who will operate, in the ambiguities of a post–Cold War era and the dawning Third Millennium, with a unitive view of history that empowers her/his people with hope, faith, love, and freedom to create their own future.

Conclusion

The liberating vision each political figure in this study articulated was generated from deep encounter with the hurts and frustrations of Caribbean existence in the post–World War II era. To a large extent, each one ought to be judged according to how he struggled to lead the Caribbean beyond the problems inherited from the legacy of slavery and colonialism to an enhanced experience of Caribbean space and humanity as free. From the depth of the encounter, Manley, Williams, Bishop, and Aristide glimpsed a transcendent unifying reality underlying and directing Caribbean and all human life toward freedom and fulfillment. The more they saw that reality, and the basic interconnectedness of all that is, the more it gave them inspired utterance to incarnate and announce a dispensation of freedom, change, and hope for their people. In such epiphanic moments biblical vocabulary burst into their speech abolishing the distinction between sacred and profane freedom, thought and action, text and context. In the struggle between the forces of slavery and freedom, some saw the cross of Christ as an historical necessity more immanently than others.

This chapter has shown important connections between the biblical text and the Caribbean context. First, it has underscored the relevance of the Bible to Caribbean history; the moral vision of the Bible makes much sense within the context of Caribbean history. From the turn of the fifteenth century to the present, Caribbean people have struggled to become the subjects of their own history. Their struggle has been fundamentally for justice and human rights. This struggle has made the Bible a valid text and a rich source of metaphors, images, and symbols for interpreting Caribbean history and articulating the vision of an alternative Caribbean future. Consequently, biblical terms such as Exodus, Pharaoh, Wilderness, Promised Land, Babylon, and others have had, and continue to have, deep resonances in Caribbean historical consciousness and search for authentic cultural identity. This chapter has shown how those connections are made in the public space of Caribbean society by outstanding political figures committed to the liberation of their people. Some, like Maurice Bishop, paid the ultimate sacrifice for their commitment to the humanization of their people; their cause and death, where applicable, was the birth and maintenance of their people or nation. It must be borne in mind that their service was to the entire Caribbean despite their island frame of reference. Caribbean people, in spite of their well-known tendency to insularity, have deep layers of psychic connection and cultural continuity, which can manifest itself in sport and in tragedy.

Secondly, the chapter indicates a sense of time and history in the Caribbean that is very similar to the biblical notions of salvation history and sacred time. As Caribbean politicians represent and articulate the voice and aspirations of their people, they announce the new; they witness to the power of resurrection faith in the face of crucifixion, death, and humiliation. It is true to say that Caribbean existence is a historical manifestation of the New Testament definition of a crucified-risen existence. Some would argue that Good Friday, which commemorates the crucifixion and death of Jesus of Nazareth, is the most solemn day observed annually in the Caribbean. One wonders whether, from a legal point of view, Good Friday resonates with the unjust humiliation that Caribbean people have had to endure throughout the course of their history. A real example of this might well have been the day when Maurice Bishop was rescued from house arrest by hundreds of daring Grenadian schoolchildren and others, carried in a triumphal motorcade to St. George's marketplace, only later to be brutally slaughtered with countless others by former friends and colleagues. Moments before his own murder, Bishop, seeing the Fort Rupert massacre of hundreds of Grenadians, declared, "Oh God, they have turned the guns on the people!"[55] Was the Fort Rupert massacre not a reversal of authentic post–World War II Caribbean politics, which, as indicated by Bishop, was a politics of resurrection, the politics of further raising up a historically crucified people for freedom and life in all its fullness? Or had violence penetrated Caribbean politics in an irreparable way? In some of the final words of Bishop, one needs to hear the words of Jesus of Nazareth to Simon Peter: "Put up your sword. All who take the sword die by the sword" (Matt. 26: 52; Luke 22: 51;

Mark 14: 47). To hear is to commit oneself to peace in the Caribbean and the world. The Bible is a text of transcendence; it is the movement of history into a new horizon of existence.

Thirdly, it must be considered that Caribbean politics, seen from the perspective of this chapter, must be considered in various ways as secularization of the Bible. This process of secularization is the struggle to bring the Kingdom of God on earth as it is in heaven. The immanence of the Kingdom of God in Caribbean history of necessity comes into conflict with the prevailing ordering of various Caribbean societies. Contrary to the way in which it is often perceived, secularization involves self-emptying. It can be conceived as the process whereby the sacred enters into the profane to transfigure it. Jesus of Nazareth had a similar concern. Politically he was committed to the renewal of Israel. His crucifixion and resurrection tell how he assimilated his people's past and transformed it through his ministry and death toward their future. The history of Jesus of Nazareth, like that of so many Caribbean politicians, was forged on the anvil of their love of liberty. The Bible, translated into the Caribbean and other contexts, does precisely this. As Jesus, not Caesar, became a hero for many of his own people, so also did Manley, Williams, Aristide, and Bishop. Paradoxically, the fate the empires planned for the Caribbean at the end of World War II did not materialize. On the contrary, post–World War II Caribbean politicians like those discussed integrated biblical language with their decolonization political rhetoric to generate new "songs of freedom" with the capacity to unite all humankind. Caribbean politicians have shown the deep political nature of the biblical text.

Notes

1. Orlando Patterson, *Freedom*, vol. 1, *Freedom in the Making of Western Culture* (New York: Basic Books, 1991), ix.
2. See Bruce Chilton and Jacob Neusner, *Trading Places: The Intersecting Histories of Judaism and Christianity* (Cleveland, OH: Pilgrim Press, 1996).
3. See Gordon K. Lewis, *Main Currents in Caribbean Thought: The Historical Evolution of Caribbean Society in Its Ideological Aspects, 1492–1900* (Baltimore & London: Johns Hopkins University Press, 1987). According to Lewis the three major constitutive elements in the evolution of Caribbean society and culture have really been: (1) The growth of colonialism. (2) The initiation and expansion of the slave and slavery systems. (3) A distinctive creole culture and creole institutions based on race and class (Lewis, 10).
4. A very useful text on this subject in general is Lawrence James, *The Rise and Fall of the British Empire* (New York: St. Martin's Press, 1994). See, for example, 542ff.

5. Gordon K. Lewis, "The Challenge of Independence in the British Caribbean," in *Caribbean Freedom: Economy and Society from Emancipation to the Present*, ed. Hilary Beckles and Verene Shepherd (Princeton: Markus Wiener, 1996), 511, also 511–27.

6. Ibid.

7. The literary output of Vidia S. Naipaul could be read as an indictment of the West Indies in this respect.

8. See Eric Williams, "Massa Day Done," public lecture delivered at Woodford Square, March 22, 1961, in *Forged from the Love of Liberty: Selected Speeches of Dr. Eric Williams,* comp. Paul K. Sutton, (Trinidad: Longman, Caribbean, 1981), 210–16.

9. No less a person than the late Caribbean philosopher and writer C. L. R. James recognized the radical nature of John's vision.

10. Jesus' Sermon on the Mount, including the Beatitudes, contain profound exegetical potential with respect to the Caribbean context. The Beatitudes announce a new day for those who follow Jesus and structure discipleship in context.

11. For an interesting study on the subject, see Ronald Segal, *The Black Diaspora: Five Centuries of the Black Experience Outside of Africa* (New York: Farrar, Strauss and Giroux, 1995).

12. For a Garveyite paradigm, see Tony Martin, "Marcus Garvey, the Caribbean, and the Struggles for Black Jamaican Nationhood," in Beckles and Shepherd, 359–69. This essay is relevant to this study.

13. Martin, 368.

14. Consider Paul and Jesus. Was Paul able to build on the foundations of Jesus of Nazareth? To what extent did Jesus of Nazareth build on "those of old"? The point is that Garvey, according to Martin's historical evaluation, is a transition point in Caribbean historical and political evolution. Garvey is also relevant to African-American history, and the history of the British Empire, that is, its rise and fall. Garvey points to the emergence of a new person on the historical stage: one who declares, "massa day done!" A continuum of emancipation is evident in Caribbean history when Garvey and his successors are taken into consideration.

15. British colonialism left a legal structure throughout the empire on which newly independent governments could build democracy. Many post–World War II Caribbean politicians were lawyers, as well as Gandhi (India) and Nelson Mandela (South Africa). Did Jesus of Nazareth speak one language to the public (multitudes) and another to his disciples (who knew the Kingdom's secrets)? France possibly left a revolutionary tradition in the Caribbean.

16. Martin.

17. See Franklin W. Knight, *Race, Ethnicity, and Class: Forging the Plural Society in Latin America and the Caribbean,* 17th Charles Edmondson Historical Lectures, Baylor University, Waco, Texas (March 27/28, 1995), 45.

18. Theophus H. Smith, *Conjuring Culture: Biblical Formations of Black America* (New York: Oxford University Press, 1994), 129–30.
19. Smith, 19.
20. See Michael Manley, *The Politics of Change: A Jamaican Testament*, rev. ed. (Washington, D.C.: Howard University Press, 1990).
21. Manley, 19.
22. Ibid.
23. Ibid., 23.
24. Ibid., 180.
25. Ibid., 178
26. Ibid.
27. Ibid., 179.
28. Ibid.
29. Knight, *Race, Ethnicity, and Class*, 45.
30. Franklin W. Knight, *The Caribbean: The Genesis of a Fragmented Nationalism*, 2nd ed. (New York: Oxford University Press, 1990), 303.
31. See Eric Williams, "American Capitalism and the Caribbean Economy," in Beckles and Shepherd, 342. Also Eric Williams, *From Columbus to Castro: The History of the Caribbean 1492–1969* (New York: Vintage Books, 1984), 408–42. Williams argued, in eschatological mode, that New World history represents a still unfinished process of the creation of autonomous, viable societies with equal opportunity for all—free from domination by Europe initially and now by the U.S. See Williams, *From Columbus to Castro*, 505. The question is also raised as to what is the prophetic task of Caribbean history.
32. For a useful compilation of Williams's speeches, see Sutton, comp., *Forged from the Love of Liberty.*
33. Williams, *From Columbus to Castro*, 503.
34. Ibid., 503–4.
35. Here I am using the biblical eschatological/apocalyptic category of the signs of the times. This category was used by the Synoptic Jesus in announcing the immanence of the Kingdom/Rule of God in history. Also Vatican II (1962–65). See Document on the Church in the Modern World (*Gaudium et Spes,* Joy and Hope). Roman Catholicism is significant in Trinidadian culture.
36. Discussion on this matter must include the thought of the late C. L. R. James, whose classic work on this matter is *Beyond a Boundary.* See C. L. R. James, *Beyond a Boundary* (Durham, NC: Duke University Press, 1993).
37. Williams, *From Columbus to Castro*, 511.
38. Ibid., 512–5.
39. Phrase borrowed from Orlando Patterson, see Patterson, 406. Indenture was not much better than slavery. The slaves/indentured servants had no voice of their own. They were socially "dead."
40. See Didachus Jules and Don Rojas, *Maurice Bishop: Selected Speeches 1979–1981* (Havana, Cuba: Casa De Las Americas, n.d.), 104.

41. On this issue, see Knight, *The Caribbean,* 324–5. See also Williams, *From Columbus to Castro,* 508–10.

42. See Jules and Rojas, 4.

43. Ibid., 5. Bishop is a son of Roman Catholicism in Grenada.

44. Ibid., 90.

45. Ibid.

46. These words are actually typed in bold in the published text of speech. Ibid., 90.

47. Ibid., 90. One is not sure how to interpret the variations in the use of upper-case letters in the spelling of church versus the consistent use of the upper-case letter when spelling State. Bishop's interpretation of Matt. 22:21 (Mark 12: 17; Luke 20: 25) is debatable, yet situational (perhaps a simple matter of quoting the text for legitimation).

48. On this, see Jean-Bertrand Aristide, with Christophe Wargny, *Aristide: An Autobiography,* trans. Linda M. Maloney (Maryknoll, NY: Orbis Books, 1993). The entire work is relevant, but see, for example, 23–41, 42–50. The place of religion in Haitian politics is traditional. The role of Voodoo in the Haitian revolution is a classic example.

49. Aristide, *Aristide: An Autobiography,* 51.

50. Ibid., 184; 120–1. Religion is intrinsic to Caribbean cultures. In addition, there is much orality in patterns of interaction in the Caribbean. Aristide's self-understanding resonates the role of the Chief as one who mediates the life of the community with that of the Spirit/spirits and the Ancestors in traditional African cosmology.

51. Ibid., 189–205.

52. Ibid. For a study on the question of the contemporary relevance of the Ten Commandments, see Walter J. Harrelson, *The Ten Commandments and Human Rights* (Macon, GA: Mercer University Press, 1997).

53. Franklin Knight claims that the Haitian revolution of the early nineteenth century resolved the racial situation in that state, by means of a constitution that declared all citizens to be black but divided the new state along racial lines. See Knight, *Race, Ethnicity, and Class,* 44–5. See also Michel-Rolph Trouillot, *Haiti State against Nation: The Origins and Legacy of Duvalierism* (New York: Monthly Review Press, 1990), 109–36.

54. Aristide, *Aristide: An Autobiography,* 120. See also selections of Aristide's sermons and messages in: Jean-Bertrand Aristide, *In the Parish of the Poor: Writings from Haiti,* trans. and ed. Amy Wilentz (Maryknoll, NY: Orbis Books, 1990), 71ff.

55. A dramatist, perhaps a Joseph Campbell, using the hero and the Christian year as paradigms, would have seen the procession of events in great tragic, yet dramatic terms, leading to a crucifixion.

Chapter 8

Recasting Identity in Ruth and Hindu Indo-Guyanese Women

Hemchand Gossai

Introduction

This chapter is an experiment in hermeneutics. It is invariably precarious when one seeks to bring together two vastly different and seemingly incongruent worlds, in this case, the Hebrew Bible and Hindu Indo-Guyanese women. Yet, I believe that this essay in part invites us to see beyond what is to what can be, in terms of the connection. As this new direction is being forged, I am cognizant that it is but a beginning; I hope it will be an impetus for other studies in the area.

A word about my background and situation in life will, I hope, lend an understanding of my point of departure. I was born and spent my formative and teenage years in Guyana. My parents, second and third generation children of East Indian immigrants, were Hindus, deeply rooted in the pervasive culture and traditions of Hinduism. As the youngest in the family, I could not fully discern the manner in which my sisters and daughters in immediate and extended family were treated early on. However, it became apparent later that the role of the Hindu woman was, for the most part, defined by the men in her life—father, husband, son. In this regard, Indo-Guyanese women share with ancient Hebrew women the experience of being always owned by or under the care of a man, as is seen in the biblical materials. As I undertake this study, I attempt to focus principally on Hindu Indo-Guyanese women and by so doing attempt to lift them out of the shadows that patriarchy has cast over them. Clearly, all women in Guyana do not have similar, let alone uniform experiences. I understand that at best my perspective will reflect a partial experience. Yet, the experiences that I shall discuss are more than merely tangential.

I am employing a kind of typological approach, which seeks to align the reality of Hindu Indo-Guyanese women with the reality of the women in Ruth. The typology underlines the roles of these women—mother, wife, and daughter—as architects of their own identity, yet planted firmly within a patriarchal tradition, where in many respects they are viewed and treated as property. While the common parlance may not suggest this overtly, the common actions do. Often property is couched in the language of protection. The tension in Ruth and in the Indo-Guyanese community regarding patriarchy and women's identity is built into the system and, though seemingly irreconcilable, nevertheless sustains itself. The cultural and religious traditions within the Indo-Guyanese community serve as the basic framework for much of the direction of their lives, as is also the case in the book of Ruth. I shall argue that the identity and transformation of Hindu Indo-Guyanese women, much like the women in Ruth, must be understood within the context of the society as a whole.

The book of Ruth begins on a note of extraordinary familial and national tragedy and ends on a note of hope and fulfillment. Between this spectrum of death and life are seemingly endless avenues of daring, risk, and newness, most of which are broached by Naomi and Ruth. What transpires specifically in the individual lives of Ruth and Naomi must be understood in the wider context: the events of the times within the family as well as throughout the society at large. As is so often the case, there is an intrinsic connection between particularity and universality. The narrative comes full circle: as it begins and as it ends, the focus rests on Elimelech and the men in his family. As the narrative begins, it is through Elimelech that everyone's identity is defined, and as the narrative concludes, male genealogy determines the future. The framework is clearly established and what freedom and identity will evolve through the women will do so in a clearly well-defined patriarchal context. Yet, by the end of this narrative, we hear a redefinition of the role of women. In this narrative, the women participate in the shaping of their identity rather than existing in the mode of passive receptivity to exterior "shapers." Their actions are all the more dramatic given that they were executed within the well-defined strictures of the tradition. The tragedy of the famine provides the backdrop for the migration of the family, a family that reflects the patriarchal orientation of the day. Phyllis Trible observes that this orientation is captured through the literary movement in the texts, such as the shifting of male to female pronouns, as Elimelech departs from the story and Naomi takes center stage.[1]

There has been an ongoing debate about the placement of the book of Ruth within the Hebrew and Old Testament canon. Some who have argued against following the Septuagint's placement of Ruth between Judges and I Samuel posit two principal arguments. First, they suggest that Ruth disrupts the Deuteronomistic history, since there is practically nothing about the narrative that fits the Deuteronomistic mode. Second, there is the argument that while Judges focuses on national and international affairs, Ruth is fundamentally a family matter. However, to proceed on this latter premise is to disregard or overlook the intrinsic intertwining of family, communal, and national life. As in war, where the personal, familial, communal, national, and international converge, so also it is the case in Ruth, a story of widespread famine. Indeed the very external factor of the placement of Ruth next to Judges underline the multifaceted effects and levels that the famine created. Ruth Putnam sees this sort of connection in Ruth from a different angle. "The communal nature of morality is acknowledged when Ruth, in the very act of choosing Naomi, also chooses Naomi's people and Naomi's God. She does not become a person without a country. . . ."[2]

As intimated by the narrator, the "death" of the situation pointedly has to do with the lack of food for the family. Extraordinary circumstances force the family to choose between familiarity of land, family, and God, on the one hand (a familiarity that appears now with inevitability of death), and foreign land, a people deemed as enemy, an alien god, but with a chance for life. One might say the family has a choice: security and death or risk and potential for life.[3] The choice is not self-evident. When one considers the various elements that enter into security, to relinquish these ties and seek hope in a place of disconnection is neither easy nor inviting. Within the story of Ruth, there is a clear sense that one's life is changed and reshaped by circumstances that are often beyond one's control. Moab is enemy territory. The stark contrast between Judah and Moab testifies to the centrality of life as the primary factor in shaping one's decision. It is not so much that Elimelech abandoned Yahweh, land, and community, but in the face of death he makes an extraordinary choice. It is, however, his choice on everyone's behalf. Further, not only does Elimelech move his family to enemy territory, but the radicality is intensified as the sons Mahlon and Chilion marry Moabite women, extending in present and potential ways the life granted them. Later, when the three women are left without husbands or sons, they are forced by their circumstances to pursue a new life. There is much within the ancient Israelite tradition to suggest that under normal circumstances an Israelite family would neither travel to, nor reside in, Moab. But dire circumstances lead to dramatic decisions, and in the midst of seeking to maintain one's cultural and religious traditions, changes transpire.

Five verses into the story, the three men in the lives of the women die. This would be a story about the women. Later the role of Boaz, while significant, will have to be understood in the context of the transformation and identity-shaping actions of Naomi and Ruth. All three of the women seek to make their own decisions. Initially, it is Naomi who decides on behalf of both Orpah and Ruth (1:8–13), though ultimately Orpah makes her personal choice and so does Ruth, each diametrically opposite from the other, but both seeking life.

Abandoning conventional wisdom, Ruth decides to cling to Naomi, thus redefining her identity. The sacrifices of Naomi are not lost on Ruth. Fundamentally three elements shape a person's identity: one's circle of family and friends, one's home and land, and the God in whom one believes. In Ruth 1:16–17, Ruth sacrifices all three as she has known them and, with enormous courage and risk, begins a new life with little evident prospect for future well-being. Each woman had reached the nadir of her existence as it was understood in that context. Alone, they are destitute, homeless, and deprived of the necessary male protection in their lives. The paradox of their existence is framed by their destitute situation, on the one hand, and the implicit evidence of their relentless pursuit of an identity, on the other. The reality of their desperate situation is captured in Naomi's concern for her daughters-in-law when she suggests that they return to their mother's house, where their chances for realization of new life would be considerably greater (1:8). Fewell and Gunn suggest, "As she [Naomi] urges them toward their mother's house to find new husbands, her language communicates that they have options. She does not."[4] This, however, is not a statement of resignation. Even in her distraught state, Naomi wonders aloud whether she would be able to bring forth sons to have her daughters-in-law marry. The narrator is not really interested in the practicality of this, or the issue of levirate marriage, but rather there is a sense here that Naomi is willing to imagine beyond reality what might bring life, recognizing as she does the implicit impossibilities.

Naomi does not allow the reality of her existence to eliminate her speech. Indeed, the very destitute nature of Naomi pushes her to challenge God regarding the unfairness of her situation. Perceiving a divine injustice, Naomi joins the ranks of Abraham and Job, faithful servants who dare to challenge God. She enters the realm of the world of challenge set aside not only for the male of the society, but this sort of challenge must be predicated on fidelity. The language and courage of Naomi might not suggest immediate change, though her words, similar to Job's, in her belief in ultimate deliverance. The hope within her complaint defies her present reality.

Emptiness of Being

When the family of Elimelech leaves Judah for Moab, the very act underlines the gravity of the situation; it is clearly a matter of life and death, and certainly they leave "empty." "Emptiness" is understood entirely in the context of the famine. At this juncture, with the focus on Elimelech, "emptiness" focuses on the lack of food. Yet, complaining bitterly to God (1:21), Naomi specifies her definition of "fullness" versus "emptiness." According to the text, Naomi was "left over." Avivah Zornberg suggests that when the men died, Naomi was the residue.[5] Like the leftovers from a meal, or as in Hebrew tradition the leftovers from a sacrifice, Naomi's residue appears to be of no significance. Ruth would cling to Naomi, and while this is clearly an extraordinary expression of selfless love, still Naomi feels that she is empty. Fewell and Gunn underline Naomi's self-perceived emptiness as she describes her void (1:20–21) stating, "She sees herself alone, apart from a vengeful God. The implication for Ruth is devastating. Ruth is nothing. Naomi speaks as though the loyal companion at her side were invisible."[6]

The text reads, *Ruth davka ba—Ruth clung to her.* This attachment, while not that of her sons or husband and clearly against societal norms, has the prospect of life for Naomi. As surely as Moab held the promise of new life for Elimelech, so surely may Naomi experience newness of life through alliance with Ruth. Particularly in the contemporary Western world, there is now more overt discontent with this patriarchal notion. Yet, what is said, both communally and individually, often does not correspond with the reality of the women's existence. In some respects, the present situation is more insidious in that rhetoric has made women and the society at large feel somewhat comfortable, though the reality in some respects has remained unaltered.[7]

Indo-Guyanese Context

The typology moves now to the Hindu Indo-Guyanese context and two case studies. First, Bharat, eldest son of Shiva and Drupatie Maharaj and hence the one to carry on the name and traditions of the family, married Lakshmi. Bharat is born into a family where the father is of Brahmin caste and highly revered as a "holy man." Lakshmi, of modest financial and social heritage though of a lower Brahmin state, is still at an acceptable level for the marriage to a Brahmin such as Bharat. In many respects, Lakshmi would exemplify as clearly as anyone in the household the ideals of being a devout Hindu, and while not formally of the Brahmin caste she would live at the level of a Brahmin. She would embody the ideal *Bhahu,* the ideal daughter-in-law, and whatever she does she does so in deference to her in-laws and her husband. For the most part, within the structure of the family and in her everyday routine she is in the "shadows." Within this Hindu Indo-Guyanese scenario, typically as daughter-in-law, Lakshmi receives few compliments or acknowledgments. Conversely, if the expectations from a daughter-in-law are unfulfilled, then this daughter-in-law quickly, though not quietly, is the recipient of unmitigated blame. The father-in-law replaces the father and thus Lakshmi continues to seek her identity from the significant men.

The extended family system is very much the norm in Guyana, particularly within the Indo-Guyanese community. Within the Shiva and Drupatie household, Bharat the son would be expected to live with Lakshmi and their children in the family house, ultimately becoming the patriarch of the household. Both Drupatie and Lakshmi outlived their husbands. Rabindranauth, Lakshmi's only son of eight children, married and left the household when his father was still alive. Thus, three generations of men, men who were destined to carry on family names and traditions, disappeared. The primary interest of Lakshmi and Drupatie, left alone with the youngest of Lakshmi's seven daughters when Bharat died, was in procuring a suitable husband for this daughter. Almost by default, the decision is made that Lakshmi and Drupatie would live together: two widows, a daughter-in-law and a mother-in-law, breaking all the norms of the patrilineal society. Both Lakshmi and Drupatie were widowed when they were in their 50s. There was never a thought of remarriage. Indeed, remarriage as such would have broken an unwritten code of conduct within the Hindu Indo-Guyanese community. Note the dramatic change in the quantitative and contextual make-up of this household: under Shiva as patriarch in the late 1960s and a total of 12 family members, to a situation in the mid 1990s where the total number of family members is three, all of whom are women, one of marriageable age. As in the case of Ruth, where Elimelech, Mahlon, and Chilion die, and decisions about life are made by the women, so also the situation in the now "emptied" household of Drupatie and Lakshmi. However, in the case of Drupatie there would not be prospects of men on the horizon who would come to their aid. While building on the traditions, reputation and most notably the names of Shiva and Bharat, they would give shape to their own identities.

In the late 1960s, when it was determined that it was time for Bharat and Lakshmi's eldest daughter to be married, the process was underway to find a "suitable boy": one of unquestionable character, high caste, good family heritage, and who is well-educated. With the exception of educational status, this "suitable boy" would be chosen on the basis of the parents' reputation. The "elders" of the family determine this process. In this case, Shiva having died, the constituency of the family "elders" include Drupatie, Bharat, and other designated family members. The process proceeded: contacts were made with desirable prospective families who had desirable sons. The eldest daughter was "shown" to three different suitors, the third of whom was chosen for her husband. In the Hindu Indo-Guyanese society, such was the norm.

Between the time of the marriage of the eldest daughter, Geetanjali, and the youngest, Devi, who was married in 1996, there has been a virtual reorientation of the entire process. In this connection, there are two points of typology that I would like to draw between Ruth and the Hindu Indo-Guyanese experience. First, the Indo-Guyanese community has been indelibly shaped by religious tradition. The male is the undisputed head of the household, thus possessing the inherent power and authority to make decisions on behalf of the family, present and future. Great importance is placed on tradition and legacy. The family name must not be soiled. Second, while traditions might be maintained, external forces and extraneous circumstances may force a family to make non-traditional decisions. This proposes a sometimes difficult and occasionally seemingly irreconcilable tension.[8] These circumstances necessitate a painful and inconclusive transformation of the role of Indian women as observed by Vinay Lal:

> She was no longer to be deprived of education; on the contrary, she would utilize her education in the service of good housekeeping, in keeping her menfolk on the straight path, in aggrandizing her feminine beauty with the armor of home science, and in enlightening the nation about the virtues of sanitation, hygiene and nutrition. There was every reason to believe that she could become modern, a participant in the affairs of the nation, even a civic leader, but this is as far as she could be allowed her resemblance with European women. Her beauty, morality and agreeableness were in no respect to be compromised.[9]

For good or ill, many of the changes within the Indo-Guyanese community have coincided with, and borne out, the transformation of the society as a whole. In its brief history as an independent state, Guyana has been through several stages of dramatic change. Through the December 1964 elections, a coalition government was formed between the Peoples National Congress, under the leadership of Forbes Burnham, and the United Force, under the leadership of Peter D'aguiar. Neither Burnham nor D'aguiar had the popular majority, but together they would rule, Forbes Burnham serving as the premier. On May 26, 1966, British Guiana was granted its independence from Britain, as both the British and the U.S. governments found the coalition government more to their ideological liking. The United Force would not play any meaningful role in the governing process.

At that time, 30 years ago, countries such as Great Britain, Canada, and the United States were for the most part mentally and physically out of reach for most Guyanese. Travel to one of these places was a major event. Typically, such a venture was set aside for those fortunate enough to have the resources to pursue an academic degree. The departure of one so fortunate, usually a male, was a time of great celebration by family and community, with an even greater celebration upon his return. So relatively infrequent was this sort of venture that even at the end of the decade of the 1960s and into the early 1970s, an atmosphere of awe surrounded such an event. The sons were expected to study, become qualified in whatever field they had chosen, and then return home.

The influence of these faraway lands was limited principally to academic endeavors, the importance of which for an Indo-Guyanese was never in question. However as the 1970s dawned, a new type of Guyanese society had been plotting and building during the previous decade and began expressing itself in ways that were foreign to the intrinsic fabric of all Guyanese people of every racial construct. Power as weapon and governmental narcissism dug deep roots, and the politics of corruption injected a renewed and deepened sense of racial divisiveness and hopelessness. It was the perception of a future of despair and wounded psyches that drove many Guyanese into self-imposed exile. Exile to lands without greener pastures is exile nonetheless. For the first time there was increased desire for, and movement to, faraway lands. Most of the migration came not as a desire to abandon the land of birth, but rather for many as a necessary choice between life and death. Because of the deterioration of the socioeconomic foundation of Guyanese life, the East Indian community sought refuge elsewhere. No longer was the quest for higher education the primary impulse for migration. Rather, the urgency was rooted in fleeing a society that was quickly becoming pervasively corrupt and a government intent on dismantling the fabric of all society, Blacks and East Indians alike. Crime, lack of food, recriminations by political forces, etc., all made life in Guyana exceptionally difficult. Many who would not ordinarily even think of migrating, did so amid great fears, great sadness, and fragile hope in a foreign land. The reality of remaining in the familiarity and security of one's natal community, where marital and spousal decisions were shaped by cultural and religious norms, yielded to a prospect of hope underlined by risk and vulnerability. This change in Guyanese political and social life coupled with the U.S. Immigration and Naturalization Act of 1965, account for the heaviest migration of Indo-Guyanese to the United States. So began in fervency the quest for new life in a foreign land. Homes, businesses, professions were all left behind and many persons and families started over in states of poverty and powerlessness.

As stated above, prior to 1965 most Indo-Guyanese came to the United States primarily with the intent of returning to Guyana, either with a good store of wealth or with a degree in higher education.[10] Those who would return to Guyana from this latter group, in later years would bring and inject new trends, norms, ideas, and values within the cultural fabric that made up the Indo-Guyanese family, and the fabric would never again be the same. Thus, whereas a generation ago the young Indo-Guyanese girl would be ostracized if she sought to choose her own husband or focus her fundamental interests on educational endeavors rather than cooking and sewing, the next generation of young adults who returned to Guyana from other countries brought new, different perspectives that would filter into the lives of Indo-Guyanese families, transforming traditional and cultural perspectives.

A generation ago, racial and religious intermarriages were simply not a viable option, and while still uncommon today, such marriages have lost some of the taboo. In Pearl Buck's novel *Mandala,* the daughter, Veera, verbally engages her mother passionately about the issue of marriage and announces that in all likelihood her brother Jai would choose his own bride. The mother says, "I must speak to his father. I would not like an American daughter-in-law, or even an English one. I like the Western people, but that does not mean taking them into our family."[11] A novel to be sure, but very much reflective of the sentiments of the Indian people within the subcontinent and the diaspora. The question Veera posed to her mother was overtly about her brother but in reality concerned herself. She was really asking whether she might have the choice of refusing the "suitable boy" chosen for her. Such an overt question would not even be entertained.[12]

Historically in Indian society, the woman about to be married is both property and pawn. Her status as property is reflected linguistically by society's reference to her as *paraya dhan,* which translates, "someone else's property." She, too, is pawn, as surely as the biblical daughters, Rachel and Leah, being used for negotiation and procurement of more property.

The role of the dowry in biblical, ancient Near Eastern and contemporary East Indian traditions within both the subcontinent and the diaspora, underlines the "property" role of the woman. One could view the dowry as the daughter's share of the parents' inheritance as she leaves the parental home for her husband's. The dowry, which may include household items in addition to other valuables, could serve as an inducement to attract prospective suitors. In the Hebrew Bible, it is recorded that Laban gives Zilpah and Bilhah as dowry to Leah and Rachel respectively on their marriages to Jacob (Gen. 29:24, 29).[13] Marriage ceremonies in contemporary Guyanese Hindu tradition include the symbolic ritual known as *Khanyadan:* the giving away of the daughter or young female. This woman, within the Hindu Indo-Guyanese society, then is treated as a servant, much as daughters are servants, only now she will be "serving" her husband and her in-laws. Servanthood is the norm. In a culture that has, at its roots, the role of *karma* and *samsara,*[14] the faithful, dedicated servile life is itself an achievement.

The second case study surrounds Suraya, a 60-year-old woman. Married for almost 40 years, she recalls being treated as a servant especially by her father-in-law. Reflecting on that time in her life, Suraya recalls that her father was aware that having his daughter marry into that particular family would in all likelihood lead to grave physical hardship for his daughter. Yet, in the end, the importance of "marrying off" one's daughter was more important than the degree of servility she would endure. It was the father's decision. In these matrimonial alliances, the issue of "love" does not factor in. Thus, it is not a question of whether Suraya's father loved her or had affection for her. Rather his singular intent was to fulfill his role as the patriarchal figure and establish a future for Suraya. She feels certain that if she were a male she would never have remained in the marriage. Yet, even on this point, one recognizes the external factor, of the influence of the United States. After having lived in the United States for six years, this kind of assertion has entered her line of thinking.

Suraya related an incident that took place early in her marriage. Soon after her wedding, she realized that she would be immersed in a servant role, subsuming her essence as a person. After only a few months of marriage, she visited her parents' house fully intending to relate the painful extent of her experiences. When she arrived there in tears, she met her brother, the primogeniture, who saw her tears and the distressed look on her face. Immediately, he told her that she is not to complain, but that she must live with it. As extraordinary as it is, Suraya's brother knew immediately what the issue was. It was as if this was not only experienced by previous sisters, or at least the knowledge was there, but it seemed expected. She never said a word! Some of her discussion with me took place in the context of her mother's funeral. Suraya's father had died some 30 years prior. As the discussion about the funeral arrangements went on, including the matter of costs, the conversation suddenly turned to whether the daughters were able to aid with the funeral expenses. The tradition holds that when the daughter is married, and the moment of the *Khanyadan* occurs, the daughter belongs to someone else. Thus she is not allowed to "give back" anything to her parents, even in death. While this may sound legalistic, the issue at hand is an understanding of the tradition. A daughter's aid to her own parents, after her marriage into a new family, must be extremely subtle, subtle enough that such aid could never be construed as "giving back" to her parents. Indeed, historically the strict Indian tradition intimates that a daughter's family should not as much as accept a glass of water from her in-laws' house!

It is true that in the Western tradition, customs of this nature are not common, and certainly to a large extent they are rejected when encountered. Yet, in subtle ways, there are instances of the role/identity of the daughter in Western tradition that suggest that she is viewed quite differently from the son. For example, occasionally today, and certainly frequently a generation ago, as part of the traditional wedding ceremony within the United States, the presiding priest or pastor asks who gives this woman in marriage, and almost without exception it is the father who answers "I do." In recent times, one sees the mother also participating in the answer, though this does not change the reality of the daughter as property. But the very tradition of the father answering the question defines the role of the woman as property, if only in the language, which for good or ill reflects our societal norms. The woman "given away" in marriage is taken by the groom, and by that understanding, she becomes his. It is never the case where the groom is "given away" in marriage. Many women and some men might be quick to say that this is only meant to be part of a tradition that really has no more meaning than simply a cultural thing. Perhaps so, but it did not simply evolve out of nothing.

Returning to Ruth and the shaping of the identity and points of intersection, we note that as the narrative develops, Naomi's concern for Ruth's welfare becomes the focus once again as the women's immediate needs are satisfied through Ruth's gleaning in Boaz's field. In 3:1ff., a text replete with sexual overtones, Naomi advises Ruth to prepare herself with anointing and wear her best clothes and go to the threshing floor to meet Boaz, where, after he has eaten and drunk and is satisfied, he will tell her what to do. This aggressive initiating behavior on Ruth's part is a risky departure from the societal convention. However, the security and future of Ruth and the family name of Naomi are such that under difficult circumstances, risks must be taken. Ruth allows Naomi to make the plans and provide the details for the encounter, and indeed Ruth says that she will do all that Naomi says. Yet, after arriving at the floor and to that point following the instructions of Naomi, Ruth takes matters into her own hands. Rather than wait for Boaz to tell her what to do, Ruth spreads her skirt over Boaz and essentially tells him what to do. Ruth is clearly aware of the risk, but equally aware that this is her life and her identity. She is the one who proposes, knowing that the next of kin bears something of a responsibility. Though she mistakes Boaz as the next of kin, she has already determined that she will pursue a future and is convinced that it is through Boaz that her redemption will come. Secrecy and propriety shape the rest of the night between Boaz and Ruth. One might say that Ruth used that which was at her disposal to shape her identity. Her actions are never questioned in the narrative, only allowed to be, and perhaps in so doing this outsider sets a new standard for women who would seek to establish their place within society.

As the narrative comes to a conclusion, the readers are reminded that the society remains patriarchal, as Ruth is described as having been acquired by Boaz (4:10). It is to Naomi that a son is born, thus to carry on the name of Mahlon. In comparing Ruth to Rachel and Leah, the narrative makes clear that Ruth also will be the one to build the house of Israel. Like Ruth, so also Lakshmi would be the one to build the house of Shiva and Bharat. Like Ruth, who determined for herself a proposal to Boaz, so also Devi would choose her own mate, a radical transformation of the convention under which her eldest sister, Geetanjali, found her husband. Yet, as Devi marries, she will undergo the *Khanyadan,* the "giving away of the daughter" to her husband. The cycle continues.

Notes

1. Phyllis Trible, *God and the Rhetoric of Sexuality* (Philadelphia: Fortress Press, 1978), 167–8.
2. Ruth Putnam, "Friendship," in *Reading Ruth,* ed. Judith A. Kates and Gail Twersky Reimer (New York: Ballantine Books, 1994), 53.
3. It should be noted here that security is not to be absolutely equated with death. Many members of the community with whom the family of Elimelech lived in Bethlehem were still there when Naomi returned with Ruth. The reality is that both parties made choices.
4. Danna Nolan Fewell and David Miller Gunn, *Compromising Redemption: Relating Characters in the Book of* Ruth (Louisville: Westminster/John Knox Press, 1990), 71.
5. Avivah Zornberg, "The Concealed Alternative," in *Reading* Ruth, ed. Judith A. Kates and Gail Twersky Reimer. (New York: Random House, 1994), 66.
6. Fewell and Gunn, 71.
7. In contemporary society, the mother-in-law has been something of a comic figure who lends herself to all sorts of jokes, from bumper stickers that read "mother-in-law in trunk" to the thoughtless comment by Ian Botham, the English cricketer, who describes the conditions in Pakistan as deplorable and fit only for mothers-in-law. This view most often references the relation of the mother-in-law to the daughter-in-law, and as sociologists have documented, this has been the case for centuries. (See Ramona Marotz-Baden and Deana Cowen, "Mothers-in-Law and Daughters-in-Law: The Effects of Proximity on Conflict and Stress," *Family Relations* vol. 36, no. 4 [October 1987]: 389; Lucy Rose Fischer, "Mothers and Mothers-in-Law," *Journal of Marriage and Family* vol. 45, no. 1 [February 1983]: 187). This portrayal of the mother-in-law has taken on a life of its own and has become the centerpiece in terms of in-law relations. In ancient, as well as contemporary, Near Eastern traditions the familial concern centers on the propagation of the family name principally through one person: the son. Thus not only would the birth of a son be significant, but also his marriage. For the most part significant relational problems with a mother-in-law center around the relationship with the daughter-in-law. The dynamics, both negative and positive, between a mother-in-law and a son-in-law most often center around secondary and refracted issues predicated upon the relational patterns long established between mother and daughter.
8. Ari Goldman in his book, *The Search for God at Harvard* (New York: Ballantine Books, 1991) speaks to this issue in a different framework where he struggles to maintain an acceptable tension between his quest to "follow" news stories, attend functions, etc., on the Sabbath, and at the same time, as a Jew, observe the Sabbath.

9. Vinay Lal, "The Nation, Nation-State, and the Cultural Politics of Hindu/Indian Womanhood in the Indian Diaspora" (unpublished paper presented at the conference, "Challenge and Change: The Indian Diaspora and its Historical and Contemporary Contexts" at the University of the West Indies, St. Augustine, Trinidad, August 11–18, 1995), 8.

10. Joseph Lopreato, *Italian Americans* (New York: Random House, 1970), 34. Joseph Lopreato uses the phrase "birds of passage," which aptly describes this group. Mahine Gosine refers to this group as "sojourners." They came for a particular purpose with no intent of residing permanently or becoming acculturated and assimilated within U.S. society. On the other hand, he sees the recent migrants as coming to the United States "for reasons pertaining to settlement, education, wealth." (Mahine Gosine, Promises of Plenty and the American Dream: Assimilation, Class and Social Mobility Among Indo-Trinidadians and Indo-Guyanese in the United States," p. 19. Paper presented at the Fourth Conference on East Indians. University of the West Indies, St. Augustine, Trinidad. August 11–18, 1995.) Gosine goes on to note that these "members do not place much emphasis on Hindu-Muslim differences, nor do they assign much credence to Brahmin, Khatriyas, Vaishyas and Sudra differences." Likewise, there is every reason to believe that the members of Elimelech's family never sought to establish their lives permanently in Moab.

11. Pearl S. Buck, *Mandala* (New York: John Day, 1970), 19.

12. See also Vickram Seth, *A Suitable Boy* (New York: HarperCollins, 1993) for an extraordinary engagement of the complexities of this issue.

13. This custom is distinguished from gifts given by the groom to the bride, as is seen in the case of Rebekah who, together with her family is lavished with gifts (Gen. 24:53). These gifts may include a payment of the "bride price" to the bride's father, as we witness in the encounter between Shechem and the brothers of Dinah (34:11–12).

14. Karma refers to the Hindu notion of the relation among past deeds, present reality, and future fate. It is the principle within Hinduism of inexorable cause and effect. Samsara refers to the sequence of change, impermanence and the cycle of birth and rebirth that affects every living being until release from this life.

Chapter 9 🎴

Identity and Subversion in Babylon

Strategies for "Resisting Against the System" in the Music of Bob Marley and the Wailers[1]

J. Richard Middleton

Jah! Rastafari! is an exclamation of enormous evocative power, as anyone who has spent much time with Rastafarians can attest. Often accompanied by a wild shake of dreadlocks, this exclamation, which is part praise to the Creator and part self-identification, communicates a positive, energy-charged, leonine roar of assertion.[2] Indeed, it constitutes a *counter*assertion, a claim to dignity and power boldly made in the face of other claims in this often dehumanizing world—claims, and a world, typically characterized by Rastafarians as "Babylonian." Counterassertion has always been central to Rastafari. From its origins as a millenarian cult of the black underclass in Jamaica during the 1930s, Rastafari has been a powerful movement of protest against the oppressive status quo. But its protest has not been simply negative. On the contrary, Rastafari has from the beginning attempted to subvert the status quo by proposing an alternative consciousness and identity for black Jamaicans. Today, Rastafari has developed into a vibrant spiritual vision and social force for black dignity throughout the world. A major carrier of this vision was reggae songwriter and musician Bob Marley who, together with Peter Tosh and Bunny Livingston[3] (originally known as the Wailers), communicated in song the power of the Rastafarian vision to many in North America, Europe, and Africa, especially in the 1970s.[4]

The burden of this chapter is to examine the lyrics of representative songs of the three Wailers, in order to elucidate their strategies for "resisting against the system,"[5] that is, for maintaining an alternative consciousness and identity in the face of the dehumanizing worldview of the dominant order. I will highlight two main strategies of resistance found in the Wailers' lyrics. The first is the appeal to historical memory, specifically to a macro-narrative of resistance, beginning with the Bible and continuing into the present day, and the second is the appeal to God's intent from the creation of the world as an alternative to the status quo. Particularly in connection with the latter strategy, I will address theological differences between Marley, Tosh, and Livingston—differences that are not ethically neutral—and will conclude by grappling with the issue of what constitutes appropriate subversion and identity-formation in "Babylon."

Speaking anecdotally, although I am, by training, a biblical scholar and not an interpreter of popular culture or music, I have been de facto applying my hermeneutical skills for years to both biblical texts and popular music, including reggae.[6] Besides utilizing popular music for the past 20 years in lectures and presentations on the relevance of the Bible for contemporary culture, I have experimented recently with a course on the spirituality of popular music. In the music of Bob Marley and the Wailers I find my interest in the function of biblical narrative, Old Testament creation theology, and especially my research on humanity as *imago Dei* (image of God) in Genesis 1, coming together with my love of reggae, which seems to pulsate naturally through my Jamaican blood. But it is not just reggae music as a genre or a cultural idiom that interests me here. As a white Jamaican Christian of British and Sephardic Jewish ancestry migrating from Jamaica to Canada in 1977, a migration "fueled" by the economic hardship of the oil crisis in the mid-1970s, the content of Marley's music (the lyrics, rhythm, and melody fusing into a unified complex) has helped me to clarify my own identity, both culturally and religiously, in the Caribbean diaspora. So there is a sense in which these reflections constitute my coming to terms with an important part of my own heritage.

Apart from the fact that biblical scholars do not usually engage in popular music analysis, it may seem more unusual for an academic essay to be so personally revealing. Here I think it is important not simply to accept the hegemony of North Atlantic paradigms of what constitutes good scholarship, but to continually press and tease the boundaries of our disciplines. Thus, I am unapologetic both about "debordering" biblical studies to include popular music analysis and about "locating" my own interests and motivations in an academic exercise. Not only are these moves quite appropriate—contrary to the idea of "pure" disciplinary distinctions and the myth of objectivity—but they are necessary moves in my case, since two of the major influences on my religious consciousness in the late 1970s and early 1980s were biblical creation theology (especially the notion of humanity as image of God [*imago Dei*] in Gen. 1:26–27) and the music of Bob Marley and the Wailers. These influences together empowered me to resist the dehumanization of North American consumer capitalism into which I was thrust and the Western progress myth, which beckoned me to join at the altar of mammon. And the flipside of that resistance is that I was empowered to sustain an alternative identity as *imago Dei,* with its gift of human dignity and its call to responsible action for justice and blessing in a world that belongs to Jah.

A Sociopolitical Reading of *Imago Dei* as Ideology Critique

It was because of the importance of the Genesis *imago Dei* text for my own worldview that I was led, as a biblical scholar, to reflect over the past several years on what it means to be created in God's image. One strand of that reflection consists in a literary-rhetorical reading of Genesis 1, which explores the model of divine power portrayed in the text and inquires into what sort of human power (in God's "image") the text's portrayal of God might authorize.[7] More relevant for our purposes in this essay, however, is a sociopolitical reading of the *imago Dei.* Here it is crucial to read the notion of image together with the mandate to rule (Gen. 1:26–28). Starting with the scholarly consensus that Genesis 1 (technically 1:1–2:3, which is a single literary unit) has its origins in the Babylonian exile, I have come to read the *imago Dei* text as making a counterideological claim. To understand that claim and the ideology that this text was countering, three sets of data are crucial. The first is the near unanimous testimony of Babylonian, Assyrian, and Sumerian creation myths that the overarching purpose of human beings is to serve the gods, by which is meant the obligation of cultic and financial upkeep of temples (with their elaborate rites) and the entire temple economy.[8] This involved providing sacrifices as food for the gods to be offered daily before their various cult statues—in which the gods were embodied—and, of course, repairing the temples when necessary and sustaining the livelihood of the priests. The mass of humanity were thus viewed as something like indentured laborers on the temple estates of the various deities, to whom they owed obligation.[9]

The second set of data is that in the ancient Near East, kings (and sometimes priests) were described as the image of a god.[10] While the idea is well-attested in Egypt over many centuries, it is less well-attested in Mesopotamia, and in fact the extant Mesopotamian texts are of Assyrian, rather than Babylonian, provenance—although one text is written by a Babylonian priest describing an Assyrian king. This designation of kings as image of Amon-Re, Horus, Enlil, Shamash, Marduk, etc., is part of the pervasive royal ideology of the ancient Near East, legitimating the divine right of the monarchy as an institution of the gods, serving to bring order to the chaos of political and social life. As image of god, the king (and, by extension, this could be applied to priests) functioned as the divinely authorized mediator of blessing from the gods, enacting the divine will on earth.[11]

The third relevant set of data for our purposes constitutes the Babylonian myth sometimes called the "Epic of Creation," also known by its first two words in Akkadian, *Enuma Elish*.[12] In the sixth century, this particular epic functioned as the charter myth of the neo-Babylonian Empire. Two facets of the *Enuma Elish* are particularly important for interpreting the *imago Dei* in Genesis 1.[13] The first facet is that the creation of the cosmos is effected by a violent act in primordial time. The young heroic god Marduk slays Tiamat, the old mother goddess *cum* sea monster (who represents the forces of chaos), and constructs the universe out of her dead carcass. Paul Ricoeur, among many others, has discerned how this primordial violent act of cosmos-making becomes the mythic legitimation of Babylonian imperial expansion, since the king, standing in for Marduk (image of Marduk) vanquishes the enemies of Babylon, who are regarded as the historical embodiments of the chaos monster, and thus reestablishes the social and political cosmos in historical time, in imitation of the god's establishment of the broader cosmos in mythical time.[14]

The second facet of the *Enuma Elish* that is relevant for our topic is that while the myth agrees with wider Mesopotamian creation theology that humans are created to serve the gods, it puts its own particular spin on this notion. According to the *Enuma Elish*, after Tiamat was defeated and the cosmos created, Marduk decided to alleviate the burdens placed on the defeated (and demoted) deities who had supported Tiamat, these burdens being precisely the upkeep of the temple economy. But instead of simply setting them free from the burdens of their labor with a full pardon, so to speak, it is decided that Tiamat's consort, the god Qingu, who had also opposed Marduk, would be killed, and from his blood humans would be made in order to take over the workload of the captive rebel gods. Not only, then, are humans created as indentured servants of the (higher) gods, but they are created out of the spilt blood of a deity who is, in effect, regarded as demonic and certainly an enemy of Marduk, the patron god of Babylon.[15]

This entire ideological complex of royal ideology and creation myths, especially the *Enuma Elish*, thus represents a worldview that would have been antithetical to the Yahwistic faith of the Judean exiles in the sixth century. For not only did it portray a god besides Yahweh as supreme, but it portrayed the world in essentially dimorphic or dualistic terms, such that order or righteousness or cosmos is imposed on (or wrested from) chaos or evil, by an essentially violent act—which is quite different from the portrayal of creation in Genesis 1. And it further portrayed the mass of Babylonian humanity—and especially any conquered and captured peoples, like the Judean exiles—as of inferior status vis-à-vis the king (and, in practice, the royal and priestly elites of Babylon), who alone stood *coram Deo* (before the face of God) and who mediated the presence and blessing of deity to the masses on earth. Genesis 1, then, and especially the notion of humans as the image of God, granted royal power in the world, is meant to resist and subvert Babylonian ideological claims about the subservient status and function of humanity. It does this by its counterclaim that God granted a royal identity at creation to all humanity, male and female (exiles included).[16]

The Importance of Alternative Consciousness in Bob Marley and the Wailers

In light of this analysis of the meaning of the *imago Dei,* it is intriguing that Peter Tosh, in the *Red X* tapes—which he recorded as his autobiographical reflections—appeals to the biblical notion of humanity as the image of God, precisely as a mode of resistance against the dehumanization of racism. Tosh recounts his exposure to the Christian Church of his youth.

> Then they started to teach me of the devil, and Satan, and hell. They teach me of the Christians. But they made sure that they teach me that Jesus, the son of God, was a white man. When I ask why am I black, they say I was born in sin and shaped in iniquity. One of the main songs they used to sing in church, that makes me sick, is "Lord, Wash Me and I Shall Be Whiter Than Snow."
>
> In my search, I heard of the name "God." I go to church and they say God made man of his own likeness and image. If I make a doll in my image it is quite obvious that the doll must look like me. Yet still I am faced with the ignorance, lost into fantasy, seeking to find the reality in what they taught me of this religion, of God.[17]

In the midst of this spiritual confusion and search, it was the "image of God" notion that provided the initial breathing room for the adolescent Tosh in a stifling, oppressive context, by evoking a sense of dissonance from the anti-black rhetoric and theology he found in the Christian Church.

But resistance to the dominant worldview is not limited to Tosh's autobiographical reflections. It is found extensively throughout the music of Marley, Tosh, and Bunny Wailer. One of the clearest examples is located in Marley's unforgettable words in the second stanza of "Redemption Song."

> Emancipate yourselves from mental slavery
> None but ourselves can free our minds
> Have no fear for atomic energy
> Cause none of them can stop the time[18]

Although concrete social and economic oppression—including the threat of nuclear war between the superpowers—is very real for Marley, he is aware that without an alternative consciousness with which to resist the "mental slavery" of the ideology *behind* the social and economic reality of oppression, it would be impossible to survive this reality (this "shitstem" or "shituation" as Peter Tosh liked to call it). So in the song "Exodus," where Marley appeals paradigmatically to the biblical memory of both the Exodus and the Babylonian exile (superimposing one on the other, as is typical among Rastafarians), he focuses not only on social and economic bondage and liberation, but also on this *inner* bondage (or mental slavery) and calls the listener to self-awareness and spiritual liberation.

> Open your eyes and look within
> Are you satisfied
> With the life you're living?
> We know where we're going
> We know where we're from
> We're leaving Babylon
> We're going to our Father's land[19]

Bunny Wailer, too, in "Moses Children," uses the exodus/bondage metaphor to describe his own present circumstances and highlights the importance of alternative consciousness.

> My burdens—sweating like a slave
> to live another day
> My burdens—if I didn't follow my mind
> I would be gone astray[20]

This emphasis on resistance by means of "following your mind," that is, an internalized alternative consciousness, surfaces in many other songs. Thus in "Could You Be Loved," Marley sings:

> Don't let them fool you
> Or even try to school you, oh! no
> We've got a mind of our own
> So go to hell if what you're thinking
> Is not right[21]

So in "Ride Natty Ride," he says:

> All in all you see wa g'wan
> Is to fight against the Rastaman

So they build their world in great confusion
To force on us the Devil's illusion[22]

Marley thus sees a spiritual battle taking place, a battle of ideologies. And in "Ambush in the Night," a song referring to both literal and ideological ambush, stanzas one and two contrast the claims of the Babylonian system with Rastafarian claims, by a change of only a few words.[23] First the lines from verse one:

They say what we know
Is just what they teach us
We're so ignorant

But in the second verse Marley sings in counterpoint to that claim:

Well what we know
Is not what they tell us
We're not ignorant, I mean it[24]

This false attempt by the system to teach or educate the masses, and the need for them to resist, is an important theme for Marley. Thus the opening words of "Babylon System" are:

We refuse to be
What you wanted us to be
We are what we are
That's the way it's going to be
You can't educate I
For no "equal opportunity"
Talking about my freedom, people
Freedom and liberty[25]

And the chorus appropriately calls on the listener to "rebel, rebel." This rebellion or resistance is celebrated in "One Drop," a song highlighting the distinctive reggae drumbeat (the third beat on the snare drum) and likening it to the pulsating of the heartbeat that sustains life.[26]

So feel this drumbeat
As it beats within
Playing a rhythm
Resisting against the system

And a little later in the song the ideological or spiritual choice is made clear as Marley sings:

> Give us the teachings of His Majesty
> For we no want no devil philosophy

And, of course, the Christian Church does not get off scot-free on this analysis, but is viewed as a part of the problem (participating in the "devil philosophy"). Besides the fact that Tosh indicts white Christianity in the *Red X* tapes, we have those powerful lyrics of protest from Marley in "Crazy Baldhead."

> Build your penitentiary,
> We build your schools,
> Brainwash education to make us the fools.
> Hate is your reward for our love,
> Telling us of your God above.
> We gonna chase those crazy baldheads out of town.[27]

Here it is crucial to realize that the operative word in the line that summarizes the content of the "brainwash education" is "above." It is the Christian teaching about a God "above"—who is disconnected from this world of suffering and blackness—that Marley protests.

An interesting commentary on this traditional religious language of transcendence and "height" is found in the first verse of "Get Up, Stand Up," a song cowritten by Marley and Tosh.[28] What follows is Tosh's version from his 1977 *Equal Rights* album, not only because I think it is better musically, but also because he adds a line about "duppy," which Marley's version does not have. By use of this term, which means roughly "ghost" (with a hint of the demonic), Tosh relegates Christian preachers to the realm of the dead.

> You preacherman, don't tell me,
> Heaven is under the earth.
> You are duppy and you don't know
> What life is really worth.

"Heaven is *under* the earth"? Is that what Christian preachers say? Tosh's implicit point is that it makes as much sense to say that heaven and God are "under" the earth as "above" it. Both notions are equally absurd. And the absurdity is expressed lyrically by using the more atypical formulation.[29]

That this absurdity is, in fact, the point, becomes explicit in the second verse, which mocks the fundamentalist Christian doctrine of the "rapture," the return of Christ to take believers out of the world. Again, this is Tosh's version.

> Cause you know, most people think,
> A great God will come from the skies,
> And take away every little thing
> And lef' everybody dry.
> But if you know what life is worth,
> You would look for yours
> Right here on earth
> And now we see the light,
> We gonna stand up for our rights.
> Come on! Get up, stand up

So it becomes clear that this ideological battle, focusing on an inner liberated consciousness, is not meant as an escape from the harsh realities of the external conditions of life (as it might be in some varieties of Christianity that counsel escape from the world), but, on the contrary, is meant to focus us resolutely on this world (on earth), while giving us power and hope for living in this world, even when we have to go against the dominant order of things.[30] How does this alternative consciousness give us hope? How does that actually work? I want to suggest that it works in two main ways. It works by appealing either to historical (especially biblical) precedent or to God's "creational" intent.

Appeal to Historical Memory to Fuel Alternative Consciousness

It is quite clear that for Marley, Tosh, and Bunny, the central historical precedent appealed to is the biblical complex of exodus and exile. That complex views the present world order as "Babylon," a system of bondage and oppression that represents everything from the West African slave trade to colonial and neocolonial class structure, racism, economic deprivation, police brutality, as well as ideological bondage or "mental slavery." In contrast to "Babylon," there is "Zion," Ethiopia, or Africa generally, which Marley calls "our Father's land" (in "Exodus"), to which Jah is guiding his people in a new exodus/return/repatriation, led by various prophetic figures.[31] "Give us another brother Moses," sings Marley in "Exodus." But in addition to Moses, Marley's lyrics mention biblical heroes like Solomon, whose lineage leads to Ethiopian emperor Haile Selassie I (in "Blackman Redemption"); the Hebrew children Shadrach, Meshach and Abednego in the fiery furnace (in "Survival"); David, who slew Goliath "with a sling and a stone;" and Samson, who slew the Philistines "with a donkey's jawbone" (in "Rastaman Live Up"). And, although not explicitly naming him, Marley also alludes to Joshua when he sings "it remind I of the days in Jericho," likening the ritual procession around the city to Nyabingi dancing at a groundation ceremony ("Jump Nyabingi").[32]

But Marley not only retells the biblical story, citing paradigmatic biblical characters and events, he updates the story to include the black struggle against slavery, racism, and oppression in the post-biblical epoch. In "So Much Things to Say," for example, he mentions, as parallel examples, the historical marginalization of Jamaican national heroes Marcus Garvey and Paul Bogle, along with the crucifixion of Jesus (pronounced Jess-us to distinguish the Rasta understanding of the Messiah from the Christian Jee-zas). He then encourages his listeners not to ignore their own history, which includes these leaders and their stories. For Marley, this historical memory is crucial to both his own and his listener's identity.

> I'll never forget, no way
> They crucified Jess-us Christ
> I'll never forget, no way
> They stole Marcus Garvey for rights
> I'll never forget, no way
> They turned their backs on Paul Bogle
> So don't you forget, no youth
> Who you are
> And where you stand in the struggle[33]

Likewise in "Rat Race" Marley appeals to the resources of historical memory as a means of sustenance in the rat race of life, full of "political violence."

> Don't forget your history
> Know your destiny
> In the abundance of water
> The fool is thirsty
> Rat race[34]

What is going on here in this appeal to biblical-historical memory is, I believe, two-fold. On the one hand, and more generally, is the well-known fact that identity is narratively formed. That is, it is by the conscious "indwelling" of a larger story of meaning, a story larger than the individual self, and beyond the confines of the dehumanizing present, that we find meaning for our lives and come to a sense of self-identity, in a manner that enables us to resist the dehumanization of a world system undergirded by its own large story or metanarrative. So memory shapes identity.[35] And counter-memory shapes alternative identity. But, secondly, and more specifically, what we find is that this larger story of redemption, stretching from the exodus to Marcus Garvey and beyond, constitutes a series of paradigmatic examples of protest, resistance, and redemption, which by their para-digmatic or precedent-setting qualities, can motivate us also to protest and resist the dehumanizing present and to work—in hope—for redemption in the present. That is, we are motivated to participate in the ongoing story. This illustrates very well the famous dictum of communitarian philosopher Alasdair MacIntyre, articulated in his book *After Virtue*. MacIntyre writes: "I can only answer the question 'What am I to do?' if I can answer the prior question, 'Of what story or stories do I find myself a part?'"[36] Both identity and ethical action are narratively shaped.[37]

Appeal to God's Creational Intent
to Fuel Alternative Consciousness

But appeal to historical precedent is only one strategy to generate a hopeful alternative consciousness and way of life. The other strategy is by appeal to creation, specifically to God's creational intent from the beginning, which can call into question the status quo, that is, the present unjust order of things.[38] Thus we have Marley's famous song, "One Love," which, in my opinion, is probably the best song Marley ever wrote.[39] The power of a cre-ation theology to sustain hope is evident in these lines found in the very cen-ter of the song:[40]

> As it was in the beginning (One Love!)
> So shall it be in the end (One Heart!)
> All right!

Notice how different this is from the *Gloria Patri*, which is often sung in liturgical churches: "As it was in the beginning, is now, and ever shall be, world without end."[41] Those lines absolutize the status quo as God's eternal will, with no hope of change, whereas Marley's lyrics assert that this world (of present injustice) will one day again manifest God's creational intent—it cer-tainly does not do so now. But "One Love" is even more profound than this. The phrases "One Love!" "One Song!" and "One Heart!" which are repeated throughout the song, constitute a reiterated call to reconciliation, even with "hopeless sinners." Marley speaks of fighting a spiritual battle (an Armaged-don) for the unification of the human race and for reconciliation with God, because he does not want anyone to have to face judgment at the eschaton:

> Let's get together to fight this Holy Armagiddyon (One Love!)
> So when the Man comes there will be no, no doom (One Song!)
> Have pity on those whose chances grow thinner
> There ain't no hiding place from the Father of Creation[42]

But perhaps the most profound lines of all come in the first verse, where Marley's creation theology leads him to challenge those who, like the Pharisees in Jesus' day, are scandalized by the radical forgiveness the Gospel offers to sinners.

> Let them all pass all their dirty remarks (One Love!)
> There is one question I'd really love to ask (One Heart!)
> Is there a place for the hopeless sinner
> Who has hurt all mankind just to save his own?
> Believe me: One Love. . . .

Like Bob Marley, Bunny Wailer also appeals to a creation theology, with fascinating consequences. And just as Marley's appeal to creation suggests that the Creator cares for *everyone,* even self-serving "hopeless sinners," so Bunny's appeal to creation opens up the boundaries of his perceptions of God's concern. Thus, in "Wanted Children," a song permeated by creation theology, Bunny evokes God's concern and care for two categories of persons not typically addressed in mainstream reggae music.[43] The first category is children. The song affirms, at the outset, that there are ultimately (from God's perspective) no unwanted children.

> I see wanted children,
> Crying from the backbone of their fathers.
> Wanted children,
> Longing for the bosom of their mothers.

The children are wanted precisely because God is their Creator. And the first verse goes on to tell the story of the creation of the cosmos, using the language of Genesis 1. The point it makes is that the created order (which manifests God's creational intent) is "originary" or primordial, and therefore exerts a normative claim on our lives.

> These creations were here from the beginning
> So accept them for what they're worth

And Bunny hints, in the last line of the first verse, at the ultimate direction the song will take: "As the freedom of a raging storm/ let the little children born."

In the second verse we find a continuation of the creation story focusing on the creation of humanity, who are granted dominion and the power to be fruitful and fill the earth. Since children—the outcome of human fertility—are thus a gift from God, verse two ends with this poignant challenge:

So who are you to try them, price them, and sell them?
Who are you to slave them, and to kill them before them born?
Who are you to hunt them down, run them down, and gun them
    down?
Who are you to judge them, and to put them to shame and scorn?

And this concern of Bunny with the well-being of children surfaces also in one of the subtle changes he makes to the lyrics of "Get Up, Stand Up," in his own recording of that song. Whereas Marley's version says twice "So (And) now you see the light/ (you) stand up for your rights," and once "So now *we* see the light/ *we* gonna stand up for *our* rights, and Tosh's has "we" consistently, Bunny's version is quite different. This is what he sings:

Now that the children have seen the light
They're gonna stand up for their rights[44]

But Bunny Wailer makes another significant, even more subtle, change in the lyrics to "Get Up, Stand Up." In the third verse (which is quite different in all three versions), one line is almost identical in the version of both Marley and Tosh. Marley sings,

We know and we understand
Almighty God is a living man[45]

In Tosh's version this reference to Selassie is similar. He says, "Almighty Jah is a living man." Bunny, however, makes two significant changes to this line.

We know and we've got to overstand
That the Creator is a living one

Besides the playful use of "overstand," the two crucial changes are that (1) God is identified explicitly as Creator and (2) we have what seems to be an intentional case of inclusive language. Now, lest it be suggested that on this last point I am being overly subjectivistic—reading my own biases into the song—let me point out that in the second verse of "Wanted Children," in which he recounts the creation of humanity, Bunny intentionally mentions both sexes twice. Not only is it explicitly "male and female" that Jah created, but "to man and woman he gave all dominion/ over all creatures that lived on creation." This inclusivity was quite unusual in male Caribbean consciousness during the 1970s.[46] I want to suggest, therefore, that here we find manifested a concern—rooted in an appeal to God's creational intent—for children and for women, both of whom are typically undervalued by Caribbean (and Rastafarian) males.

But Bunny goes further still. For he has what is, to my knowledge, the first reggae song that is concerned about ecology. On the 1977 album *Protest*, we find the song "Scheme of Things," which speaks of the pollution of the world in both spiritual and physical senses, and asks:

> What are you doing toward the scheme of things?
> What are your works to your brother beings?[47]

In other words, the alternative consciousness generated by appeal to creation, in these songs by Bunny Wailer and Bob Marley, involves seeing others in a new light, since they also are created by God and therefore have dignity and worth. Creation theology, in other words, can empower you to stand up and speak out on behalf of, and fight for the rights of, others different from yourself. It can even cause you to love your enemies. But none of this is strictly necessary. It does not work quite this way with Peter Tosh. Take, for example, two songs by Tosh that appeal to creation. "Creation" and "Igzialbher (Let Jah be praised)" utilize language from Genesis 1 and Psalm 104 respectively.[48] Both songs, though beginning with language echoing biblical creation texts, go on to quote various psalms describing God's sustenance of the psalmist in the face of opposition. This reveals quite clearly Tosh's strategy. For him, in these songs, creation functions to legitimate the justice (and victory) of his own cause, in the face of his enemies. That is, Tosh portrays the Creator as fundamentally on *his* side, aiding him in the battle against his opponents.

Now this is all quite legitimate, up to a point. A problem surfaces when this legitimate sense of God used to support one's own cause begins to resemble the Babylonian ideology represented in the *Enuma Elish*. It is quite ironic that underlying many of Tosh's songs is a worldview in which Tosh himself has appropriated the stance of Babylon towards its enemies, a stance that both in Babylonian times and in Tosh's lyrics claims divine legitimation for the favored hero and destruction of the opponents. Something of Tosh's aggressive "Babylonian" stance begins to surface in "Stepping Razor," a stance that is, however, tempered by the song's humorous undertone.

> If you eat asphalt
> You better treat me good
> If you drink lead soup
> You better treat me good
> I'm like a stepping razor
> Don't you watch my size, I'm dangerous
>   . . .
> If you wanna live you better treat me good

Cause I know say bluntly you don't go through one fifth
of the tribulation whe' I go through
Like all now, only your name would be here to represent you[49]

Especially if placed in the context of the movie *Rockers,* where this song is
used ironically in a crucial scene (depicting the showdown between the sufferers and oppressors), its sense of humor can be appreciated, whatever the
author's explicit intention. But the song "I'm the Toughest" is an entirely different matter.

Anything you can do, I can do better
I'm the toughest
And I can do what you can't do
You never try to do what I do
I'm the toughest[50]

This song embodies what could only be described as a puerile attitude. It
reeks of schoolboy one-upmanship. But this attitude is transformed into
something more than puerile in Tosh's militant "Equal Rights," which contains the following lines:

What is due to Caesar, you better give it unto Caesar
And what belong to I-an-I, you better give it up to I[51]

Note what identity Tosh appropriates for himself here. In a powerful call for
"equal rights and justice" he cites a text that recurs in three of the Gospels in
which Jesus contrasts coins with Caesar's image, which therefore belong to
the emperor, with people, who are stamped with the image of the Creator,
and thus belong to God.[52] But Tosh places himself syntactically not in the
place of the *image* of the Creator, but directly in the Creator's own place by
his use of the first person singular pronoun. The alternatives are drawn not
between Caesar and God, but between Caesar and Tosh himself. And yet a
certain ambiguity is introduced by the use of both "I," which is singular, and
"I-an-I," which can be either singular or plural, thus allowing for the possibility that Tosh is claiming a divine identity not simply for himself, but on
behalf of the entire Rastafarian community (or possibly all oppressed people).

There is no such ambiguity, however, in "I Am That I Am."
Don't underestimate my ability
Don't defame my character
Don't belittle my authority
It's time you recognize my quality, ye-ah
I said: I Am That I Am—I Am, I Am, I Am[53]

Here Tosh appropriates nothing less than God's self-revelation to Moses in Exodus 3:14 in order to assert his own *unique* identity *over against* that of the listener, who is constantly exhorted in the song to acknowledge and recognize Tosh's importance and significance.

By attending to the large number of songs in Tosh's repertoire about being alienated, estranged, misunderstood, and opposed on all sides and also to the contours of his own life story—the *Red X* tapes are quite informative here—the fact becomes clear that Tosh lived with a constant sense of outrage at the injustice and oppression he felt he received, which led him to an essentially adversarial stance towards others.[54] "I Am That I Am" simply gives (inappropriate, even idolatrous) theological formulation to that stance, not only by claiming the meaning of the tetragrammaton as the content of his own self-identity, but by defining this (divine) identity in opposition to everyone else. It is thus quite paradoxical that someone who appeals to the notion of "Babylon" to describe the dominant oppressive order should assume an identity that essentially recapitulates the very self-understanding of historical Babylon and especially of the Babylonian monarchy. According to this self-understanding, Babylon (and the king as the image of God) stands in a unique, privileged, divinely authorized (we might say self-righteous) opposition to the enemies of the empire, who represent the forces of chaos and evil.[55]

In this connection, it is significant that liberation theologian Pedro Trigo has warned that oppression can lead not only to disempowerment, which is very common, but also to a stance of vengeful self-assertion, which absolutizes those on the side of liberation while demonizing the oppressors. It is even more significant, in light of Bunny Wailer's creation theology, that Trigo also claims that a biblical faith in God as Creator can be a powerful antidote both to disempowerment and to vengeful self-assertion in the face of oppression.[56]

What sort of resistance to evil, then, might a commitment to God as Creator of all (including the oppressor) engender? One example is Marley's radical proclamation of forgiveness even for the "hopeless sinner" in "One Love/People Get Ready," appealing to creation ("as it was in the beginning") as a guide for fighting "this Holy Armagiddyon." This attempt to not demonize those who embody historical evil is also found in "So Much Things to Say."

> I-an-I no come to fight flesh and blood,
> But spiritual wickedness in high and low places.
> So while they fight you down,
> Stand firm and give Jah thanks and praises.[57]

With these words, Marley echoes the Pauline admonition in Ephesians 6 to stand firm and pray in order to resist the devil. This admonition functions as an important alternative to either acquiescence in the face of evil or the enactment of human violence in response to evil.

In Bunny Wailer's case it is his song "Amagideon" (this is his spelling) that illustrates his own, alternative mode of spirituality and resistance to evil, even in apocalyptic times. The song paints the story of the world with large strokes, from creation to eschaton, and describes the historical struggles we experience in the present, which lead to the final judgment.

> I see light fighting against darkness
> Righteousness against evil
> Right battling against wrong
> Here come bondage struggling for freedom
> But have patience I-Idren, have patience
> Don't be burdened by reasons of tribulations
> But have patience I-Idren, have patience
> Remember the call of redemption
> It says, Blessed are the poor
> They shall inherit the earth
> Blessed are the meek
> They shall have new birth
> Them that hunger and thirst after righteousness
> Them alone shall be called blessed
> In this ya Woe-de Woe-de Woe
> It's the Amagideon
> Taking place in-a Iration
> In-a Iration[58]

Drawing on language from Jesus' beatitudes and from the book of Revelation, Bunny counsels patient endurance and the humble pursuit of righteousness in the face of an apocalyptic battle of good and evil ("Amagideon") taking place in creation ("Iration"). The contrast with Tosh's use of creation theology could not be starker. Whereas Tosh believes that he is naturally aligned with the Creator and the forces of right in his battle against evil (in effect—though not necessarily in intention—relegating Tosh's enemies to the outer darkness, outside the legitimate realm of creation), Bunny is willing to stand back and allow the battle to unfold, trusting the victory (and the judgment) to God alone.[59]

Having described various strategies for "resisting against the system" in the Wailers' music, and particularly the divergence of ethical stances with regard to the function of creation theology, it remains to note that this divergence raises the important question of the ethical legitimacy of various ways of resisting evil, a question that is existentially pressing for anyone engaged in emancipatory praxis in a world of real, historical oppression.

Without answering this question in any definitive way, I would suggest that there are pertinent biblical resources for addressing both our existential resistance to evil and our alternative identity-formation in "Babylon."[60]

Let me, in conclusion, make a final comment about the subjectivity of my thesis. As a biblical scholar attempting to formulate and articulate interpretations of Wailers' songs that I have been living and working with at an implicit level for a number of years, I have noticed a significant convergence between my reading of how biblical texts—whether liberation narratives or creation theology—participate in, and resist, ideology, on the one hand, and my reading of similar strategies in the music of Bob Marley and the Wailers, on the other. My initial sense was that my biblical scholarship, in particular my research on the sociopolitical function of the *imago Dei,* must have influenced my interpretation of this music. But, of course, that isn't usually the way it works. It is life that most fundamentally affects scholarship, and not the other way around. This, taken together with the fact that I was listening to Marley's music long before I ever began graduate biblical studies, leads me to ask whether my reading of the *imago Dei* as ideology critique might not itself have been significantly shaped by the music of Bob Marley and the Wailers. Not only does this seem to be the case, but it is quite appropriate that it should be so.

Notes

1. A paper presented to "The Bible in Caribbean Culture and Tradition Consultation at the Society of Biblical Literature," San Francisco, CA, November 21, 1997.

2. On the significance of power and dignity of the African lion for understanding the Rastafari posture vis-à-vis the world, see Horace Campbell, *Rasta and Resistance: From Marcus Garvey to Walter Rodney* (Trenton, NJ: Africa World Press, 1987), p. 99. Campbell's analysis is developed by Adrian Anthony McFarlane in "The Epistemological Significance of "I-an-I" as a Response to Quashie and Anancyism in Jamaican Culture," ch. 6 in *Chanting Down Babylon: The Rastafari Reader,* ed. Nathaniel Samuel Murrell, William David Spencer, and Adrian Anthony McFarlane (Philadelphia: Temple University Press, 1998), esp.114–6 on "The Lionhearted Response."

3. Bob Marley was born Nesta Robert Marley, Peter Tosh was born Winston McIntosh, and Bunny Livingston (now known as Bunny Wailer) was born Neville O'Riley Livingston (the writing credits for his songs are usually attributed to Bunny O'Riley).

4. Although there have been many biographical and journalistic accounts of Bob Marley's life and career, none can match the historical depth and cultural sensitivity of Timothy White's portrait in *Catch a Fire: The Life of Bob Marley* rev. ed., (New York: Henry Holt, 1996).

5. From the song "One Drop," by Bob Marley. Released on the *Survival* album by Bob Marley and the Wailers (Island Records, 1979). One of the problems for the citation of popular music lyrics, which is especially true for reggae (and which will be encountered in future citations in this chapter), is that song lyrics may change significantly from one recorded version of a song to another (indeed, I will cite some of these changes as important data for my analysis). A further problem is that sometimes the copyright date of a song is considerably later than known recorded versions of the song, not to mention ambiguities about authorship. This complexity is simply to be expected in Jamaican culture, which is still largely oral in nature, and it leads Marley's biographer Timothy White to comment that compiling an accurate discography of any Jamaican musical group "would try the patience of anyone but Jah Rastafari himself" (White, 393). I will, nevertheless, consistently endeavor to give the standard copyright information for each song along with relevant information on the version I am actually quoting.

6. I have also explored (with Brian Walsh) the musical vision of Bruce Cockburn, one of Canada's premier singer/songwriters, in a coauthored article, "Theology at the Rim of a Broken Wheel: Bruce Cockburn and Christian Faith in a Postmodern World," *Grail: An Ecumenical Journal* vol. 9, no. 2 (June 1993): 15–39.

7. J. Richard Middleton, "Creation Founded in Love: Breaking Rhetorical Expectations in Genesis 1:1–2:3," in *Sacred Text Secular Times,* ed. Leonard Jay Greenspoon, Klutznick Studies in Jewish Civilization, 10 (New York: Fordham University Press, 2000).

8. As far as scholars can tell, this understanding of human purpose is universal to all the cultures of Mesopotamia. Some of the better-known Mesopotamian myths that articulate this purpose include the *Enuma Elish,* the *Atrahasis* epic, *Enki and Ninmah,* the *Myth of the Pickax,* and *Cattle and Grain.*

9. According to H. F. W. Saggs, Mesopotamian creation myths did not simply propound abstract ideas. Rather they constituted "an explanation of a particular social system, heavily dependent upon communal irrigation and agriculture, for which the gods' estates were primary foci of administration" (Saggs, *The Encounter with the Divine in Mesopotamia and Israel* [London: Athlone Press, 1978], 168).

10. The most comprehensive study of the sources is Edward Mason Curtis, *Man as the Image of God in Genesis in the Light of Ancient Near Eastern Parallels* (unpublished Ph.D. diss., University of Pennsylvania, 1984). For accessible essays that summarize the relevant references, see Phyllis A. Bird, "'Male and Female He Created Them': Gen. 1:27b in the Context of the Priestly Account of Creation," *Harvard Theological Review* 74 (1981) 2: 129–59; D. J. A. Clines, "The Image of God in Man," *Tyndale Bulletin* 19 (1968): 53–103; and Jeffrey H. Tigay, "The Image of God and the Flood: Some New Developments," in *Studies in Jewish Education and Judaica in Honor of Louis Newman,* ed. Alexander M. Shapiro and Burton I. Cohen (New York: KTAV, 1984), 169–82.

11. Since I am proposing a sixth century Babylonian context for Genesis 1, something needs to be said about the underrepresentation of Mesopotamian (and especially Babylonian) references to kings as image of god in the extant archeological record. This is not the place to discuss the matter fully, except to note the paucity of manuscript finds in general from Mesopotamia from approximately 1500–1000 B.C.E. (when most of the Egyptian references occur) and especially during the sixth century in Babylonia. As Saggs cautions, "It is self-evident that the random nature of archaeological discovery may result in gaps in the evidence and false emphases" (*Encounter with the Divine,* p. 18). Another factor is that it is extremely perilous to limit the reconstruction of a worldview from textual sources alone, as if every influential idea in a people's cultural life must find written attestation, especially in a predominantly oral culture. In the case of Babylonian kings as image of God, although the archeological record is spotty, this notion fits well with what we know of the Babylonian worldview and social order.

12. English translations of the *Enuma Elish* include E. A. Speiser, "Akkadian Myths and Epics," *Ancient Near Eastern Texts Relating to the Old Testament,* ed. James B. Pritchard, 3rd ed. with *Supplement* (Princeton: Princeton University Press, 1969), 60–72; Alexander Heidel, *The Babylonian Genesis: The Story of Creation,* 2nd ed. (Chicago: University of Chicago Press, 1951), ch. 1: "Enuma Elish"; and more recently Stephanie Dalley, *Myths from Mesopotamia: Creation, the Flood, Gilgamesh and Others* (Oxford: Oxford University Press, 1989), "The Epic of Creation," 228–77.

13. For a very helpful commentary on the *Enuma Elish,* see Thorkild Jacobsen, *The Treasures of Darkness: A History of Mesopotamian Religion* (New Haven: Yale University Press, 1976), ch. 6, which bears the unwieldly title: "Second Millennium Metaphors. World Origins and World Order: The Creation Epic."

14. Ricoeur's analysis of the *Enuma Elish* is found in *The Symbolism of Evil,* trans. Emerson Buchanan (Boston: Beacon, 1969), part II, chap 1: "The Drama of Creation and the 'Ritual' Vision of the World."

15. The creation of humans out of the blood of Qingu is recounted in tablet VI of the *Enuma Elish.*

16. Further references to particular points in the above analysis may be found in the notes of two essays in which I have previously sketched a sociopolitical reading of the *imago Dei.* These are J. Richard Middleton, "The Liberating Image? Interpreting the *Imago Dei* in Context," *Christian Scholar's Review* vol. 24, no. 1 (1994): 8–25 and J. Richard Middleton and Brian J. Walsh, *Truth Is Stranger Than It Used to Be: Biblical Faith in a Postmodern Age* (Downers Grove, IL: InterVarsity, 1995), ch. 6: "The Empowered Self." I am presently working on a monograph on the *imago Dei,* which will contain a more extended exploration of the sociopolitical background of Genesis 1 and humanity as God's image.

17. From the *Stepping Razor—Red X* video documentary, © 1992 by Bush Doctor Films, Inc., directed by Nicholas Campbell.

18. "Redemption Song," by Bob Marley. Released on the *Uprising* album by Bob Marley and the Wailers (Island Records, 1980).

19. "Exodus," by Bob Marley. Released on the *Exodus* album by Bob Marley and the Wailers (Island Records, 1977).

20. "Moses Children," by Bunny O'Riley, © 1977 by Solomonic Music/Island Music (BMI). Released on the *Protest* album by Bunny Wailer (Island Records, 1977).

21. "Could You Be Loved," by Bob Marley. Released on the *Uprising* album by Bob Marley and the Wailers (Island Records, 1980).

22. "Ride Natty Ride," by Bob Marley. Released on the *Survival* album by Bob Marley and the Wailers (Island Records, 1979).

23. Marley survived an assassination attempt on December 3, 1976, which was clearly ideologically motivated.

24. "Ambush in the Night," by Bob Marley. Released on the *Survival* album by Bob Marley and the Wailers (Island Records, 1979).

25. "Babylon System," by Bob Marley. Released on the *Survival* album by Bob Marley and the Wailers (Island Records, 1979).

26. "One Drop," by Bob Marley. Released on the *Survival* album by Bob Marley and the Wailers (Island Records, 1979).

27. "Crazy Baldheads," by Rita Marley and Vincent Ford. Released on the *Rastaman Vibration* album by Bob Marley and the Wailers (Island Records, 1976).

28. "Get Up, Stand Up," by Bob Marley and Peter Tosh. Released on the *Burnin'* album by the Wailers (Island Records, 1973), on the *Equal Rights* album by Peter Tosh (Columbia Records, 1977; live version released on the *Captured Live* album by Tosh, EMI, 1984), and on the *Protest* album by Bunny Wailer (Island Records, 1977).

29. This ironic turning of language on its head is also part of the well-known Rastafarian playfulness with words in general to make a worldview point, such that "oppression" becomes "*down*pression" and "understanding" becomes "*over*standing." Or, in what is perhaps the best-known example, the object pronoun "me" (which is used in Jamaican patois as both grammatical subject and object) becomes consistently "I" (in both subject and object situations), thus replacing the traditional objectification of the speaker with a perpetual grammatical subjectivity (furthermore, "me" is sometimes replaced with "I-an-I," an ambiguously singular/plural expression, which renders the speaker intrinsically part of a community, thus countering modern isolationism and individualism). Other examples of Rastafarian wordplay that are dependent on the significance of "I" include "Idren" for "brethren" and "Iration" for "creation." Although the significance of "I" for Rastafarians may have originated in a simple misreading of the roman numeral in the throne name of the emperor of Ethiopia, Haile Selassie I, this "misreading" has turned out to have powerful subversive potential.

30. Brian Walsh and I have critiqued the unbiblical character of this escapist, otherworldly Christianity in *The Transforming Vision: Shaping a Christian*

World View (Downers Grove, IL: InterVarsity, 1984), especially chs. 6 and 7. The contours of a fundamentally this-worldly Christianity, rooted in Scripture, are sketched in chs. 3–5.

31. On the significance of Babylon for Rastafarians, see Ennis B. Edmonds, "Dread 'I' In-a-Babylon: Ideological Resitance and Cultural Revitalization." ch. 1 in Murrell et al.

32. "Survival" by Bob Marley. Released on the *Survival* album by Bob Marley and the Wailers (Island Records, 1979). "Blackman Redemption," by Bob Marley and Lee Perry, "Rastaman Live Up," by Bob Marley and Lee Perry, and "Jump Nyabingi," by Bob Marley. Released (two years after Marley's death) on the *Confrontation* album by Bob Marley and the Wailers (Island Records, 1983). "Blackman Redemption" previously released as a single (Tuff Gong, 1978).

33. "So Much Things to Say," by Bob Marley. Released on the *Exodus* album by Bob Marley and the Wailers (Island Records, 1977).

34. "Rat Race," by Rita Marley. Released on the *Rastaman Vibration* album by Bob Marley and the Wailers (Island Records, 1976).

35. Brian Walsh and I have explored this function of narratives—and of the biblical narrative in particular—in *Truth Is Stranger Than It Used to Be*, chs. 4 and 5.

36. Alasdair MacIntyre, *After Virtue: An Essay in Moral Theory*, 2nd ed. (Notre Dame, IN: University of Notre Dame Press, 1984), 216.

37. The biblical scholar who has been most formative in developing this analysis concerning the function of Scripture to shape identity and action is James A. Sanders. See his seminal essay, "Adaptable for Life: The Nature and Function of Canon," in *Magnalia Dei: The Mighty Acts of God*, ed. Frank Moore Cross, Werner E. Lemke, and Patrick D. Miller, Jr. (Garden City, NY: Doubleday, 1976), 531–60, reprinted in James A. Sanders, *From Sacred Story to Sacred Text: Canon as Paradigm* (Philadelphia: Fortress, 1987).

38. This is the basic argument of J. Richard Middleton, "Is Creation Theology Inherently Conservative? A Dialogue with Walter Brueggemann," *Harvard Theological Review* 87/3 (1994): 257–77. This paper was presented at the 1992 annual meeting of the *Society of Biblical Literature* in San Francisco, CA.

39. Significantly, it was continual listening to this very song in the days before the 1992 *Society of Biblical Literature* annual meeting which gave me the existential courage to stand before an audience of over 200 biblical scholars at that meeting and critique so renowned a scholar as Walter Brueggemann on his largely negative opinion of creation theology.

40. "One Love," by Bob Marley. Released on the *Exodus* album by Bob Marley and the Wailers (Island Records, 1977). Note that an earlier version of this song, entitled simply "One Love," was released on *The Wailing Wailers* (Studio One, 1965), credited to Marley alone.

41. This traditional second century hymn is found in a number of different musical settings in many hymnal traditions. For example #805–807 in *The Wor-*

shiping Church: A Hymnal (Carol Stream, IL: Hope Publishing, 1990);
#577–579 in *The Presbyterian Hymnal: Hymns, Psalms, and Spiritual Songs*
(Louisville, KY: Westminster/John Knox, 1990); #622–623 in *The Hymnal
for Worship and Celebration* (Waco, TX: Word Music, 1986); #538 in *The
New National Baptist Hymnal* (Nashville, TN: National Baptist Publication
Board, 1977).

42. The spelling "Armagiddyon" is phonetic for Marley's patois pronunciation of
Armageddon in the song.

43. "Wanted Children," by Bunny O'Riley, © 1977 by Solomonic Music/Island
Music (BMI). Released on the *Protest* album by Bunny Wailer (Island
Records, 1977).

44. "Get Up, Stand Up," by Bob Marley and Peter Tosh. These lyrics are from
the *Protest* album by Bunny Wailer (Island Records, 1977).

45. "Get Up, Stand Up," by Bob Marley and Peter Tosh. These lyrics are from
the *Burnin'* album by the Wailers (Island Records, 1973).

46. For recent analysis of the role of women in Rastafari, see Maureen Rowe,
"Gender and Family Relations in Rastafari: A Personal Perspective," and
Imani M. Tafari-Ama, "Rastawoman as Rebel: Case Studies in Jamaica," chs.
4 and 5 in Murrell, et al.

47. "Scheme of Things," by Bunny O'Riley, © 1977 by Solomonic Music/Island
Music (BMI). Released on the *Protest* album by Bunny Wailer (Island
Records, 1977).

48. "Creation," by Peter Tosh, © 1988 by EMI Records Ltd. Released on the
Bush Doctor album by Peter Tosh (Rolling Stones Records, 1978). "Igzialbher (Let Jah be praised)," by Peter Tosh, © 1976 by Sony Music Entertain-
ment Inc. Released on the *Legalize It* album by Peter Tosh (Columbia
Records, 1976).

49. "Stepping Razor," by Joe Higgs, © 1977 by CBS Inc. Released on the *Equal
Rights* album by Peter Tosh (Columbia Records, 1977).

50. "I'm the Toughest," by Peter Tosh, © 1978 by EMI Records Ltd. Released
on the *Bush Doctor* album by Peter Tosh (Rolling Stones Records, 1978).

51. "Equal Rights," by Peter Tosh, © 1977 by CBS Inc. Released on the *Equal
Rights* album by Peter Tosh (Columbia Records, 1977).

52. The contrast is implicit only, since Jesus does not explicitly mention what it
is that belongs to God. The text is found in Matthew 22:15–22, Mark
12:13–15 and Luke 20:20–26.

53. "I Am That I Am," by Peter Tosh, © 1977 by CBS Inc. Released on the
Equal Rights album by Peter Tosh (Columbia Records, 1977).

54. The interviews, news conferences, and autobiographical reflections in the
Stepping Razor—Red X documentary vividly illustrate the depth and inten-
sity of Tosh's alienation and outrage.

55. This taking on the image of the enemy is what some psychologists have described as a "reaction formation."

56. Trigo makes this argument in *Creation and History*, trans. Robert R. Barr,
part II: "From Chaos and Cosmos to Faith in Creation" (Maryknoll, NY:

204 J. Richard Middleton

Orbis, 1991), 69–108. A similar argument concerning the theological and ethical significance of beginning the biblical story of liberation (centered around the exodus) with an account of creation is made in Middleton and Walsh, ch. 5. This framing of liberation by creation is also central to James Sanders's previously cited essay, "Adaptable for Life: The Nature and Function of Canon," and to Terence E. Fretheim's *Commentary on Exodus* (Louisville, KY: John Knox, 1991). This emphasis on creation is a relatively new departure for Old Testament studies, which has tended to be suspicious of creation themes, while valorizing liberation or deliverance themes. On the reasons why this has historically been the case, see Walter Brueggemann, "Response to J. Richard Middleton," *Harvard Theological Review* 87/3 (1994): 279–89, esp. 281–3.

57. "So Much Things to Say," by Bob Marley. Released on the *Exodus* album by Bob Marley and the Wailers (Island Records, 1977).

58. "Amagideon," by Bunny O'Riley, © 1976 by Solomonic Music/Island Music (BMI). Released on the *Blackheart Man* album by Bunny Wailer (Island Records, 1976).

59. Lest it be thought that I am unambiguously recommending Bunny Wailer's stance here, there is a significant complication that needs to be noted. Although I am impressed by much (though not all) of Bunny's musical vision represented by his first two solo albums (*Blackheart Man,* 1976 and *Protest,* 1977), it is well known that after these albums he underwent a significant shift, beginning with *Dub Disco Volume I* (Solomonic Music, 1978), and moved from producing socially critical or religiously profound songs to turning out rather superficial dancehall music (almost 20 albums in the past 20 years, about half of which is new material, the rest being dancehall versions of older songs). This is not an absolute distinction in Bunny's repertoire, since he has produced some "conscious" music in these 20 years, but it does represent a significant change of emphasis. This seeming abdication of moral responsibility has been commented on by chroniclers of the Jamaican music scene as well as by reggae musicians and Rastafarians including Peter Tosh who was quite outspoken about the matter (to which Bunny typically responded by saying that the youths need to let off steam and he is simply providing the music for this). It might also be noted that Bunny quite astutely aligned himself with a commercially successful musical trend and thereby preserved a market for himself in present-day Jamaica, where "conscious" reggae has become a rarity.

60. This is not to suggest that the Bible is unambiguous on these matters. I have taken to heart Walter Brueggemann's continued warnings about the oppressive ideological potential of creation theology in the Old Testament to simply legitimate the status quo, warnings which he continues to sound, despite his acceptance of my critique and his appreciation of the new work being done on creation in the Old Testament. Brueggeman's warnings suggest a critical question, which cannot here be answered, concerning the relationship between Bunny Wailer's theological/ethical stance rooted in creation

and his dancehall "turn." Are these in some way connected to each other, such that creation theology can serve to relativize the struggle against oppression? Or are there other factors to be taken into account, since neither Marley's nor Tosh's appeal to creation seem to have led in this direction? Relevant factors in Bunny's case include his well-known elusive, reticent personality and his back-to-nature, isolationist tendency, which caused him to disappear to his farm for long periods of time, remaining out of touch with the wider world. Finally, what is the connection between Bunny's avoidance of political topics, his theological/ethical stance, and his quite legitimate desire to simply stay alive? Six months after Tosh's brutal killing in 1987, Bunny commented in a newspaper interview (possibly recalling also the 1976 assassination attempt on Marley and that Marley was also dead, of cancer in 1981): "Me nuh inna nuh sacrifice business. Me have ta be here ta see the victory of good over evil" (Balford Henry, "I Will Not Be a Reggae Martyr, Says Bunny, Last of the Wailers," *Sunday Gleaner* [March 20, 1988]). But these are questions, perhaps, for another essay.

Part III

Playing with Text in the Caribbean Context

Rastafari, Hermeneutics, and the Politics of Liberation

Chapter 10

Biblical Hermeneutics in Modern Caribbean Experience

Paradigms and Prospects

Noel Leo Erskine

Personal Theological Anecdotes

Because my family were Christians in Jamaica, I had the privilege of growing up in the Church. Since I did not know any existence outside of the Church it was not strange, when it was time for me to make a vocational decision, that that decision was to become a minister of the Gospel within the Church. Apart from the fact that the decision brought cheers to my father who served the Jamaica Baptist Union as president and missionary secretary, it seemed to me then, that if I were to serve my country in a way that sought to put the "liberative" agenda of the Gospel in conversation with a society that was harsh for most of its citizens, that to be situated within the Church was most propitious. The Church in the Caribbean has had a paradoxical relationship to the society. At times the Church used the Bible to challenge the assumptions on which "slaveocracy" thrived. At other times the Church and the Bible became instruments of oppression. What is not well-known is the fact that the Jamaica Baptist Church, in an attempt to alleviate the pain of post-slavery colonialism, bought large plots of lands and subdivided them to parishioners. Thus, the Jamaica Baptist Church built schools, hospitals, clinics, and water tanks for the masses of people in Jamaica. So it was not strange that I would seek vocational clarity within this Church.

I entered theological school in the Caribbean at a time of transition from colonial rule to an ever-increasing consciousness and moves toward national identity and self-determination. I was caught up in the post-independence search for personal and national identity. Like many of my contemporaries, I set out, Bible in hand, on a quest to learn more about who I was and how the social and historical situation in the Caribbean shaped my Church's reading of the Bible. In the Caribbean the pastor's interpretation of the Bible is held in high esteem by the parishioners, who regard the clergy as God's sole authority on biblical and theological matters. But the Caribbean pastor's approach to the Bible has traditionally been limited to an exploration of the context of the text with a view to exegeting some spiritual truths for the spiritual formation of the hearer and, to a lesser extent, providing answers to one's existential situation. The preacher began his exposition by analyzing the ancient text in its original context and then tried to find a meaning or meanings from the word for the Church and the society. Often the word was strange since it did not know or engage the context to which it was addressed. The existential needs of the preacher's parishioners and the populace at large did not pierce the consciousness of most pastors, and the congregants themselves were not conscientized to the fact that the word was able to address their physical needs as it does the spiritual. Since the biblical methods that the preacher employed were European, God was often presented to us through other peoples' cultural experiences. The Bible was often not in conversation with our life situation. There was not yet any consciousness that the God of the Bible was involved in the ordinary affairs of the people other than for spiritual formation. What happened in the Church's reading of the biblical context of the text was unrelated to the struggle in society for human dignity and meaning. This divorce of the Church, the Scriptures, and the school from the "bread-and-butter" issues of our daily lives made it very difficult for us to have any clear understanding of "self." When we listened to the Scriptures it was always in the cloister of the church or seminary, always insulated from the real world.

One of the memories that stand out for me is a protest against a mainline Church's reading of the Bible. Prior to the Sunday morning service at a local Baptist church of which my father was the pastor, a Rastafarian stood in front of the church and demonstrated his disgust at the way the church interpreted the Scriptures, by burning a Bible in full gaze of many of the parishioners. He complained that the Bible was being used as a weapon against the masses of the people. The Bible, he contended, was not being used to "free up" poor people.[1] I discovered, after my seminary training, that one of the big challenges facing the mainline Churches in Jamaica, as elsewhere in the Caribbean, is not for us to stop listening to the Bible as word of God—or throwing out the proverbial baby with the bath water—

but to figure out what it would mean for Caribbean people to listen to the Bible in their world: discovering what it means to read the social and historical context of the biblical text in our social, cultural, historical, and political context.

In fairness to the mainline Churches, I must point out that one of the reasons for the divorce between the Bible and the contemporary situation is the fear of the ideological captivity of the biblical text, the fear that the reading of the Scriptures would be colored by our reading of the contemporary context in a form of eisegesis (reading one's own ideas and interpretation into the text). This is one of the reasons for the reservation concerning the Caribbean Church's engagement of black theology and Latin America's theology in critical discourse. The Caribbean church has been afraid that if we learned from black theology we would read the Scriptures from the perspective of our own bias, the prejudice of race. If we learned from Latin American theology, we might read the Scriptures through the lens of class. What the Church hoped to accomplish was to present a Gospel that was free of ideological captivity, the same way Martin Luther, the great reformer, sought to free the Church from what he called "the *Babylonish Captivity of the Church*" the "imprisonment of the Scriptures to the Roman Catholic Church's teachings of the "Seven Sacraments.""[2] But no one ever reads the Scriptures or presents the Gospel from a completely neutral position. We all bring our prejudices and ideologies to bear on the Bible.

Perhaps the root of this fear of ideological captivity imprisoning the Bible in the region goes back to the kind of instruction that the colonial Church in Britain gave to its missionaries in the Caribbean. The following is an example of the instruction that was sent out in 1865 by the Baptist Missionary Society to missionaries in Jamaica:

> You are going to people in a state of slavery and require to beware lest your feelings should lead you to say or do anything inconsistent with Christian duty. Most of the servants whom the Apostle Paul addressed in his epistles to the churches were slaves, and he exhorts them to be obedient to their own masters in singleness of heart, fearing god, and this not only to the good and gentile.[3]

This was also true of instructions given to missionaries in the Wesleyan Methodist Churches. Consistent with notions of Christian duty in colonial Jamaica was the upholding of the institution of slavery. This also meant honoring the Eurocentric hermeneutics that supported the system.

The truth here is that the hermeneutics that the foreign agencies advocated represented a certain social class that was certainly not neutral on biblical interpretation. It represented an investment in the colonial economic system. The interpretation of the Scriptures advocated was on the side of the plantocracy and against the masses of poor people. In this setting and with this approach to the Scriptures, which did not recognize the Eurocentric ideological captivity of the Scriptures to the brokers of power, the Bible was able to liberate neither the oppressor class nor the oppressed. In a real sense, one could say the Bible was held in "Babylonian captivity" ideologically, as the church was held at Avignon in the 1500s. The Bible was read in a way that affirmed the blindness and insensitivity of the Church to the suffering masses. The colonial Church, in denying a role for the Bible in the transformation of culture, in the fear that the Bible would be acculturated, used the Bible to keep intact the status quo. Biblical materials read from the perspective of the oppressor were used as a weapon against the oppressed.

This approach to the Bible held sway into the late colonial period and up to the eve of Jamaican independence in 1961. As recent as the early 1960s, some of the questions students had to grapple with in seminary in Jamaica were: Who wrote the biblical text? When was the text written? Who was the audience? What were the historical and social conditions of the first hearers? The answers given by Church leaders ignored the context in which people sought to make sense of their lives. The question of the text transforming the social-political structure was left to the "nonconformists." Using the proper academic tools, the mainline Churches excelled at the level of interpreting the text in its own setting, but the church failed to place this interpretation of the text in conversation with the identity of the hearers. And, of course, no one inquired about ways in which the context of the hearers can influence the meaning of the text; this was a potential heresy. Yet, the Church needed to ask the question, at what points the perspectives of the hearers intersect with the perspective of the text. Perhaps one reason for the alienation of the text from the context of many Christians in mainline Churches is the fact that the text does not interact with their world. The teaching of the Bible often represents the world of the experts, the world of the biblical scholar.

Hermeneutical Paradigms In The Caribbean

The fear of overpowering or corrupting biblical truths with human ideas is a real one. There is already an existing hermeneutic in our communities seen in the following four approaches to the Bible in the Caribbean to which I now turn. First, I examine the approach of David Jelleyman, former professor of New Testament at United Theological Colleges of the West Indies, my own New Testament professor who has had a tremendous impact on the Church in the Caribbean. Then I will examine briefly the approaches of Pastor Fletcher of the Seventh Day Adventist Church (SDA) and that of Professor John Holder of Codrington College of the Anglican Church in Barbados. Finally, I will look at the approach of Rastafari, an approach that is of primary importance since Rastas provide a perspective from outside the Church.

A Hermeneutic of Protest

In his important essay, "Protest, Pattern and Power," David Jelleyman gave an interesting discussion on the phrase "And sitteth at the right hand of God, the father Almighty,"[4] an important Pauline creedal text that forms an essential part of the historic Apostles Creed of the Church. Jelleyman points out that this is the historic answer to the question: "Where is Jesus Christ today?" The importance of discussing this phrase here is that it highlights the Church's attitude to authority and power in the world and to its exercise of authority and power in the Church. Jelleyman points out that an aspect of this disclosure is made in a familiar Gospel narrative, which related what is described as the ambitious request of two of the Lord's disciples. According to Mark, the Evangelist, "And James and John, the two sons of Zebedee, came forward to him and said to him, 'Teacher, we want you to do for us whatever we ask of you.' And he said to them: 'What do you want me to do for you?' And they said to him, 'Grant us to sit, one at your right hand and one at your left, in glory'" (Mark 10:35–37, RSV). The first major point Jelleyman makes, as he reflects on Jesus' use of power and authority in the Gospels, is what he refers to as the paradox of power. In the biblical context, Peter had witnessed on the day of Pentecost that "it is this Jesus, crucified and killed by the hands of lawless men, whom God raised up (Acts 2:23, 24 cf. 32). This claim is made expressly in terms of Ps. 110.1. Therefore Peter declares: "Let all the house of Israel . . . know assuredly that God has made him both Lord and Christ, this Jesus whom you crucified" (v. 36). This paradoxical interpretation of Ps. 110 is an apt expression of the Gospel, a paradox that goes back to Christ himself (Mark 14:62). As Jesus stood before Caiaphas he acknowledged his messiahship in the statement, "you will see the Son of Man sitting at the right hand of Power, and coming with the clouds of heaven."

The paradox here, states Jelleyman, is that it is this same Jesus who taught people to despise the best seats in the synagogues and the places of honor at feasts (Mark 12:39), who commanded people to love their enemies and to pray for their persecutors (Matt. 5:44). This is the same Jesus, now bound and on trial for his life, who is destined to enjoy divine approval and ultimate vindication. This is the paradox that did not make sense to the exponents of religion in Jesus' time; a paradox that Jesus himself proclaimed and that is repeatedly restated by the Apostolic Church. It was a paradox on

Holy Thursday. It was a paradox on Whitsunday. It was a paradox when the word went forth in Jerusalem. It was a paradox to Jew and gentile; it was a paradox in the ancient Roman world and it is a paradox in the Caribbean. The coveted positions of prestige and power, which James and John so eagerly desired, Jesus has emphatically and vigorously repudiated and rejected. The sons of Zebedee were in quest of prestige, power, and status in society; but all that Jesus did ran counter to the spirit of the age, of that age and every age. His ministry was therefore a ministry of protest, and such a ministry did his apostles inherit from him. Such is the Church's proper ministry today.

So Jelleyman takes us in the direction of what I call a hermeneutic of protest. He implies that biblical hermeneutics in the Caribbean must be one of protest against the misuse of Scripture for the misuse of power. But there is more. Jelleyman maintains that the lives of Christians should be a sustained and vigorous protest against the love of prominence, prestige, and power, which comes all too naturally to people; and I gather he means primarily people in the Caribbean. There is a selfish or self-centered love for greatness and glory in the Caribbean, against which the followers of Jesus have steadfastly to set their face. Christians are called to exemplify the mind of the servant, who did not grasp but gave, who did not elevate self but who emptied self. It is a career of this character that receives the stamp of God's approval. "Therefore, on the strength of such ministry, God has highly exalted him" (Phil. 2:9).

Jelleyman has a healthy respect for the State. He puts it this way: "The State is of Divine appointment, necessary for the regulation of human society and for the organization of life in community. Existing in the world, in which the rebellious powers are still in operation. The State serves in God's design to hold these powers in check, but this it can do with only limited success, because it is itself a part of the system in which these rebel forces are not yet subdued."[5] Because of the Church's loyalty to the State, the Church may work for reformation but never for revolution. This hermeneutic of protest is directed inward, to a person's own renunciation of prominence, power, prestige, and elevation in this society. Jelleyman does not ask that the hermeneutic of protest turn outward to systems and institutions of power that oppress the poor. This hermeneutic of protest leaves unchallenged the principalities and powers in the society that reduce the lives of people to meaninglessness. But the key to the Gospel story has to do with the paradox of power. The paradox is that the lowly are exalted, the humble are elevated and the kingdoms of this world must become the kingdom of our Christ and our God. The one who sits at the right hand of the father almighty, sits in judgment on the social ordering of Caribbean society, which excludes those of poor estate and magnifies those who oppress the poor.

A Hermeneutic of Responsibility

The perspective of the Seventh Day Adventist (SDA) Church in Jamaica, as represented by Pastor L. H. Fletcher, president of the West Indies College, Mandeville, Jamaica, is a good case study in the hermeneutics of responsibility. In his article, "The SDA Facing the Challenges of the 80's," Fletcher speaks from Tim. 3:15, "The household of God which is the Church of the living God, the pillar, and ground of the truth."[6] (RSV) He identifies the words Church, Living God, Pillar, and Ground of Truth as key words and phrases he wants to emphasize as he talks about the challenges the SDA Church faces throughout Jamaica. He suggests that there are three meanings of the word Church, from a Pauline perspective. First, when Paul speaks of the Church he is talking about the Holy Catholic universal Church, the whole company of regenerated individuals throughout the world in all times and places. In the verse under study, Fletcher claims that Paul addresses himself not only to the Church at Ephesus, but to the Catholic Church, which he here refers to as the House of God—the Church of the living God, which is the pillar and ground of truth. The second meaning in Paul's use of the word Church comes from the Greek word *ecclesia,* which means an association or congregation of people, called out by God, for the service of Jehovah. Fletcher points out that the word Church forms a bridge between the Church of both the Old and New Testaments, so that the called out ones of the Old Testament find fellowship with the saints of the New Testament. They unite in faith and hope and love so that God may work out in us and through us his eternal purpose.

The third meaning of the word Church is the community of saints gathered in the SDA Church in Jamaica: those who have accepted the call of Jesus to come out of the thinking and the lifestyle of the world and enter into a covenant relationship with him. These Christians are a chosen generation, a royal priesthood, a holy nation, a peculiar people. All who are children of God in Christ Jesus are members of the body and in this relationship they may enjoy fellowship with each other and fellowship also with their Lord and master. Fletcher makes two claims: (a) We have the truth; (b) This truth must be proclaimed to all the world. To us, as to no other people, is entrusted the truth. God has given to the faithful in the Church a unique understanding of the truth. Citing the founder of the Seventh Day Adventist faith, Ellen G. White, who states "It is as certain that the SDA have the truth as that God lives,"[7] Fletcher begins to develop a hermeneutic of responsibility for the Jamaican Church. The Church has responsibility because God has chosen it and given to it the truth. This responsibility is expressed in a number of challenges the Church faces in Jamaican society. The first challenge is rebellion against all forms of legitimate authority, and this expresses itself even in relationship to the word of God. There is a direct attempt to stifle truth. There are those who compromise biblical truth to make it fit the desires of a new morality within the Church. The second challenge concerns those who seek to neutralize the Church's teaching of the truth. Fletcher reminds his audience that as the Church seeks to fulfill its mission the gates of hell cannot prevail against it. The central challenge facing the Church in Jamaica concerns its unswerving commitment to the Word of God. "We must say to the people, 'Put your trust in God. Obey his commandments. Do all in your power to establish his kingdom on earth.'"[8]

Another challenge the Church faces is it must never be a political or an economic instrument even though it "carries weight" in political and economic matters. It is the role of the Church to sense the needs of humanity, and it must address those needs by handing a cup of cold water, or a loaf of bread in the name of Jesus. But let the Church concentrate on its basic mission: the preaching of the Gospel to everyone. "For this gospel of the kingdom shall be preached to the whole world for a witness to all the nations; and then shall the end come" (Matt. 24:14). "For I am not ashamed of the gospel of Christ for it is the power of God unto salvation" (Rom. 1:16). The Church as it addresses moral issues must not take sides. It must not be involved in politics or political arenas. Let the Church concentrate on its fundamental mission, the conversion of men, women, and youth to personal faith in Jesus Christ. These converted men, women, and youth will deal with the political, social, and economic issues much better than any pronouncements from the Church. The final challenge that confronts the Church is the need to take its responsibility to the family seriously. The family is an index of the Church's health. The Church must address itself to the issues that face the family such as finance, matters of import and export, inflation, and devaluation. Pastor Fletcher suggests that what is needed is a sense of balance between addressing these critical needs of the family and the program of evangelism for the world. According to Fletcher, this hermeneutic of responsibility must not take sides, it must aim at balance.

That Fletcher faces a dilemma that is not unique to the SDA Church in Jamaica, is quite clear. The dilemma has to do, on the one hand, with the Church's attempt to talk about its identity in a way that signifies its distinctiveness as "being in the world but not of the world" and, on the other hand, to articulate the Church's relevance to the world. Many Churches take sides when confronted with these alternatives and Fletcher indicates that the SDA Church in Jamaica is no exception. In order to preserve its identity, the Church turned inward. The temptation to turn inward is real as Fletcher is well aware of (Matt. 5: 13), "You are the salt of the earth; but if the salt has lost its taste, how shall its saltness be restored? It is no longer good for any thing except to be thrown out and trodden under foot by men." (RSV) The problem here is that in the attempt to hold onto its identity, the Church has sacrificed its relevance to Jamaican society and runs the risk of becoming a sect on the margins. Further, the Church's silence in relation to issues of governance in Jamaican society puts the Church in complicity with corruption in that society as it fails to confront issues of power with the truth of the Gospel. The challenge is for the Church to be willing to risk its identity and discover a larger space to be as she seeks to be relevant in the world.

Further, Fletcher's call for a spiritual responsibility of the Church in the world is not in keeping with the role sectors of the Church have played in the history of Jamaica. Fletcher presents the SDA Church in Jamaica as having a rather narrow view of truth. According to him, the SDA Church in Jamaica has the truth and is the sole repository of truth. Granted, he does not state what he means by truth. But if Christ is the truth about God and God's plan and purpose for humanity, it is clear Fletcher will have to make room for a public space for truth. This openness to the truth would allow for an ecumenical conversation with believers from other faiths. The prayer of Christ in John 17 would begin to become a reality in our time. This openness leads to religious tolerance and encourages a sense of unity.

A Hermeneutic of Identity

The next approach to reading the Bible in the Caribbean is offered by John Holder, professor of Old Testament at Codrington College, Barbados, who uses the biblical text to raise questions that are present in the existential situation. He posits as a goal of his study the need to hear the Bible as the living Word of God in the Caribbean context, but only after we have set the text within its original context. Holder proposes to look at the book of Deuteronomy to discover what God's Word is for the Caribbean situation. First, he contends that the book of Deuteronomy emerged within the Manasseh era with one primary purpose, the generating of hope within a hope-denying context. Israel lived in the tension between promise and fulfillment. The issue concerns land. At a time when Israel was in danger of losing its land, the community was reminded of the ties that bind Israel, Yahweh, and the land together. It is these bonds with the people, Yahweh, and the land that constitute the reason for hope. What Holder proposes to do is to isolate the themes of land, identity, and leadership from the biblical text and then see their relevance for the Caribbean.

According to Holder, the land is a gift from Yahweh. The stress on the gift-like character of the land is important because this sets up some space between the land and the people. The land is sign and signal of Yahweh's covenant with his people, and can never become a substitute for Yahweh.

The land and its resources should never serve to block out Israel's memory of Yahweh's goodness. Because of the space between Israel and the land it was clear to Israel that the real owner of the land was not the ancestors, as in African communities, but Yahweh. This space between Yahweh and the land does not only mean that Yahweh owns the land but also that responsibility goes with owning the land. At the very heart of Israel's responsibility to the God of the covenant was the acknowledgment that the neighbor had a right to the land. The author of Deuteronomy urged that the neighbor's landmark shall not be removed: "In the inheritance which you will hold in the land that the Lord your God gives you to possess, you shall not remove your neighbor's landmark" (Deut. 19:14, RSV). Each citizen of Israel is entitled to a bit of land. There is an awareness here of the debilitating effect of landlessness. In the context of Deuteronomy, landlessness severs the binding relationship between Yahweh and Israel, for which there can be no substitute. There is something sacred about the land, especially when it comes from God.

At this juncture, Holder converges the biblical horizon with the horizon of the Caribbean in a contextual conversation, a conversation that preexisted in the sense that the biblical text, read in the context of the granting of the land in ancient Israel, is not read in the Caribbean context of landlessness. Caribbean history is one in which the majority of the people have been excluded from land ownership. But Holder only alludes to the problem; there is no sociocultural criticism at this point. The biblical text is not an offense to the large landowners in the Caribbean of which the Church is "the first among sinners." It would have been most helpful for Holder to explore in the Caribbean context what it means to assert that the land belongs to God. Does this mean that the people have a right to the land? Does Holder's interpretation of the Deuteronomist view of land lend credence to the Cuban model, which in principle claims that the people ought to have access to the land? The land is of critical importance to Caribbean people as the homestead often provides space to cultivate food for the home, space for games, and meeting for family and friends. In the Caribbean it is not unusual to meet and socialize in the yard, to sit under a tree for a game of dominoes, or to stay outdoors all day for a game of cricket. It is in the yard that food is prepared and eaten. In many cases, the house plot is also used as family cemetery, especially in rural areas. Because identity issues in the Caribbean cannot be properly addressed without a discussion of land, it is of first importance that Holder go further than he has in this article and indicate at what points the Deuteronomist view is helpful for the Caribbean situation. Does Holder have any suggestions regarding land distribution and ownership? Where is the land to be found? Should the Caribbean

Church, one of the largest landowners in the region, subdivide and share its land with the peasantry?

Holder moves on to the issue of identity, which the text raises. The people that Deuteronomy addresses have moved out of slavery, but have not yet reached the goal that their release has set in motion. They were a people in the process of becoming. They lived in the tension between slavery's past and the future prospect of liberation. Israel's identity was being carved out of her dehumanizing past and her hopeful future. Hope and memory are always kept in tension as Israel articulates her future. Israel cannot grasp the new future unless she is willing to take the memories of her past into that future. Holder concludes this section with several lessons that the Caribbean must also learn from the text. First, there is the challenge to know our past and be willing to learn from it. Our past should be used as a pedagogical resource to assist us in improving the present and shaping the future.

The second lesson that Holder offers from Deuteronomy is that Caribbean people can only cope and embrace themselves if they know their roots. They must also guard against adopting and imitating the ways of Canaan. To the Caribbean, according to Holder, the United States is Canaan. Caribbean people must pray, "Lord lead us not into imitation." Holder puts it this way: "This is a warning that we here in the Caribbean need to take very seriously. If we want to remain on the world stage as a distinct group of people with well-defined, readily recognizable elements of culture that we can call our own, then we must resist the seductions of the gods of Canaan. In other words we must avoid trading our history, our memories, our (understanding) of God, for those offered by other cultures."9

I have analyzed three approaches to biblical hermeneutics in the Caribbean: first, the position of David Jelleyman, which I referred to as a hermeneutic of protest; the position of the SDA pastor, Pastor Fletcher, which we called a hermeneutic of responsibility; and that of John Holder, which we referred to as a hermeneutic of identity. The hermeneutic of protest asked us to turn inward and renounce power, prestige, and prominence in the society. Pastor Fletcher, who articulates a hermeneutic of responsibility, forbids the Church to take sides, because the Church is responsible to all sides. And so the Church is left with the Bible in hand but unable to engage the culture. Professor Holder, who seeks to place the biblical interpretation in conversation with Caribbean identity, articulated a hermeneutic of identity in which landlessness is sign and signal of the loss of identity. Since all of these positions are flawed and inadequate in more ways than one, I inquire now of the Rastafarian faith to see if help may yet come from outside the Church to address this social, cultural, and theological problem.

A Hermeneutic of Hope and Empowerment

The move now to consider Rastafarian hermeneutics represents a paradigm shift from the perspectives advocated by Jelleyman, Holder, and Fletcher. The perspectives considered so far originate from a theological seminary in Jamaica, the Anglican Church in Barbados, and the Seventh Day Adventist Church in Jamaica. These attempts to translate the Bible into the language of the people represent conversations within the Church and presuppose the centrality of the Bible as an authoritative document. The Bible constitutes the central authority of faith for these communities. There is a shift in perspective and outlook when the paradigm shifts come to the Rastafarian faith. First, the Rastafarian's engagement with the Bible occurs outside of the Church and is not informed by the traditions and teaching offices of the Church. Rastafarians are critical of the Church often pointing out that in the Caribbean it is an extension of the European and North American Church and, as such, has not invested in the alleviation of the grinding poverty in the region. Moreover, they regard the Church as representing the bourgeois class, and the Church's biblical exegesis as representing their theological and exegetical interests. They connect their struggle in Jamaican society for solidarity and dignity with the struggle of oppressed Israel and claim that they are the true Israelites.

As far as the Rastafarians are concerned, the Bible exists for serving the needs of the community. Biblical interpretation does not begin with a consideration of the historical-critical method as it does in biblical scholarship, but with national and global circumstances that impinge on the lives of the Rastafarian community. Their primary concern has to do with the ways in which the biblical text affirms Rastafarian identity and addresses issues of dignity in Jamaican society. Because the Bible exists for the community, Rastafarians take from it whatever is helpful for their struggle to eke out a meaningful existence in "Babylon," i.e., Jamaican society. Rastafarian hermeneutics involves a critical reflection on historical experience in Jamaican society and on the global scene.[10] The Bible is not the authoritative source of truth for Rastafarians. The authoritative source of truth is "Jah," as Jah reveals "Jah's" ways in national or world events, or through the Bible. Jah's activities are not limited to the Bible. Jah is active in national and world events and Rastafarians turn to the Bible often to find an explanation of what Jah is up to in the world. Because of this the Rastafarians are busy exegeting both the sociological and the biblical text. They often begin with the sociological text and then move to the biblical text for elucidation and confirmation of what they presume Jah is doing in the world.

This seems to be what happened in the 1930s with the founding of the Rastafarian movement in Jamaica. According to Leonard Barrett, who worked closely with the Rastafarians, the economic and political situation in Jamaica during the 1930s and the coronation of Ras Tafari as emperor of Ethiopia were the triggers that led the Rastafarians to search the Bible for the meaning of these events. Commenting on the socioeconomic situation in Jamaica, Barrett states:

> The decade beginning in 1930 may well be called the "decade of despair" for the average Jamaican. The political situation was stagnant. The country was still in the hands of men who had little or no feeling for the hungry masses. The average wage for a full day of unskilled labor was twenty-five cents for men and fourteen cents for women. . . . These were the years of the Great Depression, which saw lines of hungry people. . . . Most scholars agree that the movement originated soon after the coronation of Haile Selassie in Ethiopia. The coronation of this African king caused some Jamaicans of African descent both on the island and in New York to study their Bibles more closely. They remembered a pronouncement by Marcus Garvey: "Look to Africa where a Black king shall arise—this will be the day of your deliverance."[11]

The events in Ethiopia, coupled with the prophecy of Marcus Garvey, led the Rastafarians to consult the Bible for answers. The Jamaican scholar Barry Chevannes supports the claims made by Barrett:

> The year, 1930; the month, November. In the remote kingdom of Ethiopia, then also known as Abyssinia, kings, princes and heads of state from all over the Western world assembled to witness the elevation of Prince Tafari Makonnen as the new Emperor of Ethiopia, Haile Selassie 1. "Haile Selassie" means "power of the Trinity." . . . Not only is Ethiopia one of the earliest countries to have adopted Christianity, but a part of the Ethiopian nobility, including the Makonnens, had at least since the middle ages claimed descent from King Solomon of Judah and the Queen of Sheba. Self-consciously, therefore, the new Emperor in appropriating as his title "King of Kings," "Lord of Lords," "Conquering Lion of the Tribe of Judah," was reaffirming the ancient roots of Ethiopian civilization and its independent place in Judaeo-Christian traditions.[12]

A biblical text that became crucial for the founders of Rastafari, as they sought to make theological sense of events that were unfolding in Ethiopia, was Rev. 5:2–5, "And I saw a strong angel proclaiming with a loud voice, Who is worthy to open the book and loose the seals thereof ? And no man in heaven, nor in the earth, neither under the earth, was able to open the book neither to look thereon. And I wept much because no man was found worthy to open and to read the book, neither to look thereon. And one of the elders saith unto me, Weep not: behold, the Lion of the tribe of Judah, the Root of David, has conquered, hath prevailed to open the book, and to loose the seven seals thereof." (KJV) Another text that the Rastafarians have found helpful in interpreting the titles chosen by Haile Selassie is Rev. 19:16, " And he hath on his vesture and on his thigh a name written, King of Kings and Lord of Lords."

In their search for biblical theological paradigms, the Rastafarians looked to Africa and to the Bible and became convinced that Ras Tafari was none other than Jesus Christ returned to redeem Africa and people of African descent. Robert Hill points out that what also convinced the Rastafarians that Ras Tafari was Christ was the homage paid to him by the Western heads of state. According to Hill, one of the dignitaries to visit the new emperor and pay obeisance was the Duke of Gloucester, the son of His Majesty King George V. The Duke presented to the emperor as gift, "a sceptre of solid gold twenty seven inches long which had inscribed on one side "Ethiopia shall make her hands reach unto God" and on the other side "King of Kings of Ethiopia." The gift, accompanied by obeisance of the royal envoy, convinced the Rastafarians that prophecy was being fulfilled.[13] Howell, one of the early founders, read Ps. 72:9–11 for validation, "They that dwell in the wilderness shall bow before him; and his enemies lick the dust! The kings of Tarshish and of the isles shall bring presents: the kings of Sheba and Seba shall offer gifts. Yea, all kings shall fall down before him, and all nations serve him." The reading of Gen. 49:10 was another confirmation by the group that Haile Selassie was of divine origin. "The sceptre shall not depart from Judah, nor a lawgiver from between his feet, until Shiloh come; and unto him shall be the gathering of the people be."

How did the Rastafarians know these things, and how could they be sure that these Scriptures referred to Haile Selassie? They would say, the answer is found in Jah's revelation to the righteous, which was made plain both in world events taking place in Ethiopia and in their interpretation of the Bible.[14] Rastafarians also found conclusive evidence in the Bible that their messiah was black: Song of Solomon 1:5–6, "I am Black, but comely, O ye daughters of Jerusalem, as the tents of Kedar, as the curtains of Solomon. Look not upon me because I am Black, because the sun hath looked upon me." For the Rastafarians, this was conclusive evidence that Solomon was black, as was David his father. Since the Scriptures trace the lineage of Jesus back to David, son of Jesse, Jesus is also seen as a black man. According to the Rastafarians, the color of God is also made clear in Jer. 8:21, "For the hurt of the daughter of my people am I hurt; I am black; astonishment hath taken hold of me.

As the Rastafarians looked to the Bible and at what was happening on the world stage in Africa, it was clear that the redemption of black people was at hand through the messiah Haile Selassie. The twin concepts of the divinity of Haile Selassie and the redemption of black people have distinguished Rastafarians from other Afro-Caribbean movements that have sought to promote an awareness of Black consciousness in the Caribbean. It must be kept in mind that the discourse concerning the divinity of Haile Selassie and the assertions concerning biblical warrants that justify this claim are being made in a sociopolitical context in which the vast majority of Rastafarians are at the base of the social and economic ladder. But not only is the Bible being read in a social setting in which inequalities are rife and the Rastafarians are at the base of the society economically, but it is being read in a cultural and social setting in which many Jamaicans value those with lighter complexions more highly than their darker compatriots. So to picture one's God in one's image was a meaningful way of redeeming the image of black people in Jamaica from disrespect and indignity.

As Rex Nettleford of Jamaica comments, the Rastafarians are not the first in Jamaica to use this strategy of fashioning their own religion as a means of survival in a hostile environment. The Rastas are borrowing from their ancestors, the Revivalists and Myalists, who also used religion as a means of survival.

> The Rastafarians have turned into a major strategy of demarginalization of religion. Having one's own God in one's own image was a grand flowering in Rastafari of what earlier begun in Myal and developed in Zion Myalism and Pocomania, with the hijacking of the oppressor's God in a move that sought to discommode the oppressor. . . . Wresting **the Christian message from the Messenger** as a strategy of demarginalization helped bring slaves and free peasants nearer a perceived mainstream as "children of God." . . . The divinity of all black people—in fact, of all human beings—here becomes the basis for the equality, liberty, dignity, and mutual respect, and equity in terms of access to economic resources, and all the values claimed by civil or democratic society but yet to be achieved in what, to exiles from Africa, is Babylon.[15]

The blackness of God ensures the sanctity and divinity of black people. This means that "blackness" is no longer a curse but is taken up into the divinity of God and becomes a point of departure for talk about the divinity of black humanity. Rastafarians even claim that they are "sons" of God. Membership in the Rastafarian community has to do with the unique relationship of the Rastafarian to Haile Selassie. One does not simply join the community to become a Rastafarian. One has to be born again through a "spiritual rebirth," or self-awakening. The believer becomes a son of "Jah Rastafari who is God" and, as such, shares in God's divinity for it is recorded in John 10:34, "I said ye are God's," and in 1 John 3:2, "Beloved, now are we sons of God, and it doth not yet appear what we shall be: but we know that when he shall appear, we shall be like him; for we shall see him as he is"[16] (KJV).

Obviously, the Rastafarians' use of the Bible is self-serving; they use the biblical text to legitimate all of their beliefs and practices. This is the case not only in their use of the Bible to justify the blackness of God but also in their use of marijuana, which is popularly known in Jamaica as ganja. Although ganja is illegal in Jamaica, the Rastafarians, with the help of biblical quotations, have designated ganja as "holy herb," which then functions as a religious sacrament for the community. The Rastafarians will say that God, who created all things, made the herb for human use and will cite Gen. 1:12 as their proof text: "And the earth brought forth grass, and herb yielding seed after his kind, and the tree yielding fruit, whose seed was in itself, after his kind: and God saw that it was good."[17] But according to Leonard Barrett, ganja smoking by members of the Rastafarian faith was one of the first signs of protest to show their freedom from the laws of "Babylon."[18]

But ganja smoking is not the most import vehicle of Rasta protest against Babylon culture; and it is certainly not a significant contribution to Rastafarians' interpretation of the Scriptures. Perhaps the most significant contribution the Rastafarians have made to biblical interpretation and Jamaican society is their theology of blackness: the claim that God is black and that African peoples are spiritually connected to the blackness of God via Christ and Selassie. Rastafarians find the European Christ unsuitable and inappropriate for their struggle for identity and meaning and so they turn to a black God. But it is in the Bible they find an indispensable resource for establishing their identity and developing their concept of a community lived under the domain of Jah that is free from oppression, exploitation, depersonalization, and domination in Jamaican society. Their model for reading the Bible as a tool of self-definition and social, economic, and political transformation certainly complements the Jelleyman and Holder paradigms for reading and hearing the words of Scripture in the Caribbean context. There is much admiration in society for the contributions the Rastafarians have made to Jamaican life and thought. I believe that the time has come for the Church to repeat what it did in the early 1970s: invite Rastafarians for conversations centered around the role of the Bible in Caribbean cultural and economic redevelopment.

Notes

1. I find it intriguing that Robert Hill, the noted Garvey scholar, in an article, "Dread History: Leonard P. Howell and Millenarian Visions in Early Rastafari Religions in Jamaica," in *Epoch—Journal of the History of Religions at UCLA* vol. 9 (1981): 41, points out that Rastafarianism as preached by Leonard Howell found fertile soil in the village of Trinityville, where I lived as a child and where my father's church was located, as early as April 1933.

2. On Luther and the Seven Sacraments, see Williston Walker, *A History of the Christian Church* (Edinburgh: T&T Clark, 1976), 309.

3. John Clark, W. Dendy, and J. Phillippo, *The Voice of Jubilee: A Narrative of the Baptist Mission, Jamaica, from its Commencement, with Biographical Notices of Its Fathers and Founders* (London: Baptist Missionary Society, 1865), 74.

4. David Jelleyman, "Protest, Pattern and Power," in *Caribbean Journal of Religious Studies*, vol. 1, no. 2 (July 1976): 7–29.

5. Ibid., 25.

6. L.H. Fletcher, "The SDA Facing the Challenges of the 80's," in *The Caribbean Pulpit*, ed. C. H. L. Gayle and William W. Watty (San Fernando, Trinidad: Rahaman Printery, 1980).

7. Ibid., 35.

8. Ibid, 36.

9. John Holder, "Some Deuteronomic Themes in a Caribbean Context," *Caribbean Journal of Religious Studies*, vol. 14, no. 2 (September 1993): 14.

10. See Leonard E. Barrett, *Soul—Force* (New York: Anchor Press, 1974), 182–3.

11. Ibid., 157–8.

12. Barry Chevannes, ed., *Rastafari and Other African-Caribbean Worldviews* (London: Macmillan Press, 1995), 9.

13. See Robert A. Hill, "Dread History: Leonard P. Howell and Millenarian Visions in Early Rastafari Religions in Jamaica," in *Epoch—Journal of the History of Religions at UCLA* vol. 9 (1981): 43–44.

14. Ibid., 44.

15. See Rex Nettleford, "Discourse on Rastafarian Reality," in *Chanting Down Babylon,* ed. Nathaniel Samuel Murrell, William David Spencer, and Adrian Anthony McFarlane (Philadelphia: Temple University Press, 1998), 315.

16. See Leonard Barrett, *The Rastafarians* (Boston: Beacon Press, 1997), 111–2. Rasta exegetes found many texts in the Bible that seemed to corroborate their claim concerning the title of their messiah and his divine status. "Sing unto God, sing praises unto his name: extol him that rideth upon the heavens by his name JAH, and rejoice before him" (Ps. 68:4). Another biblical text that often represents the belief in racial redemption is Ps. 68:31, "Princes shall come out of Egypt; Ethiopia shall soon stretch out her hands unto God." According to the Rastas, Ps. 87:3–4 offers conclusive evidence that Haile Selassie was the awaited one: "Glorious things are spoken of thee, O city of God. Selah. I will make mention of Rahab and Babylon to them that know me: behold Philistia, and Tyre, with Ethiopia; this man was born there."

17. Ibid., 129.

18. Ibid. Of course, to claim that smoking ganja is a general protest against the state is certainly untrue; this practice is rather pervasive in Jamaican society. Ganja smoking has become one of the practices of "Babylon." But for the Rastafarians, ganja smoking is part of their ritual of protest and dissonance against Babylon.

Chapter 11 🎴

Daughters of Jah

The Impact of Rastafarian Womanhood in the Caribbean, the United States, Britain, and Canada

Loretta Collins

> ... a real "roots" girl
> Inna mi stance mi nuh paper soldier
> Mi move like Sister Winnie and the Queen Omega...
>
> —Sister Carol[1]

Paradoxically, anthropologists, historians, and sociologists have portrayed the socioreligious phenomenon of Rastafari as a source of inspiration for colonized freedom fighters but a force of oppressive dogma for women. Rastafarians reiterate Marcus Garvey's vision for an African repatriation and his demand to end "mental slavery"; criticize political corruption, imperialism, neocolonialism, and racism; preach black pride and "one love and unity"; and, as prophets of Jah, attempt to usher in a "new dispensation during which man will fully recover his God-like nature and injustice, suffering, and oppression will be eradicated from human affairs through the intercession of the divine."[2] Reggae, in its global manifestations and translations, has emerged over the last 25 years as the most salient soundtrack for the transnational anticolonial liberationist ethics, aesthetics, spiritualities, and power strategies of the "Black Atlantic" and beyond.[3] Reggae "continues to function as the principle medium through which people the world over have acquired their knowledge and awareness of Rastafari."[4] Reggae also offers many examples of messages sympathetic or affirming to women, especially in songs by Bob Marley ("No Woman No Cry"), Peter Tosh ("Whatcha Gonna Do?"), Burning Spear ("African Mother"), Lucky Dube ("Hold On"), and reggae dub poems by Mutabaruka, Oku Onuora, Michael Smith, Yasus Afari, and Benjamin Zephaniah. Women reggae artists, such as Rita Marley, Marcia Griffiths, Judy Mowatt, and Sister Carol, as well as Jamaican, Canadian, and British dub poets Jean "Binta" Breeze, Cherry Natural, Lillian Allen, Afua Cooper, and Carmen Tunde promote the strength of Rastafarian women.

Yet reggae also includes a tradition of denigration of women based on Old Testament morality and Jamaican folk traditions, such as proverbs, "Man is like an arrow, woman is like a shadow. Women will hurt you, no doubt about it" (Reggae group, The Meditations). Reggae idealizes African queens and mothers and condemns "fallen women" ("Pimper's Paradise," by Bob Marley), while ragamuffin and dancehall music—musical genres often differing in ideologies from but influenced by roots reggae/Rastafari—often denigrate women with "slack" lyrics and sexual boasting ("Gone Up," "Cocky Rim," and "Flesh Axe" by Shabba Ranks, "Waan Mi Virgin" and "Titty Jump" by Yellowman, and "Pull Up to the Bumper" by Patra). As both a religious practice and a pop-cultural product, Rastafari presents challenges to womanist critics interested in issues of the representations of women in an international context.

The Early Phase In Rasta Women Research

When I first began to examine representations of Rastafari womanhood, I was primarily interested in pop-cultural and literary manifestations. I started with the following questions: If the roots reggae performer functions as a mystic or prophet, who in this role emphasizes a need for historical redress and a nonimperialistic spiritual rebirth? How have woman reggae performers, dub poets, and Rastafarian women novelists understood their roles as conscious Rastafarian- influenced teachers? In my initial research, I examined various representational discourses of Rastafarian and reggae codes of womanhood as constructed in magazines and newspapers (*JAHUG, Rastafari Speaks, Rasta Voice, Coptic Times, Dub Missive, Reggae Report, Reggae Times, The Beat,* and *Uprising International*), reggae and dub poetry by women, novels featuring Rastafarian women as main characters (including *Dread Culture: A Rastawoman's Story* by the Jamaican-Canadian writer Masani Montague and *A Daughter's Grace* by the Barbadian-British writer

Zindika), and fictive and documentary films on Rastafarian womanhood (*Burning an Illusion, Omega Rising, Rastafari: Conversations Concerning Women,* and *Roots Daughters*). As I accumulated background research, I also became interested in the myopic way Rastafarian women have been represented by both androcentric and feminist-oriented academics. It seems evident that articles intending to pay tribute to the contemporary strides of the Rastawoman only provide brief references to specific activities, events, associations, or tasks performed within domestic and labor economies. After talking with and interviewing Rastafarian women in London, Kingston, and Toronto over the last three years, I want to advocate a new directive in Rastafari scholarship that will consider the recent shifts in theorizing and practicing global feminisms and accurately reflect the accomplishments and goals of women who choose a Rastafarian lifestyle.

In "Under Western Eyes: Feminist Scholarship and Colonial Discourse," Chandra Talpade Mohanty delineates the challenges and problems of representational discourses, stating that "the relationship between Woman—a cultural and ideological representational discourse (scientific, literary, judicial, linguistic, cinematic, etc.)—and women—real, material subjects of their collective histories—is one of the central questions the practice of feminist scholarship seeks to address. This connection between women as historical subjects and the representation of woman produced by hegemonic discourses is not a relation of direct identity, or a relation of correspondence or simple implication." Neither pop-cultural and literary representations of the Rastafari sistren nor academic representations have accurately embodied the complex range of lived experiences or fully documented the histories of female participation in Rastafari. Even the most politically savvy histories of the movement and ethnographic studies most sensitive to women's issues have not escaped simplistic hegemonic paradigms of what it means to be a Rastawoman. In contrast, the explorations of Rastafari womanhood in fiction, music, and poetry at least acknowledge acts of *agency* and self-determination, political and spiritual agenda-setting, and individual subjectivities.

By means of reviewing the discursive representations of the Rastawoman in academic discourse, and by documenting the activities and goals of particular women's organizations, this chapter seeks to redress prevailing scholarly misrepresentations and challenge analytical modes that reduce Third World women's issues to the overriding problem of sexual domination. I provide a critique of scholarship that sustains notions of "First World" superiority in feminist liberation efforts, without exploring the complex effect of "structural elements in many developed countries," ethnic and racial strife, global capitalism, and neocolonial views on the lives of women in "underdeveloped" countries (all of which provide benefits to "First World" women).[5] However, I also criticize "womanist" analyses of the revolutionary power of Rastafari womanhood and other African women's movements that applaud global feminism within the "New Rastafari" in theoretical terms. This I do without grounding the discussion in documentation of particular Rastafarian practices and women-associated projects.

Because there are so few publications on the subject of women in Rastafari, scholars tend to repeatedly cite a few early keystone articles that delineate patriarchal codes. Although those articles attempt to avoid a totalizing or homogenizing portrait of Rastafarian womanhood, they emphasize dogmatic oppression and material victimization. The majority of recent articles repeat the same list of subordinating elements—Rastafarian doctrines and taboos concerning women. Rastafari woman is defined first by her gender oppression—rather than by her adherence to the visionary/revisionary ideologies of Rastafari or by her socioeconomic, racialized, or politicized experiences. As Mohanty notes, in the sort of Western imperial feminist framework set up in most of these articles, the "average third world woman leads an essentially truncated life based on her feminine gender (read: sexually constrained) and being third world (read: ignorant, poor, uneducated, tradition-bound, religious, domesticated, family oriented, victimized, etc.)." This, Mohanty suggests, is in contrast to the "(implicit) self-representation of Western women as educated, modern, as having control over their own bodies, and sexualities, and the freedom to make their own decisions."[6] Thus, I object to discursive constructions in academic writing that reinscribe the Rastawoman as subordinated victim rather than as a dynamic, heterogeneous source of social transformation. I advocate a research directive that examines acts of *agency*, provides a detailed documentation of local women-centered activities and testimonies, recovers neglected histories, traces international ties between women, searches out Rastafarian women in global settings not yet well-researched in Rastafari scholarship, and promotes collaborative projects among researchers and Rastafarians.

As Rastafari and reggae continue to influence worldwide liberationist ideologies, adherents must interrogate aspects that potentially hinder women. Several researchers have pointed out the often dire financial status of Jamaican women in the urban informal economy—in a situation of underemployment, unemployment, poorly paid domestic day-labor, and marketplace "higglering." As Faye V. Harrison argues, "The sexism that shapes and inhibits the political behavior of women active in the informal economy impedes the political development of the entire informal and casual work force." In order for the economically "downpressed" sector of Jamaican urban society to "trod forward," women must gain access to a wide range of economic strategies for the maintenance of their households. This is especially urgent since a high percentage of women in urban Kingston function as head of household, cannot depend on income from their babies' fathers, and may receive lower rates of remuneration for labor in "female-specific jobs."[7] Ideologies that impede female participation in the wage-economy sector and in community mobilization efforts damage the survival and development of the sector at large. Rastafarian livity and reggae prevalent in these areas promote spiritual empowerment, opportunities for community formation, and the consciousness-raising rhetoric of public dissent, on one hand. If, on the other hand, Rastafarians articulate contradictory messages of respect and denigration of women, it is imperative to interrogate detrimental ideologies or practices. Perhaps this is a process that should take place primarily from within Rastafarian communities. Currently, Rastafari-identified women live in several countries and come from all economic classes, educational levels, and labor fields or professions. Rastafarian women have been vocal participants in recent years and have written on the status of women. Unfortunately, as women have often pointed out to me in conversation (especially women living in the Caribbean), their publications are often either self-financed or appear in ephemeral Rastafarian pamphlets and newspapers with limited circulation and haphazard archiving. Regardless of who conducts the research, Rasta and non-Rasta commentators must clearly define the specific situations of the women they include in their studies. It is especially imperative that outside researchers (who often have much greater access to prime publication opportunities) examine their motives, methods, and preconceptions before ascribing the label "sexism" to Rastafari livity.

At the same time, Western feminist academics should consider the sexual and cultural hegemony their own discourses produce when creating representations of the "oppressed" urban Jamaican or Rastafarian woman. Rather than generalizing about a "group" as if it is a unified, homogeneous entity— the generic Rastawoman—researchers must attempt to document the multiplicity of ways in which women in particular local secular and religious segments mediate material resources, conceptualize their experiences, and create alliances to exert control over the contingencies of everyday life and counteract objectionable local actions or national systemic/ institutional policies. While women are subject to religious mores, societal norms, and coercive state regulations concerning capital, labor, industry, property, legal rights, human services, race relations, family structures, conjugal contracts, and sexual conduct, women are social catalysts, as well.

Obiagele Lake, Maureen Rowe, Carole D. Yawney, and other scholars of Rastafari have pointed out that the actual position of Rastafari women "has been given very scant attention."[8] The most substantial, book-length works on Rastafari, dating from the early 1970s to 1995, including studies by Ernest Cashmore, Ivor Morrish, Anita M. Waters, Jack A. Johnson-Hill,

Leonard E. Barrett, Barry Chevannes, G. E. Simpson, Hon. Rex Nettleford, Joseph Owens, and Horace Campbell, neglect to provide detailed commentary on the contributions, experiences, political histories, roles, or representations of Rastafarian women. Gender concerns are either omitted entirely or relegated to a cursory sentence, footnote, paragraph, or at most a few pages.

Of the early book-length studies, Horace Campbell's *Rasta and Resistance: From Marcus Garvey to Walter Rodney* (1987) provides one of the most lengthy discussions of Rastafari women (a full page and a half). In a study that traces Rastafarian movements in Jamaica, Britain, and Ethiopia, Campbell merely dismisses the involvement of women in these various manifestations. He claims that there "were no overt signs of striving Rasta women in Britain in the early days," marking Rastawomen's resistance as "in the main passive" to the "tendencies of capitalism to shape women into mindless consumers." Attempting to distinguish the political imperatives of black women's organizations from Western feminism, Campbell equates "those who babble feminist slogans and generalize about the sexism of Rasta" with "those feminists who reinforce racist myths about black men as rapists." Even though one might argue that Campbell's point about the interconnectedness between a key issue of the Western feminist agenda and discrimination against black men is undeniably well-taken, his use of conventionally insulting phrases, such as "mindless" and "babble," in regard to women is tinged with misogyny.[9]

To Campbell's credit, he does mention Makeda Patricia Silvera and Charmaine (Masani) Montague, leaders of the Toronto-based Rasta Cultural Workshop. In 1980, Silvera had traveled to Jamaica to discuss with leading reggae performers the pervasiveness of lyrics degrading to women. At that time, Silvera was an undergraduate student at York University, working under the supervision of Professor Carole D. Yawney, who has carried out extensive research on Rastafari. In the original article, Silvera (now editor of Sister Vision Press in Toronto) describes her thesis project, "Images of Women in Reggae Music," and characterizes how she envisions the role of a Rastawoman in the Canadian context. She claims that too often reggae lyrics portray women as either "some 'gal upon de street corner' running after different men, or adolescent mothers with several children they cannot support by themselves." While she criticizes derogatory lyrics and has traveled to Jamaica with the express purpose of urging popular reggae artists to respect women in their songs, Silvera does not dispute basic male-female hierarchies. Rather, she emphasizes common goals. The Rastawoman's purpose, according to Silvera, is "similar to that of the man, which is to struggle with progressive forces towards the destruction of Babylon." Acknowledging that the Canadian Rastaman can be "puritanical" in his lifestyle, dietary practices, and relations with women (refusing to eat food prepared by women, for instance), Silvera claims that these ideologies have not provoked struggles over leadership between men and women. "What is important is how we are going to feed our children and educate them in Babylon." The Rasta Cultural Workshop, undocumented in academic writings, is one example of the influential role a Rastawoman can play in the attempt to promote Rasta livity and improve conditions for women and children.

Masani Montague, who started the Rasta Cultural Workshop (1977–80) with her sister, a community worker, says that at the time, besides the Ethiopian Orthodox Church, the workshop was the first attempt to organize Rastafarians in Toronto.[10] Although the primary purpose of the workshop was to promote economic self-sufficiency, craft-making, and education, organizers also felt the imperative to counteract the flood of negative media coverage, characterizing Rastafari as a "bizarre cult" associated with violent crime, that appeared in the Toronto press after Bob Marley's concert tour of Canada in 1975. The Workshop ran a film series and a Bible study group, as well. Later, Montague also helped organize the First International Rastafarian Conference in Toronto (1982) and the Voice of Thunder: Dialogue with Nyabinghi Elders (1984), a month-long program that brought three Rastafarian Elders from Jamaica. She has organized reggae concerts and cultural fests—Culture Jam in 1985, 1987, and 1989, and Rastafests in Toronto and Ottawa between 1993 and 1997. Masani has examined social issues in the Rastafarian community in her theatrical plays and her novel, *Dread Culture*, and in an in-progress book titled "Reasoning with My Sisters." Mentioned briefly by Campbell, the Rasta Cultural Workshop and the long-term work by Makeda Silvera and Masani Montague deserve more extensive academic attention.

Few researchers mention actual organizations of Rastafarian women by name. Faye V. Harrison, in "Women in Jamaica's Informal Economy: Insights from a Kingston Slum," a study based on primary research conducted during the late 1970s in "Oceanview," a slum in downtown Kingston, cites Sheila Kitzinger and Maureen Rowe on Rastafarian male dominance. She fails to include any conversations she may have had with Rastafarian women, but she does assert that during the 1970s, women became "more visible and vocal within the Rastafari movement."[11] As an example of new perspectives on women in Rastafari, she states—in a footnote—that in 1980 three women's organizations were established. Unfortunately, these organizations remain unnamed and no further information or citation is provided. One can only assume that she has no firsthand knowledge of these groups, but is referring to the three that the Rastafarian Sistren Maureen Rowe names in the much-cited 1980 *Caribbean Quarterly* article, "The Woman in Rastafari."

Carole Yawney has attributed the critical omission of Rastafarian women in research to both the ethnocentrism on the part of most academics (most of whom are male) and the perceived urgencies of the early researchers who attempted to combat Rastafarian harassment campaigns in the Caribbean, the United Kingdom, and Canada. Yawney claims that academics, having been socialized in sexist societies and into professions with largely unexamined male biases, do not generally consider women's experiences to be serious, independent subjects of study. "This orientation," she states, "would be reinforced in societies such as Rastafari where its patriarchal ideology would confirm Western ethnocentrism and encourage us to identify with the male definition of what is culturally significant."[12] Since "leadership" is a prime issue in patriarchal systems, those researchers interested in power structures within the more-or-less acephalous Rastafari movement focus on the Patriarchs and Prophets of particular Rastafari compounds. One such study, John Paul Homiak's 1985 doctoral dissertation, "The 'Ancient of Days' Seated Black: Eldership, Oral Traditions, and Ritual in Rastafari Culture," examines, in part, the Rastafari Elders. Women receive minute, peripheral attention in the analysis and figure only in descriptions of the proceedings of the tabernacle. Homiak describes women as dressed in "ankle-length skirts and heads covered in colorful wraps," and positioned "around the circular fringes of the Tabernacle" where they "dance passively" during the Nyabinghi—compared to the more ecstatic dancing by men— and refrain from the ganja "chalice." The degree to which he cites Yawney and repeats the same signifiers of female subordination that she emphasizes indicates that Homiak's observations of female participation were not a primary priority and his interpretations were overly reliant on prior discursive representations.[13]

Jack A. Johnson-Hill, in *I-Sight the World of Rastafari* (1995), a study that provides an "interpretive sociological account of Rastafarian ethics" through the analysis of Rastafarian poetry, exemplifies the male-orientation in Rastafari studies. By praising what he discerns as a progressive "non-chauvinistic awareness" in recent poems by Rastamen, he ironically defends his own choice to neglect works by Rastawomen in his analysis of relationships between the sexes:

> Although there is still a tendency to romanticize the black woman, there is also an emerging predilection to view her as more than a sexual object, baby producer, handmaiden, or source of male ego gratification. While the poetry of Rasta sistren provides insights regarding relations between men and women in Rastafari, the analysis in this section will be limited to examples of poetry written by men, because the change in male consciousness is particularly noteworthy in such a traditionally patriarchal movement.[14]

The "new" more egalitarian and respectful treatment accorded to women in texts by men is justifiably praised, but perhaps a more noteworthy approach for the Rastafari scholar would be an inclusion of poetry written by women and statements on male-female relationships from the perspectives of Rasta sistren.

Women scholars such as Obiagele Lake and Diane J. Austin-Broos emphasize the disproportionate participation of men and women in Rastafari as a reason for the neglect of Rastawomen. According to one of the most recent population surveys completed by the Statistical Institute of Jamaica (1982), 2,588 women and 11,661 men claimed Rastafarian identification out of a population of 2.5 million in Jamaica. Undoubtedly, these figures, by now outdated and also subject to inaccuracy—assuming that not all Rastafarians will claim a Rastafarian identification in response to a governmental survey conducted in a society that has been less than accepting of the brethren and sistren—do not adequately reflect the participation rates of women. According to early newspaper and academic accounts of Rastafari, women were visibly present during activities—including those viewed as socially rebellious—in numbers large enough to warrant mention. *The Star,* March 24, 1958, reports: "The city of Kingston was 'captured' near dawn on Saturday by some 300 bearded men of the Rastafarian cult along with their women and children." This revolutionary attempt was preceded by a convention, well-attended by both men and women: "For the first time in local history members of the Rastafari Cult are having what they call a 'Universal Convention' at their headquarters known as the Coptic Theocratic Temple in Kingston Pen. Some 300 cultists of both sexes from all over the island have assembled at Back-O-Wall headquarters since Saturday, March 1."[15]

Leonard Barrett, in *The Rastafarians: Sounds of Cultural Dissonance* (1977), documents the noticeable involvement of women, while categorizing their status as secondary: "In special meetings women act as mistresses of songs or, in the case of the Rastafarian African National Congress, they may be used as recording secretaries." Barrett also observes that a "large segment" of Rastafarian women during this period were selling "Rastafarian products such as knitted clothing, baskets, mats, brooms, art works, and other sundries."[16] None of the early studies investigate the essential role Rastafarian women played in sustaining their households through self-help economic enterprises or in the development of a Rastafarian aesthetic in handicrafts and arts. Rastafarian crocheted outfits, tams, sandals, purses, leather goods, bedspreads, jewelry, wood carvings, T-shirt art, and souvenir crafts have not only been vended locally and internationally, sold as fundraisers for Rastafarian causes, and showcased at the biannual Jamaican national crafts fair at Devon House in Kingston, but have influenced Caribbean visual and plastic artists and fashion designers.

Barrett includes a brief summary of his discussion with a woman well-known "for her Rastafarian crafts." He argues that "this female opinion is important because, for years, the women of the movement have remained in the background of this male organization." In addition to agreeing with the Rasta proscriptions against birth control and a belief "in the superiority of men," the informant says that she enjoys the Sunday services of the Ethiopian Orthodox Church, "its Amharic language classes on weekdays, and the social get-together of the women." Missing an opportunity to inquire in more depth about the economic, educational, and social functions that Rastawomen participate in, Barrett chooses to pose the more typical ideological questions about Rasta dogma and women. He does not pursue an inquiry into the activities women participate in at the E.O.C. or the craft skills practiced by this particular informant. He also mythologizes the Rasta Queen as parable-of-the-woman-fallen-from-grace, in a cinematic scene in which another woman who has been expelled from a Rasta camp for bad sexual conduct stands at the bottom of a hill, gazing up towards the tabernacle: "Her gaze . . . reminded me of the scripture which reads: 'I will lift up mine eyes unto the hills, from whence cometh my help.' The queen looked lost."[17]

The problem for early researchers of Rastafari may not have been primarily the statistically low participation of women within Rastafari, but an inquiry narrowly directed at dogma and "narrativized" through heavy allusion to what was perceived as an Old Testament, fundamentalist positioning of women. Contemporary researchers might, instead, attempt to document the activities and beneficial experiences of women who have participated over the years in the Women's Guild at the Ethiopian Orthodox Church.[18] Although the E.O.C. promotes Christian Orthodoxy, the Maxfield Avenue church in Kingston has a high percentage of parishioners who practice Rastafarian lifestyle and share Rastafarian perspectives. Many women Elders attend E.O.C., as well, and might be able to offer testaments about the woman-centered activities of the Church.

Barry Chevannes's doctoral dissertation, "Social Origins of the Rastafari Movement," and its revision, *Rastafari: Roots and Ideology* (1995), is the only extended study by a male researcher to investigate the "remarkable developments" by women in post-1970s Rastafari movements. Although he documents strict gender and sexual taboos observed by the Bobo Shanti, a more fundamentalist sect once led by Prince Emmanuel, he argues that these taboos have undergone changes within the larger Rasta communities. He notes that in recent Rasta celebrations women were present in large numbers. Women have been invited speakers at occasions as auspicious as the 100th anniversary of the birth of Marcus Garvey rally in Half-Way-Tree park in Kingston held August 17, 1987 by the Ethiopian International Unification Committee (EIUC). Women have been included in a Rastafarian delegation to the Smithsonian Institution in the United States. Women have spoken out against sexual subordination in Rastafarian publications. Chevannes offers as an instance Daughter Loi's statement delivered in a September 1985 issue of *Rasta Voice:*

> For black sisters who recognize themselves to be assets to our liberation struggle, the role of inferiority is unacceptable. In the quest for the liberation and oneness of our people, the black man must discontinue the practice of subordination of black sisters, and come to grip with the facts; we are just as needed as the brothers in the struggle for liberation and continuous prosperity of the black race.[19]

The Sistren Theatre Collective, an education-and-social-action-through-drama organization based in Kingston and founded by working-class women during the 1970s, has also conducted research and workshops on Rastafari gender relations. Sister Imani M. Tafari-Ama, the project organizer, brought together "eighty dreadlocks, evenly distributed between genders and spanning the major groupings."[20] Maureen Rowe, who participated in these workshops and has served over the years as an organizer and commentator on the roles of women, remembers the Sistren project for its success in generating a dialogue between men and women on divisive issues, such as polygamy.[21] Unfortunately, after the workshops finished, the Rastafarian communities failed to productively carry forward the dialogue in any organized way. Although Sister Tafari-Ama documented the workshops in a master's thesis, titled "An Historical Analysis of Grassroots Resistance in Jamaica: A Case Study of Participatory Research on Gender Relations in Rastafari" and a video, later researchers have failed to make use of these valuable materials.[22]

In a recently published anthology, Tafari-Ama's chapter, "Rasta Woman as Rebel: Case Studies in Jamaica," briefly describes the Sistren Theatre Collective-sponsored "Gender Relations in Rastafari" project, noting its unprecedented attempt to raise and clarify gender issues such as Rastafari ideology, sexuality, women's roles, and images of women. Tafari-Ama's article provides excerpts of several interviews with women who follow the path of Rastafari but also declare their autonomy. This study is particularly valuable in its examination of contradictions between ideologies and practice in a faith that proclaims the man "Kingman" and head of household, when the common economic reality is of households headed and supported by women. In addition, analyzing patriarchal structures, "family survival strategies," and class divisions between Rastafarian women and men, Tafari-Ama also tackles more controversial issues, including a woman's rights to procreative decision-making and the need to confront and combat domestic violence.[23] Chevannes had access to Sister Tafari-Ama's unpublished work, but did not provide any detailed summary or textual analysis of her documentation. However, a positive quality of Chevannes's study is his contextualization of the advancements for Rastafari women in terms of other political and ideological triumphs by women's movements within the Jamaican society during that era. Within five pages, Chevannes briefly introduces several aspects of contemporary Rasta womanhood worthy of further study, yet none of these instances of agency have been taken up in later studies by Chevannes or other researchers.[24]

The Second Phase Women Research and Sistren Agency Initiatives

In the second phase of academic response to Rastafari—a phase dominated by women researchers, including Diane J. Austin-Broos, Sheila Kitzinger, Carole D. Yawney, Teresa E. Turner, Ella Ray, Obiagele Lake, Maureen Rowe, and Imani M. Tafari-Ama—a handful of articles have appeared. In one of the most often cited but dated articles, "The Woman in Rastafari" (1980), Maureen Rowe delineates the subordinating attributes of Rastafari—which then get repeated and elaborated on in subsequent articles on Rastawomen. At the time of publication, Rowe was criticized by her detractors as a reactionary apologist for the subordinated status of women within Rastafari. Some critics told her that she should have focused more vehemently on the victimization of women. However, she had a more positive objective. Although a few researchers, including Obiagele Lake and Ella Ray, have reasoned with Rowe since the publication of her article, most of the academics who repeatedly cite her have not had personal communication with her. She believes a strongly worded assertion that research on Rastafari must be conducted by participants in the movements, which appears in the introduction of the essay, accounts for why non-Rastafarian researchers might have shied away from interviewing her about more recent developments in gender relations.

Rowe's 1980 article delineates several well-known stereotypic characterizations of Rastafarian doctrines but defends the positive role of women in Rastafari.[25] Even though Rowe argues that from the beginning sisters drawn to Rastafari were "'conscious' of Afrika" before sighting the faith, and that Rasta daughters from the 1960s and 1970s were independently attracted to Rastafari because of the pan-Africanism, politics, and economics, researchers who cite Rowe emphasize the sighting of Rastafari through the Kingman. Rowe said that women in the 1970s and thereafter joined the Twelve Tribes of Israel, an organization that involves women in official capacities, asserted themselves more vocally at Rasta gatherings, modified Rasta dress codes, and reasoned together. Rather than rally for independence, women were calling for an acknowledgment of the interdependence of men and women in liberationist efforts. Rowe mentions "three groups of daughters" organized in 1980, the King Alpha and Queen Omega Daughters; International Twelve, among the Twelve Tribes of Israel; and Dawtas United Working Towards Africa (DAWTAS). These groups addressed the need for educational/social services and self-help industries. However, the histories and projects of these daughters' organizations remain untold in scholarship. Researchers citing Rowe and adhering either to a Western imperial feminist agenda or a male-biased orientation, readily excerpt sections on dogma while omitting references to autonomy and activism. Citing an extended passage from Rowe's description of Rastafarian doctrine on women, Diane J. Austin-Broos downplays the positive aspects of womanhood provided by Rowe: "Rowe details a number of modifications to this doctrine among Rastafarians with whom she is familiar. Nevertheless she acknowledges, like other commentators, that women play a subordinate and very minor role in working-class Rastafarianism."[26] Each of the organizations mentioned by Rowe and ignored by other scholars is obviously worthy of documentation.

Rowe participated in King Alpha and Queen Omega Daughters and its offshoot, Daughters United Working Towards Africa (DAWTAS). She also knew of a group of Elder Rastafari women known as King Alpha and Queen Omega Theocracy Daughters. Both King Alpha and Queen Omega Daughters and DAWTAS were attempting to address the educational needs of Rastafari youth, self-development activities, the establishment of social services, and international outreach. Farika Birhan, an activist in several Rastafarian activities and the director of a small press whose activities are described in more detail later in this chapter, provided documentation of some of the Elder group's agendas. According to Maureen Rowe, the King Alpha and Queen Omega Daughters were attempting to establish a basic school and devise self-development activities for women. Rita Marley donated quite a few books to the organization. Land for the school had been donated in Irish Town, but funds were needed to clear the land, build a school, acquire buses, and provide a staff. The women organized fund-raising events, primarily within the Rastafarian community. At Family Fun Day, held at Hope Botanical Gardens in Kingston, the organization sold pledges and raffled cakes donated by a corporation. During 1986–87, Rowe and another sistren, also an educator, surveyed Rastafarian parents with school-aged children and, disappointingly, found that only parents who were either incapable of affording mainstream Jamaican basic schooling or had children not yet of school age expressed an interest in enrolling their children. More affluent Rastafarian families preferred to send their children to an established Jamaican school with a demonstrated success rate in exam preparation and scholarship programs for higher education. Under these circumstances, it was difficult to project a financially viable school. The school project was further complicated by the inconvenient location of the Irish Town land and the need for transportation. Disillusioned by the survey results and the financial and logistical difficulties, the women were unable to build the school. However, Rastafari women have successfully participated in designing curriculum for Afrocentric schools or have run other Rasta-centered schools. Rowe served as principal at Rastafarian Leahcim Semaj's Sankore School in Stony Hill, Jamaica. Although not exclusively Rastafarian, this school featured an African-centered curriculum. Both Sister Petinaud and Sister Faye have operated Rastafarian basic schools on the north side of the island.

Unfortunately, the activities of the King Alpha and Queen Omega Daughters, DAWTAS, and the achievements of individual Rastafarian women educators remain undocumented. Rowe believes that during the 1980s, the Twelve Tribes of Israel also had a women's group, which concentrated on traditional craft skills, such as sewing. During the 1990s, a loosely affiliated group of women brought Queen Mother Moore, an African American activist, to Jamaica.[27] In 1997, JAFA, a new federation of women in the Jamaican music industry, presided over by attorney Rastafarian Sandra Alcott, promises to champion the rights of and support the development of women artists and promoters. In a more recent article, "Gender and Family Relations in RastafarI: A Personal Perspective," Rowe attempts to place Rastafarian ideologies concerning women within the historical context of larger Jamaican society and the creolization of European and African practices and worldviews. Rowe reveals that the two groups that she participated in during the early 1980s disbanded under charges of sexual deviance by the brethren, a strategy that had the effect of intimidating the Rastawoman from organizing exclusively female service groups. However, Rowe argues that despite this pressure, women continued to reshape and have a positive impact on RastafarI. According to her analysis, Rastafarian women were the first to gain acceptance in a society that denigrated the dread brethren. Instead of limiting their citations to Rowe's earlier article, researchers should draw upon her more recent elaborations.[28]

Another early text by a Rastafari woman is less frequently quoted, but also taken by a few researchers as evidence of the restrictiveness of fundamentalist Rasta dogma. In the first edition of *Rastafari: The New Creation* (1981), Barbara Makeda Lee expresses an acceptance of conventional sex-specific roles for men and women. Jamaican Makeda has at one time or another been an author, filmmaker, cultural journalist, novelist, and former Independent senator in the Jamaican Parliament (1984–87). According to Makeda, the traditional domestic roles of man as primary "breadwinner" and woman as "childbearer" do not necessitate a situation of inequality. She describes the "Rastafari Queen," "the Mother of Creation," as a woman who with "humility and grace" "acknowledges that the Man is leader of the union, but in this there is no inequality, for as Queen, she is a strong partner." The Rastafari Queen "uses her womanly intuition and perspective to assist her man," but she also finds her own "means of industry and productivity." Makeda praises the custom of modest dress, since Rasta garments do not "reveal the beauty" of the woman's body "to the casual observer, reserving this sensual sight for her man alone." The use of make-up is also discouraged: as a role model to other sisters for "priestess and prophetess," a woman should allow her face to radiate with the natural "Vibrations of Holy Love."[29]

Western feminists have protested against fundamentalist dress codes, arguing that under a guise of religious piety the patriarchy uses female coverings and admonitions of sexual fidelity as means of enforcing the status of women as physical property. However, Rastafari dress codes cannot be equated with other fundamentalist clothing traditions. While it is relatively common to see young Jamaican women appearing in public in short dresses, shorts, jeans, or dancehall-style clothing, in general the conventions of dress in public for most Jamaican women of all ages and economic levels is still fairly conservative. The Rastawoman who wears dreadlocks, a head-wrap or tam, a long skirt, and perhaps African cloth or the Rasta colors—red, green, and gold—is marking herself as distinctively Rasta in a society that has considered Rastas to be threatening to the social fabric of the bourgeois class. As one Rastawoman informant remarks to Obiagele Lake in defense of the dress conventions: "When you see a Rasta dawta come, you know she's a Rasta because of the way she adorns herself. We wear no pants, we wear no shorts, you know. In the good old ancient way that's the way we dress."[30] Thus, while Western feminists might balk at discursive descriptions of "modest" Rastafari dress, in praxis the clothing functions as a triple-signifier *against* oppressive gender, racial, and post-colonial practices. It signifies resistance to the sexual-objectification and commodification of women's bodies in Western capitalist society. In *Perceptions of Caribbean Women: Towards a Documentation of Stereotypes,* Erna Brodber argues that in a Jamaican context, the pressure to conform to European definitions of beauty impede Jamaican women: "This effort to change body form diverts time and mental energy from more creative activities and, most detrimental of all, crystallizes an inferiority complex." Illustrating that the enforcement of European definitions of beauty have been connected to the repression of popular expressions of black racial pride, Brodber cites a 1971 case in which the headmistress of Wolmers Girls School, "one of Jamaica's oldest and most prestigious educational institutions," forbade girls from wearing "soul hair-dos."[31]

In a 1997 pamphlet, "The Rastafari Queen," Makeda updates her reasonings on Rastafarian womanhood. Acknowledging the impossibility of providing a universal definition of what a contemporary Rastafarian woman is, Makeda first addresses beliefs that were held pervasively. She rationalizes menstrual blood pollution taboos and offers justification for new guidelines. She claims that during the early days of the movement, Rastafarians living in the more impoverished areas lacking in modern conveniences of sanitation and accessible water supply, customarily obeyed "Levitical laws of cleanliness which deemed that a woman should stay separate from the community" during her period. She argues that those sisters who live in sanitized conditions might no longer adhere to these taboos: "If a Brother considers his partner 'unclean' during 'that time' and the Sister is not pleased with this, this is one of the things which they should have come to an understanding about, before becoming yoked together. Some Rastas live according to liberating New Testament doctrines, while others are comfortable with Old Testament ways." Makeda urges the Rastawoman to "impart to her children an education in the heights of Black Culture, History, and Religion," continuing the emphasis on motherhood that has been so vital within Rastafari, but she also assertively places the woman side-by-side with man, with "neither more equal than the other half."[32]

Sheila Kitzinger and Carole D. Yawney, early researchers of Rastafari who each initially gained entrance into the communities they researched by reasoning with Rastafari brethren, focus primarily on the livity of the Rastaman. Yawney has attempted to reevaluate her earlier lack of emphasis on the issue of Rasta womanhood. Kitzinger states that although "at one time there was a camp consisting solely of women," women play a peripheral role in the movement. Oral histories from this woman's camp might have revealed alternative visions of Rastawoman identity. However, no more is said of the camp, including how Kitzinger knew of its existence. Instead Kitzinger focuses on domestic arrangements between men and women. She cites a Rastafarian belief that good Queens must obey their Kingmen, as an indicator of a male insistence on female subservience. Other aspects of domestic partnership noted by Kitzinger include a stance against legal marriages and an abhorrence of contraception. In two different articles, she provides contradictory appraisals of Rasta nonlegal unions. In "The Rastafari Brethren of Jamaica," she states: "They do not bother with legal marriage, but in this they are no different from the majority of peasant Jamaicans for whom marriage is a sign of a successful relationship established over the years, rather than the ticket to one. Marriage exists 'when two people come to each other to support each other.'"[33] Yet she implies a differentiation between Rastafarian and rural peasant values of legal marriage in another version presented in "Protest and Mysticism: The Rastafari

Cult of Jamaica": "Rastas would be ashamed to marry legally. . . . Other peasant Jamaicans, although they may never achieve it, look forward to legal marriage as a possible reward for economic success in middle age, and as the symbol of a successful relationship established over the years."[34] Legal marriage, part of a Western Judeo-Christian and colonial system of verification not available to enslaved Africans under early Jamaican plantation codes and, furthermore, not part of traditional African conjugal agreements, is valorized here as a sign of ultimate achievement.

In 1986, 70 percent of Jamaican households were headed by women, and many researchers have documented the traditions of baby fathering, visiting unions, and "outside children" in Jamaican society. Characterizing these domestic arrangements as unstable and undependable for women, researchers often imply that Jamaican women would be better off, in economic and child-rearing terms, if the society was structured upon legal and monogamous marital agreements.[35] However, in "Colonial Policy towards Women after the 1938 Uprising" (1986) and *Wid Dis Ring* (1987) Joan French, a member of the Sistren Theatre Collective, documents the way that the Jamaica Federation of Women, a bourgeois organization of the 1940s that promoted legal marriages, actually played a vital role in the pauperization of Jamaican women. In a massive public campaign preaching "up-lift" messages in the press, through churches, and local and national organizations, "poor women were encouraged to accept the 'dignity' of marriage as a solution to their economic problems." Modeled upon the Women's Institute of Great Britain, the Federation, supported by a membership of 30,000, sponsored mass weddings. One of the main promoters of legal marriage, Mrs. Marry Morris-Knibb, purchased inexpensive wedding rings in bulk and sold them for 10 shillings, making them affordable for poor women. One hundred and fifty mass weddings were held. According to French, the overall effect of the marriage campaign and the glorification of dependent housewifery was a reduction of women's participation in the wage economy and unionization movements, which provide settings for economic improvement, individual achievement, and political activism.

In Jamaican history, unionization was a powerful move towards better wages and work conditions, as well as decolonization and the construction of the two major rival political parties, the Jamaica Labour Party and the People's National Party. As French argues, "the solution to female poverty, then, was not to pay women 'proper' wages for work they did, but to deprive them of what little wages they had through the establishment of 'proper' families, in which men were seen as the providers, and therefore as having the primary right to a wage." British ideologies about the connections between "Home" and "Country," which were used as a model by the Federation, ran counter to traditional practices of Jamaican female self-reliance, as well. According to Brodber, the twentieth-century emphasis on "house-wifery and a high degree of sex role differentiation in work were not before part of the black woman's behavior. Nor was dependency on one man."[36]

On the subject of birth control, Kitzinger states that Rastafarians disapprove of contraception, labeling it "internal murder." Indeed, many Rastafarian documents speak out against the use of birth control devices and the pill; however, this stance may not be examined solely in terms of Western feminist conceptions of sexual domination. In a July 21, 1972 issue of *Rasta Voice*, Ras Colquhoun cites several Bible verses in support of the anti–birth control stance, including Mark 10:15: "Verily I say unto you whosoever shall not receive the Kingdom of God as a little child, he shall not enter the gates of Zion."[37] Sister Farcia, in "Forward Up Daughters," denounces governmental birth control programs, as well. According to Kitzinger, Rasta informants justified the belief against unnatural birth control barriers by stating that they believed in "life upon creation, because the old soon dead off" and were anticipating the day when children would be needed to till the soil when repatriation to Africa became possible. Kitzinger states that natural means of birth control, such as abortifacient bush teas, were approved of and used by some Rastafarians. Several researchers have documented the use of bush teas, including those brewed from pennyroyal, for birth control in Jamaica. What becomes apparent after examining many Rastafari periodicals, books of poetry, and oral histories recounted by researchers, is the high degree to which Rastafarians have been concerned about cherishing and providing for "the youth." Both Rastafarian men and women discuss the importance of taking responsibility for children and providing them with enlightened education and a strong sense of black pride. Children are regarded as natural resources. Rastafarian women are characterized in academic discourse as oppressed, in part because of the Rastafarian glorification of Mother Africa, motherhood, and a perceived lack of reproductive freedom. Researchers attempting to understand Rastafari proclamations against birth control during the 1970s might consider the way abortion, birth control, and motherhood were viewed in Jamaican culture at large, the biblical injunctions, the positions of other "Orthodox" religions, Black Power ideologies of the times (the Nation of Islam, for instance, held a similar stance against birth control), and the way population-control programs have functioned in First World-Third World interaction.

Cheryl Johnson-Odim, in "Common Themes, Different Contexts: Third World Women and Feminism," argues that one cannot simplistically attribute an anti-birth control stance to a lack of development and modernization or a patriarchal and fundamentalist socioreligious power structure within the society. One must take into consideration the complicated economic and ideological systems at work in the global rhetorics and programs of "population control," especially considering that the early development of population-control arguments and stratagems was not unrelated to the philosophies and "science" of eugenics. Rastafarians have expressed strong anti-imperialist philosophies. One might argue that Western contraception ideologies and practices are a product of and contribute to the foundational management principles and goals of global capitalism.[38] Furthermore, no researcher has yet surveyed contemporary Rastas of both genders about the impact of recent HIV awareness on sex practices and the use of barrier protection. A survey of young Rastafarians would probably reveal a variety of opinions about unprotected sex. Jamaican television networks broadcast several AIDS and pregnancy awareness public service announcements utilizing popular actors and singers. Certainly, the use of condoms has been advocated in recent ragamuffin reggae music. Buju Banton, hailed as a new roots-conscious singer with the release of his (1995) *Til Shiloh* CD, urges, "Ragamuffin don't be silly/ Put some rubbers 'pon the willy."

Carole Yawney questions the role of non-Rasta feminist scholars in evaluating gender issues. In "Moving with the Dawtas of Rastafari: From Myth to Reality," Yawney urges both outside feminist researchers and Rastafari sistren to examine their ideological biases when playing the role of evaluator or defender of Rasta gender norms. She acknowledges the failings of Western feminism to adequately address itself to the needs and agendas of international women or women of color and the resulting required precautions for scholars grounded in feminist theories. Yawney argues that non-Rastafarians need to find means to "understand more about women's experience of Rastafari," citing as a case in point an article written by Rastafarian women who advocate polygamy. Yawney advocates fieldwork research conducted from a feminist perspective and based on "social relationships with women." However, Yawney also argues that prescribed gender roles within Rastafari cannot be deemed just solely because individual women choose to accept them. She criticizes a stance taken by Rowe as an example of false consciousness. Rowe argues that "The concept of male dominance can have no validity where the female understands, accepts, and operates within the parameters of a prescribed role. It is only when the female resists this role that the concept acquires significance."[39] In a 1983 article, "Rastafarian Sistren by the Rivers of Babylon," Yawney argues that sistren living within the Caribbean have more passively accepted male hegemony, while their Canadian and U.S. Rastafarian sistren have "vigorously defended their interests in the face of much opposition." By locating an assertive and politicized element of Rastafarian womanhood in Canada and the United States, Yawney seemingly attributes the activism of Rastafarian women to their immigration from restrictive Caribbean communities and their "exposure" to the superior First World formulations of gender equality.[40]

But Yawney sets up what is, perhaps, a false dichotomy between the more "liberated" Rastafarian woman of North American and Canada and her more subjugated Caribbean sistren. The Jamaican *Rasta Voice* often reports and pays tribute to the active participation of women in international and local events. For instance, a July 21, 1972 issue mentions the Local 41 division of the Ethiopian World Federation, which consisted solely of women. An August 9, 1974 issue announces a speech to be given at the head office of the Rastafari Movement Association by Sister Norma Hamilton, who had just returned from the Sixth Pan-African Congress held in Dar es Salaam in Tanzania. During the same year, the journal announces Sister Hamilton's initiative to start a Montessori method school for children aged two to five years old—the Royal Ethiopian Basic School—in the yard of Jah Bond of the Twelve Tribes of Israel. Later assuming the name Iyawata Farika Fayola Birhan, Hamilton published many Rasta poems, wrote radio dramas, television and film scripts for the government's Information Service, campaigned for adult literacy, organized Rasta sistren within the King Alpha and Omega Daughters Theocracy I, edited *Queen Omega News,* started a Rastafari press, Queen Omega News Communication Company (which followed her from Jamaica to Palo Alto, San Jose, and Berkeley, California), and mothered five children. Hamilton had been trained as a journalist at *The Daily Gleaner* and at the London School of Journalism.

King Alpha and Queen Omega Daughters Theocracy I, headquartered in Jamaica, in its statement of purpose, calls for the development of respect, knowledge, and Omega balance in the movement; a review of the traditional and prophetical role of Rastafari women; protection from economic exploitation, the opening of trading posts and cultural training centers; the establishment of an educational network; the recording, documentation and broadcasting of the contributions of Rastafari women's efforts to liberate her people; and the liberation of Africa, repatriation, peace and justice.[41] In the introduction to Kongo Pidow's volume of poetry, *Rastafari Poems of Reality, Truth and Naturality,* published by Queen Omega News Communications, Birhan (Hamilton) states that her press is one of the educational projects of the Daughter's Theocracy: "Its aim is to bring news to the world of Rastafari from the Nyabinghi vision, focusing on telling the world who Queen Omega is."[42] Birhan's messages of upliftment and her agendas for educational advancement were consonant with the statements of racial and gender pride by women issued by *Rasta Voice* and the Rastafarian Movement Association.

Yawney cites as progressive the uncovering of women's locks during the leisurely moments of the First International Rastafarian Conference in Canada: "Several of these sistren, temporarily freed from domestic and economic duties, sought out each other's company to bask in the sun.

Dressed in traditional African-style, bare-arm robes (as opposed to Jamaican tailored attire) they shook their locks free from their head ties and relaxed. Were things getting out of hand?"[43] Yet, during the same time period, many women within the Caribbean were contributing significantly to and influencing the emergence of Rastafari, sometimes with the respect and support of the brethren and sometimes in the face of more ardent opposition. Although Iyawata Farika Fayola Birhan (Hamilton) was at that time a vocal spokesperson, no researcher has since attempted to interview Birhan or provide commentary on her poetry or work as an educator. According to Chevannes, Birhan came into Rastafari during a time when the children of the middle classes, intellectuals, and professionals began sighting Rastafari in larger numbers. Influenced by Black Power and women's civil rights movements of the 1970s and 1980s, Rastafarian women began asserting their interest in coming into the faith without a Kingman. By the time of the Rastafari International Theocracy Issembly, which took place on the University of the West Indies, Mona, Jamaica, campus and in Montego Bay, Westmoreland, Trelawny, St. Catherine, and St. Thomas, from July 18–26, 1983, the issue of sexual equity within Rastafari was urgent enough to feature in the controversial opening address delivered by Brother Iration:

> I respectfully implore this Theocratic Issembly to acknowledge that the Creation is administrated by two complimentary heads, male and female.
>
> Being the sexual individualisation of Rastafari Supreme life, thus sexual equity is a fundamental principle of nature for the harmonisation of the Rastafarian family. It is of the fundamental concept of the Rastafari Inity that male and female are the continuation of each other. Daughters are indispensable, and even more so at this stage of our struggle.
>
> No liberation, national or international, can ever be accomplished without the in depth involvement of daughters . . . (cheers and applause). . . .
>
> We must realize that our daughters cannot give their needed potential contribution from an inferior status. We must give our daughters their natural respect and dignified recognition, thereby addressing the core and rudiments of our cultural disorder.[44]

Undeniably, women within the Caribbean are influencing the contemporary directives of Rastafari. As Yawney says, "Some of the sisters who have been raised abroad or who have lived some time abroad are asking very pointed questions about their role within the movement."[45] While it is true that many of the most visible and vocal women within Rastafari in Jamaica have spent time abroad and have ties with women in the larger international Rasta community, one may be certain that their perspectives and goals for social justice are influenced as much from their experiences in the Caribbean (or their travels to Africa) as from their exposure to Black Power struggles and feminist influences in Britain, Canada, or the United States.

Researchers such as Teresa E. Turner have more directly attributed a post-1970s to 1990s shift in gender dynamics within a more secularized "New Rastafari" to the influences of black feminist movements: "the 'new Rastafari' is part of an international social movement of resistance to structural adjustment and affirmation of a new society which transcends the limitations of the male deal." In "Rastafari and the New Society: Caribbean and East African Feminist Roots of a Popular Movement to Reclaim the Earthly Commons," Turner identifies new Rastafari as a more potent force for global reform. She recognizes the historical contributions of black women to resistance against "'gendered, racial and racially-gendered hierarchies' of slavery, colonialism and today's super-exploitation." Employing a Marxist, C. L. R. James–type analysis, Turner links three historical junctures in anti-colonization movements in which women were active—the Nyabinghi movement in East Africa (which she locates in southwestern Uganda), the Mau Mau movement (Kenya), and Rastafari (Jamaica). In the interest of documenting the submerged "herstory" of these militant movements, Turner insists upon women as catalysts and essential agents.[46] Turner's womanist agenda and global perspective—although a positive move in Rastafari scholarship—unfortunately leads the author into simplifying and generalizing complicated histories, ultimately doing little to inform readers about specific daily acts of local resistance, militancy, or organization among the "new Rastafari" women.

Of the recent articles, the best in terms of allowing Rastafarian women to speak for themselves on the subject of their experiences and concepts of identity, Obiagele Lake's "The Many Voices of Rastafarian Women: Sexual Subordination in the Midst of Liberation," is the first to include excerpts of interviews with Rastafarian women. These interviews, which Lake conducted in Jamaica, attest to the pluralities of responses of Rastafarian women to traditional Rastafarian doctrines and include strong statements of autonomy. Several women emphasize the ways in which Rastafari doctrines and practices regarding women have changed. Or, better yet, informants discuss how they have personally responded to, modified, and reshaped Rastafarian concepts according to their own perspectives. Women discuss "sighting" Rastafari on their own volition, the positive aspects of Rastafarian dress, flexibility in the menses taboos, and the relative gentleness of Rastafarian men. One informant explains that since Rastafarians are interested in liberation and education, they are more conscientious about their family than men who spend time at the rum shops after work.

But the article still models itself upon representations of oppression and subordination. Rowe's list of subordinating elements provides the structural outline of the essay in sections titled "Women and Pollution," "Women's Dress and Hair," etc. Lake clearly has an ultimate agenda of establishing that "although Rastafarian men may differ in their rhetoric of liberation and their Afrocentric symbolism compared to other Jamaican men, their de facto relationship to women is retrogressive." In the final quoted interview, a Rastafarian sistren mentions briefly the cooperative effort by an organization of Rastafarian women to bring Queen Mother Moore to Jamaica. No further mention is made of Rastafarian women's experiences and efforts of achieving social agency. Lake argues that the creation of a more egalitarian society requires not only a greater access to material resources for women, but a production of "positive cultural images that would resonate with their newly acquired positions in society."[47] She views this access to creation as a difficulty for Rastafarian women because men have "control over cultural resources," such as media and religious texts. Yet, Rastafarian women have been spokespersons, activists, artists, poets, playwrights, crafts people, journalists, vendors, vocalists, pop music singers, church or organization participants, conference organizers, educators, publishers, and professionals. Researchers need to seek out and document the positive cultural images that the women of Rastafari have already fostered and continue to create.

Conclusion

No academic article on Rastafari womanhood has yet attempted to research and analyze the positive aspects of Rastafarian women's identity and societal efficacy or document the agendas of distinct women's organizations. As Marnia Lazreg notes in "Feminism and Difference: The Perils of Writing as a Woman on Women in Algeria," "the overall effect of this entrenched paradigm based on oppression deprives women of self-presence of being. Because women are subsumed under religion presented in fundamental terms, they are inevitably seen as evolving in non-historical time. They have virtually no history. An analysis of change is therefore foreclosed." However, Lazreg says, Rastafarian women in Jamaica, North America, Britain, and Canada, and elsewhere "make history," banning together to form sisterhoods for social change and self-help. A substantial amount of work remains to be done in documenting the history of women within both the early and contemporary movements. Many of the male Elders involved in the formative period of Rastafari have now passed on. As Barry Chevannes has pointed out to me, it is possible that because of a more extended longevity for women, Elder women might still be able to recount their memories.[48] Oral histories provided by Elders and women sighting Rastafari during the 1970s and 1980s should be collected as expediently as possible.

Researchers should also direct their attention and support to contemporary alliances of women that are setting agendas for the future. One such organization, RASSIS (Rastafarian Sisters) International, founded by a dynamic trio of women, Denise Miller, Damali Robertson, and Marcia Henry, and based in Kingston, Jamaica, provides music managing, booking, and public relations services. Devising creative entrepreneurial ideas and a line of culturally conscious products, RASSIS has been involved in Afrocentric bookfairs and concerts, and markets hand-painted Rastafarian "rods" (walking staffs), jewelry, and crocus sack clothing. The sistren plan to open wellness centers that would focus on mind, body, and soul—offering ital nutrition counseling and products, conferences, and workshops.[49] Undoubtedly, Rastafarian women in the many Caribbean nations, South America, North America, Africa, and Europe are organizing equally ambitious enterprises and creating vital cultural spaces for women. Rastafarian women in London have actively participated in the Twelve Tribes of Israel, the SIMBA Rastafari Organisation, and Rastafari Universal Zion (a community-based organization that has assisted in housing, welfare rights, health, education, and run an Afrocentric Saturday school). Their activism remains undocumented in scholarship even though Rastafari brethren have received considerable coverage by both the British media and black British cultural studies essayists.

The academic and popular debates generated by Western feminisms, black womanisms, "Third World" or global feminisms, cultural studies, and post-colonial theories have provoked productive and radical reorientations within academia. They have promoted a proliferation of rigorous interrogations of the complex impact of global capitalism, nationalist struggles, post-empire, imperialistic, neo-colonial regimes, militarism, local economic strategies, ethnicity, cultural imperatives, race and racism, traditional values, and gender oppressions on the lives of men, women, and their families. Issues of sexual subordination within liberationist religious and secular movements must be confronted. Rastafarian women have certainly experienced instances of gender oppression. As the reggae singer Judy Mowatt has said, "Man and woman are like two wings of creation, as one cannot ascend without the other, because if one ascends without the other, then creation will not be as it should have been with just one wing."[50] Gender equity is an essential issue in achieving social justice. However, far too often the limited focus on gender oppression and dogma precludes a more holistic and/or participatory research directive that has an agenda of documenting specificities. The time has come to record the detailed histories of the innumerable *courageous* individual acts of agency and the successes of particular organizations of women. Molara Ogundipe-Leslie advocates positions emerging from feminism in the African context. Some of the key points she cites are worth reiterating as applicable to the study of pan-African movements of Rastafari and womanhood:

- That the total configuration of the conditions of women should be addressed rather than obsessing with sexual issues.
- That motherhood is idealized and claimed as a strength by African women and seen as having a special manifestation in Africa.
- That certain aspects of women's reproductive rights take priority over others.
- That women's conditions in Africa need to be addressed in the context of the total production and reproduction of their society and that scenario involves men and children. Hence, there has always been an emphasis on economic fulfillment and independence in African feminist thinking.
- That the ideology of women has to be cast in the context of the race and class struggles that bedevil the continent of African today, that is, in the context of the liberation of the total continent.[51]

In historicizing an international movement as influential in the pan-African fight against the legacies of slavery and colonialism as Rastafari, researchers interested in the impact and relevance of woman-centered collective action, agency, and autonomy must address themselves to the full range of activities, experiences, values, and herstories of Rastafarian sistren.

Notes

1. I wish to give thanks to Rastafari sistren Barbara Makeda Lee Blake Hannah, Maureen Rowe, Denise Miller, Masani Montague, and Professor Carole D. Yawney for their assistance and conversations. The research for this article was funded by a Fulbright Graduate Fellowship to Jamaica and a grant from the International Council for Canadian Studies and the Canadian Embassy.
2. John Homiak, "The 'Ancients of Days' Seated Black: Eldership, Oral Tradition and Ritual Rastafari Culture" (unpublished Ph.D. diss., Brandeis, 1985).
3. Paul Gilroy's term in *The Black Atlantic: Modernity and Double Consciousness* (Cambridge, MA: Harvard University Press, 1993).
4. Obiagele Lake, "The Many Voices of Rastafarian Women: Sexual Subordination in the Midst of Liberation," *New West Indian Guide* 68:3,4 (1994), 235–57, esp. 236; Neil J. Savinshinsky, "Transnational Popular Culture and the Global Spread of the Jamaican Rastafarian Movement," *New West Indian Guide* 68:3, 4 (1994), 259–81, esp. 260.
5. Chandra Talpade Mohanty, "Under Western Eyes: Feminist Scholarship and Colonial Discourses," in *Third World Women and the Politics of Feminism,* ed.

Chandra Talpade Mohanty, Ann Russo, and Lourdes Torres (Bloomington: Indiana University Press, 1991), 53; Cheryl Johnson-Odim, "Common Themes, Different Contexts: Third World Women and Feminism," in *Third World Women and the Politics of Feminism,* 322.

6. Mohanty, *Under Western Eyes,* 56.
7. Faye V. Harrison, "Women in Jamaica's Urban Informal Economy," *Third World Women and the Politics of Feminism,* 187, 180.
8. Lake, 241.
9. Horace Campbell, *Rasta and Resistance: From Marcus Garvey to Walter Rodney* (Trenton, NJ: Africa World Press, 1978), 200, 199. See Johnson-Odim, 323: "We also remember that rape, or even the perceived or concocted threat of rape, has historically posed nearly as great a danger to the safety of black men as to that of black women. For centuries, besides fearing for their own security, black women have feared the maiming, lynching, or jailing of their husbands, brothers, and sons on charges that they were rapists, no matter how unsubstantiated." See also Angela Davis, "Rape, Racism and the Myth of the Black Rapist," in *Women, Race and Class,* ed. Angela Y. Davis (New York: Random House, 1981).
10. Phone interview, July 30, 1997.
11. Harrison, 187.
12. Carole D. Yawney, "Moving with the Dawtas of Rastafari: From Myth to Reality," in *Arise Ye Mighty People? Gender, Class & Race in Popular Struggles,* ed. Teresa E. Turner (Trenton, NJ: Africa World Press, 1994), 66.
13. Ibid; Homiak, 6.
14. Jack A. Johnson-Hill, *I-Sight the World of Rastafari: An Interpretive Sociological Account of Rastafari Ethics* (Metuchen, NJ: American Theological Library Association and Scarecrow Press, 1995), 242.
15. *The Star,* March 6, 1958, 1; as cited by Leonard Barrett, *The Rastafarians: Sounds of Cultural Dissonance* (Boston: Beacon Press, 1988), 93, 92.
16. Barrett, 209.
17. Ibid., 184–5.
18. Barrett, 209, 184–5; The Ethiopian Orthodox Church is a Christian Church. The Kingston, Jamaica, Church unofficially recognizes Haile Selassie as an earthly prophet rather than a divine being. However, about 70 percent (by the author's estimate) of the congregation is either Rastafarian or Rastafarian-affiliated.
19. Barry Chevannes, *Rastafari: Roots and Ideology* (Syracuse, NY: Syracuse University Press, 1995), 403.
20. Chevannes, 404, 406.
21. Personal interview, Kingston, Jamaica, July 8, 1997.
22. See Imani Tafari-Ama, "An Historical Analysis of Grassroots Resistance in Jamaica: A Case Study of Participatory Research on Gender Relations in Rastafari" (master's thesis, Institute of Social Studies, The Hague, 1989).
23. Imani Tafari-Ama, "Rasta Woman as Rebel: Case Studies in Jamaica," in *Chanting Down Babylon: The Rastafari Reader,* ed. Nathaniel Samuel Mur-

rell, William David Spencer, and Adrian Anthony McFarlane (Philadelphia: Temple University Press, 1998), 89–106.

24. See Len Garrison, "Out of Exile: A Study of the Historical Development of the Rastafari Movement in the Jamaican Society" (unpublished Ph.D. diss., Ruskin College, Oxford University, 1973), esp. 87. Some of the organizations mentioned were not predominantly Rastafarian in orientation. Although researchers mention the large percentage of participation by women in The Ethiopian World Federation (EWF) and other organizations that existed between the 1970s and the present, much could be done to document women's roles in earlier Jamaican groups such as EWF, The National Liberation Study Group, Youth Black Faith, Youth for Social Change, Abeng, Jamaican African Liberation Front, Rastafarian Movement Association, Black Cultural Renaissance Movement, the Harambee Theatre, and the Socialist Study Group.

25. Maureen Rowe, "The Woman in Rastafari," *Caribbean Quarterly* 26, vol. 4 (December 1980): 13–21. The custom of calling women "daughters" has been repeatedly mentioned as a signifier of subordinate female status—evidence of the paternalistic and patronizing relationship between Kingmen and Daughters—rather than as a signifier of respect taken from Biblical rhetoric. However, a survey of Rastafari periodicals suggests a more egalitarian use of gender terms. For instance, in the full run of *Rasta Voice,* a Kingston journal published between the 1970s and 1980s, nearly every article begins with the inclusive addresses of "Sons and Daughters" or "Brothers and Sisters." The terms "Queen" and "Empress" are commonly heard, as well. Haile Selassie's wife, Empress Menen, called Queen Omega by Rastafarians, serves as a role model. As Sister Farika Birhan explains, "Empress Menen's effect on the Rastafari during her earthly reign was profound. Rastafari addressed the woman in the Congregation as Queen. The Rastafari Woman had a female model to model herself after and followed Empress Menen's movement with close scrutiny. The Rastafari saw Empress Menen in every Rastafari Woman, and respect was high. . . . The psychological effect upon the Black Woman to have an Afrikan Woman reigning as Empress in regal splendor, and being paid homage has never been stressed by so called writers on Rastafari culture. It must never be overlooked by those of us searching for the Woman in the Rastafari Culture." See "Rastafari Woman," *JAHUG* 2 (1992): 36–8. Sister Imani Tafari-Ama also argues that the Rastafarian woman takes pride rather than offense at the titles of respect she is given. See "Rastawoman as Rebel: Case Studies in Jamaica," in *Chanting Down Babylon,* 92.

26. Diane J. Austin-Broos, "Pentecostals and Rastafarians: Cultural, Political, and Gender Relations of Two Religious Movements," *Social and Economic Studies* 36, vol. 4 (1987): 1–39, esp. 19.

27. Queen Mother Audley Moore was the founder and president of the Universal Association of Ethiopian Women and a member of the Universal Negro Improvement Association and the National Council of Negro

Women. During the late 1950s, she submitted petitions to the United Nations, demanding acknowledgment of the genocide of slavery and reparations for former slaves. F. Len Wilson, "African-American Research and Discussions list," electronic mail, May 6, 1997.

28. Maureen Rowe, "Gender and Family Relations in RastafarI: A Personal Perspective," in *Chanting Down Babylon.*

29. Barbara Makeda Lee, *Rastafari: The New Creation* (Kingston: Jamaica Media, 1981).

30. Lake, 247.

31. Erna Brodber, "Perceptions of Caribbean Women: Towards a Documentation of Stereotypes" (Cave Hill, Barbados: Institute of Social and Economic Research [Eastern Caribbean], 1982), mimeograph at Jamaica National Library.

32. Makeda Blake Hannah, "The Rastafari Queen," pamphlet, Kingston, Jamaica (1997).

33. Sheila Kitzinger, "The Rastafarian Brethren of Jamaica," *Comparative Studies in Society and History* vol. 9 (1966): 38; and Kitzinger, "Protest and Mysticism: The Rastafari Cult of Jamaica," *Journal for the Scientific Study of Religion* 8 (fall 1969): 240–62, and 253.

34. Ibid., 253.

35. See references to this bias in Olive Senior, *Working Miracles: Women's Lives in the English-Speaking Caribbean* (Institute of Social and Economic Research, University of the West Indies, Cave Hill, Barbados, 1991, in association with Indiana University Press); Dorian Powell, "The Role of Women in the Caribbean," *Social and Economic Studies* 33:2 (1984): 97–121; Powell, "Caribbean Women and Their Response to Familial Experiences," *Social and Economic Studies* 53:2 (1986): 83–130.

36. Joan French, *Wid dis Ring* (Kingston: Sistren Research, 1987), 29; "Colonial Policy towards Women after the 1938 Uprising: The Case of Jamaica," paper presented to the Conference of the Caribbean Studies Association, Caracas, Venezuela, May 28–30, 1986, 21, 5, mimeographed copy at Jamaica National Library; Brodber, 36.

37. Ras Colquhoun, "No Birth Control," *Rasta Voice* vol. 21 (Kingston, Jamaica: July 1972): 3. *Rasta Voice* is one of the ephemeral Rasta publications that are very inconsistent and hard to find. *Rasta Voice* is a cyclostyled publication mimeographed. It is now out of print.; Sister Farcia, "Forward Up Daughters," *Rasta Voice* (Kingston, Jamaica), 86:16.

38. Ibid., 323.

39. Yawney, "Moving with the Dawtas," 72; Yawney, "To Grow a Daughter: Cultural Liberation and the Dynamics of Oppression in Jamaica," in *Feminism: From Pressure to Politics* (Montreal: Black Rose Books, 1989), 143; Rowe, 16.

40. Carole D. Yawney, "Rastafarian Sistren by the Rivers of Babylon," *Canadian Woman Studies* 5:2 (winter 1983): 73–5, esp. 75; *Rasta Voice,* (Kingston, Jamaica) vol. 91 (1983): 14, 15, 20.

41. See "Daughters of the Theocracy," *JAHUG* 2 (1992): 30.
42. Kongo Pidow, *Rastafari: Poems of Reality, Truth and Naturality* (Palo Alto, CA: Omega News Communications Unlimited, 1982).
43. Yawney, "Rastafarian Sistren," 75.
44. "Rastafari International Theocracy Issembly: Word- Sound Higher-Lights," *JAHUG* 2 (1992): 20–2.
45. Personal interview with Barry Chevannes, Kingston, Jamaica, February 17, 1997; Yawney, "Moving with the Dawtas," 142.
46. Teresa E. Turner, "Rastafari and the New Society: Caribbean and East African Feminist Roots of a Popular Movement to Reclaim the Earthly Commons," Arise Ye Mighty People! Gender, Class & Race in Popular Struggles, 10; Turner citing Brand (1987), 29, and Young and Dickerson (1993); Turner, p. 33; Rastafarians have adopted elements of Nyabinghi. For a discussion of the role that women played in East African Nyabinghi, see Elaine Hopkins, "The Nyabinghi Cult of Southwestern Uganda," in *Rebellion in Black Africa,* ed. Robert I. Rotberg (London: Oxford University Press, 1971).
47. Lake, 252, 251.
48. Marnia Lazreg, "Feminism and Difference: The Perils of Writing as a Woman on Women in Algeria," *Feminist Studies* 14:1 (spring 1988): 81–107; Paul Gilroy, *There Ain't No Black in the Union Jack: The Cultural Politics of Race and Nation,* foreword by Houston A. Baker, Jr. (Chicago: University of Chicago Press, 1987), 11; Personal interview with Barry Chevannes, Kingston, Jamaica, February 17, 1997.
49. Phone interview with Denise Miller, Kingston, Jamaica, July 13, 1997. See also Sheryl White, "Women in the Biz: RASSIS International," *Reggae Times* 1:10 (1997): 8–9.
50. Carol Anne Clark, "Judy Mowatt: Insights into Reggae's Light of the Moon," *The Reggae and African Beat* (December 1985): 15–6.
51. Molara Ogundipe-Leslie, "Stiwanism: Feminism in an African Context," in *Recreating Ourselves: African Women and Critical Transformations* (Trenton, NJ: Africa World Press, 1994), 207–41: 225–6. Cited in Shelah Moody, "Judy Mowatt," *Reggae Report* 10:4 (1992): 18–9.

Chapter 12

Riddim Wise and Scripture Smart

Interview and Interpretation with Ras Benjamin Zephaniah

Darren J. N. Middleton

Labeled a "streetwise, post-criminalized artist" by the editors of *The Routledge Reader in Caribbean Literature*, Benjamin Zephaniah has been crafting verse for many years, and the burden of this essay is to capture a spark from his powerful poetic fire.[1] To this end, after providing a brief biography of Zephaniah's life, I reproduce (with permission) three important poems from his wide-ranging *oeuvre*. I follow this with some hermeneutical reflections, a kind of theologically informed literary criticism, which attempts to show the biblical background to the aforementioned verse. Finally, I conclude with a word-by-word account of an interview with Zephaniah, which was conducted in 1995.

Born in Birmingham, England, in 1958, Benjamin Zephaniah spent some of his childhood in Jamaica where he experienced and internalized a certain Caribbean cultural ethos that pulses throughout his later work. Forced out of "regular school" at the age of 12, largely because he was perceived to be an obdurate ruffian, he was sent to an "approved school" for immediate "correction." Interestingly enough, as part of a new generation of black creative writers in modern Britain, writers who believe art's first function is social engagement, Zephaniah now devotes the bulk of his time and energy to the task of helping out in schools, in youth clubs, in prisons, in universities, and in teacher training centers. By the time he was 15 he developed an impressive following in his home town of Handsworth, an English inner-city area that became the scene for black uprisings against the

Thatcherite government in 1981; it was from here that he spoke out on both local and international issues of sociopolitical concern. Also, in these formative years, his interest in Rastafarian spirituality—an Afrocentric, Caribbean theology with Haile Selassie I as its Christ-figure—began to blossom and grow. Rastafarianism then, as now, played a dominant influence in the lives of disenfranchised blacks in the projects of British cities.

Zephaniah As Scholar And Artist

Arriving in London at 22, Zephaniah published his first book, *Pen Rhythm* (Page One Books), to critical acclaim. Although enormously popular within the Caribbean and Asian expatriate communities, he soon sought a wider, more mainstream audience. *The Dread Affair* (Arena Books), his second published book, caused a stir because of Zephaniah's idiosyncratic use of Standard English to launch a savage attack on "the Establishment." He has since published *In a Liverpool* (Africa Arts Collective) and *Rasta Time in Palestine* (Shakti Publishing), and the latter text poeticizes his journey through occupied territories. More recent books include *City Psalms* (Bloodaxe Books), a collection of poems crafted with the printed page in mind, which stands in contrast to his earlier volumes of performance poetry, as well as *Talking Turkeys* (Viking), a bold and brassy collection of poems for children.

A poet who has toured every continent with his unique brand of verse, Zephaniah caused considerable controversy when he was shortlisted for the post of creative artist in residence at Cambridge University. A similar outrage occurred when he was shortlisted to become professor of poetry at Oxford University. Scrutinized and attacked by the British press, largely because of his "approved school" background, Zephaniah nonetheless regrouped himself and moved on to spend a year as writer-in-residence for the city of Liverpool. This post gave him the chance to work with young people and students.

The subject of one of the first documentaries ever shown on British Channel 4 TV, Zephaniah has appeared on chat shows, music and poetry programs, as well as political debates. At the end of 1991 the BBC produced his first television play, namely, his "uproariously" funny *Dread Poets Society.* Here Zephaniah confronts Mary Shelley, Percy Bysshe Shelley, Lord Byron, and John Keats; in an engagingly imaginative way, they all come together to debate poets both past and present. In 1993 he also wrote and presented *Crossing the Tracks,* a documentary for the BBC about black/Asian culture. *Big Boys Don't Make Girls Cry* and *Free South Africa* are among his most notable musical recordings. Others include *Dub Ranting; Rasta* the album; and *Us and Dem.* His many and diverse dramas include *Playing the Right Tune* (Theatre East), *Job Rocking* (Riverside Studios), *Hurricane Dub* (BBC Radio), *Streetwise* (Temba), *Delirium* (Union Dance Company), and *The Trial of Mickey Tekka*. Of these plays, *Hurricane Dub* was published as one of the winners in the BBC's Young Playwrights Festival in 1988. Significantly, Benjamin Zephaniah was nominated for the post of British Poet Laureate in 1999; he lost to Andrew Motion.[2]

In person, Benjamin Zephaniah is a jovial Rastafarian man who wastes no time in exploring the finer points of politics, veganism, spirituality, music, and, of course, the nature and status of poetry today. Although he has been dealt some very cruel cards in his career thus far, he remains (and is) a buoyant spirit—driven by the *élan* that works at the heart of his Rastafarian religiosity, propelled forward by an intoxicating sense of mission. In conversation, he will readily confess his love for language, his intuitive feel for the mystical quality of words. Enthralled by their magical power, their imaginative allure, he twists and turns phrases like a decorated general might use murderously destructive weapons in mortal combat. Agitated by structural and societal injustice, Benjamin Zephaniah sees his poetry (among other things) as "an alternative news broadcast" on pertinent local and international issues. The following three poems reflect not only Benjamin's political ideology but they demonstrate his fascination with and understanding of Judeo-Christian Scriptures.

A. "I Dwell Here"

Carry go
bring it come
you have lot
I have some,
I dwell here
you rest there
distribute
equal share,
all I can see
poverty
let the mind
be so free,
yes for hire
no is bought
someone must
protect the fort,
Africa, Africa
reaching out
Africa,

righteous ting,
Africa, Africa
I need you
Africa, Africa
I love you
Africa.
Some they say
go your way
right now I
demand pay,
all nations
there they seek
some black people
will not speak,
Jamaica
don't want you
Arawak land
yest dat true,
England did

was down here
as a slave
only fit
for the grave,
now to talk
talk aloud
very black
very proud
now to sing
rejoicing
now seeking.³

reject me
I must cling
to my tree,
Africa, Africa
reaching out
Africa
very black
very proud
shouting loud
AFRICA

B. "Can't Keep a Good Dread Down . . ."
The seed of Abraham grows
it will not stop
and he who sees it knows
Rastafari is on top,
great schools and churches have been built
to hide us from the real,
but those who built burn in their guilt
as prophecies reveal.

Sympathizers come
to dance to rasta sound
we can't live in the atmosphere
we must live on the ground,
businessmen are some
they buying rasta sound,
they have no love for riddim
their interest is the pound.

The Lion of Judah has prevailed
the Seven Seals is I
no living in the grave no more
King Fari will not die,
no brainwashed education
for wisdom must top rank,
if you want riches
you must check Selassie I bank

The root of David grows
weakheart get on your toes
and check the dread go sight JAH head
'cause he who sees HIM knows,
the Bible did not end the seed won't disappear

the only difference is that now
the rastaman is here, and,

Selassie I keeps on coming
can't keep a good dread down
those that stood start running
when JAH JAH comes to town,
greater love keeps coming
Alpha is here wid us,
so stop praying to polluted air
and give rasta your trust.[4]

C. "Dread John Counsel . . ."
Here I scribe just doing what comes to me naturally
everything I write is my account of history
just like an ambassador without an embassy
in my manifesto there is dread democracy,
I am here to take the good and throw the bad away
I represent a kingdom that has lived from time I say
in the counsel there are wise men with no mind to betray
in this kingdom there is love for all for love will not decay,
and this is me in exile so far away from home
no labour or conservative can give me what I own.

In this land my brothers and some sisters fight me down
therefore in the dark place and the jailhouse I am found
but I have a weapon that shall burn the enemy
and it has a fallout that shall rule equality,
the court is revolutionary the righteous ones shall stand
and in the tabernacle there doth play a reggae band
there is no House of Commons and everyone is high
and this kingdom is governed by a upfull one called I,
but I am here in exile so far away from home
still in this sick captivity I will not use their comb.

Tafari is my partner and Hannah is my tool.
David is my tuning key, Isaiah is my school,
dread John is my thinking, Obadiah is my aim,
Ezekiel is part of me I would like to make this plain,
in no case will we sit here in this democracy
believing what they tell us 'bout black equality,
when flies are caught in spiders' webs the spider must return
so if a one should stay here with them that one will with them
burn,
we are not too fussy 'bout being British free

> the kingdom's international a kingdom we can see,
> they will never give us what we really earn
> come our liberation and see the table turn,
> still this is me in exile so far away from home
> still recruiting soldiers to break this modern Rome.[5]

The aim of this section is to accentuate, by brief interpretative commentary, some of the scriptural references in Benjamin Zephaniah's three poems. In several places he refers to biblical names, themes, and books. By capitalizing on those references, I intend to show how Zephaniah reads the Hebrew Bible and the Christian New Testament through Rastafarian spectacles. Although there are no biblical allusions in "I Dwell Here," the first stanza of "Can't Keep a Good Dread Down" calls to mind the Abraham Saga, which takes up 13 chapters of Genesis. Zephaniah proclaims that "the seed of Abraham grows/it will not stop/and he who sees it knows/Rastafari is on top." This reference points to Abraham, son of Terah (Gen. 11:26–29), the so-called "friend of God" who probably lived around 1800 B.C.E. (Isa. 41:8; 2 Chron. 20:7). Originally called Abram, his name was changed to Abraham, which was understood to signify "father of a multitude"; Abraham was the father of the people who were later called the Jews (Gen. 17:5). Thus, Zephaniah takes us right back to God's promise to Abraham that he would be the father of many people, to show that Rastafari (God, for Zephaniah) was guiding all true devotees from the dawn of time and shaping their future. Furthermore, Zephaniah believes that the Rastafarians are the People of Jah (and "Jah" is the Rastafarian rendering of "Jehovah," the English rendering of the Hebrew tetragrammaton YHWH, the unpronounceable name of the God of Israel), through whom Jah will benefit the rest of creation.

Allusions to the Christian New Testament book of Revelation can be found in the third stanza of "Can't Keep a Good Dread Down." Here Zephaniah declares that, "The Lion of Judah has prevailed/the Seven Seals is I/no living in the grave no more/King Fari will not die." Also, in the fourth stanza, he asserts that, "The root of David grows." Now, the text of Revelation 5:1–5 is behind both remarks. First, this passage speaks of a kingly messiah ("the Conquering Lion") who will come from the royal tribe of Judah (Rev. 5:5). While traditional Christian preaching associates the lion metaphor with Jesus of Nazareth, Zephaniah connects it to Ras Tafari, who took the title "Lion of Judah" at his coronation, and who, to Rastafarians, is a direct descendent of King Solomon/ Queen Makeda of Sheba and thus of the stock ("root") of David. Second, the idea of the "Seven Seals" is a reference to the apocalyptic scroll fastened with seven emblems (Rev. 5:1). It would not be far wrong to suggest that the number of seals means that it is difficult for an "unworthy" soul to gain access to this unique papyrus roll. In

Zephaniah's view, Haile Selassie I ("King Fari") is authorized to open and read the sacred document. Such worthiness is linked to the emperor's Davidic ancestry. Moreover, every Rastafarian man is worthy ("the Seven Seals is I") by virtue of his association with Haile Selassie I; indeed, the divine spirit of King Fari is invested in every devotee of the King of Kings, the Lord of Lords, the Conquering Lion of the Tribe of Judah. Thus, for Zephaniah, every Rastafarian man is able to play a part in Jah's final plan for the destiny of the world.

It is interesting to notice that "Can't Keep a Good Dread Down" closes with a line inspired by Revelation 1:8; 21:6; and 22:13: "Alpha is here wid us/so stop praying to polluted air/and give Rasta your trust." A title of Christ, Alpha is the first letter of the Greek alphabet—Omega is the last—and, when taken together, the Alpha and the Omega, the beginning and the end, the first and the last, is a phrase that expresses the divine power over all creation. While Zephaniah would agree with all that I have said here about the Alpha and the Omega, we should notice how he appears to use his own theological immanentalism to counter the traditional Christian belief in theological supernaturalism. Indeed, he seems to regard the Christian belief that God, or Alpha, lives in the sky, up there in heaven, as little more than white man "trickery," a "kind o' nonsense" used to pacify marginalized black women and men. Thus, Zephaniah enjoins us to "stop praying to polluted air," that is, to abandon theological supernaturalism, to believe that the true Alpha is Rastafari, and to trust that the greatest embodiment of Rastafari is found in the person of the Holy Emperor.

A similar reverence for the Holy Emperor is set within the framework of Zephaniah's third poem, "Dread John Counsel . . ." Here Zephaniah describes himself as a scribe in a kingdom characterized by deathless love. It is interesting to notice that the word "kingdom" is repeated five times in this poem; it probably means the absolute rule of Jah Rastafari revealed in Haile Selassie I to vanquish Jah's enemies, creating a community over whom Jah reigns, the whole mass of creation, and issuing in a sphere in which the authority of Jah is experienced. Although I should be careful not to make the parallel between Zephaniah's verse and the Christian New Testament too close, perhaps I can say that the Gospel picture of the "kingdom of God/heaven," like that of Zephaniah's "kingdom" of Jah, is chiefly one in which the believer voluntarily submits to the divine rule (John 3:3–5; Matt. 19:23–24; Mark 10:23–25; Luke 18:24–30). Of course, Zephaniah does not share the Johannine view of an other-worldly kingdom (John 18:36); indeed, his kingdom theology is this-worldly, secular, and Afrocentric.

Finally, Zephaniah closes "Dread John Counsel . . ." by invoking the names of several heroes and heroines of the Hebrew Bible. In doing so, he takes us to the heart of his vocational self-understanding: "Tafari is my part-ner and Hannah is my tool/David is my tuning key, Isaiah is my school/dread John is my thinking, Obadiah is my aim/Ezekiel is part of me I would like to make this plain." At least five items of theological interest are worth noting at this point. First, I have said that Zephaniah versifies the Rastafarian man's sense of oneness with the spirit of Rastafari; thus, to refer to Tafari as a "partner" is once again to express the idea that the secret of life is found through the divine inspiration of the Holy Emperor.

Second, it seems that Zephaniah references Hannah, the gracious mother of Samuel, in order to draw attention to his own Nazirite heritage. The Nazirite was an Israelite who sanctified himself and took a vow of isolation and self-imposed discipline for the purpose of some higher mission. He re-fused to consume wine, to use a razor, and to touch dead bodies. There are at least three Nazirites in Scripture, namely, Samson (Jude 13:5–7), Samuel (1 Sam. 1:11) and John the Baptist (Matt. 11:18; Luke 1:15). In 1 Samuel 1:11 Hannah promises God that Samuel "shall not drink neither wine nor intoxicants, and no razor shall touch his head." The last clause in the last sentence is especially noteworthy; indeed, dreadlocked Rastafarians often claim that the Nazirite vow not to use a razor and/or a comb is an ancient sign of moral holiness (Lev. 19:27–28). Since the penultimate stanza of "Dread John Counsel . . ." ends with a defiant refusal to use "their comb" in "this sick captivity" (the non-African world), it seems that Zephaniah uses Hannah as his "tool" in order to assert his own status as a modern, conse-crated Nazirite.

Third, the writer of 1 Samuel 16:21–23; describes David as a skillful sol-dier who was appointed to play the lyre to Saul, Israel's first king, requested by popular demand against Samuel's wishes, when he (Saul) was depressed. Thus, Zephaniah's claim that David is his "tuning key" is almost certainly a reflection of Zephaniah's belief that he, like David, is being chosen for great things. The connection is clear: just as David was the musician chosen to slay the feared Philistine, Goliath of Gath (1 Sam. 17), so Zephaniah is fa-vored to use music and poetry in his fight against "this modern Rome," the non-African world, (Babylon).

Fourth, Zephaniah claims that he belongs to the "school" of Isaiah. Now, the prophet of Isaiah 1–39 is known as First Isaiah, or Isaiah of Jerusalem, and his task in the southern kingdom of Judah was to condemn social and religious evils. In particular, this eighth-century B.C.E. prophet told the lead-ers of Judah that they were heading for disaster unless they changed their ways. Preaching against Assyria's foreign gods, Isaiah of Jerusalem advised Judah to put their trust in God alone, whose power extended over all nations (Isa. 30:15). Finally, during one political crisis, Isaiah of Jerusalem used symbolic actions—he wore sackcloth and walked barefoot—to accentuate his message that Judah would be stripped of her special status if she trusted in Egypt to assist them in the campaign against Assyria (Isa. 20:2–3). Like Isaiah, Zephaniah is a Rastafarian prophet-statesman: if one glances through his entire literary *oeuvre,* or indeed any of the albums and tapes that record his words and beliefs, one will notice that much of it addresses social and religious evils. "Dread John Counsel . . ." is a good example. Here Zephaniah asserts that British black women and men are blind to the truth about themselves as African sons and daughters of Jah, because of their false trust in Britain's political process ("no labour or conservative can give me what I own"). Like Isaiah, who advised Judah to trust in God alone, Zephaniah preaches single-minded devotion to Rastafari.

Fifth, Zephaniah supplements his interest in Isaiah by associating himself with two other prophets, namely, Obadiah, the fourth of the Minor Prophets, whose concern was for the destruction of Edom, one of Israel's archenemies and, with Ezekiel, the last of the Major Prophets. The aim of the short book of Obadiah is clear: the writer pronounces judgment on Edom and declares an imminent restoration for Israel. Thus, when Zephaniah says that "Obadiah is my aim," we can perhaps interpret this as a sign of Zephaniah's own mission, that is, to pronounce judgment on Britain, the modern Edom, and to declare a restoration for all sincere Rastas, the true Israelites, in the day of the Holy Emperor.

Ezekiel's early message was one of doom and gloom (Ezek. 7) until Jerusalem was destroyed in 586 B.C.E. After the worst happens, Ezekiel begins to sing a new song: the same God who brought the two Israelite kingdoms to their knees is the same God who will raise them up once more. Indeed, Ezekiel's famous vision of the valley of dry bones illustrates his theology of hope (Ezek. 37:1–10). For Ezekiel, the bones represent the Israelite kingdoms, in ruins but able to be restored by the mighty power of God. The last nine chapters of the book of Ezekiel record the prophet's vision of the restoration: of the holy temple, the holy city of Jerusalem, and the holy land of Israel. Like Ezekiel, Zephaniah views himself as a performance prophet, that is, as a man blessed with words he feels in his body, which he cannot hold in, and as a man who sees fantastic visions and has experiences of being beside himself with emotion. Parts of "Dread John Counsel . . ." seem to foretell doom and gloom for those British Blacks who place their trust in so-called "democracy"; for he talks of "flies caught in spiders' webs," and yet he writes this poem to rally the dispirited and the downtrodden. Indeed, Zephaniah preaches that Jah will one day make a new beginning for Jah's people, illustrated most vividly in Zephaniah's Ezekiel-like vision of a new tabernacle (the second stanza of "Dread John Counsel . . .").

Zephaniah As Cultural Critic Up Close

During the week of September 11–17, 1995, Benjamin Zephaniah was guest artist in residence in the Department of Theater and Dance at the University of Memphis. In addition to visiting theater classes and poetry classes in the Department of English, Zephaniah launched the Department of Theater and Dance's 1995–96 season with two public performances on Friday and Saturday, September 15 and 16. In the midst of such frenetic activity, Zephaniah nonetheless agreed to meet me for lunch in a restaurant close to the University's main campus.

MIDDLETON: *What made you turn to poetry in your youth?*

ZEPHANIAH: Long before I understood what the word "poetry" meant, I just loved words. I am told that before I could speak, I quickly discerned whether a word was "angry," "loving," "challenging," or "funny" by sound only. I quickly identified words that rhymed. Also, I enjoyed listening to the different accents people spoke. In the mid 70s, when I was very inspired by the Rastafarians (and the National Front began to roam British streets, peddling their racist views to the working class), I realized exactly what poetry could achieve as an alternative news broadcast. Poetry has always been with me. The unfairness of the world troubled me. It was one of the main reasons why I became so keen to make myself heard.

MIDDLETON: *You place strong emphasis on your role as a performance poet. How far, and to what extent, do you find that people rally around the spoken word today?*

ZEPHANIAH: The popularity of the spoken word varies from place to place. I feel very much at home performing in South Africa, Zimbabwe, India, Pakistan, and especially the Middle Eastern countries. Here the oral tradition is still important. In America, I find that my audiences do not come to hear me on account of their love for poetry. Rather, they come because they are keen to hear my "message," to hear an alternative version of the British news or news from a black point of view. In England, there have been times when poetry has received good exposure. We have had Poems on the Underground, Poems on the Box, National Poetry Days, etc. Regardless of the hype, there's a hardcore group that continues to rally around the spoken word. I can earn a living by going around community centers, clubs, and pubs. I do not need to advertise this in the mainstream media. It never ceases to amaze me that in the age of video and the Internet, people still want to hear and see a single poet on stage.

MIDDLETON: *In one of his few interviews, Rastafarian Mikey Smith once spoke of poetry as a pedagogical tool, able to challenge "the dependency attitude" felt by the lower socioeconomic classes. Do you see yourself as someone who has tried to keep the conscious flame burning? If so, what do you make of Muta-baruka's ambiguous remark, "The solutions that you seek will not be found in the streak of a pen, or even ten lines of mine"?*

ZEPHANIAH: I believe there are many examples where political struggle has been fuelled and driven by poetry and song. I would like to think that Mutabaruka is here telling the reader that the solution to life's problems is not simply in reading his poems, or even in writing one's own. Rather, one has to get involved. After all, Mutabaruka's album (from which you got this quote) is entitled *Any Which Way, Freedom.* Why not freedom in-spired by the word? Many people feel they are doing enough by purchas-ing a Bob Marley record, signing a petition and reading radical poetry. I know that Mutabaruka hates this "type"; I don't have much time for them myself. The poetry, the popular and traditional music I grew up listening to was always created to keep the "conscious flame burning." I used to laugh at love songs and see them as quite silly. Coming from a generation that had no voice on the airwaves, it was always important to me that our aspirations should be articulated through my work. I would use every line—recording or TV interview—to do so.

MIDDLETON: *What function does Rastafarian spirituality play in your poetry?*

ZEPHANIAH: Much of my early writing is concerned with spirituality. Handsworth Rastafarians saw me as their scribe; I tended to see myself as a messenger of Rastafari. Over time, though, I began to realize that this limited me to a Rastafarian audience. Eventually, I came to the belief that preaching to the converted was not such a great idea. At this point, my poetry went in many directions but it was still inspired by Rastafarian po-litical ideas. My focus was still Africa but with the rest of the world in view. I still believe I can get across a Rastafarian message without men-tioning the word "Rastafari." Humor is a great way to do this. In fact, I know that I have inspired many people to ask after Rastafari without my preaching it at all. These people would have been "turned off" if all I did was chant "blood and fire" to sinners and that we, meaning Rastafarians, are the "chosen few." My present work is targeted toward children. I cer-tainly do not believe in preaching to children, but poems about plants, animals, and even the life of the universe has got many of my young read-ers interested in Rastafari spirituality. Rastafari appears in my work even though you may not come across the word itself.

MIDDLETON: *In "I Dwell Here" it appears you do not look to Jamaica or En-gland for hope, solace, or salvation. You seem to be affirming Africa as the Black Man's Vine and Fig Tree. Is Africa an integral feature of Rastafarian consciousness? Are you comfortable or uncomfortable with the label "Afrocen-tric poet"?*

ZEPHANIAH: I do not mind the label "Afrocentric Poet" if that means that I see the world through African spectacles. Artists always complain about labels. I know I do. Along with "Afrocentric poet" I can wear "reggae poet," "performance poet," "dub poet," "rhythm poet," "rasta poet," "revolutionary poet," and "black poet." There was a time when black people arrived in England. There was a time when black people arrived in Jamaica. Tell me of a time when black people arrived in Africa and I will tell you of the beginning of time. I am an African who just happens to be born in England. I shall fight for my political rights here. A "United States of Africa" is still important to me. Everything about Rasta points to Africa, Marcus Garvey, Haile Selassie I, the Garden of Eden. Personally, I don't think there is such a thing as a Rastafarian without Africa. Even "white Rastas" should have Africa in mind.

MIDDLETON: *In "Can't Keep a Good Dread Down," you seem to be saying that Selassie I lives on (in spite of 1976, the year he allegedly died) in the hearts and minds of Rastafarian believers. Is this the meaning of the lines, "no more living in the grave no more/ King Fari will not die"?*

ZEPHANIAH: Yes, if I was told by someone that my father had died I would want to see proof. I wouldn't believe it until I did. That is earthly. Spiritually, I do not accept death.

MIDDLETON: *Clearly, politics is very important to you. In "Dread John Counsel," you lament the inability of the two major political parties in Britain to help you discover your own identity as a black man. Why is that? Has anything changed since you wrote that poem? If not, why do you think that is the case?*

ZEPHANIAH: Most people now realize that most politicians concern themselves with their career only. Politicians tend to see black people as "the black vote." As black people, we should rise above that. When the racists hounded our streets attacking black people, politicians did not protect us. Too much political debate is about controlling immigration and containing the children of immigrants. Not much has changed. We still have to organize ourselves to fight racism. We still have to police the police. Things haven't changed because the system remains the same. We are still educated to respect racist "heroes." Politicians are distant from the people. They earn too much money. One of the major problems is that a "race industry" has been set up. We have a couple of black people in Parliament and some people feel that this is enough. I don't. That probably makes me a revolutionary!

MIDDLETON: *How important is live performance?*

ZEPHANIAH: I write most of my poetry with performance in mind. Long after I had a large black audience, I was convinced that no white publisher would publish my work. More importantly, I wanted to reach the very people who did not read books. I wanted to reach people on the dance floors, in the clubs, and on the streets. Poetry on the page was way down on my agenda. Live performance, TV, records, and even radio were of greater interest to me. These reached the masses. In what we call the "oral tradition," the poet must bring words to life. This may mean acting, crying, or chanting, but I also believe that we must work on the literary front. This is not because of any need to feel "accepted" but simply to reach a wider audience. I've always been frustrated by the fact that many good British dub poets will go unheard and unfortunately (in my view) many refuse to be published. Poets are always keen to see how a new poem will go down with the public. So, one of the other reasons why performance is important to me is that you have an immediate response to your work. When I publish work, I already know what the public think about it. They may even know it better than the publisher.

MIDDLETON: *Many know about your being shortlisted for the Oxford Chair in Poetry. What poetic contribution were you prepared to make in the city of dreaming spires?*

ZEPHANIAH: I think it would be fair to say that Oxbridge has very little awareness of performance poetry. This is not to say that they have no knowledge of contemporary poetry. Students can now be found dissecting the works of writers such as Seamus Heany, Bob Dylan, and even Bob Marley. Much oral poetry is not written. As such, it is out of the reach of Oxbridge students. Had I been awarded the Oxford Chair, I would have organized whole sessions of performance poetry. Not just dub poetry but Asian, African, Gaelic, Native American, and Eastern European. This would be done not only for poetic style but also for general educational reasons.

MIDDLETON: *Which poets/creative writers have influenced you?*

ZEPHANIAH: When I started creating poetry, I knew very little about poetry or poets. I was more influenced by Marcus Garvey, Malcolm X, C. L. R. James, and Angela Davis. The writers I have grown to love are Langston Hughes, Shelley, Dylan Thomas, The Last Poets, Maya Angelou, and Mahmood Darwish. I should add that none of these influenced my style, I just love their work. Many people see parts of my work connecting with other ideas in other writers. If I see such things, I look for another course. Poetry is me trying to be original.

MIDDLETON: *Will the dub poetry of the future involve a "black focus" or do you view dub poetry as part of a wider, universal vision?*

ZEPHANIAH: I don't think dub poetry will focus on the "black thing" in the future. However, most dub poetry is created by black people. Race will inevitably be high on the agenda. As for me, my own poetry took on a change for the better when I began to travel and understand the international scene. Many of the poets I meet today also want to understand the struggles of others, their culture. For dub poets to survive in the future, well, they must get involved in a more open debate. They need to create something new. I think the younger generations know this.

Notes

1. Alison Donnell and Sarah Lawson Welsh, ed., *The Routledge Reader in Caribbean Literature* (London: Routledge Press, 1996), 349.
2. I want to record my grateful appreciation to Benjamin Zephaniah, and especially to his literary agent, for help with this brief biography of his life and career (to date).
3. Benjamin Zephaniah, *The Dread Affair: Collected Poems* (London: Arena Books, 1985), 47.
4. Ibid., 24–5.
5. Ibid., 54–5.

Chapter 13 🏃

Holy Piby

Blackman's Bible And Garveyite Ethiopianist Epic With Commentary

Nathaniel Samuel Murrell

Introduction

For justifiable reasons, people of the African diaspora have attempted to produce their own liberating versions of sacred scripture and theology since the days of slavery. This practice not only provided them an anti-slavery theology but also formed a basis for self-definition and affirmation of their African heritage, as they proffered their own idea of the divine and visions of human hope for the future. Some of the early classic versions of the black vision and self-definition in written text are: U.S.-bred "David Walker's Appeal," Alexander Young's *Ethiopian Manifesto*, and Henry MacNeal Turner's "Black Christ"; Caribbean-born Athlyi Rogers's *The Holy Piby*, published in 1924 in Newark, New Jersey; *The Royal Parchment Scroll of Black Supremacy*, first published by the Reverend Fitz Balentine Pettersburgh of Jamaica in 1926; and Leonard Howell's *The Promised Key*, also published in Jamaica in 1934. Under the influence of Marcus Garvey's pan-African vision, Athlyi Rogers, in the *Holy Piby*,[1] attempts to indigenize Judeo-Christian Scriptures in an early twentieth-century African-Caribbean-American context. This highly prized piece of ephemera survived for over 75 years in its essential form and found an important place in formative Rastafarian thought. In fact, alongside the Bible, this pamphlet-sized religious text has been, and continues to be, a source of inspiration to "roots" men and women in Rastafari[2] since the 1930s. As Timothy White observes, "The true foundation of Rastafarianism is the *Holy Piby,* the *Black Man's Bible,* compiled by Robert Athlyi Rogers of Anguilla from 1913 to 1917."[3] In the *Holy Piby,* as in other publications, early Rastafarians found language and ideas for their nascent ideology and the vision of their Afro-centric world that provided the hermeneutics with which they interpret the Bible.[4]

This brief introduction and commentary on the *Holy Piby* examines its religious and political ideas and their impact on the Rastafarians. Published at least six years before the founding of Rastafari but recognized, next to the Bible, as the earliest Rastafarian revered sacred document, the *Piby* was designed especially for members of the African Athlican Constructive Church (AACC), called the Hamitic Church, and popular among the Rastafarians of the 1930s. Much has been written about the use of the KJV in Rastafarian theology; and in *Chanting Down Babylon: The Rastafari Reader* (1998), William David Spencer made *The Promised Key* accessible to the reading public with an impressive commentary and interpretation. But since its publication by the Athlican Strong Arm Company, in January 1924, *The Holy Piby (Piby)* has not appeared in any literary form. Scholars doing research on Rastafari occasionally reference the *Piby* but mainly from secondary sources; the booklet is hardly ever quoted directly because of its unavailability to the public. Featuring the *Piby* in this volume therefore adds another chapter to the preservation of rare primary sources on Afro-American and Caribbean cultural and religious movements of the early twentieth century. Through the kind courtesy of my Jamaican colleague, Rev. Clinton Chisholm of Spanish Town, Jamaica, I am able to present the *Piby* in its entirety for the reading public.[5]

In the midst of the economically depressed and socially alienating climate for African-Americans of the 1920s, the Anguillan-born pan-African nationalist and staunch supporter of Marcus Mosiah Garvey, Robert Athlyi Rogers—self-styled "His Holiness, Shepherd Athlyi, IST of the House of Athlyi, supreme lord of the Afro-Athlican Constructive Church" (see cover page to the *Piby*)—sought new ideological paradigms for living for his Afro-centric religious organization, the AACC. Drawing heavily on Jewish and Christian traditions, Rogers began preaching his message in the streets of Newark, New Jersey, in 1917, at the height of World War I, just when Marcus Garvey's United Negro Improvement Association (UNIA) was in full gear (*Piby,* Second Book (SB), Ch 4 v1). In July of the following year, the Athlians declared themselves a Church "at the Israel Memorial A.M.E. Church, West Kinney Street, Newark, New Jersey (SB, Ch 5 v1). After Rogers appointed himself shepherd of the flock in 1919, he "paraded the streets of Newark with a host of Negroes, protected by riding officers of the city and accompanied by a Salvation Army carrying banners, proclaiming a universal holiday for Negroes and foretelling of their industrial and national independence" (SB, Ch 4 v4).

In their religious celebrations and "cultus," Athlians practiced water baptism by immersion, a sanctifying act that they called "concretation," (SB, Ch 6 vv1–3) and in their monthly "Solemnityfeast" observed the Christian sacrament of communion in both elements, bread and water. The "Ordained cleffs" (Elders) served bread and water to celebrants "saying, eat in remembrance of your pledge to God, yielding yourselves into actual work for the welfare of your generation through the up building of Ethiopia and for the rescue of suffering humanity" (SB, Ch 6 vv2, 6). Celebrants were told: "Drink in remembrance of your baptism when thy sins hath been washed away" (v7). The *Piby* teaches the existence of one God who functions in concord with the Holy Spirit and Angel Douglas (SB, Ch 6 vv3, 7, 20 and 25; Ch 8 v12). Annually, a three-day celebration marked the anniversary of the Church from July 29 to August 1, with the divine presence supposedly in attendance "in celestial and terrestrial concord led by the mighty angel Douglas" (v8). On "the First of August all members of the A.A.C. Church . . . join[ed] in with the Universal Negro Improvement Association that there be a united day of joviality" (*Piby,* cover page).

So from its very inception, the AACC had a dual purpose: salvation through spiritual formation and justice and social-economic upliftment for Ethiopians, people of African descent (SB, Ch 2 vv6–8). The movement became geographically a three-legged operation with footings in Kimberley (South Africa), Kingston (Jamaica), and Newark (New Jersey). Like Garvey, Rogers had visions of an African kingdom inhabited and governed by Africans for Africans. He dreamed of a promised land where "Ethiopians," all peoples of African descent, would live in peace and harmony with control over their own economic and political destiny. This social, political, and religious *communitas* was constructed on an Ethiopian, *qua* African, philosophy, a vision that is seen clearly throughout the *Piby,* the text of which is reproduced in its entirety here with commentary.[6]

THE HOLY PIBY[7]

QUESTIONS AND ANSWERS

Questions and answers concerning the works of God among the children of Ethiopia and the principles of Athlianity:

Q1. What is the house of Athlyi?

A. A house created by the Almighty God through his apostle Athlyi, giver of the gospel and the law commanded by the Lord for the salvation of Ethiopia's posterities.

Q2. What is the right wing to the house of Athlyi?

A. The Afro Athlican Constructive Church.

Q3. What is the left wing to the house of Athlyi?

A. The Athlican green pasture.

Q4. Can there be any other Church or denomination save the Afro Athlican Constructive Church upon the Law of the Gospel commanded by God to save the generations of Ethiopia?

A. No.

Q5. What is Athlicanity?

A. The Law and the Gospel administered by Athlyi.

Q6. Why can no other [C]hurch be established upon this gospel?

A. Because the Athlicanity is sent by the Lord our God not to teach confusion and hatred but to set up a real religious and material brotherhood among the children of Ethiopia.

Q7. What is the Holy Piby?

A. A Holy book of God written unto the generations of Ethiopia.

Q8. Do the Athlians believe in Jesus Christ?

A. As a true servant sent by God to seek and to save the lost house of Israel.

Q9. Who did Athlyi, Marcus Garvey and colleagues come to save?

A. The down-trodden children of Ethiopia that they may [raise] to be a great power among the nations and in the glory of their God.

Q10. What is the Dictuary?

A. The most holy place in the Afro Athlican Constructive Church or in the house of Athlyi, where the Shepherd or his apostles occupies to administer the gospel.

Q11. What is God's holy law to the children of Ethiopia?

A. A written document handed to Athlyi by an angel of the Lord whose name was Douglas.

Q12. What is the difference between God's holy law to the children of Israel and God's holy law to the children of Ethiopia?

A. There is much difference, the holy law to the Israelites was given to Moses, but God's holy law given to the children of Ethiopia was handed to Athlyi by a messenger of the Lord our God, notwithstanding in the law given to the Israelites there are ten commandments, but in the law given to the children of Ethiopia there are twelve.

Q13. What Church is already established on God's holy law given to the children of Ethiopia?

A. The Afro Athlican Constructive Church.

Q14. By what other name shall this church be known?

A. The House of Athlyi.

Questions & Answers: Afrocentric Articles of Faith

Preceding "The First Book of Athlyi" are articles of faith and understanding in 14 "Questions and Answers concerning the works of God, . . . the children of Ethiopia and the principles of Athlianity." These articles of faith function as a preface to the *Piby* and seem to juxtapose Moses' reception of "God's holy law to the Children of Israel" and "God's holy law to the children of Ethiopia," *qua Africa*. The *Piby* claims to be "A written document handed to Athlyi by an angel of the Lord whose name was Douglas . . . a messenger of the Lord our God." Whereas the children of Israel got only ten commandments, 12 were given to the Athlians and children of Ethiopia (Q&A 11–13). Moses is a receiver of revelations, but Athlyi Rogers received more than Moses thus making the Athlican Church superior to the Church in the wilderness, the Israelites. The *Piby* reflects here an unorthodox Judeo-Christian idea—one seen in Rabbi Matthews's Black Jews of Harlem, Rastafari, and other black neoorthodox "Christian" groups—that Blacks are the new Israelites. This belief is at the heart of Rastafarian theology, which claims that Rastas are Falashas, black Jews, the real Children of Israel or people of Jah.[8]

In a kind of parallel, the *Piby*'s "Questions and Answers" attempt to explain rudimentary principles of faith and doctrine to recently "concretized": communicants of the AAC Church. But just as clearly they give voice to the Afrocentric ideology of this pre-Rastafarian movement. Children of Ethiopia, Negroes, "Athlicanity," and Marcus Garvey provide the vocabulary key, historical reference, and philosophical framework for the "vision" articulated in the sacred pages of this epic, the *Piby*. That the word Ethiopia or Ethiopian should punctuate every page of this short document and occur over 100 times is no accident. Athlyi Rogers was committed politically to the Africanist vision of Marcus Garvey, a major focus of the *Piby*. Especially in the "Third Book of Athlyi," the Afrocentric political agenda is carefully blended with Rogers's salvific mission of bringing a social, religious, and political message to all African peoples. The house of Athlyi is even seen as "created by the Almighty God through his apostle Athlyi, . . . for the salvation of Ethiopia's posterities" (Q&A 1).

Pushing the Afrocentric Ethiopian ideology beyond the limits of ecumenical tolerance and cooperation, only the AAC Church is regarded as authorized "by God to save the generations of Ethiopia" (Q&A 4). Such a partisan pan-African idea that only Africans can save Africa, or the continent must be only for the Africans, is not unique to the Athlians but has a long history in the black struggle. At the close of the 1700s the cry was "Haiti for the Haitians! Down with French oppression!" In the 1840s a small but vocal group began voicing the ideology of Cuba for the Cubans against American annexationists and Spanish loyalists; later in the century it was Puerto Rico for the Puerto Ricans. Africa for the Africans was at the heart of Marcus Garvey's UNIA. This message also became a platform on which African countries began forging their freedom from European domination through the

African independence movement, which followed about a quarter of a century after Garvey's demise. In the 1950s and 1960s, Trinidad, Jamaica, Barbados, and other Caribbean states picked up the Afrocentric baton as a battle cry for independence from Britain.

In spite of its apparent "intolerance," the *Piby* is unlike Leonard Howell's anti-White, anti-Vatican, anti-Christian, and misanthropic *Promised Key*. In fact, the *Piby* makes it clear that the AAC Church is not designed "to teach confusion and hatred" toward other ethnic and religious groups "but to set up a real religious and material brotherhood among the children of Ethiopia." The idea was to lift "the down-trodden children of Ethiopia that they may rise to be a great nation among the nations" (Q&A 9). In this context, the *Piby* is "a Holy book of God written unto the generations of Ethiopia" (Q&A 7), or Africa; and Athlyi Rogers, Marcus Garvey, and their colleagues came to save the "down-trodden children of Ethiopia that they may rise to be a great power among the nations and in the glory of their God" (Q&A 9). This was a message of hope for some African Americans in the very trying and painful episodes of the second decade of the twentieth century.

Also prefacing the first book are three commands called "The Shepherd's Command by Athlyi:"[9]

> 1st Let all literature for the instruction of Athlian's children be of a constructive nature, looking toward Ethiopia.
> 2nd Let the eye of a star be the eye of the Shepherd and the ear of a star be the ear of a Shepherd, for they are his stars.
> 3rd Fight for that which is yours and ye shall obtain it, for there is nothing hard against the power of God.

These commands are designed to induce allegiance to the shepherd, Athlyi Rogers, as well as give credence to the "divine origin," assure reverent reception, and establish the doctrinal authority of the *Holy Piby*. The text portrays Rogers as having a divine vision from God and praying that the *Holy Piby* will live on forever. Here Rogers seeks to establish divine legitimacy for his role as apostle to Africa and head of his religious movement. The recurring divine presence of a "mighty angel robed in four colors" (SB, Ch 1 v17) and "descending from among the great heavenly host" (Ch 2 v1) is obviously the making of a mythic sacred story, an anthropomorphic allusion (or illusion?) designed to legitimize a theological claim—in this case, Rogers's authority as spiritual leader and shepherd of the flock—as well as provide divine warrant for doctrinal beliefs (that is, showing that the Athlican Church has divine origin or endorsement). The four colors in the angelic robe are the "colors of the Great Negro Civilization" (Ch 6 Aggregation v15), probably representing those of the UNIA or the AAC Church. But, as we shall see later, they are for the robing of Athlyi Rogers.

THE FIRST BOOK OF ATHLYI CALLED ATHLYI

CHAPTER II. THE CREATION.

1. From the beginning there was God and he spake and all things were made that are made.
2. The sixth day God made man for his glory, and all things were given unto him for his possession and for his use the woman hath God made of man and for the glory of the man that she serve him and raise up seed unto him.
3. And God rested the seventh day and hallowed it that men should do also.
4. Now when the man saw the woman that was made of him and for his glory, he loved her and married with her, consequently she bore children unto him and they became the father and mother of all men.
5. And God called the man Adam and the woman Eve. They were of a mixed complexion.
6. And it came to pass that God commanded the man to give names to all things that are made.

ATHLYI. CHAPTER II.

DEAD BECAME ALIVE.

1. And it came to pass that God entered the body of an unknown dead and the dead became alive, then did he walk about the earth in person.
2. He dwelt among men and wrought many miracles so that the kingdom of heaven might be verified.
3. He suffered persecution and privation as an example of what ministers of the gospel must suffer to maintain the kingdom of God among men.
4. And it came to pass that God gave his name Elijah, and he called upon the name of the Lord God even though he himself was God.
5. Now when the time had appeared for God to return, the supreme angel commanded the chariot of heaven to meet him.
6. And when the chariot appeared unto Elijah, he ascended and returned to his throne in heaven where he reigned from the beginning and shall [reign] unto the end, king of kings, and God of gods.
7. Had the men in the days of Elijah's visit on earth taken a right record of his administration, long before this day the inhabitants of this earth would have known him as God of all men.

8. For in Elijah do the heavenly host worship as God of the universe and in him do I, Athlyi, believe as the only God.

9. He is the Lord of righteousness and of love, an industrious God, jealous, brave, omnipotent, omnipresent, a king of sympathy and of justice, giver of power and salvation, upon this God, and him only, his Law and the Holy Ghost shall the Athlians build their church.

10. We shall endeavor to please and serve him, for he is our God. We shall worship him with all our hearts and with all our souls, for unto us there is none so good as the Lord, our God.

11. When the Lord God of Ethiopia is with us in the battle for that to which we are entitled, show me the foe so powerful to set us down? Verily I say unto you there is none.

12. But who can be so good as to please the conscience of the people that they say ye are of God? Who will pay such a price? Will you? Then, if so, lay down and let the public trod upon your head for a good name.

13. Verily I say unto you for this the Athlians are bad, but on the scale of justice, let them not be found wanting. Then shall they please the Lord God, maker of heaven and earth, and great shall be their reward in the kingdom of heaven.

Commentary: Athlican Creation Mythology

The "First Book of Athlyi Called ATHLYI" (FB) opens with a narrative on creation in six verses mimicking the biblical creation myth in Genesis chapters 1 and 2, although it begins only on the sixth day of creation rather than on the first. God is seen as existing from the beginning and speaking all things into existence. On the sixth day God made "man" for his glory, and gave all things unto him for his possession and use. Even the woman that God made of man was created for the glory of the "man"; she must "serve him and raise up seed unto him" (vv 1–2). After his six-days creation, God "rested on the seventh day and hallowed it that men should do [so] also" (v 3). God names Adam and Eve, the first humans. Adam loves the woman God made of him and he is commanded to "give names to all things that are made" (Ch 1 vv1–6).[10] This traditional view on women and the subservient role that the *Piby* ascribes to them here is rather surprising given the admirable "feminist" consciousness that is demonstrated in the Second and Third Books. As I will argue later, this clearly reflects the androcentric thinking of Athlyi Rogers's time and not an exclusively personal gender bias.

Narrated in 13 verses of Chapter II, titled "Dead Became Alive," is a strange conflated reading of biblical materials on Elijah, God, and Christ.

God is seen as entering the body of "an unknown dead and the dead became alive" and "walk[ed] about the earth in person." This mysterious creature becomes a sort of God-man who "dwelt among men and wrought many miracles so that the kingdom of heaven might be verified." After suffering persecution and privation among humans, God gave that strange personage the name Elijah, who "called upon the name of the Lord God even though he himself was God" (Ch II vv 3 and 4). In Rogers's heterodoxy, the Elijah-God-Christ "is the Lord of righteousness and of love, an industrious God, jealous, brave, omnipotent, [and] omnipresent," and the "Lord God of Ethiopia," upon whom the Athlians built their Church. The reason for the centrality of Elijah in this unorthodox theological exposition is unclear. The odd discourse on Elijah's coming out of a dead man's body and becoming God the suffering deliverer probably indicates that Rogers believed he cracked the "Messianic secret" and thus regarded Christ as not only coming "in the spirit of Elijah" (Luke 1:17), but the very "Elijah who must first come" (Matt. 17:9–13; Mark 9:9–13, NIV).

Rogers's interpretation of the messianic secret may have countenanced I Corinthians 2:7–8: "But we speak God's wisdom, secret and hidden, which God decreed before the ages for our glory. None of the rulers of this age understood this; for if they had, they would not have crucified the Lord of glory" (NRSV). At any rate, in Rogers's mind, the messiah or deliverer is going to be a divine human being, a God man, or Elijah-Christ. Rogers's novel theological idea of this strange character of the God-Elijah-Christ that was to come (FB, Ch. II vv 8 and 11) associated with Ethiopia would, six years later, form an important part of the "Rasta-Garvey" revelation that the expected Messiah comes out of Ethiopia in the person of Haile Selassie I. As an ideological rallying magnet for his pan-African movement, Garvey was fond of citing the biblical passage in Ps. 68:31: "Princes shall come out of Egypt; Ethiopia shall soon stretch out her hands unto God." But the pan-Africanist Garvey had absolutely no intentions of turning Selassie—whose political leadership in the developing world Garvey regarded as inert—or any African ruler into a religious messiah.[11] The God who will help Ethiopia (Africa) in her struggles is the God to deliver all Africans from oppression and domination.[12]

The *Piby* follows Garvey's philosophy and uses of the name "Ethiopia" to represent all of Africa and her peoples. This is implied in the rhetorical declaration and confession: "When the Lord God of Ethiopia is with us in battle for that to which we are entitled, show me the foe so powerful to set us down. Verily I say unto you there is none" (FB, Ch. II, v11; SB, Ch 6, v32). The *Piby*'s Ethiopianism has a more overt theological focus than the theology in Garvey's pan-Africanism; but Rogers is very Afrocentric in his ethnocentrism. Throughout the preamble and "First Book," spiritual salvation, liberation, protection, and "upliftment" of Ethiopia, *qua Africa,* and African peoples are the primary ethnographic foci of the *Piby.* The fact that Rogers even established branches of his Church in South Africa and Jamaica demonstrates how much he was committed to this Afrocentric vision and mission. This mission was shared by other leaders of independent black nationalist groups in the metropolitan United States, such as Noble Drew Ali, founder of the Moorish Science Temple, forerunner of the Nation of Islam; Rabbi Matthews, founder of Black Jews of Harlem; Father Divine; Daddy Grace; and Rogers's South African Church itself. The mission represents common indigenous theological themes of the black nationalist religious movement of the early twentieth century.

THE SECOND BOOK OF ATHLYI CALLED AGGREGATION
CHAPTER 1. HEAVEN GRIEVED.

1. For as much as the children of Ethiopia, God's favorite people of old, have drifted away from his divine majesty, neglecting life [economic], believing they should on spiritual wings fly to the kingdom of God, consequently became [a convenient] for the welfare of others.
2. Therefore the whole heaven was grieved and there was a great lamentation in the kingdom of God. Ethiopian mothers whose bodies have been dead a thousand years, weeping for their suffering generations and would not be comforted.
3. And behold two angels of the Lord resembling two saints of Ethiopia appeared before Athlyi and he inquired of them what is the cry?
4. And they answered him saying, Ethiopian mothers who have been dead a thousand years [are] pleading before Elijah for the redemption of suffering Ethiopia and her posterities who by the feet of the nations are trodden.
Convention in Heaven.
5. There is a great convention in heaven, saith the angels of the Lord, unto you this day [whom] we are sent by the Lord to felicitate, for thou art appointed shepherd to lead Ethiopia's generations from the oppressive feet of the nations, and there are appointed also prophets to prepare the way before thee.
6. And it came to pass when Athlyi heard these sayings he feared with great astonishment and turned his face from the angels of the Lord.
7. And there appeared unto him his divine highness Jesus Christ, Prince of the Kingdom of God, and said quickly behold the messengers of my Father.
8. At this saying Athlyi turned again to the angels of the Lord and said, thy will be done, O God of Ethiopia, but how can I be shepherd to

lead millions of millions even from the end of the earth [when as]
I am but a twig before the eyes of men?

The Heaven Open.

9. And the angels of the Lord answered him saying, a twig that is made
by the Holy Spirit, an instrument to lead men is great in the sight
of God, over which the armies of the earth or the hosts shall not
prevail.

10. And it came to pass that the angel who had [the less] to say lifted
her eyes to heaven and stretched forth her arms over the earth and
cried, blessed be thou Ethiopia, glory be the Father, thou Elijah,
Hosanna, Hosanna to Jehovah, praise ye Douglas the convention
[have] triumph.

11. There appeared a beautiful light on earth and when the light
flashed Athlyi looked toward the heaven, and behold the heaven
was open and there was a great host of saints robed in blue, millions
of millions, as far as his eyes could see there was a mighty host.

12. When Athlyi sought the angels of the Lord they were not and he
heard a voice say Athlyi and another Athlyi, and he looked up and
saw the two angels ascending toward the celestial host.

Ethiopia Anointed.

13. And when the two messengers of the Lord were midways they cried
out unto the earth saying, blessed be thou Ethiopia for this day
thou art anointed, thou art blest with a blessing, be ye forever
united and stand up, let the world know your God.

14. And when the two angels of the Lord neared the multitude, the
whole host roared with a thunder of joy that shook the earth like a
mighty earthquake.

15. And it came to pass that an angel robed in four colors came forward to receive them and the whole celestial multitude stood and
quietly formed an aisle.

16. And when the two messengers appeared before the heavenly host
they bowed to the multitude and turned themselves around and
bowed also to the earth.

17. Then came forward the mighty angel robed in four colors and
placed a gold ring upon their heads, and [there] came forward also
two mothers of Ethiopia, each with a star in their right hand, and
pinned them on the left breast of the two messengers of the Lord.

18. And it came to pass that heaven and earth shook three times and
the two angels marched up the aisle and joined with the multitude.

Rejoicing in Heaven.

19. There was great rejoicing in heaven and singing hosanna to Elijah;
praise ye Douglas; blessed be thou Ethiopia forever and forever; the
people at the end of the known world, and world unknown shall
look for the coming of thy children with food and with raiment.

20. And when the two angels had joined the multitude and the mighty angel had finished his performance, the said angel who was robed in colors turned to the heavenly host and said:

21. Mothers of Ethiopia, the convention has triumphed, your sorrows have brought joy to Ethiopia, your tears have anointed her soil with a blessing, your cries have awakened her children throughout the earth, yea in the corners of the unknown world are they aroused, and [is] prophesying, saying prepare ye the way for a redeemer.

Shepherd Anointed.

22. For unto Ethiopia this day a Shepherd is anointed, yea, as a shepherd gathers his sheep so shall he gather unto God, the generation of Ethiopia even from the end of the earth and lead them high, a nation among nations.

23. Then shall the inhabitants of the earth know that the Lord our God has not forsaken Ethiopia, and that the mighty is weak against his command, and unto no nation has he given power forever.

24. Verily I say unto you, woe be unto the persecutors of the shepherd for he is anointed by the Lord our God, therefore one drop of his blood or the least of his apostles whom he has anointed to administer the law to the generations of Ethiopia, or the blood of a prophet within the law, shall break to pieces the oppressors of Ethiopia.

The Mighty Angel.

25. When the mighty angel had finished speaking to the heavenly host he then turned to the earth and said: Children of Ethiopia, stand, and there flashed upon the earth a great multitude of Negroes knowing not from whence they came; then shouted instantly the whole heavenly host, behold, behold Ethiopia has triumphed.

26. And it came to pass that the mighty angel spoke to the multitudes of Negroes, saying, woe be unto those who say to the shepherd, thou fool, or [thou fool] to the least of an apostle anointed to administer the law, for it is not the desire of the shepherd but the will of the Lord who is God.

Dominion Over the Shepherd.

27. For as much as the Lord has dominion over the shepherd and the shepherd over his apostles and the apostles over all the generations of Ethiopia; then shall the Lord our God administer to the shepherd and the shepherd to his apostles and the apostles to all the children of Ethiopia.

28. Woe be unto an apostle who is anointed to administer the law and neglect or deny it. Verily he shall be cast out and the hand of the Lord shall come upon him with sorrow and disgrace.

29. Woe be unto those who saith I will not be united, neither will I follow the shepherd, they shall be as sheep without a shepherd only to be destroyed by the wolf of the field.
30. Woe be unto those who saith I hearken not to the voice of the shepherd but go the way of the majority, for in the majority the spirit of the Lord will not be found.
31. Woe be unto those who saith I will not worship in the house of the Lord subsidiary to the house of Athlyi.

Purification.

32. For as much as the house of Athlyi is founded by the holy spirit to purify the children of Ethiopia and to administer the holy law commanded to them by the Lord God of all mercies, that they in the end shall be ushered in the kingdom of his Divine majesty by faith through consecration in love, justice and by the pledging of life's loyalty to a prolific and defensive cause for the welfare of mankind. Let not the least or the greatest of the children give a deaf ear to the saying of the shepherd thereof, for through the mouth of the shepherd cometh the word of the Lord to the adherents of the Holy Law.

CHAPTER 2. PRESENTATION OF THE LAW.

1. And it came to pass that the mighty angel robed in four colors descended from among the great heavenly host.
2. When the Athlyi saw the angel descending he feared with great fear and hid behind the root of a tree.
3. But the angel of the Lord came up unto him and said, Athlyi, come forth for the Lord has made thee shepherd of his anointed children of Ethiopia.
4. And Athlyi answered saying, who are thou? I am Douglas, a messenger from the Lord, replied the angel. I am sent to robe thee and to give in thy hands and in thy care the Lord's articles.
5. Verily no man shall take away that which the Lord giveth, for the word of the Lord who is God, will not come unto any save he who is appointed by the Father.

Athlyi Robed.

6. The angel of the Lord robed Athlyi in four colors and commanded him to put forth his right hand, and the messenger presented in his right hand a staff and in his left hand the Holy Law saying, Go and administer this law through thine apostles unto the children of Ethiopia and command them to rise from the feet of their oppressors. Great is the penalty if there be any failure on your part to deliver the law; the hand of the Lord shall come upon thee with horror and thou shalt regret the day [ye was] born.

7. The angel of the Lord hesitated, then said to Athlyi, swear before the Lord God that thou wilt administer the law unto the children; then Athlyi lifted his eyes to the heaven and said, the heaven and the earth bear witness to my saying I will.

8. Then the messenger of the Lord touched Athlyi on his left breast with the first finger of his right hand saying, be thou brave, then disappeared from the presence of the shepherd.

Chapter 3. God's Holy Law To The Children Of Ethiopia.

Great and manifold are the blessings bestowed upon us the oppressed children of Ethiopia, by His Divine Majesty, Lord God Almighty, King of all mercies, when by his most holy command his divine highness, Christ, Prince of the heavenly kingdom, descended and anointed us that we may be prepared to receive these noble men, servants of God and redeemers of Ethiopia's posterities, his honor, Marcus Garvey and colleague, his holiness the shepherd Athlyi, supreme minister of God's holy law to the children of Ethiopia, may we show gratitude to our God by being submissive to his teachings through these his humble servants, and submitting ourselves in obedience to his holy law that we a suffering people may reap the fruit thereof.

When as it was the intention of others to keep us forever in darkness, by our faithfulness to the law we shall in time prove to the nations that God has not forsaken Ethiopia.

The Holy Law—Commandments.

I. Love ye one another O children of Ethiopia, for by no other way can ye love the Lord your God.

II. Be thou industrious, thrifty and fruitful, O offsprings of Ethiopia, for by no other way can ye show gratitude to the Lord your God, for the many blessings he has bestowed upon earth free to all mankind.

III. Be ye [concretize] and ever united, for by the power of unity ye shall demand respect of the nations.

IV. Work ye willingly with all thy heart, with all thy soul and with all thy strength to relieve suffering and oppressed humanity, for by no other way can ye render integral service to the Lord your God.

V. Be thou clean and pleasant, O generation of Ethiopia, for thou art anointed, moreover the angels of the Lord dwelleth with thee.

VI. Be thou punctual, honest and truthful that ye gain favor in the sight of the Lord your God, and that your pathway be prosperous.

VII. Let no people take away that which the Lord thy God giveth thee, for the Lord shall inquire of it and if ye shall say some one hath taken it, ye shall in no wise escape punishment, for he that dieth in retreat of his enemy the Lord shall not hold him guiltless, but a people who dieth in pursuit of their enemy for the protection of that which the Lord God giveth them, shall receive a reward in the kingdom of their Father.

VIII. Thou shalt first bind up the wound of thy brother and correct the mistakes in thine own household before ye can see the sore on the body of your friend, or the error in the household of thy neighbor.

IX. O generation of Ethiopia, shed not the blood of thine own for the welfare of others for such is the pathway to destruction and contempt.

X. Be ye not contented in the vineyard or household of others, for ye know not the day or the hour when denial shall appear, prepare ye rather for yourselves a foundation, for by no other way can man manifest love for the offsprings of the womb.

XI. Athlyi, Athlyi, thou shepherd of the holy law and of the children of Ethiopia, establish ye upon the law a holy temple for the Lord according to thy name and there shall all the children of Ethiopia worship the Lord their God, and there shall the apostles of the shepherd administer the law and receive pledges thereto and concretize within the law. Verily he that is concretized within the law shall be a follower and a defender thereof, moreover the generations born of him that is [concretize] within the law are also of the law.

XII. O generation of Ethiopia, thou shalt have no other God but the Creator of heaven and earth and the things thereof. Sing ye praises and shout hosanna to the Lord your God, while for a foundation ye sacrifice on earth for his divine majesty the Lord our Lord in six days created the heaven and earth and rested the seventh; ye also shall hallow the seventh day, for it is blessed by the Lord, therefore on this day thou shall do no manner of work [or] any within thy gates.

The Shepherd's Prayer by Athlyi.

1. O God of Ethiopia, thy divine majesty; thy spirit come in our hearts to dwell in the path of righteousness lead us, help us to forgive that we may be forgiven, teach us love and loyalty on earth as to heaven, endow us with wisdom and understanding to do thy will, thy blessing to use that the hungry be fed, the naked clothed, the sick nourished, the aged protected and the infant cared for. Deliver us from the hands of our enemies that we prove fruitful, then in the last day when life is o'er, our bodies in the clay, or in the depths of the sea, or in the belly of a beast, O give our souls a place in thy kingdom forever and forever. Amen.

CHAPTER 4. THE LAW PREACHED.

1. Now in the year of 1917 A.D., Shepherd Athlyi first went about the city of Newark, New Jersey, U.S.A., telling of the law and preaching

[concretation] saying, I com not only to baptize but to concretize for the rescue of suffering humanity, for verily I say unto you, first seek ye righteousness toward men and all things will be added unto you, even the kingdom of God.

2. There came to him many to be concretized and he concretized them with water, men and women. And the names of his stars were: Rev. J. H. Harris, Sister R. J. Hamilton, Brother J. Reid, Rev. and Mrs. J. Barber, Brother C. C. Harris, Sister Leila Best, Sister Thurston, Brother H. Pope, Rev. and Mrs. Flanagan, Brother Charles McLaurin, Sister Letica Johnson, Brother and Sister Adam Costly, Brother and Sister W. D. Sullivan, Sister Sarah Johnson, Brother G. W. Roberts, Rev. J. J. Derricks, Rev. A. J. Green, Rev. W. Barclift, Sister Bertha Johnson, Her Holiness the Shepherdesss Miriam, Her Holiness Shepherd Miss Muriel, Brother F. L. Redd. These are those who followed the shepherd from place to place.

3. And it came to pass that his holiness, the shepherd, traveled to Springfield, Mass., U.S. A., there he concretized with water, and the names of his stars who followed him around were: sister Sylvie Randall, Brother and Sister Eugene Kitchen, Brother and Sister Joseph Rutherford, Rev. R. G. Gaines, Brother J. When, Sister Ellen Frazier, Sister Minnieolo Walker, Sister M. A. Bryant, Irene Chambers, E. Dempsey. From there he traveled all around South America and the West Indies, preaching of the law and concretation by water for the sake of suffering humanity.

4. Moreover in the year of 1919 Athlyi, after he was anointed shepherd, paraded the streets of Newark with a host of Negroes, protected by riding officers of the city and accompanied by a Salvation Army carrying banners, proclaiming a universal holiday for Negroes and foretelling of their industrial and national independence.

CHAPTER 5. AHTLYI PREACHED.

1. For as much as the doctrine preached by Athlyi gained favor in the hearts of the people, and that I was efficient for the salvation of Ethiopia's generations: On the thirteenth day of the seventh month, in the nineteen hundred and eighteenth year the followers of Athlyi assembled at the Israel Memorial A. M. E. Church, West Kinney Street, Newark, New Jersey, U. S. A. They declared themselves [Athlyians] by name and in faith:

2. And they consolidated themselves within the faith.

3. They sang songs of praises and offered thanksgiving to the Lord God of Ethiopia.

4. And it came to pass that a committee was appointed from among them to confirm the Shepherd, and the names of those appointed

and consolidated were Sister Rachel Hamilton, Rev. James Barber, Sister Gilby Rose, Brother C E. Harris and Brother James Reed.

5. The committee decorated the Shepherd in four colors and committed in his right hand a staff so as to confirm the authority conferred upon him by the heavenly officials.

6a. Now when the Shepherd was adorned and anointed by prayer, the [Athlyians] shouted with great joy and cried Lead on, Shepherd of the [Athlyians].

7b. And it came to pass after the performance, the Shepherd stood up, and he was in four colors which were blue, black, red and green, and he explained the meaning of the colors of the staff.

8. Saying Ethiopia's generations shall respect the heaven while for a foundation they sacrifice on earth; moreover a king sits on the throne of his organized government, but a shepherd must seek his sheep and prepare a pasture for them that they be fed.

9. Then the Shepherd commanded his followers to stand, and he taught them saying great is his divine majesty, the Lord God of all mankind, Father of Ethiopia; who is greater than the Lord God? Even from the beginning of the world hath he prepared for his children unto the end.

10. The sun, the moon, the stars, the wind, the rain, the land and the sea hath he given free to mankind; who is so philanthropic, so magnificent, who can give such a gift? There is none so great as the Lord our God.

11. Let all the generations of Ethiopia hear the voice of Athlyi, for in his hands the law is given unto them.

12. Let not the devil persuade you that you turn your back against the lord god of Ethiopia.

13. Woe be unto you should the heavenly father because of your ingratitudes turn against thee, revengely the hands of thy enemies shall come upon thee with horror.

14. Let the [Athlyians] walk in the path of righteousness and all impediments shall be their foot stool and the spirit of the Lord shall dwell with them for ever and ever.

15. Blessed are the industrious hearts for they are those who use the blessing and the power of God for the good of mankind. Great shall be their reward in the kingdom of heaven.

16. Blessed are those who seek the Lord and by actual work prove to the nations that they have found him; for the power of God shall be as two kings feeling in darkness for an electric switch and [he that] found it immediately there was light throughout his palace and all the people rejoiced because of its splendor, but in the palace of him that found it not, there was no light, therefore his people wandered and became the servants of others.

17. Blessed are a people who seek their own, beautify and maintain it, for in their barns there shall be plenty; great shall they be among men. The Lord shall glory in them and their daughters shall be the wives of mighty men.

18. Woe be unto a people, a race who seek not their own foundation; their wives shall be servants for the wives of other men, and their daughters shall be wives of poor men and of vagabonds, and there shall be tears because of privation, then in the end hell everlasting for there shall be no reward in the kingdom of heaven for the slothful nor the unconcerned.

19. Woe be unto a race of people who forsake their own and adhere to the doctrine of another. They shall be slaves to the people thereof.

20. Verily I say unto you O children of Ethiopia, boast not of the progress of other races, believing that thou are a part of the project for at any time thou shall be cast over the bridge of death both body and soul.

21. Forget not the assembling of [thyselves] and unitedly working for the up building of Ethiopia and her generations.

22. Then shall the nations of the earth respect thee and thy commodities shall be for their gold and their commodities for thy gold, but there shall be none to fool thee neither shall ye be their slaves.

23. For thy emblem shall rank among their emblems; thy ships among their ships and thy men of war among their men of war; great shall be thy name among the nations.

24. The Lord God, Father of Ethiopia, shall glory in thee, with thee shall all the angels rejoice, great is thy reward in the kingdom of heaven.

25. Thy daughters shall work with clean hands and in soft clothing, thy sons shall enjoy the fruit of their colleges.

CHAPTER 6.

1. The following meeting after the Shepherd was confirmed, there came to him men and women to be concretized, and he concretized them with water.

2. And the Shepherd taught the form [of] Solemnityfeast, which the Christian call sacrament, and he taught the form of baptism [also concretation] and the period of concord according to the Athlican faith.

3. Let the people be baptized with water by submersion for the remission of their iniquities in the name of one God, his Holy Law and the Holy Ghost.

4. Let the people be concretized also with water that they be [binded] into one united band form one generation to another and let them pledge their lives loyally to the cause of actual work for the up

building of Ethiopia and for the rescue of suffering humanity; suffer them to wash their hands against the slothful and fruitless life of the past.

5. Then shall the parson give to them a hand of fellowship, bringing them forward into a new and ever productive life.

6. Let the people assemble once a month on their knees before the Altar at Solemnityfeast, then shall the parson and ordained cleffs administer to them bread and water, saying, eat in remembrance of your pledge to God, yielding yourselves into actual work for the welfare of your generation through the upbuilding of Ethiopia and for the rescue of suffering humanity.

7. Drink in remembrance of your baptism when thy sins hath been washed away, bid far the devil and his iniquities; arise and go in the name of one God, his Law, and the Holy Ghost.

8. For as much as angel Douglas [binded] the heaven and earth for the rescue of Ethiopia and her posterities, suffer the children of Ethiopia to assemble for three days celebration, beginning from the setting of the sun on the twenty-ninth day of the seventh month unto the setting of the sun of the first day of the eighth month of the year, which shall be known throughout the world as the period of concord in accordance with the celestial and terrest[r]ial concord led by the mighty angel Douglas.

9. Hear, oh generations of Ethiopia, for I, Athlyi, speak not as a mere man but with authority from the kingdom of God.

10. Verily, I say unto you, the first and second days of the concord thou shall not eat the flesh of any animals, nor large fishes, neither shall ye drink of their blood or of their milk; thy victuals shall be of fowl and tiny fishes; devote thyself in communing with the Lord God of Ethiopia.

11. Be aware of improper conduct, for the angels of heaven are participating in the concord.

12. On the third day, which is the last day of concord, let there be a great feast and joviality among the people.

13. Let the atmosphere be teemed with balloons of colors carried in the hands of the people; let also the possessions of all Ethiopia's generations be adorned with the colors.

14. During the concord the house of Athlyi shall order the release of the people from all Athlican factories, or other enterprises so that they can commune with the Lord their God.

15. In time of concord let the Athlican ships fly the colors of the Great Negro Civilization wheresoever they are; pray that the captains thereof are of the Athlican faith so as to celebrate concord in its fulness.

16. Hear ye, O' generations of Ethiopia, for I, Athlyi, speak unto you, for as the Lord God of Ethiopia liveth, this is a serious affair which must not be forsaken.

17. The Holy finger print of the almighty God signed the issue in the name of his majesty, his Law, and for the sake of suffering humanity.

18. And it came to pass that one of the new comers into the Athlican faith who sat in the midst of the audience spake, saying, may I ask his holiness, what is the principal belief of the Athlians.

19. Straightway the Shepherd answered saying, the fundamental belief of the Athlican faith is justice to all, but hear ye, also, the Athlian's creed:

THE ATHLIAN'S CREED.

20. We believe in one God, maker of all things, Father of Ethiopia and then in his Holy Law as it is written in the book Piby, the sincerity of Angel Douglas and the power of the Holy Ghost. We believe in one Shepherd Athlyi as an anointed apostle of the Lord our God, then in the Afro Athlican Constructive Church unto the most Holy House of Athlyi. We believe in the freedom of Ethiopia and the maintenance of an efficient government recorded upon the catalog of nations in honor of her posterities and the glory of her God, the establishment of true love and the administration of justice to all men, the celebration of concord, the virtue of the Solemnityfeast and in the form of baptism and concretation as taught by our Shepherd Athlyi.

We believe in the utilization of the power and blessings of God for the good of mankind, the creation of industries, the maintenance of colleges and the unity of force, then in the end when earth toil is over we shall be rewarded a place of rest in the kingdom of heaven, there to sing with the saints of Ethiopia, singing Hallelujah, hosanna to the lord our God for ever and ever—Amen.

21. Then the Athlians shouted hosanna to the Lord God, surely the lord has sent us not only a Shepherd but a savio[u]r.

22. Straightway the Shepherd Athlyi spake saying upon those words the Afro Athlican Constructive Church stand firm over which the hosts of hell nor the armies of the earth shall not prevail.

23. And the Shepherd being full with the Holy Spirit recited from his heart saying:

24. Father, thou God of all, closer to thee even though afar we stray; thou has called us back, now all in one we come, children of Africa: closer, oh God, to thee; closer to thee.

25. And he began to tell his followers about the wonderful works of God; how he hath sent apostles of the twentieth century, to save Ethiopia and her generations from the oppressive feet of the nations that they prove themselves fruitful for the good of their children and the glory of their God.

26. Know ye that I am not the only one sent by the Lord our God to rescue the children of Ethiopia, for before me there were two oth-

ers sent forth to prepare the minds of the people for the great things that shall come to pass.

27. I saw an angel resembling a mighty Negro, and upon his head were horns of a great structure and on his breast was a map of life.

28. I heard a great voice uttered from the end of the world saying, behold the map of the new Negroes, by this shall ye know the apostle of the twentieth century whom the almighty God hath commanded to save Ethiopia and her posterities.

29. At the sound of the mighty voice the structure descended from the head of the angel and stood upon the ground and the map surrounded it, then was the writing plain to be understood.

30. And the Shepherd showed the people a copy of the map, and said behold the map as I have seen it, straightway at midnight I reproduce the mystery.

31. Then the Athlians shouted for joy and the Shepherd spake with a loud voice saying thou sun that shines upon the waters of the utmost world, that gives light to the earth, stand thou still over mountains of Africa and give light to her righteous armies.

32. Where are those; there is none to compare with the Athlians in united spirits and a determination; a people lovers of freedom and of justice, fearless of death.

CHAPTER 7.

1. Now in the year of nineteen hundred and nineteen on the thirtieth day of the seventh month, when the Athlians were celebrating concord in the city of Newark, New Jersey, U. S. A., and on the third day of the period a paper was read by the Rev. Bonfield telling of Marcus Garvey in New York City.

2. And the Shepherd hesitated, then spake, saying:

3. I almost believe this is one of the apostles of the twentieth century, but where is the other? For I look for two, however by the map of life I shall know him.

4. Raise not the weight of your finger on Marcus Garvey, neither speak ye against him.

5. In the year of 1921 Garvey spake, saying: I have no time to teach religion.

6. Because of this saying Athlyi took up his pen and was about to declare him not an apostle of the twentieth century.

7. And it came to pass that the word of the Lord came to Athlyi saying, blame not this man, for I the Lord God hath sent him to prepare the minds of Ethiopia's generations, verily he shall straighten up upon the map.

8. Nevertheless, in the year nineteen hundred and twenty-two Apostle Garvey issued a religious call throughout the world which fulfilled the last item upon the map of life.
9. Therefore, Athlyi yielded him a copy of the map, and declared Marcus Garvey an apostle of the Lord God for the redemption of Ethiopia and her suffering posterities.
10. And the word of the Lord came to Athlyi saying, I am the Lord God of Ethiopia, three apostles of the twentieth century have I sent forth unto Ethiopia's generations to administer the Law and the Gospel which I have commanded for their salvation, let not the hands of men ordain them.
11. For I, the Lord, hath anointed mine apostles that they may ordain and give authority to ordain.

CHAPTER 8. ATHLYI SENT ABROAD.

1. And it came to pass that the word of the Lord came to Athlyi saying get thee into foreign countries and provide stars of the Law and of the gospel of the twentieth century.
2. Go the way of the Atlantic and return by way of the Pacific, and Athlyi obeyed the Lord.
3. And when he was in the Strait of Magellan, the Lord spake to him saying:
4. My holy house of Athlyi let her be of two wings, the Church to the right and a green pasture to the left.
5. Let the Church teach and the green pasture to provide for the people; let the house of Athlyi be the director thereof, and I, the Lord, shall dwell in the house of Athlyi and give light to her wings, then shall the inhabitants of the earth know that I am the Lord God of Ethiopia.
6. Let there be but one church or denomination upon the law and the gospel commanded for the salvation of Ethiopia's generations.
7. In entering the inner door of the Church let the people bow with reverence to the holy dictuary.
8. Suffer no one to preach upon or in the dictuary save a teacher of the law and a believer in the gospel commanded to the children of Ethiopia.
9. Let the people take interest in the apostles, but he that boost not the green pasture to provide for the people is not worthy of compensation.
10. Let the people give to the green pasture for their own good and for the welfare of their generations.
11. Oh, Athlians, love ye one another, forget not the assembling of yourselves together that no corruption gather between thee, for

thou art the light and guide unto salvation; let all the children of
Ethiopia follow thee.

12. May the Lord God of Ethiopia watch between us whil'st we are absent one from another. May he endow us with unity of spirit and
anxious hearts to again assemble for the rise of falling humanity
through the guidance of the house of Athlyi and in the name of one
God, his Law and the Holy Ghost for ever and ever-Amen.

Aggregations on Theology

The "Second Book of Athlyi Called Aggregation" (SB), with its eight chapters, is the longest and most organized theological section of the *Holy Piby.*
The Elijah-Ethiopia motif opens this narrative section, declaring that the
children of Ethiopia are God's favorite people; they "have drifted away from
his divine majesty" and, for them, "the whole heaven is grieved" so that there
is "a great lamentation in the kingdom of God." Here Rogers recalls strange
apocalyptic visions of two angelic beings representing Ethiopian saints and
"Ethiopian mothers, who have been dead a thousand years, pleading before
Elijah for the redemption of suffering Ethiopia" (Ch 1 v4). These visions are
coded with biblical imagery and language from the Apocalypse of Revelation. At a "convention in heaven," the heavenly personages are commissioned to confirm the appointment of Athlyi Rogers as "shepherd to lead
Ethiopia's generations from the oppressive feet of the nations" (Ch 1 v5).
The "Holy Spirit" makes Rogers, called a mere "twig before the eyes of men"
but "great in the sight of God," an "instrument to lead" Ethiopians to freedom. With that, an angel blesses Ethiopia with triumphant shouts reminiscent of Christ's triumphal entry into Jerusalem on Palm Sunday: "glory be
to the Father, thou Elijah, Hosanna, Hosanna to Jehovah, praise ye Douglas
the convention [have] triumph" (SB Ch 1 vv9 and 10).

Rogers's indigenized theology of law and purification, clothed in a kind
of Ethiopianist Beta Israel for the children of Africa with a mysterious Elijah overlay, is very strange. This is a new Judaism baptized into Christian
thought and clothed in an apocalyptic Elijah theology whose true identity
is yet to be unveiled. Rogers claimed to receive the Holy Law for this new
legalism in his very hand from the angel of the Lord when "Christ, Prince
of the heavenly kingdom, descended and anointed" them "servants of God
and redeemers of Ethiopia's posterities." But whereas God, the Holy Spirit,
and the Holy Law are central to Roger's theology, Christ plays an insignificant role, if at all, in his thoughts. Roger's "Holy Law-Commandments"
urge: brotherly love, industry, concretizing or baptism, willing work to deliver the oppressed, cleanliness, pleasantness, punctuality, honesty, truthful-
ness, preserving what the community has, correcting mistakes in one's own

house before seeking to do the same to others, shedding no blood, being contented, and having no other God but the Creator (SB, Ch 3 vv1–12). Although love and industry are the first laws, the 12 commandments are designed to induce subservience, cooperation, and obedience to Rogers and the AAC Church.

Unlike Moses' Ten Commandments, reverence for God in Rogers's commandments is secondary to respect for Rogers and the AAC Church; no mention is made of honoring parents or keeping the Sabbath. However, Rogers's teaching of forgiving in order to be forgiven, showing love and loyalty on earth, being wise and understanding to do God's will, feeding the hungry, and clothing the naked are some of the noblest ideals of traditional Jewish and Christian theology. When these are proffered with reference to the suffering, misery, challenges, and hopes of African peoples, they let down the gauntlet on the plea for justice and racial equality in Western society. Essentially, the underlying theological message of the *Piby* is this: God has a program for the "upliftment" of the African peoples and He will bring that program to fruition through the leadership of Athlyi Rogers (in his Athlican church), Marcus Garvey, and the other "apostles."

Two other dominant emphases surface in this section, and in much of the *Piby* as a whole: the triumph of Ethiopia and the entrenching of the leadership of the "Shepherd anointed," Rogers himself, in a form of self-serving personality cult. Rogers is so obsessed with his own authority that the whole vision pageantry is designed to support his appointment as shepherd and undisputed leader of the flock. In speech after speech, vision after vision, Rogers undergirds his own position of authority and divinely appointed right to rule, a characteristic of cult leaders. He will gather "the generations of Ethiopia unto God" as "the shepherd gathers his sheep," and "the inhabitants of the earth shall know that the Lord our God has not forsaken Ethiopia." God is the only one who is above the shepherd, Athlyi Rogers, who pontificates: "Woe be unto the persecutors of the shepherd," to those who oppose him and reject his leadership, and on those who refuse to obey his voice. The shepherd claims divine authority to "administer the Holy Law" through his apostles unto the Ethiopians; and he swears before the angel that it will be so (SB, Ch 1 vv22–32). Athlyi says, "for I, Athlyi, speak not as a mere man but with authority from the Kingdom of God" (SB, Ch 6 v9).

The fact that "The committee decorated the Shepherd in four colors and committed in his right hand a staff so as to confirm the authority conferred upon him by the heavenly officials" (SB, Ch 5 v5), shows the power of myth, ritual, and symbols in the making of the Athlican sacred epic story that undergirds this religious movement. Here, myth marries theology to provide a basis for faith and praxis, and also to authenticate religious leadership. Rogers has the Athlians shouting " . . . surely the

Lord has sent us not only a Shepherd but a saviour" (SB, Ch 6 v21). While his people shout his praises, Rogers takes on the persona of the biblical Joshua and, as an insane man, commands the sun to stand "still over mountains of Africa and give light to her righteous armies" (Ch 6, v31). Rogers may have even intended to portray himself as the "Natural Man" who is deified in this section and somehow conflated with the mysterious Elijah. If that was his intent, then he is the Elijah who is to come, "conveyed to the throne of Elijah, God of heaven and earth," for "God hath exalted him in the spirit Prince over the children of Ethiopia" (TB, Chs 2–4 v4).

After a careful reading of the *Piby,* William David Spencer asked some serious questions of Rogers's sanity and integrity. Since Rogers claims that "one drop of his blood" will "crush his opponents" and pronounces woes on any disagreeing with him, was he a megalomaniac who usurped a kind of papal authority under the guise of a divine call and commission (SB, Ch 1 vv24–30)? Is he a power-hungry autocrat who dominated his flock with claims of authority from higher powers or headquarters? Was he just a dreamer who left the action to others while he spun daydreams of having a divine commission and hordes of people following him? Or was he a self-styled potentate who had his own harem and lived a cushy lifestyle on the backs of his faithful, allegedly appointed by heaven to follow him with unquestionable devotion because of the mandates of his divine book? Spencer concludes that the political-ecclesiastical structure in the *Piby* "is pretty heavy hierarchy with a demand for blind allegiance. A study of Rogers's lifestyle might tell us if he was a charlatan, megalomaniac (Joan of Ark?), or a timid guy who couldn't brook opposition and brought in BIG BROTHER [the divine] to back him up."[13] A good biographical study of this pro-Garvey leader could indeed provide revealing answers to these sentient questions; for in spite of Rogers's devotion to the Garvey mission and vision, Garvey's interest in leadership and power among Africans in the diaspora pales in the face of Rogers's cunning thirst for domination of his flock under the guise of divine legitimacy.

Notwithstanding Rogers's obviously contrived and autocratic rule of his flock under the guise of divine call and commission, characteristic of Hebrew prophets, the true subject of the *Piby* is nonetheless Africa and its people. That Africans are the true focus of this epic vision is made clear by the sudden presence of "the multitude of Negroes" who are the recipients of an angelic address concerning the protection and triumph of the Ethiopians under the shepherd of God's flock (vv 25, 26, and 27), none other than Athlyi Rogers. "The house of Athlyi is founded by the Holy Spirit to purify the children of Ethiopia and to administer the holy law commanded to them by the Lord God of mercies" (v32). This is all grounded in indigenized Judeo-

Christian theological concepts related to God as Father, creator, sustainer, provider, and protector of Ethiopia; Jesus Christ as messenger and a form of Elijah-messiah; and the Holy Spirit as energizer of the Church of Athlyi. The "kingdom of God" and the Holy Spirit, Moses and God's holy law, righteousness and justice, and Ethiopian mothers weeping for their children and "would not be comforted" (SB, Ch 1 v2), are but a few of the biblical themes and allusions that color the pages of this ephemeral epic. Most of the didactic "Aggregations" in Chapter 5 are written in the mode of biblical legal traditions, "hortatory" exhortations, beatitudes ("Blessed are those who seek the Lord"), apocalyptic woes in synoptic Gospel style ("Woe be unto a race of people who forsake their own and adhere to the doctrine of another," v19), and the typical "antithetical affirmative" of Jesus: "Verily! Verily! I say unto you O children of Ethiopia" (v20).

The explicit commitment of the *Piby* to the upliftment of the African peoples, "the rescue of suffering humanity" (SB, Ch 6 v6), and the belief "in the utilization of the power and blessings of God for the good of mankind, the creation of industries, the maintenance of colleges and the unity of force" ("the Athlian's Creed") is a testimony to its humanistic Afrocentric philosophy and adaptations of Garvey's pan-African vision. The entire Chapter 7 of the Second Book is devoted to Rogers's relationship with Garvey, whose political rhetoric occasionally overshadowed the role of religion in his movement and puzzled Rogers (Ch 7 v5). Garvey's religious sensitivity, biblical preaching, and theological pronouncements of the early 1920s, however, erased any doubts in Rogers's mind of Garvey's spirituality and sense of divine call and commission. Rogers could therefore declare "Marcus Garvey an apostle of the Lord God for the redemption of Ethiopia and her suffering posterities" (Ch 7 vv8 and 9). Though colored by the Rogers cult, the Afrocentric Ethiopian vision of Garvey is clear.

Rogers's Feminist Consciousness

To Athlyi Rogers's credit, his feminist consciousness takes center stage in the apocalyptic vision where the "two mothers of Ethiopia, each with a star in their right hand, . . . pinned them on the left breast of the two messengers of the Lord" and sparked off earthquake-like reactions on the earth while there is "great rejoicing in heaven and singing hosanna to Elijah" (SB, Ch 1 vv13, 17, 18 and 19). Through the beautiful act of the "mothers of Ethiopia," Africa's people experience joy, blessing, and continued protection from "the Lord God." God shall lead succeeding generations of Ethiopians, and the world will take notice that "the Lord our God has not forsaken Ethiopia" (SB, Ch 1 vv21–23). Because of the bravery of the "mothers," "the

Lord God of Ethiopia" is portrayed as eulogizing Mother Henrietta Vinton Davis "whom the whole heaven adore because of her greatness of faith and loyal way in which she fights to save Ethiopia and her generations from everlasting downfall" (TB, Ch 2 v8). The Lord then gives instruction to put Henrietta at his (Rogers) and his colleague's (Garvey) side; "for great is her wisdom, saith the Lord" (v8).

Rogers's respect for women should come as no surprise; he belonged to a movement, the UNIA, in which women not only outnumbered men but held prominent positions. As Tony Martin narrates: "The first member of the UNIA, founded in the summer of 1914, shortly after Garvey returned from England, was . . . Amy Ashwood, who would in due course become Amy Ashwood Garvey . . . A list of the original UNIA executive in Kingston reveals that almost half the members were women." Garvey encouraged "the appointment of women to regular positions at the very highest levels of the organization." Prominent women like Garvey's sister, Indiana, joined him in many debates in Jamaica on the subject, "Is the intellect of woman as highly developed as that of man?" Martin continues: "Once the UNIA relocated to New York in 1916 and Garvey settled down to organize, we find once more that women tended to play a fairly well-integrated role in the movement. Some of the highest positions in the UNIA were held by women. The best-known of these women is Henrietta Vinton Davis, a woman who had been an associate of Frederick Douglass, the great Afro-American leader."[14] Orator, Shakespearean actress, abolitionist, and pan-Africanist, Henrietta served the association "as vice-president on various occasions."[15] Other prominent women in Garvey's life included: international organizer Madame de Mena; printing press manager Lillian Galloway; famous African-American vocalist, Marian Anderson; well-known pioneer of NAACP and Women's Club, Wells Barnett; legendary cosmetologist, Madame C. J. Walker; and European-American Rosa Pastor Stokes,[16] to name a few.

When the feminine consciousness in Rogers's myth-making theological thought and vision again resurfaces in the Third Book, it shows the creation of a space for women in this avant garde religious organization, as it did in the UNIA. But this adulation of women in the Athlican Church is blatantly absent in the Jamaican-born Rastafarian movement led by Leonard Howell in particular. In fact, in spite of his use of positive feminine imagery in his discourse on Ethiopia and the Queen of Sheba in *The Promised Key,* Howell deliberately debased feminism by flipping the adulation of women in the *Piby* on its head and turning it into a litany of damnation against Eve, the mother of all living. For Howell, Eve is "the mother of Evil," sinful, dirty, and deceitful. He said the "gross beauty is the Queen in hell" a representative of "all white people if you please."[17]

This male chauvinism in Howell is quite surprising given the fact that Howell knew of the prominence of women in the UNIA in Jamaica and the United States. He was a Garvey admirer and even recruited women from the Jamaica UNIA for his new Rastafari Movement. That he had knowledge of the *Piby*, whose Ethiopianism provided the doctrinal basis and linguistic key for the ideology of his movement, is widely accepted. His discourse in *The Promised Key* opens with the Ethiopianist vision, which punctuates every section and almost every verse in that pamphlet.[18] As the Garvey scholar Robert Hill notes: "There had been in existence in Jamaica, prior to the coronation event in Ethiopia in 1930, a considerable tradition of 'Ethiopianism' that was traceable back over a lengthy period" of time. "Ethiopianism was also manifested in the series of eight essays written by James M. Lowe of Jamaica and published in the *Crusader* in New York City in 1919–1920 under the title, 'A Revealed Secret of the Hamitic Race.'"[19] Even more important, Hill declares definitively:

> The doctrine that would provide the actual interpretative basis of Rastafari ideology, however, was contained in two books introduced into Jamaica in the period 1925–27, which the *Daily Gleaner* characterized as "publications of the new Ethiopian religion." The first of the two books was *The Holy Piby*, otherwise known as "the Black Man's Bible" . . . It formed the doctrinal basis of Roger's Afro-Athlican Constructive Gaathly, with headquarters in Kimberly, South Africa. The Jamaica branch of the AACC went under the name "Hamitic church," and was established jointly by Grace-Jenkins Garrison and Rev. Charles F. Goodridge, who encountered *The Holy Piby* in Colon, Panama.[20]

So the *Piby* was seen as setting up "new doctrines," and enumerating "the creed of a new religion of which Marcus Garvey is pronounced the Apostle."[21]

What is puzzling here is why the *Piby* and Garvey, two of Howell's primary ideological sources, failed to mollify his incendiary diatribe on women. No anti-Christian vitriol plagues the *Piby*, no diatribe against the Roman Catholic Church, and no male chauvinist, patriarchal, and overtly misogynist reading of the biblical narratives on Eve and other women—as is evident in *The Promised Key*. To the contrary, the *Piby* magnifies the place of women in the Athlican Church and the envisioned new African community. One is left to speculate on what might have happened had Howell been influenced by Rogers's and Garvey's respect for women as much as he was inspired by their Ethiopian-Africanist ideology. The use of a Rogers-Garvey appreciation for the role of women in society by the early founders of Rastafari could have given the movement a very different approach to the place of the sistren in the movement, in its early days.

THE THIRD BOOK OF ATHLYI NAMES
THE FACTS OF THE APOSTLES

CHAPTER 1. APOSTLES ANOINTED.

1. Just at the time when the nations of the earth through their ill education and oppression, believed that they had ruined the children of Ethiopia for ever, and that they would be satisfied with the crumbs of life.
2. Behold the great God Almighty hath commanded his angels to anoint them that they be a new and prolific people upon the earth.
3. Then did the Lord God with his own hands ordain three apostles and sent them forth to save Ethiopia's generation from doom.
4. Now when Marcus Garvey, God's foremost apostle, heard the voice of his colleague, apostle Robert Lincoln Poston, preaching in the City of Detroit, Michigan, United States of America, he knew that this was his colleague for the Lord God hath revealed, notwithstanding the tree apostles had met in the spirit before they came to administer the law and gospel for the full salvation of Ethiopia's posterities.
5. And it came to pass that apostle Garvey journeyed to Detroit and there met his colleague and they greeted each other with great joy, and the heart of one was the heart of the other.
6. Now when the amalgamation of their apostleship was verified, apostle Poston came to New York City, United States of America, and then teamed with apostle Garvey in the work for the redemption of Ethiopia and her trodden posterities, whom through the oppression, the nations and the ignorance of the Negro ministers of the Christian faith, were hanging over the bridge of death, both body and soul.

CHAPTER 2. GOD SPOKE TO HIS DISCIPLES.

1. Now in the year nineteen hundred and twenty-three, the word of the Lord God of Ethiopia came to apostle Marcus Garvey saying, where is thy colleague?
2. And he answered, Father, behold he is with me.
3. Call together the children of Ethiopia, saith the lord, that they may know my request, and send forth a mission unto the land of Ethiopia which I hath given to her children from the beginning of the world, that they prepare a foundation for all the posterities of Ethiopia, even unto the end.
4. For I, the Lord God, shall come to judge between the three races of men; woe be unto the empty handed, the slothful and the coward. I shall bring judgment upon them with fire and with brimstone, even the baby at the mother's breast shall not escape, saith the Lord.

Prepare ye a bill of arrangement, saith the Lord, and give it in the hands of thy colleague that he go to the land of Ethiopia (Africa) and to the nations at the entrance of the land and request them to open the door for the return of thy children.

5. And I, the Lord, shall go with him, and I will touch the hearts of the nations and they shall yield to the request.

6. Then shall the children of Ethiopia return to their own land and there establish a light with which no nation shall compare, nor will there be any power sufficient to douse it.

7. For I am the Lord God of Ethiopia and I shall dwell with mine anointed and they shall be my people as long as they follow the teachings of my apostles.

8. Moreover, behold at thy side is the noble woman Henrietta in whom the whole heaven adore because of her greatness of faith and the loyal way in which she fights to save Ethiopia and her generations from everlasting downfall. Place her at the side of thy colleague, for great is her wisdom, saith the Lord, and send ye also another that they go and prepare a home for mine anointed.

9. And it came to pass that apostle Garvey obeyed the Lord, and he called the children of Ethiopia and there gathered a great host in the City of New York.

10. And when the apostle put before them the Lord's request they leapt for joy and confirmed the will of the Lord God of Ethiopia.

11. There was a delegation of three sent forth according to the words of the Lord.

Chapter 3. Standing Before Elijah.

1. And it came to pass that on the night of the fifteenth day of the third month of the nineteen hundred and twenty-fourth year, Athlyi spake aloud, saying:

2. Behold I saw the heaven draped in black, and I saw Angel Douglas sitting in a mourning robe, moreover the celestial saints of Ethiopia were in deep sorrow.

3. And it came to pass that I continued to look, and behold I saw a natural man standing before Angel Douglas, and after a brief conversation, the mighty Angel conveyed him to the throne of Elijah, God of heaven and earth.

4. Then upon the head of the natural man did Elijah place a crown and on the front part of the crown there was a brilliant star whose light extended from heaven to the earth.

5. Now when the crown was bestowed upon him, behold the mourning apparel disappeared and there was joy in heaven.

6. And it came to pass that I saw a great host of Negroes marching upon the earth and there was a light upon them, then I looked to-

ward the heaven and behold I saw the natural man standing in the east and the star of his crown gave light to the pathway of the children of Ethiopia.

CHAPTER 4. APOSTLES EXALTED.

1. The following morning after Athlyi's vision, Athlyi looked toward the rising sun and cried out saying, my God, my God, what shall happen to the apostles of the Twentieth Century? Father if it's me, even I that shall pass from the presence of men grant that the Piby live forever that the children of Ethiopia, through the teaching of the Afro Athlican Constructive Church, may obtain salvation forever.
2. And it came to pass that the Lord spake unto Athlyi, saying:
3. In the flesh did he go to prepare a foundation for the generations of Ethiopia, but in the spirit will he return to lead them there upon.
4. For I, the Lord God, hath exalted him in the spirit Prince over the children of Ethiopia; he shall see with all seeing eyes; in vain shall the nations of the world lay traps before mine anointed, for the Prince of the children shall lead them.
5. Woe be unto the proud, the hard hearted, unto those who shall say I have my treasures here and I will not leave them, neither will I follow the host led by the apostles of the Twentieth Century.
6. I shall bring vengeance upon them, saith the Lord, they be better boiled in oil, for I shall have no mercy upon them.

Apostle of the Ethiopianist Vision

In the "Third Book of Athlyi Named the Facts of the Apostles," the apocalyptic "Elijah image" is again summoned and associated with the "God-man-Christ," the apostles (Rogers, Garvey, and Robert Lincoln Poston), Ethiopia, and God. This is done probably to show the ideological link connecting Garvey's well-known prophesy of a prince arising out of Africa and Rogers's African messianic theology. The messiah is coming out of Ethiopia because "the Lord God, with his own hands, ordained three apostles and sent them forth to save Ethiopia's generation from doom." Only two of the apostles are named: Marcus Garvey and Robert Lincoln Poston of Detroit who, when he moved to New York City, "teamed [up] with apostle Garvey in the work for the redemption of Ethiopia and her trodden posterities" (TB, Ch 1 vv4 and 6). But who is the third apostle? Rastafarians fill in the blanks: one Rasta says Emperor Haile Selassie I, the Lion of the Tribe of Judah himself, and another says Leonard Howell. But Rogers is the third apostle who sees a vision of himself in the same way that Sun Myung Moon would eventually present the Lord of the Second Advent in the third person;

filling in the blanks with a personality is left to loyal followers to "discover" on their own under the tutelage of their "anointed" teacher.

In this section of the *Piby,* one again hears clear echoes of repatriation to Africa and the Garveyite vision to establish a kingdom for Blacks on the continent. According to Rogers, the word of the Lord came to Garvey in 1923, in the presence of his colleague, Athlyi Rogers, saying: "Send forth a mission unto the land of Ethiopia which I hath given to her children from the beginning of the world, that they may prepare a foundation for all the posterities of Ethiopia," *qua Africa,* and warn of God's judgment. "Then shall the children of Ethiopia return to their own land and there establish a light with which no nation shall compare, nor will there be any power sufficient to douse it." In the repatriated and reconstituted African kingdom, "the Lord God of Ethiopia" will dwell with his anointed and they shall be his people "as long as they follow the teachings" of his apostles (Ch 2 vv3, 6, and 7). Garvey is reported to have obeyed the heavenly vision in 1922 and called a large meeting in New York City, during which he unveiled the political plan to the joy and elation of the crowd (v8). By putting Garvey's vision for an African kingdom and Rogers's dream to bring God's message to the peoples of Africa in the form of a divine call and commission, the *Piby* legitimizes a political religious mission through divine agency and myth-making. That is, it gives the whole mission divine origination, vindication, and theological warrant.

Summary: The *Piby* and Rastafari

In Chapter 3 of the Third Book the narrative moves into first person singular, as Athlyi Rogers reports, on March 15, 1924, another apocalyptic vision involving Elijah and Angel Douglas. The cryptic 6 verses leave me with as many questions as when I began writing this introduction: Who is this Angel Douglass sitting in a mourning robe, and appearing throughout the *Piby?* Who are the celestial saints of Ethiopia and why are they in deep sorrow? Who is the "natural man" upon whose head Elijah placed a crown with a brilliant star shining from heaven before "a great host of Negroes marching upon the earth?" (v6) Is the crowned "natural man" Garvey or Rogers himself? Or could this be a later interpolation into the pamphlet by a Rasta attempting to give an apologetic connection to Haile Selassie's messiahship[22] after his coronation in 1930 but skillfully worked back into the *Piby?* Is the vision of a natural man's crown giving "light to the pathway of the children of Ethiopia" a precursor to Rastafari? Even if Athlyi Rogers had written this about himself or Marcus Garvey, Howell and other early Rastafarians interpreted it as referring to Selassie and made it essential to their Ethiopian vision.

This Ethiopianist vision is at the heart of Howell's cosmology and punctuates all but two pages of *The Promised Key*. Howell said: Ethiopia is "a country of great contrasts"; its "black people" are "extraordinarily blended into a refined fusion that cannot be met with in any other part of the world"; Ethiopia is written on the "Sceptre of His Majesty Rastafari the King of Kings and Lord of lords"; "Queen Omega" is the empress of Ethiopia (pp. 1–2); "The glory that was Solomon greater still reigns in Ethiopia" (p. 3); there is going to be a "resurrection of the Kingdom of Ethiopia," and "Queen Omega the Ethiopian woman is the crown woman of this world" (p. 4); "Ethiopia is the succeeding kingdom of the Anglo-Saxon Kingdom," and her "rule book leads us into different departments of the Kingdom" (p. 5). Ethiopia has a "balm yard" against leprosy (p. 6). "Ethiopia knew the perfect value of holy baptism in water" (p. 7); "Ethiopia's Repository will charge and qualify the fallen angels deadly poisonous . . . lying tongue" (p. 8). "Ethiopia is the crown head of this earth field since heaven has been built" (p. 10); and "she is that rich national woman that has charmed the men of nations to lie with her" (p. 11). Although "slave traders went to Ethiopia and damaged her seeds, beyond any earthly cure," Ethiopians will "build anew" (p. 12). The "keeper of the tree of life . . . owner of this earth" is the owner of Ethiopia," and "The royal name of this Ethiopian dignity is called Black supremacy" (p. 13).

The apocalyptic discourse on Elijah, "the natural man," and Ethiopia has the language of the book of Revelation, a trademark and apocalyptic fancy of Rastafari. If Howell and other founders of Rastafari were looking for divine pronouncements and allusions that would connect Athlyi Rogers's vision with Haile Selassie, the last two chapters of the *Piby* offered great theological ideas and mythic political language. "The Lord God, hath exalted him in the spirit Prince over the children of Ethiopia; he shall see with all-seeing eyes; in vain shall the nations of the world lay traps before mine anointed, for the Prince of the children shall lead them." In fact, Rogers's construction of the divine Godhead minus the person of Christ, left room for a third personality which he probably believed he filled in the elevated Elijah-natural man savior myth. But the Rastas seized the opportunity and supplied their own savior in the person of Selassie, a Christ indigenized in Afro-Caribbean culture for the liberation and salvation of the oppressed.

Like its successor, Rastafari reasonings, the *Piby* shows that one way to make scripture relevant to a community is to indigenize biblical materials by interpreting them with local paradigms, comprising a special ideological conception of reality, a people's historical experiences, and the community's dreams and hopes for future salvation, liberation, or "upliftment." The Ethiopianist paradigm with which the *Piby* interprets the Bible, of necessity, required a black philosophical "preunderstanding" of one's self, the social-political-economic context of interpreter/reader and text. As New Testament scholar Rudolf Bultmann reminded biblical scholarship a few decades ago, no one reads or interprets a biblical text *tabula rasa* (without a presupposition); "exegesis without presupposition is impossible." Everyone approaches the text with a *Vorverstaendnis* (preunderstanding) that comes from one's cultural context, educational and religious background, life experiences, tradition, and prejudice or prejudgment.[23] Athlyi Rogers's Ethiopianist reading of the Bible is therefore probably as legitimate as Bultmann's "demythologizing" interpretation of the Gospels. Rogers made the Bible an instrument for black dignity, pride, and hope in the God of the future.

Notes

1. The Piby shows evidence that it may have been written at different settings and probably under very different circumstances. Timothy White noted that Rogers compiled the *Piby* from 1913–17, and some of his "believers" published it in New Jersey (Timothy White, *Catch a Fire: The Life of Bob Marley*, rev. ed. [New York: Henry Holt, 1991], 9). Robert Hill, on the other hand, contends Rogers wrote the *Piby* in Newark, New Jersey ("Leonard P. Howell and Millenarian Visions in Early Rastafari," *Jamaica Journal* vol. 16 no. 1 [February 1983]: 27).
2. William David Spencer, "The First Chant: Leonard Howell's The Promised Key," in *Chanting Down Babylon: The Rastafari Reader*, ed. Nathaniel Samuel Murrell, William David Spencer, and Adrian McFarlane (Philadelphia: Temple University Press, 1998), 362.
3. White, 9. Compiled between 1913 and 1917, the *Piby* was published in Newark in 1924 and distributed in Woodbridge, New Jersey.
4. Rastafarian pathfinders found furtive political ideas and religious concepts in many sources in early twentieth-century Jamaica: the Jamaican militant resistant tradition of the 1800s, the preaching of the late nineteenth-century Jamaican prophet Alexander Bedward, pan-African nationalists Robert Love and Marcus Garvey, to name a few.
5. My research investigation reveals that the copyright statute of limitation on this work expired in 1999 (after 75 years) and that the work has not been reissued in any form recognized by the Library of Congress or the University Library Network in North Carolina. The publisher is also nonexistent. My copy of the *Piby* was discovered at the Jamaican Archives in Spanish Town, Jamaica, by my research colleague Rev. Clinton Chisholm and French Journalist Hèléne Lee during their research on Jamaican culture.
6. The pagination of the three major sections of the booklet suggests that it may not have been written at the same sitting. My photocopied edition from Jamaica came with "The Third Book" sandwiched between "The First Book" and "The Second Book." These I rearranged in their sequence but left

individualized pagination in tact. My working copy of the *Piby* also came arranged in three books of irregular length, each beginning a new pagination sequence. "The First Book of Athlyi Called ATHLYI" (FB) has only three meager pages (1–3). "The Second Book of Athlyi Called AGGREGATION" has 26 pages (numbered 1–26), and is the greatest source of theological ideas in the *Piby.* "The Third Book of Athlyi, Named THE FACTS OF THE APOSTLES" (TB) has only five pages (numbered 1–5) and appears to be missing the conclusion or ending page. On the other hand, the Second Book (SB) ends on a misplaced expanded version of the well-known Jewish Mizpah used as a benediction in many Christian religious gatherings: "May the Lord God of Ethiopia watch between us whil'st we are absent one from the other . . ." that should come at the end of the "Third Book," rather than at the end of the Second Book.

7. No name is given on the prima facie of the *Piby* regarding its real author. The cover page reads "distributed by The House of Athlyi, Woodbridge, NJ, U. S. A." and "Published by Athlican Strong Arm Company, January, 1924." In spite of the January date, it also reads: "The House of Athlyi, Woodbridge, N. J., U. S. A. March, 1924 . . . His Holiness, Shepherd Athlyi, IST of the House of Athlyi, supreme lord of the Afro-Athlican Constructive Church, requests that all Negroes the world over celebrate concord in its fullness . . ."

8. H. L. Wilmington and Ray Pritz observe that though "often referred to in Israel as Falashas," the Ethiopian Jews call themselves "Beta-Israel," the "House of Israel." They consider the name "Falashas," an Ethiopian slave, meaning "stranger" or "exile," to be derogatory, although "the tribe has indeed been perceived since ancient times as a stranger or exile." (*Israel at Forty: 1948–1988* (Wheaton: Tyndale, 1987), 126.

9. These give the impression, at least to me, that they continued on a fourth page, but this is a personal speculation.

10. The purpose of the creation myth at the beginning of the *Piby* is unclear; it is connected neither to what precedes it nor to what follows. I can only guess that the author wanted to give his received vision or revelation a sense of "divine" beginning.

11. See Clinton Hutton and Nathaniel Samuel Murrell, "Rastas' Psychology of Blackness, Resistance, and Somebodiness," in *Chanting Down Babylon,* 42. The orthodox Christian activist Garvey believed the Rastafarian view of Haile Selassie as messiah was both misguided and heretical, and disavowed association with the movement.

12. Ibid., 39–41. Ethiopia, to Garvey, was the popular designation for all of Africa in the late 1800s.

13. Personal correspondence from Gordon-Conwell Theological Seminary, commenting on my first draft of this introduction and commentary (April 13, 1999), 1.

14. Tony Martin, "Women in the Garvey Movement," in *Garvey, His Work and Impact,* ed. Rupert Lewis and Patrick Bryan (Mona, Jamaica: Institute of

Social and Economic Research & Department of Extra-Mural Studies, 1988), 67–8.

15. Ibid., 68.

16. Ibid., 68–71. See the especially helpful essay by Honor Ford-Smith, "Women and the Garvey Movement in Jamaica," in *Garvey, His Work and Impact,* 73–83.

17. William David Spencer, "The First Chant: Leonard Howell's *The Promised Key,*" in *Chanting Down Babylon,* 379.

18. See *The Promised Key* by G. G. Maragh, published by Dr. Nnamdi Azikiwe (Accra, Ghana: The African Morning Post Head Office, 1930); Also Spencer, "The First Chant," 362. In "Leonard P. Howell and Millenarian Visions in Early Rastafari" *Jamaica Journal* vol. 16, no. 1 (February 1983), 9, Robert Hill discusses "Ethiopianist ideas that had become dormant by the end of the 1920s" but which had a powerful influence on "the wave of millenarian beliefs in Ethiopia's link with divinity" by Howell and others.

19. Hill, "Leonard P. Howell," 26.

20. Ibid., 27. Hill notes that in *The Promised Key* Howell extensively plagiarized *The Royal Parchment Scroll of Black Supremacy* in 1935. But Howell also made The *Holy Piby* one of the interpretive bases of Rastafari. Timothy White also contends that the *Piby* was brought to Jamaica in 1925 (*Catch a Fire,* 9).

21. Hill, 27.

22. But neither the print not the text's style seem to change as it does with interpolations into *The Promised Key.*

23. See Rudolf Bultmann, "Is Exegesis without Presuppositions Possible?" (1957) in *New Testament & Mythology and Other Basic Writings,* selected, ed., and trans. Schubert M. Ogden (Philadelphia: Fortress Press, 1984), 145–52.

Notes on Contributors

HEMCHAND GOSSAI, coeditor, is Associate Professor of Religion at Muhlenberg in Allentown, Pennsylvania. Born in Guyana, South America, Gossai has studied in the United States and Scotland. He is the author of a number of articles and two volumes, *Justice, Righteousness and the Social Critique of the Eighth Century Prophets* (Peter Lang Publishers) and *Power and Marginality in the Abraham Narratives* (University Press of America). Gossai is one of the original members of the Consultation on the Bible in Caribbean Culture and Tradition.

NATHANIEL SAMUEL MURRELL, coeditor, a Grenadian-American, is Assistant Professor of Philosophy and Religion at the University of North Carolina at Wilmington, as well as an Examiner in Religion for the University of the West Indies, Cave Hill, Barbados. He is coeditor of the award-winning *Chanting Down Babylon* (1998) and coauthor of a forthcoming textbook *Introduction to Afro-Caribbean Religions* (2001). Murrell is also a contributor to the forthcoming landmark work *African Americans and the Bible* (2000), and an original member of the Consultation on the Bible in Caribbean Culture and Tradition.

GERALD M. BOODOO, a native of Trinidad, is Associate Professor and Chair of the Department of Theology at Xavier University of Louisiana. He is an active member of the annual Catholic Conference on Theology in the Caribbean Today and convenes the World Church Theology Group of the Catholic Theological Society of America. Among his recent publications is a contribution on Caribbean Christologies in the forthcoming *Dictionary of Third World Theologies,* and an article on "Gospel and Culture in a Forced Theological Context" in the *Caribbean Journal of Religious Studies.*

LORETTA COLLINS from the University of Iowa is an Assistant Professor in the English Department at the University of Puerto Rico, and a continuing member of the American Academy of Religion Seminar, "Rastafari in Global Context: Religion and Culture." She has done extensive research on and among women in Jamaican Rastafari.

JANET L. DECOSMO is Associate Professor of Humanities and Director of the Center for Caribbean Culture at Florida A&M University in Tallahassee, Florida, where she has taught for 19 years. Her research focuses on religious and cultural expressions (reggae, Rastafari and festival arts), both in the Caribbean and in Bahia, Brazil. DeCosmo is a member of the American Academy of Religion Seminar, "Rastafari in Global Context: Religion and Culture."

MIGUEL A. DE LA TORRE teaches Theologies of Liberation at Hope College in Michigan. He has two forthcoming books: *The Quest for the Historical Cuban Christ*, and *Introduction to Hispanic Theology: Latino/a Perspectives*. He has several published articles, all dealing with the religiosity of Exilic Cubans based on their social location.

NOEL LEO ERSKINE is an Associate Professor of Theology and Ethics at the Candler School of Theology, Emory University in Atlanta. A native of Jamaica, Erskine taught at Cornwall College in Montego Bay, Jamaica, and served churches there for six years. He did graduate work at Duke Divinity School and at Union Theological Seminary and is the author of *Decolonizing Theology: A Caribbean Perspective*. Erskine has contributed to several books on Caribbean and African American religions.

JOHN HOLDER, Barbadian-born, is Professor of Bible at Codrington College in Barbados and a Canon (Clergy) in the Anglican (Episcopalian) Church in the Caribbean. Holder has published two books and has contributed to several other works in the Caribbean. Holder contributed to the Society of Biblical Literature's Consultation on the Bible in Caribbean Culture and Tradition.

LESLIE R. JAMES, a Grenadian-American, is assistant Professor of Religion at DePauw University, Indiana. He teaches religion, African-American, Latin American, and Caribbean Studies. He has also contributed to the Society of Biblical Literature Consultation on the Bible in Caribbean Culture and Tradition.

DARREN J. N. MIDDLETON is Assistant Professor of Religion and Literature at Texas Christian University. Educated in England and Scotland, he is the author of two book-length studies of Nikos Kazantzakis, the Cretan novelist, and a member of the steering committee for the American Academy of Religion Seminar, "Rastafari in Global Contexts: Religion and Culture."

J. RICHARD MIDDLETON is a Jamaican-American of Jewish-European ancestry. He is Assistant Professor of Old Testament at Colgate Rochester Divinity School and was a member of the Society of Biblical Literature's

Consultation on Bible in Caribbean Culture and Tradition. He has coauthored two books and contributed to several other volumes.

HORACE RUSSELL is the Dean of the Chapel at Eastern Baptist Theological Seminary in Pennsylvania. He is an authority on Caribbean church history and former President of the United Theological College of the West Indies in Jamaica. He has written two books and contributed to several volumes. Russell was one of the earliest contributors to the Society of Biblical Literature's Consultations on the Bible in Caribbean Culture and Tradition.

Index